A New Deal for All?

D1484208

A book in the series

RADICAL PERSPECTIVES

A Radical History Review book series

Series editors: Daniel J. Walkowitz, New York University

Barbara Weinstein, New York University

A New Deal for All?

Race and Class Struggles in Depression-Era Baltimore

ANDOR SKOTNES

DUKE UNIVERSITY PRESS   *Durham and London*   2013

© 2013 Duke University Press
All rights reserved
Printed in the United States of America
on acid-free paper ∞
Designed by C. H. Westmoreland
Typeset in Minion Pro with Verdana display
by Tseng Information Systems, Inc.

FRONTISPIECE:
Photograph by Paul Henderson.
Courtesy of the Afro-American
Newspapers Archives and Research
Center.

Contents

About the Series

History, as radical historians have long observed, cannot be severed from authorial subjectivity; indeed, from politics. Political concerns animate the questions we ask, the subjects on which we write. For more than thirty years, the *Radical History Review* has led in nurturing and advancing politically engaged historical research. Radical Perspectives seeks to further the journal's mission: any author wishing to be in the series makes a self-conscious decision to associate her or his work with a radical perspective. To be sure, many of us are currently struggling with the issue of what it means to be a radical historian in the early twenty-first century, and this series is intended to provide some signposts for what we would judge to be radical history. It will offer innovative ways of telling stories from multiple perspectives; comparative, transnational, and global histories that transcend conventional boundaries of region and nation; works that elaborate on the implications of the postcolonial move to "provincialize Europe"; studies of the public in and of the past, including those that consider the commodification of the past; histories that explore the intersection of identities such as gender, race, class, and sexuality with an eye to their political implications and complications. Above all, this book series seeks to create an important intellectual space and discursive community to explore the very issue of what constitutes radical history. Within this context, some of the books published in the series may privilege alternative and oppositional political cultures, but all will be concerned with the way power is constituted, contested, used, and abused.

The city of Baltimore, with its unique geographic location and demographic profile, provides the singularly illuminating prism through which *A New Deal for All? Race and Class Struggles in Depression-Era Baltimore* views race and labor reform in the mid-twentieth-century United States. Baltimore was at once the most northern of the country's major Southern cities and among the most southern of its leading industrial cities. As a segregated Jim Crow city, Baltimore and its environs experienced the horrific racial violence, including Klan lynchings, that riddled postwar border states; as an industrial center, it attracted the large East European (and substantial Jewish) immigrant and black migrant populations who came to the city for jobs in its large and dynamic garment factories, steel plants, and service sector. The coming of the Great Depression allowed race reformers, radicals, and trade unionists to make common cause in their fight against race discrimination and labor exploitation.

Historians have usually associated the histories of the radical labor and black freedom movements with northern cities—and told their stories separately. In *A New Deal for All?*, Andor Skotnes establishes a new paradigm that sees these histories as imbricated in each other and uniquely visible in this border metropolis. As Skotnes demonstrates in this wide-ranging and conceptually ambitious book, the movements for black freedom and industrial reform, from the 1930s through the onset of the Second World War, must be told as part of the same story. The Black freedom movement in Baltimore provided some of the nation's most renowned civil rights leaders, Juanita Jackson Mitchell and Thurgood Marshall among them. Skotnes, who began his career as an associate director of the Columbia University Oral History Program, and is one of the country's premier oral historians, allows their voices and those of leading union and communist labor leaders in the nascent CIO movement to animate his story. Making it clear that the "long civil rights movement" has its origins in these struggles of the 1930s, Skotnes makes it equally clear how thoroughly the histories of the struggle for racial and class justice are entwined. At times, the two movements work in solidarity; at other times, they conflict. Yet they are always profoundly shaping each other.

Illustrations

Abbreviations

AAISTW   Amalgamated Association of Iron, Steel, and Tin Workers
ACLU   American Civil Liberties Union
ACW   Amalgamated Clothing Workers
AFL   American Federation of Labor
AFM   American Federation of Musicians
AME   African Methodist Episcopal
A&P   Atlantic & Pacific Tea Company
ASCO   American Stores Company
BCHA   Baltimore Citizens' Housing Committee
BERC   Baltimore Emergency Relief Commission
BFL   Baltimore Federation of Labor (AFL)
BHA   Baltimore Housing Authority
BIUC   Baltimore Industrial Union Council (CIO)
BTA   Building Trades Association
BTC   Building Trades Council
BUL   Baltimore Urban League
CIO   Committee for Industrial Organization, then Congress of
         Industrial Organizations
CP   Communist Party
CSB   Centralized Shipping Bureau
CWA   Civil Works Administration
CWCL   Cooperative Women's Civic League
DWOC   Distillery Workers Organizing Committee
FEPC   Fair Employment Practices Committee
FERA   Federal Emergency Relief Administration
GEC   General Executive Council (IUMSWA)
ILA   International Longshoremen's Association
ILD   International Labor Defense
ILGWU   International Ladies' Garment Workers Union
ISU   International Seamen's Union
IUMSWA   Industrial Union of Marine and Shipbuilding Workers of America
IWW   Industrial Workers of the World
LID   League for Industrial Democracy
LWIU   Laundry Workers International Union (AFL)
MDCFL   Maryland-District of Columbia Federation of Labor (AFL)
MDCIUC   Maryland and District of Columbia Industrial Union Council (CIO)
MHS   Maryland Historical Society
MOWM   March on Washington Movement

MWIU   Marine Workers Industrial Union
MWL   Marine Workers League
NAACP   National Association for the Advancement of Colored People
NARA   National Archives and Records Administration
NIRA   National Industrial Recovery Act
NLC   Negro Labor Committee
NLG   National Lawyers Guild
NLRB   National Labor Relations Board
NMU   National Maritime Union
NNA   New Negro Alliance
NNC   National Negro Congress
NRA   National Recovery Administration
NYPL   New York Public Library
PUL   People's Unemployment League of Maryland
SDC   Seamen's Defense Committee
SP   Socialist Party
SWOC   Steel Workers Organizing Committee
TUUL   Trade Union Unity League
TWOC   Textile Workers Organizing Committee
UAW   United Auto Workers
UFW   United Federal Workers
UMW   United Mine Workers
UTW   United Textile Workers
WAA   Workers' Alliance of America
WPA   Works Progress Administration
WUC   Waterfront Unemployed Council
YCL   Young Communist League
YMCA   Young Men's Christian Association
YWCA   Young Women's Christian Association

Acknowledgments

This book has been a very long time in the making. In the process of writing it, I received assistance and guidance from a great many individuals and institutions, some of whom I am able to acknowledge here.

I want to start with those who were influential from the inception of this project. Ronald J. Grele was there way before the beginning as a mentor and intellectual collaborator from my undergraduate years; he introduced me to and schooled me in oral history and in social theory, and more than once read and reflected on various iterations of this book manuscript. Daniel J. Walkowitz was also there before the beginning, and introduced me to what was then known as the "new social history." Over the years he has often given me excellent creative feedback on my work and my thinking, and he is, along with Latin American historian Barbara Weinstein, editor of the Radical Perspectives book series in which this volume is published. I also want to warmly acknowledge Warren Susman, a remarkably creative mind and my first dissertation adviser, who passed away at a tragically young age, and Norman Markowitz, who picked up the ball as my second adviser and greatly helped me complete my dissertation some years later.

A number of historians and colleagues were important in helping me shape this book, including a group of colleagues who were once all based in Baltimore. Jo Anne Argersinger, Roderick N. Ryon, and Linda Zeidman shared their sources and ideas with me, and gave me much encouragement; Linda Shoppes, in addition, read and commented very perceptively on versions of my manuscript; Cindy Gissendanner hosted me on several visits to Baltimore City and offered useful suggestions. Non-Baltimoreans Michael Frisch, Bruce Nelson, and Jim O'Brien also read and commented on the manuscript, and Jim did a really wonderful job editing my prose. In addition, the late Roy Rosenzweig shared with me his research and interpretations for one section on my book, Joseph E. Moore did the same for another section, and Nelson Lichtenstein gave me early encouragement and direction on my project.

Oral history interviews were crucial to the writing of this book, and all of my interviewees contributed significantly to the process; they are acknowledged in the text and endnotes. However, I want to emphasize here my special gratitude to one of my interviewees. Over a period of five years, Juanita Jackson Mitchell gave me over twenty hours of rich, recorded testimony on her life and on the Black freedom movement of the 1930s, 1940s, and beyond. All oral history informants offer much more than their account of the "facts"; they also offer their interpretations of history. This was very much the case with Juanita Jackson Mitchell. She was (although she would never have described herself this way) a fine and passionate historian in her own right. Her interpretations and her passion greatly informed many portions of this book. I would love to have her reflections on it in its published form, but, sadly, she passed away some years ago.

I am grateful to the staffs of a number of libraries and archives for their assistance to me, including those of the Enoch Pratt Free Library, the Morgan State University Library, the University of Maryland libraries and archives at Baltimore County and College Park, the Kheel Center for Labor-Management Documentation and Archives at Cornell University, the Sheridan Libraries of Johns Hopkins University, the Maryland Historical Society, the Maryland State Archives, Baltimore County Public Library, the Columbia University Oral History Collection, the Library of the University at Albany, the Library of Congress, the National Archives, and my very own Sage Colleges Libraries. I want to make special mention of John B. Gartrell, archivist, Afro-American Newspapers Archives and Research Center for the help he gave me.

The research and writing of this book was supported by several faculty development grants and two competitive sabbatical awards at the Sage Colleges in Troy and Albany, New York, where I teach. I am grateful for these.

I want to thank Valerie Millholland, my editor at Duke University Press, and the whole staff there for their work and guidance. I want to particularly thank Miriam Angress, associate editor at Duke, who worked diligently and cooperatively with me during the publication process—she was terrific!

My parents—Arthur Skotnes, who passed away several years ago, and Pearl Skotnes—did not really contribute directly to this book, but their long-term encouragement, dedication, support, and love ultimately did much to make this project possible. My children, Darren Meade Skotnes and Claire Rita Meade Skotnes, literally grew up with this project as a part of their lives—too much so, I fear, at times. Nevertheless, they have always been a great inspiration to me in all my endeavors, and their implicit, and occasionally explicit, encouragement was crucial to this effort.

Finally, I want to state my tremendous gratitude to and admiration of my closest colleague, best friend, and wife, Teresa Meade—a most accomplished historian of Latin America, and of women and gender—whose support, knowledge, critical abilities, and guidance on every level were utterly crucial to this project. Some years ago she dedicated her first book to me. I am extremely happy finally to be able to do the same for her: with much love and thanks, I dedicate this book to Teresa.

A New Deal for All?

1. Members of the Baltimore NAACP Youth Council, with symbolic nooses around their necks, demonstrate in support of the National Demonstration against Lynching in Washington, D.C., February 12, 1937. Photograph by Paul Henderson. *Courtesy of the Afro-American Newspapers Archives and Research Center.*

Introduction

I am very happy to welcome you to Baltimore and Maryland, a city and state that have been in the vanguard of the struggle for freedom.
— JUANITA JACKSON MITCHELL

When Juanita Jackson Mitchell, a veteran Black[1] freedom movement leader, welcomed a conference of oral historians to Baltimore some years ago, she greeted them with this perhaps surprising statement. She was right, though, for as this book will endeavor to show, the Baltimore metropolitan region has been integral to struggles for freedom of various types in the United States, especially during the Great Depression and the early years of the Second World War. Juanita Jackson Mitchell knew this well, because from 1931 on she was a major leader of these struggles.

This is a study of race, class, and social struggle in Baltimore, and in Maryland more generally, from the late 1920s to the early 1940s. During this period, contradictions of race and class in the region generated powerful social movements that challenged the established order and effected significant social change. The key movements of the era were the workers' movement, the Black freedom movement, and a few smaller progressive and radical movements. All of these developed in a complex web of interrelationships: sometimes they allied, sometimes they interpenetrated, always they influenced each other. Since the upsurges of the 1950s, 1960s, and 1970s reawakened historians of the United States to the central importance of social struggle, many valuable accounts of social movements have been produced, but most of these histories have focused primarily on a single social movement. The labor movement, Black freedom movement, women's movement, gay and lesbian movement, and student movement have generally been investigated in near-isolation from each other. This, however, is a study of social movements *in the plural*. The perspective here is that, within a given social context and period, the social movements that arise, like the social contradictions that produce them, are deeply, complexly, and subtly interconnected, and that these movements are best examined together.

The Depression era is widely known, of course, as a period of intense class struggle that resulted in the rise of modern industrial unionism in the United

States. Many historians have focused their research on the workers' movement regionally and nationally during this era, although only occasionally on the Baltimore region, where a strong labor movement arose. Some historians, especially in recent years, have recognized that struggles around race and racism were crucial to the industrial union movement, and they have produced valuable studies of workers of color, of racial/ethnic contradictions, and of racial/ethnic identities within the movement. Some historians have even argued that a "civil rights unionism" emerged in some locales toward the end of this era, a phenomenon that, as this study will show, was emerging in Baltimore.

But relatively few have investigated the African American movement, based in the neighborhood and public spheres, during the years after the Great Crash of 1929. Such investigations, it seems, have been discouraged by the widely held myth that the modern Black freedom movement, in the form of the Civil Rights Movement, appeared suddenly, autonomously, and almost spontaneously in the mid-1950s, in the wake of the U.S. Supreme Court's decision in *Brown v. Board of Education*. In a challenge to this view, a number of historians are constructing an alternative picture of the "long civil rights movement." In the process, they are extending the origins of the modern freedom movement back through the Second World War into the Great Depression years, claiming that, rather than being essentially autonomous, the modern freedom movement has always been connected with other social movements—especially, in its early phases, with the workers' movement. The present study is part of this scholarly trend. In this book, I will argue that a powerful, mass-based Black freedom movement emerged from the multiclass African American neighborhoods of Baltimore, and of Maryland, during the Depression, helping to resuscitate and transform the national freedom movement. Indeed, the new freedom movement in Maryland created the "legal laboratory" for the strategy that eventually resulted in *Brown v. Board of Education*, developed the prototype for the national Youth Movement of the National Association for the Advancement of Colored People (NAACP) that swept the country after 1936, and contributed several major leaders, including Thurgood Marshall, to the national struggle. Moreover, this new freedom movement arose alongside the region's new, mass-based industrial workers' movement, which, as the site of much struggle around racism and Black workers' rights, developed its own internal freedom movement. The two movements, with the involvement of various radical groupings, interconnected with and overdetermined each other throughout the Depression years. For the Baltimore metropolitan region, and no doubt elsewhere, the modern long civil rights movement began in the early 1930s.[2]

If the object of this book is to investigate the interactions of social movements in the Depression era, why focus on a single locale? To be sure, this is a local study, but it is one that aspires to say something of more than just local interest. Sometimes the forces and interactions that give shape to social movements are most accessible to a historian at a relatively localized level, especially if they are explored within a broad theoretical and historical framework. Sometimes the contradictory tendencies and the potentialities of these movements, including possibilities never realized, are more apparent when they are viewed up close. Sometimes underlying processes, even those of national and international dimensions, are most visible locally. Sometimes—and this is of special concern to this study—the intricate interconnections between social movements are clearer when they are examined "on the ground."

Many local studies of modern social movements choose a "city" as their locale without really defining or problematizing this entity. The approach here is somewhat different. The urban theorist Manuel Castells once wrote that the "metropolitan region," not the city, as popularly understood, is "a central form of the organization of space of advanced capitalism." If Castells is right, a metropolitan region is a particularly good socio-geographic focus for a study like this one, for it allows the historian to locate and define the object of study within a historical space that is conceptually linked to the basic structures and processes of a modern society. Metropolitan regions are generally composed of concentric, intersecting, and overlapping areas of varying size, function, and character, linked in a definite network to the other regions within a given social formation. The local histories of urban social movements unfold in large part within the structured spaces of metropolitan regions and are deeply conditioned by them. The structured space of the movements in this study is the Baltimore metropolitan region. But why Baltimore? While this question will be addressed at greater length below, the short answer is that Baltimore and Maryland were, as they had been for many decades, a "border" city and a "border" state occupying the "middle ground" between South and North. This "in-betweenness" catalyzed a rich variety of struggles around *both* race and class, allowing close investigation of the character, interconnections, and potentials of such struggles in the United States under the conditions of the Great Depression.[3]

This study is a historical narrative, and its sections and chapters reflect the periods and phases of the social struggles in the Baltimore metropolitan region of the period. To anticipate these briefly, part I, "The Context," consists of a single chapter that sets the stage for the struggles that emerged in the Depression years by exploring the character of the Baltimore metropolitan region and its social geography and by examining the culture and traditions of resistance of the region's working-class and African American communities.

Part II, "Emergences, 1930–1934" (chapters 2–4), focuses on the first phase of the struggles of 1930–41, during which the Black freedom and workers' movements, left in disarray by the crash, began to reconstruct themselves, drawing largely on local resources. This was a particularly fluid and experimental period during which various groupings in both movements worked closely together; radicals of different sorts played key roles; antiracism became central to the campaigns they launched; and the foundations for new forms of both movements were constructed.

Part III, "Transitions, 1933–1936" (chapters 5–8), discusses the "take-off phase" of the regenerating workers' and freedom movements during the initial phase of the New Deal, as mass mobilizations occurred and large campaigns were mounted. As these movements developed, and their activities expanded, they continued to intersect and collaborate. However, while continuing mainly to function in the forms created in the previous phase, both movements in Baltimore became less regional and more involved with national efforts.

Part IV, "Risings, 1936–1941" (chapters 9–12), deals with the rapid growth phase of Baltimore's social movements during the country-wide surge of social struggle that marked the second New Deal. The mainstreams of both the regional workers' and freedom movements embraced national organizational forms—the Congress of Industrial Organizations and the NAACP, respectively—while retaining many of their regional dynamics. During this period, both movements won significant victories that began to transform the region. However, the level of direct interaction between them declined as they each grew rapidly and as the main forces in each increasingly responded to national mandates and focused on discrete areas of activity. Nonetheless, each movement continued to profoundly influence the other, and important secondary interconnections between them developed. Then, as the Second World War raged in Europe, and as war loomed for the United States, both movements consolidated their positions as influential forces in the region and turned toward greater collaboration with each other. Finally, the epilogue sums up the main themes of the struggles around race and class in the region during the Depression era and briefly projects these struggles through the war years into the postwar period.

It bears mentioning that significant portions of this study depended on oral histories—retrospective interview accounts by witnesses of and participants in the history under consideration. Oral history has especially great potential to provide unique perspectives on history, despite some recognized limitations. Sections of this study could not have been written without the oral histories I used, because the information contained in them simply does not exist apart from personal testimony. Other parts are far richer because of the insights added by oral histories to information provided by more traditional sources. But most of all, what oral history best provides is a glimpse into the interior of a story, into the lived and felt experience. My oral history informants offered more than data; they offered their interpretations and something of their lives. I am grateful to them, especially to Juanita Jackson Mitchell, who spent many hours with me sharing her memories and whose words open this introduction. I hope that I have retold their stories well.

I. The Context

2. The financial, commercial, cultural, and governmental center of the Baltimore metropolitan region was located in the city's downtown, northwest of the Inner Harbor. *Courtesy of Legacy Web, Baltimore County Public Library.*

1

Communities, Culture, and Traditions of Opposition

In its industrial development Baltimore is northern;
in its social customs it is more southern than Virginia.
—CHARLES JOHNSON, National Urban League

The social movements of the Baltimore metropolitan region during the era of the Great Depression emerged within a definite context and on particular historical foundations that had been constructed over a long period. To understand these movements, and to locate them within a national framework, this chapter will consider six features of the Baltimore region on the eve of the Great Crash; its location on the middle ground between North and South; structure and community of its metropolitan space; economic and political power in the region; the working class and its traditions; race and ethnicity; the African American community and its culture.

On the Middle Ground

Baltimore, situated fifty miles below the Mason-Dixon Line, was at the time of the Crash the pre-eminent border city of the pre-eminent border state. It remained, as it had long been, the proverbial "middle ground" between South and North, between historic territories of slavery and of free labor, between the subsequent homelands of Jim Crow ruralism and U.S. corporate capitalism. The region had a dual nature, an *in-betweenness*.

By the time of the Crash, Baltimore was a major industrialized metropolis of a type familiar in the North and on the West Coast but hardly known in the South. With a municipal population of 804,874 and a metropolitan population approaching 1 million in 1930, it was the seventh largest city in the country. By contrast, the two largest comparable southern cities, New Orleans and

Houston, ranked far below in population, at sixteenth and twenty-third, respectively. Baltimore had a huge, diversified industrial sector; it was a center of food processing, iron and steel production, copper smelting and refining, fertilizer and chemical production, men's clothing fabrication, aircraft construction, and electronics and automobile manufacturing. It was also a major commercial center with road and railroad links to the rest of the country, and a harbor that connected the city to the nation and the world (see figure 2). By the end of the 1920s, its port was the third busiest in the United States; by 1937, it was second.[1]

Baltimore was a very northern-like, working-class metropolitan region. By 1930, those holding working-class jobs represented a large majority of the total employed. Sharply divided by hierarchies of skill, race, ethnicity, and gender, the region's complex working class spread across the industrial, transport, and service-commercial sectors of its economy. A large fraction of the working class was composed of first- and second-generation European immigrants, who often lived in traditional or newly formed enclaves with others of the same national background. In addition, Baltimore's working class had long traditions of class struggle and organization comparable to those of workers in the older industrial regions of the country. In all of these ways, Baltimore was similar to northern and western urban centers; more than that, it was a *constituent part* of the emerging northeastern megalopolis, the largest urban system in the United States. It was a southern anchor of a chain of metropolitan regions that extended along the northern Atlantic seaboard from Baltimore and Washington, D.C., in the south, through the commercial-industrial port regions of Philadelphia and New York, to Boston in the north. Moreover, Baltimore's hinterland in northwestern Maryland—with its small Black population, Appalachian subsistence agriculture, commercial dairy farms, wheat fields, coalmines, railroads, local small industries, and occasional small cities with a few large industrial concerns—had deep historical ties to the Susquehanna River Valley and mountain regions of Pennsylvania; it was strongly oriented to the U.S. North.[2]

However, Baltimore, in its in-betweenness, was also profoundly southern, and several of its socio-demographic features indicated this fact. While the proportion of immigrant White ethnics in its population (29.1 percent) placed it between the major northern cities, on the one hand, and southern cities, on the other, its "White American" population in 1930 was about 53 percent of its total—much closer to the southern than the northern pattern (see table 1). Moreover, much of Baltimore's White population had roots in and strong ties to the rural South. Baltimore's African American population of nearly 130,000, about 18 percent of the total, was proportionately larger

TABLE 1. Race and Ethnicity in Selected Cities, 1930
(ranked by percentage African American)

City	% African American	% White 1st and 2d Generation in U.S.[a]	% White American[b]	% Other Races[c]
Boston	2.6	71.5	25.7	0.2
New York	4.7	73.3	21.8	0.2
Chicago	6.9	64.4	28.0	0.7
Detroit	7.7	57.6	34.2	0.5
Cleveland	8.0	64.9	27.0	0.2
Pittsburgh	8.2	51.1	40.6	0.1
Philadelphia	11.3	50.6	38.0	0.1
Baltimore	*17.7*	*29.1*	*53.1*	*0.1*
Houston	21.7	14.0	59.4	4.9
New Orleans	28.3	18.6	52.8	0.3
Richmond	29.0	7.8	63.2	0.0
Atlanta	33.3	5.1	61.6	0.0
Norfolk	33.9	9.9	56.0	0.2
Memphis	38.1	7.6	54.3	0.0
Birmingham	38.2	7.3	54.5	0.0

[a] Foreign-born or U.S.-born with at least one foreign-born parent.
[b] U.S.-born with U.S.-born parents.
[c] In this census, "Other Races" included "Mexican," and "Indian, Chinese, etc."

Source: U.S. Bureau of the Census, *Fifteenth Census of the United States: Population* (1930), vol. 2, table 24, vol. 3, tables 12, 18–19.

than the Black populations of major northern urban areas. Although a few northern cities had bigger absolute numbers of Black residents because of explosive immigration during the Great Migration of the previous decade and a half, the large African American community in Baltimore, unlike the communities in the North and similar to those in the South, was not mainly the result of recent immigration. In fact, the proportional size of Baltimore's Black population had remained virtually the same for more than a century.

Baltimore's southern features were most readily apparent in its system of racial relations: it was a profoundly Jim Crow town. Its strict legal and customary system of segregation was comparable to those of cities in the Deep South, although not as severe and terroristic as some. Southern-style segregationist ideology was hegemonic in many sectors of the White population, where "Whiteness" was constructed in the most supremacist terms. Conversely, the region's large, long-established Black community had, over many decades, created on its side of the color line a rich array of social institutions and cultural traditions, including a durable freedom movement.[3]

Finally, although Baltimore was embedded in the northeastern megalopolis, and its hinterlands in northwestern Maryland were northern in character, its overwhelming rural hinterlands in southern Maryland and on the Eastern Shore, with economies based on small-scale tenant farming and oyster and crab harvesting, were strongly oriented toward the U.S. South by commerce and culture. What little industry the region had was almost entirely limited to canneries along the shores of the Chesapeake Bay. "Native" Whites, with generations of forebears in the United States, predominated demographically over a tiny European immigrant population while holding the large Black population—about 30 percent of the total—in strict segregationist subjugation. Local White elites held much of the land, controlled the commerce, and ran the courthouse rings and county governments. Baltimore was the commercial and transportation hub, the main urban cultural center, and the chief emigrant destination for eastern and southern Marylanders and for those in the upper South beyond the Maryland border. The regions to the south of Baltimore could hardly have contrasted more with those of the north and west; Baltimore was a border city, not only in the national context, but also in the context of its own hinterlands.[4]

Space, Neighborhood, and Community

In 1930, the "border city" of Baltimore radiated out from its harbors on the branches and bays of the Patapsco River a dozen miles from the Chesapeake Bay, and extended far to the north and west. This space—structured not only by geography, but also by economics, politics, and culture, as well as by race, ethnicity, and social class—was the stage on which the struggles of the Depression years played out.

The annexation of 1918 had tripled the size of the city within its formal municipal boundaries to nearly eighty square miles of land (see figure 3). Rail lines surrounded the port areas, with major terminals at Camden station to the west of the Inner Harbor; at Canton, to the east; at Locust Point, to the south, and at Fairfield and Curtis Bay farther south, with industry concentrated around the harbors and railways. The downtown area, directly north and west of the Inner Harbor, contained the city's main financial, commercial, cultural, and government locations. Moving to the north and west of the harbor complex, the number of industrial and commercial establishments progressively diminished, with the exception of an important group of textile mills several miles north on the Jones Falls waterway. Working-class residen-

3. The industrial, commercial, and residential zones of Baltimore radiated out from its downtown area at the Inner Harbor. *Courtesy of Legacy Web, Baltimore County Public Library.*

tial areas clustered around the commercial and industrial concentrations, fanning out with population densities dropping (and class status rising) as the urban gave way to the suburban and then to the semi-rural.[5]

The residential areas of Baltimore congealed from a number of autonomous towns and villages, including Oldtown and Fells Point (established in the early 1700s), the former cotton mill towns of Hampden and Woodberry on Jones Falls (1830s), and the company-organized industrial towns of Canton (1828) and Brooklyn (1880s). Many of these areas retained distinct identities as working-class neighborhoods through the 1920s and were still, to a large degree, "walking" communities, with residents working locally. Wealthy commuter villages of the late nineteenth century (Roland Park, Mount Washington, and West Arlington) and the early twentieth century (Guilford and Homeland) also continued to function as cohesive, semi-independent "suburbs" within the post-1918 city limits.[6]

Ethnicity, race, and class frequently defined neighborhoods. The more recent European immigrant ethnicities—Jews, Poles, Russians, Italians, and Lithuanians—tended to concentrate in the poor, densely populated row houses of the working-class residential belts around the harbors. Sometimes they resided in relatively homogeneous communities such as Little Italy, in more mixed neighborhoods such as Locust Point, or in ethnically distinct sections of multiethnic communities such as Old Town or Highlandtown. By the late 1920s, however, many people in these poor White ethnic communities were migrating to areas formerly inhabited by more affluent "natives" and longer-resident nationalities. Eastern European Jews, for example, began to follow the earlier route of German Jews, moving to sections of northwestern Baltimore, where they established fairly homogeneous working-class and lower-middle-class neighborhoods. Others, such as the Italians, tended to disperse in several directions to less ethnically defined neighborhoods. As newer immigrant ethnics began to migrate away from the harbor area, they pushed longer-resident White ethnics farther to the north and west, often to the new "row house suburbs" of West Baltimore. Generally, geographic mobility within the city was the result of improvements in economic circumstances and resulted in a dilution of immigrant ethnic community and culture. Moreover, geographic mobility tended to weaken the vitality of residential community life, as work was ever more separated from neighborhood and home.[7]

More affluent White groups also migrated out of the central city area during the 1920s, in part to escape class and racial/ethnic change. Upper-class residents from Mt. Vernon and Bolton Hill, wealthy neighborhoods to the north of downtown, settled in growing numbers in the more remote suburbs of Roland Park, Guilford, and Homeland. Increasing numbers of elite families moved beyond the city boundaries to the countryside at Green Spring, Worthington, and Dulaney Valley. The urban historian George H. Callcott sees this decade as a watershed, during which modern suburbanization was truly established and Baltimore County and Anne Arundel County were decisively pulled within the city's orbit.[8]

African Americans, however, were all but excluded from this residential movement. At the turn of the century, Baltimore's Black population was concentrated in three areas of the city: west of the Inner Harbor near the Camden yards of the Baltimore and Ohio Railroad, in Old West Baltimore northwest of the downtown, and, to a lesser extent, in Oldtown. Over the next three decades, the African American population grew steadily, especially during the Great Migration after 1914; nonetheless, African Americans remained ringed in by White residential areas, where they were constrained by segregationist covenant, custom, and violence from breaking through. As a result, African American neighborhoods suffered from the greatest population densities, the worst poverty, the highest incidence of disease and crime, and the most oppressive social conditions in the city. Some changes, however, took place in the residential distribution of the city's Black population. Old West Baltimore grew the most rapidly, and by the 1920s it had become the demographic and cultural center of Black Baltimore, while new warehouse construction displaced much of Camden, the oldest of the three Black concentrations. In addition, with rising population densities, predominantly Black residential areas became more racially homogeneous, and African Americans resided on block fronts and thoroughfares, as well as on alleys and back streets, the traditional residential areas for African Americans in many U.S. cities. African Americans' residential experience was typical of the "ghettoization" of Black urban communities that occurred in the late nineteenth century and early twentieth century. True to its border-city character, Baltimore's ghetto formation occurred about a decade earlier than that of the major northern cities and perhaps two to three decades behind the process in major southern cities.[9]

Finally, characteristic of the rapid post–Civil War industrialization of northern urban areas, Baltimore's growing industrial and commercial zones surged over their municipal boundaries. The land annexation of 1918 brought most of the region's industries back inside city lines, with one major exception: the steelworks at Sparrows Point. Located twelve miles southeast of the city center at the mouth of the Patapsco River, the giant Sparrows Point complex was founded in 1892 and purchased by Bethlehem Steel in 1916. It had its own company town, with planned residential segregation along lines of class, race, and skill level, and its own middle-class suburb in Dundalk.[10]

Then, during the nationwide boom of the First World War and the 1920s, industry grew inside the city limits to the north, west, and south of the harbor areas. To the east, industry again leapt over the city lines, and major concerns such as Standard Sanitary Manufacturing, Crown Cork and Seal, Standard Oil, Western Electric, and Anchor Fence built new installations in the area between Sparrows Point and Baltimore proper. To the northeast at Middle River, Glenn Martin Aircraft, the showpiece of Baltimore's new aircraft industry, located its central production facilities on a huge, two-mile-square tract of land far beyond the city's borders. Bethlehem Steel invested another $1 million at Sparrows Point during these years, making it the largest tidewater steel mill in the world. Some working-class residential development followed the eastward extension of the industrial region, but the vast majority of the workers in the new industries commuted from the city by rail or bus, further weakening neighborhood-based community. The extra-municipal expansion of industry also weakened the city government's control over the region's industrial base while strengthening the hand of a number of the business-dominated boards and bureaus that operated across the city boundaries.[11]

Economic and Political Power

From the mid-nineteenth century on, Baltimore's industrial and commercial sectors flourished; however, the city failed to develop a strong financial sector. During the last quarter of the nineteenth century, when financial capital was engineering great concentrations of industry across the United States, outside investment largely fueled the expansion of the city's industries. As the historian Sherry H. Olson has written, Baltimore had been one of the last remaining U.S. industrial centers characterized by "family ownership of industry"; during this period it became a "branch-plant town." By 1896, a group of Chicago financiers had purchased the Baltimore and Ohio Railroad, once the flagship of the city's economic expansion, and by 1916, Bethlehem Steel, based in Pennsylvania, had acquired the homegrown steel complex at Sparrows Point (see figure 4). Although locally owned enterprises in industry (garments, brewing, secondary metal fabrication), retail and wholesale trade, and regional transportation remained, large national firms predominated, and the region's business community, which now included the top regional managers of nationally owned firms, had come to embrace its financially subservient position. In 1919, Baltimore's business leaders created the Industrial Bureau to attract branch plants to the region—the first such organization in the country. Its efforts were apparently successful, for plants built by national corporations such as Western Electric, Glen L. Martin Aircraft, Berliner-Joyner, Doyle Aero, Curtis Caprivi, American Sugar, Lever Brothers, McCormick Spice, and Procter and Gamble were among the 103 new industrial concerns of the 1920s. The growing financial dependence of Baltimore on outside financial capital by the late 1920s was another expression of the city's "southern" position within the emerging northeastern megalopolis. But if much of the region's capitalist power structure had been "nationalized," out-of-town business elements rapidly adapted to certain local traditions, especially Baltimore-style Jim Crow.[12]

The city government, charged with managing social space and basic social processes within municipal boundaries, underwent waves of renovation from the late 1890s through the 1920s that were linked to the region's economic changes. Beginning with the new city charter of 1898, Progressive reformers in Baltimore, as elsewhere in the country, campaigning under the banner of efficient, business-oriented government, successfully undermined the existing city machine, tamed its ward-based political apparatus, and "modernized" municipal administration. The post-reform Democratic Party, however, retained effective clubs in many neighborhoods and was especially strong among most European ethnics. In contrast, the Republican

4. Located outside Baltimore's city boundaries, the Bethlehem Steel complex, shown here in the late 1930s, included the largest tidewater steel mill in the world. *Courtesy of Legacy Web, Baltimore County Public Library.*

Party received consistent support from wards dominated by African Americans, Jews, and Germans. Unlike many cities, South and North, there was real competition between the two parties for municipal office.[13]

A second wave of renovations to Baltimore city government began in 1918 at the climax of the region's First World War economic expansion. A home rule amendment to the state constitution allowed Baltimore City, alone among the municipalities of Maryland, the combined powers of city and county government, freeing the city's power elites from the interference of the rural- and town-based elites who controlled Maryland's county governments. Also, a unicameral City Council replaced the old bicameral body, and the number of election districts was reduced from seventeen to six, thereby weakening the influence of neighborhood-based forces. The African American community in particular suffered from this redistricting, which diluted its voting power and undermined its ability to elect Black City Council members, as it had done since 1890. Taken together, these reforms concentrated effective power in the hands of the White business elites at the very time that national finance capital was becoming increasingly influential within the region. To further strengthen its position, the business community formed the

Baltimore Association of Commerce in 1924, which developed a close relationship to the city government, and great influence throughout the city, the
industrial region, and the state. During the later 1920s the lobbying efforts
of this association were an important factor in the defeat of a minimum-
wage law, workmen's compensation legislation, the eight-hour workday for
women, a child labor amendment, a nonpartisan state insurance fund, and
a soldiers' bonus. By 1930, governance in Baltimore was, from the standpoint of the regional economic elite, rather "modern," business-oriented,
and distinct from both southern municipal cronyism and northern machine
politics.[14]

The Working Class and Its Traditions

Baltimore's working class at the end of the 1920s was large, internally differ-
entiated, multiethnic, and multiracial, and it boasted a long history of social
struggle, the legacy of which was inscribed in its structure, its traditions, and
its institutions.

Most historians use the term "working class" in vague and intuitive ways.
The definition of the working class used here, however, is quite specific: the
families and communities of those who own no productive property, exercise no essential control over the labor of others, and sell their ability to labor
for a wage or salary. From this point of view, the working class includes wage
and salary earners in factories, offices, shops, transportation concerns, educational bodies, government institutions, and the like. However, it excludes
supervisors, managers, bureaucrats, and certain categories of professionals
who have significant authority, delegated from above, over the labor process, even though they receive a salary. This latter group forms the nucleus
of a different social class, which analysts refer to using labels such as the
professional-managerial class, the salaried middle class, or the bureaucratic
petty bourgeoisie. The working class, despite its internal complexity, shares
essential class interests distinct from those of this managerial-professional-
bureaucratic class—and distinct from those small property holders, and of
the owners and agents of large capital—which gives it a particular unity and
basis for collective action.[15]

According to the 1930 federal census, 253,733 people, or 70 percent of the
gainfully employed, occupied working-class positions in Baltimore. A majority of the members of all of the major racial/ethnic groups in the city were
working class, although there were differences in the relative concentrations
of workers in each group: 58 percent of all employed U.S.-born Whites had
working-class jobs, as did 61 percent of employed foreign-born Whites and

more than 88 percent of all employed African Americans. Whites, whether U.S.-born or foreign-born, participated at similar rates in working-class labor; Blacks participated at a significantly higher rate; the African American community was, in its internal composition, the most working class in Baltimore. Working-class employment was, of course, gendered as well as racialized. Men held just over 70 percent of all working-class jobs, and women held just under 30 percent. Moreover, Black women (those older than fifteen) engaged in wage labor far more frequently (56%) than White U.S.-born women (30%) or foreign-born women (17%), and only African American married women worked in significant numbers.[16]

If Baltimore in 1930 was a working-class town, it was, more precisely, a "blue-collar" town. Nearly two-thirds of its workers were located in the industrial sector (manufacturing and transport), with just over 50 percent located in manufacturing alone. The remaining workers had various commercial, clerical, and personal-assistance jobs in a heterogeneous "service" sector. A very definite racial/ethnic and gendered division of labor distributed wage earners between and within these sectors of the working class. According to census data, employment in the industrial sector was nearly 85 percent male, with both native-born and foreign-born White men significantly overrepresented relative to their proportions in working-class employment as a whole. Despite a fivefold increase over the previous three decades, Black men remained underrepresented in manufacturing jobs, where they held about a fifth of the positions. Furthermore, White men, immigrant or U.S.-born, were overrepresented on the skilled and semi-skilled levels of the industrial sector, and African American men were decisively underrepresented. Black men were nearly always employed as unskilled manual laborers, and they disproportionately held the dirtiest and most dangerous jobs, such as those in fertilizers (89%) and rolling mills (67%). The relatively few women present in the industrial sector were almost all White and were largely operatives in textile, food processing, and, above all, clothing production—industries related to traditional conceptions of women's tasks. The tiny number of Black women in the industrial sector was mostly classified as laborers.[17]

The service sector of Baltimore's economy contained more than a third of the city's workers, although only about half of them worked in stores, shops, and offices that resembled the "service sector" workplaces of a modern capitalist economy. The other half worked as personal servants, maids, and domestic workers mostly in private households, and they often labored under preindustrial, premodern, and almost precapitalist conditions. While wage earners in "modern" service jobs were just over 60 percent male and tended to be U.S.-born Whites, 75 percent of all domestic workers and personal servants were women, and 75 percent were Black.[18]

In summation, the economic distribution of Baltimore's employed working class in 1930 contained some clear polarities. White men, foreign- and native-born, were clustered toward the skilled and semi-skilled ranks of the critical industrial sector, while Black men were relegated to the least skilled laboring positions in the industrial and service sectors. Similarly, White female workers were concentrated in commercial and clerical jobs in "modern" service work and in a few industries; Black women were overwhelmingly restricted to employment in domestic and personal service. On the macro-level, there is very little indication that European immigrant ethnicity was a powerful and systematic factor in working-class occupational distribution. Concentrations of particular European ethnicities did occur in some industries, but the overall picture is one of real dispersal across skill levels. However, it is clear that the racial division of labor rigidly compartmentalized and marginalized African American workers, especially when it combined with the gendered division of labor.

As they initiated collective resistance early in the Great Depression, Baltimore's working class drew on a number of occupational, racial/ethnic, and class traditions, especially labor unionism. At the end of the 1920s, Baltimore had the reputation of being a rather weak union town; only about 6–8 percent of its workers were organized. The relative weakness of the region's union movement may, however, be overstated, since it ranked seventh of the eleven largest cities in the country in average strikes per million residents per year for 1919–29, slightly below St. Louis, Philadelphia, Cleveland, and Buffalo, but above Detroit, Pittsburgh, and Chicago. Moreover, the city had a continuous history of workplace struggle, dating back to at least the 1790s, that was broadly similar to that of other large port cities and manufacturing centers. If the workers' movement was at low ebb in the late 1920s, labor unionism was nonetheless alive. There were in fact three major local union traditions, each based in particular sections of the working class: White craft unionism, industrial unionism, and African American trade unionism.[19]

Craft unionism, based in the skilled White male ranks of the industrial sector of the working class, dominated the small, organized labor movement at the end of the 1920s. The craft unions formed a large majority of the approximately 114 locals affiliated with the Baltimore Federation of Labor (BFL), a regional council connected to the national American Federation of Labor (AFL). In general, the craft unions and the BFL itself stood for conservative, bread-and-butter unionism, promoted self-help over government assistance, and were uninterested in organizing semi-skilled and unskilled workers. At least fifty-four of the region's craft unions organized skilled occupations closed to Black employment, and several more, especially in the building trades, had rules barring African American members. The best that could be said for BFL unions on the question of race, as the sociologist Ira De A. Reid put it in 1934, was that they "in the main have put forth no effort to secure Negro members." However, belying the federation's overall conservatism, a number of radicals and socialists were active, long-term members, and the BFL did include a number of industrial unions and a few predominantly African American unions in its ranks. In the 1920s, the BFL supported Progressive campaigns for state workmen's compensation, the eight-hour workday for women, and a ban on child labor. In 1924, in alliance with leading Black activists, it supported Robert La Follette's third-party bid for the presidency of the United States. Hence, progressive impulses existed within conservative BFL craft unionism, leading the federation to play an important, sometimes paradoxical, role in the social struggles that emerged in the 1930s.[20]

The industrial unions were carriers of the most militant and democratic traditions of the Baltimore workers' movement. Based mainly in older branches of the manufacturing sector, these unions sought in principle to organize workers industry-wide across skill levels, racial-ethnicity, and gender. For example, the International Ladies' Garment Workers Union (ILGWU) included workers from several European immigrant ethnicities and many women, and the United Textile Workers (UTW) was composed mostly of White, male, "native" Americans; both organized the unskilled, semi-skilled, and skilled. Some industrial unions in Baltimore, such as the locals of the ILGWU and the UTW, were affiliated with the craft-dominated BFL, but the most important and influential industrial union, the Amalgamated Clothing Workers (ACW)—based in men's clothing, the largest division of the region's garment industry—was not. Ethnically, the Baltimore ACW comprised mainly Eastern European Jews but also significant numbers of Italians, Bohemians, and Lithuanians, many of whom were foreign-born or first-generation U.S.-born, and most of its locals consisted of a single ethnicity. In fact, ACW locals conducted much of their business in languages other than English; the first explicitly English-language local was not formed until 1932. To mobilize support, the ACW appealed to the various European ethnic traditions of its members, and its locals frequently functioned as ethnic institutions, especially in the Jewish community. However, because of ongoing problems of ethnic contention between and within locals, the union leadership mounted an educational "Americanization" campaign in the 1920s to create a common "class consciousness" and to turn union members into citizens of a U.S. industrial democracy.[21]

In sharp contrast to many unions in Baltimore, the ACW and the ILGWU made attempts to organize Black workers, and the ACW actively promoted interracial solidarity during the 1920s through its workers' education program. It appears that the ethnic and at times racial discrimination that many immigrant garment workers, especially Jews, experienced made some of them more receptive than other Whites to an antiracist message. Nonetheless, the success of these unions in organizing Blacks was minimal, for African Americans represented only a small fraction of the garment workforce. The attempts at interracial unity were nonetheless symptomatic of a tradition of ethnic tolerance within industrial unionism in Baltimore that would become increasingly important in the 1930s. The more democratic, egalitarian ethos of these unions was also evident in the many female workers they organized, and especially in the case of the ACW, in the important local and national female leaders they produced. Still, gender equality was uneven, at best. As Jo Ann Argersinger shows, through much of the 1920s, ACW women struggled with very mixed success to improve their status in the union.[22]

Several currents of radicalism, from socialism and communism to Labor Zionism, colored the industrial unionism of the ACW and the ILGWU. Particularly pronounced in the Baltimore Joint Board of the ACW, the delegate assembly of the locals, such radicalism was reflected in the ACW's goals, which included carving out areas of workers' control on the job, replacing supervisors with union shop chairmen and chairwomen, creating independent boards of arbitration and labor courts, and establishing a negotiated "rule of law" to limit management prerogatives in the workplace. The ACW referred to this approach as "co-management." With its radically tinged industrial unionism, the ACW was to be a crucial player in the 1930s.[23]

The third major union tradition in Baltimore in the 1920s was that of African American labor, which had a long history. According to the historian Bettye C. Thomas, the Caulker's Association, organized in the late 1830s by free Blacks, was "one of the first black labor unions in the country." During the following decades, the African American workers' movement experienced ebbs and flows until the collapse of the Knights of Labor, the full imposition of segregation, and the rise of the BFL after the mid-1880s put Black labor seriously on the defensive. Nonetheless, the movement survived and underwent a minor renaissance in the region in the 1910s. In the early 1920s, Charles S. Johnson found about 3,880 mainly male Black union members in

transport and construction. Only a few Black workers were members of integrated locals, while many more belonged to independent African American
unions such as the Railway Men's Benevolent and Protective Association,
the Consolidated Hod Carriers No. 1, or the Colored Projectionists' Association of Baltimore. The largest number was members of the segregated
locals of White-dominated unions such as the International Hod Carriers
and Common Laborers, the Musicians Association, and the International
Longshoremen's Association (ILA). The experience of Black locals within
predominantly White-dominated unions varied. Some Black locals had their
own leadership and some autonomy, while others had White officers or were
largely controlled by an affiliated White local. Although some White trade
union locals cooperated with related Black locals, others worked actively to
undermine Black trade unionists, such as the White union bricklayers who
often employed non-union Whites rather than Black union hod carriers.
Black workers did, however, have real power in one AFL union: the ILA.[24]

African Americans in Baltimore fought for decades to defend their jobs
on the docks and their position in the longshoremen's movement. As a result, in 1930 69 percent of Baltimore longshoremen, and at least 60 percent of the city's ILA members, were Black. Although the ILA locals were
not strictly segregated, they were largely so. Of the five locals in town, three
had small minorities of Black members and one, composed of more highly
skilled checkers and shipping clerks, barred Blacks and immigrants. However, the largest and most important ILA local, No. 858, had a membership of
about 1,000 and was 90 percent African American. Local 858, with its independent Black leadership, formed the core of Baltimore's African American
labor movement at the time and was destined to play a key role in the 1930s
and early 1940s.[25]

The 1920s were nowhere a friendly decade for organized labor in the United
States, and by the end of the decade, all three segments of Baltimore's labor
union movement were in disarray. The BFL's membership had deteriorated
significantly. At a time that textile firms were beginning to relocate plants to
non-union areas farther south, the UTW fought and ultimately lost a bitter
eight-week-long strike in 1923. The men's clothing industry was in crisis, and
the ACW's membership fell drastically from its wartime high of more than
10,000 members to fewer than 3,000 by 1930. African American labor suffered, as well, and a number of predominantly Black unions disappeared over
the last half of the decade. Nevertheless, although the White craft, industrial,
and African American labor unionist traditions in the region were in decline
at the time of the Crash, they were surviving.[26]

Race, Ethnicity, and Community

Race and ethnicity have been discussed thus far without clear definitions. Given the importance of these concepts to this study, and the controversies among historians and others over them, a few definitional comments are necessary. Historically speaking, capitalist social formations, as they consolidate their territory under a centralized state apparatus, undertake to forge a single nation, with a single national identity, out of the nationalities, ethnicities, and peoples occupying that territory. This is an ongoing process, made more complicated when the territories and populations under the control of a "nation"-state change because of geographic expansion or immigration. The process of subordinating and assimilating minority ethnicities into the nation is always complex and seldom fully realized. Tendencies toward amalgamation often encounter opposing tendencies, including the resistance of subjected populations who seek to reproduce their own identities and cultures. Nationality is therefore an arena of social struggle. Moreover, from the point of view of the dominant power, there is no single method of subordination, amalgamation, or assimilation; there are, rather, a variety of possibilities, depending on history and context.[27]

In the United States—especially since the Civil War largely resolved the problem of regionally based nationality—two main systems of ethnic subordination have existed, one associated with the immigration of European nationalities (referred to in the dominant discourse as the "problem of ethnicity") and one involving peoples of color (the "problem of race"). Neither of these systems really has anything to do with human physiognomy or race as a biological category; both, in fact, have to do with ethnicity and "peoplehood." The roots of these two systems, and of the "color bar" that differentiates them, extend back to fifteenth-century European expansionism and colonialism, when notions of race developed to justify, on the nominal basis of physiological features, the aspirations of European ruling groups to dominate everything non-European. The color bar and the two related systems of ethnic subordination were structured into the settler-dominated society of North America from the beginning and evolved as that society expanded.

In the United States one system of ethnic subordination functioned to integrate members of European immigrant nationalities—most of whom were poor, working people—by relegating many of them to the margins of economy and polity, but only temporarily. Over a few generations, as these "alien" groups moved up the economic ladder, lost nationality-based cultural characteristics, experienced geographic dispersal, saw members marry outside their ethnicity, and assimilated into the dominant White American identity; they became "White." Certain remnants of European nationality often remained among "White ethnics" for generations as secondary notions of personal identity, holiday ritual, and sentimental attachment. Such remnants can affect behavior, but after two or three generations they seldom provide a foundation for a defined peoplehood or, in the strong sense of the word, an ethnicity.

The system for people of color, especially African Americans, has operated in a diametrically opposed manner. Blacks have been continuously relegated and re-relegated to the lower economic levels of society and to its political-cultural margins, and they have been subordinated and re-subordinated to all peoples defined as White. Their economic mobility has been severely circumscribed, and their ability to disperse into the larger population largely has been blocked—especially in terms of marrying outside their group. No matter how distantly separated from the lands and cultures of their ethnic origins, Black Americans never fully assimilated into the dominant national identity—that is, White identity. As a result, they have, over many generations, produced a distinct, separate, evolving African American ethnic identity and culture.

It is important to emphasize that European ethnic cultures were *immigrant* cultures that faded as their heirs became "Americanized" and "Whitened." African American culture also originated in a complex of foreign cultures, but it has not faded into the dominant ethnic culture. Instead, through continual reproduction and evolution over many generations, African American culture has developed as a distinct but thoroughly "American" culture, as American as any form of White culture. But the dominant racialist ideology continually casts the Black American people (and other people of color) as the "other," not White, not truly and fully American—indeed, not truly and fully human. To put it differently, nationality in the United States is formed in a permanent two-tier manner, with the top tier for Whites and the bottom tier for Blacks and other people of color. African Americans and, say, Irish Americans may both belong to ethnic groups, but they are ethnic groups of different types, with African Americans as a racialized ethnicity, or a racial/ethnic group.

The European immigrant ethnicities present in Baltimore in the early decades of the twentieth century, to varying degrees, formed communities with distinct traditions and institutions similar to those found in other U.S. cities, particularly northern ones. Ethnically based benevolent and self-help organizations, religious institutions, cultural formations, and, less frequently, political groupings abounded. However, the evidence suggests that by the late 1920s, a half-decade after the legal proscription of most immigration and a decade and a half after its effective end, the assimilation of European ethnicities in Baltimore into the dominant Whiteness was so advanced that the cohesiveness of their communities was in serious decline.

A partial exception to this general picture of decline of European ethnicity through the late 1920s was Baltimore's Jewish community, despite (or perhaps because of) its enormous internal class and ethnic contradictions. The 1930 federal census listed only country of origin and race, not religion, so the Jewish population was hidden among the census statistics for Russians, Poles, Germans, Lithuanians, and others. A reasonable guess, though, is that Jews in Baltimore may well have numbered as many as 70,000–80,000 at the end of the 1920s, and they were probably the largest European immigrant group in the region. However, they were an immigrant ethnicity with some significant differences.[28] While other European immigrants had been part of subjugated social classes in their own national homelands, or had come from homelands ruled by an imperial power of another nationality, immigrant Jews came from countries and regions in which they formed ethnically oppressed *minority* nationalities over a very long period. The memories and myths of this centuries-old oppression were inscribed in and permeated immigrant Jewish culture and were passed down to the U.S.-born generations. Consequently, Jewish culture, more than other European ethnic cultures, was in significant part a culture of ethnic resistance.[29]

In addition, Jews were subjected to more extreme forms of ethnic oppression in Baltimore and the United States more generally than other European minorities. Only Jews among Baltimore's White ethnics in the 1920s, for example, were systematically and overtly excluded from residing in certain neighborhoods; notices that Jews were forbidden in new housing developments even appeared on billboard advertisements. Nominally, discrimination against Jews was based on religious difference—and, indeed, in a decade during which Christian godliness was especially close to Americanism, religion was particularly important. In addition, semi-racial stereotyping of Jews, far more widespread than was the case for other white ethnic groups, reinforced discrimination. Anti-Semitism in the United States in the 1920s, like that in Europe, had a resurgent tendency to cast Jews as perpetual others, regardless of degree of assimilation to the dominant culture or the number of generations in residence. To put it differently, since Jews were, in the view of the dominant Jim Crow culture, not quite White, themes of resistance from their European Jewish backgrounds were reinforced by experience in the United States. Despite the greater ethnic subjugation they faced, however, Jewish Americans experienced geographic and occupational mobility like that of other European ethnic groups, and quite unlike that of African Americans.

Interestingly, far from being a unified immigrant nationality in terms of class and ethnicity, Baltimore Jews were among the most divided. The central contradiction in the community was the ethnic antagonism between German Jews and Eastern European Jews. The community of German Jews in Baltimore was founded in the mid-nineteenth century and by the end of the 1920s was well established, with a status similar to that of Baltimore's large German Christian community. German Jews largely spoke English, practiced Reform Judaism, were middle or upper class, and lived uptown. In contrast, the Eastern European Jews who arrived later spoke Yiddish, were Orthodox in religion, were overwhelmingly working class, and lived downtown. In fact, there was significant social, cultural, and geographic distance between the two groupings, and their members had little to do with each other on the level of daily, neighborhood-based intercourse.[30]

However, the relationships between Eastern European and German Jews in Baltimore were complicated. In the first place, German Jews created philanthropic institutions that primarily aided the poorer, later arriving Eastern European Jews, thereby strengthening their common Jewish identity. This philanthropy, though, was often extremely paternalistic and sometimes openly based on German Jews' embarrassment over the supposedly less civilized Eastern Europeans. In addition, many Eastern European Jews labored for little pay in clothing firms owned by German Jews; as a result, the union struggle in the garment industry sometimes took on the complexion of class war within the Baltimore Jewish community. Nonetheless, Jewish-owned firms allowed Orthodox Jewish workers to maintain their religious practices, and wealth from garment production was spread throughout the Jewish community (albeit unequally). As a result, the internal social complexity of the Baltimore Jewish community included institutions that crossed lines of differences (the Jewish Court of Justice, the philanthropies), and institutions representing distinct ethnic sections of the community (the Reform temples, the Orthodox *shules*, the *landsmanshaftn*[31]). In addition, drawing on Jewish cultural traditions of resistance, the Baltimore community had a socially active wing that was expressed in working-class-based radicalism (Labor Zionism, the Socialist Bund, the Workmen's Circle), as well as in middle- and upper-class-based urban Progressivism. The socially active wing contained some of the city's most prominent social liberal intellectuals and philanthropists, as well as some of its most militant and radical proletarians.[32]

Finally, more than the city's other European ethnicities on the eve of the Depression, the Jewish community had the cohesiveness and sense of identity (despite its internal contradictions) to generate a distinct, mass social movement, primarily in the garment industry, where some local branches of the ACW functioned as Jewish community institutions. Nonetheless, trade unions are prototypically class, not ethnic, organizations, and even the largely Jewish garment unions in Baltimore included workers of other national backgrounds, especially Italians and Italian Americans.[33]

Black Baltimore: Conditions, Culture, and Resistance

African Americans, who formed Baltimore's largest ethnic community, numbered some 142,106 persons in 1930 and were situated on the other side of the color bar from the European ethnicities. The only racial/ethnic community of significant size, African Americans had struggled for generations against sharp, continuous racial oppression—first under slavery, then under various forms of segregation. In the process, they had developed an ethnic culture and identity in which traditions of resistance—overt, subtle, unconscious, and sometimes contradictory—were particularly strong. By 1930, after 150 years of continuous existence, the African American community was not only the metropolitan region's largest and oldest minority community, it was also the only ethnic group with a tradition of resistance strong enough to fully mount a distinct oppositional movement. Indeed, alongside the Baltimore working class and overlapping with it, the region's African American community provided the social basis for one of the great social movements that would arise in the region during the Depression.[34]

The segregationism under which African Americans in Baltimore lived at the end of the 1920s was ubiquitous. Blacks had separate and inferior schools, cinemas, concert halls, restaurants, recreational facilities, and health-care services. Many department stores were segregated, and in those that were not, Blacks were often barred from trying on clothes. The few facilities that were available to both Blacks and Whites maintained separate, less desirable sections for Blacks. According to testimony, by 1930 there were only two places in the city, outside the African American neighborhoods, that Blacks and Whites could easily hold an integrated meeting: Homewood Friends Meeting House and the Young Men's Christian Association (YMCA) at Levering Hall, both on the campus of Johns Hopkins University. In the nominally integrated public places in the city, the White power structure still made it clear that it considered Blacks outsiders. As Thurgood Marshall, who often referred to Baltimore as "way up South," recalled from his childhood, "Another thing I remember very well is that there were no toilet facilities available to Negroes in the downtown area. One day, I remember, I had to go. The only thing I could do was get on the trolley car and try to get home. And I did almost get in the house, when I ruined the front doorsteps. That gives you an idea of what we went through."[35]

Yet unlike in much of the South, by 1930 African Americans in Baltimore could sit anywhere on most municipal public transportation, and while there were obstacles to voter registration and to voting, they were less formidable than in many southern states. In fact, the African American community had a strong tradition of electoral activity; of the eighteen City Council elections between 1890 and 1930, Black candidates won seats in thirteen. The city was, in the words of the historian Suzanne Ellery Greene, "almost unique in the continuing presence of blacks in high public office," although the municipal redistricting of the 1920s ended this. Also, Maryland was the only state in the country to have, as a part of its state government, an Interracial Commission (albeit an ineffective one) with the stated purpose of alleviating racial tensions. Nonetheless, formal and informal Jim Crow had a calamitous effect on Baltimore's Black community. Blacks suffered from devastatingly high rates of poverty, crime, and disease; low life expectancy; and high rates of infant mortality and illegitimacy. Relatively few could afford to own homes in a city that prided itself on widespread home ownership among all classes. Even the limited gains in geographic and economic mobility experienced by some Blacks in the 1920s were severely circumscribed by legal and extralegal means, and these gains were in no way analogous to the progress made by the assimilating generations of White ethnics.[36]

The other side of this dismal picture was that, in resisting and surviving Jim Crow, African Americans built a culturally and institutionally rich community despite having a relatively weak business sector. According to a study conducted in 1934 by Ira De A. Reid, Baltimore, with the fourth largest African American population in the country, was ninth in the number of stores with Black proprietors. There were a few truly capitalist concerns with wage-earning employees, only six of which grossed more than $100,000 in 1931, and only two took in more than $150,000. Among the largest Black-owned businesses that supported the community's tiny upper class of capitalists were the Afro-American Publishing Company, the Druid Hill Laundry, the Dunbar Theater Amusement Company, and the Metropolitan Finance Corporation. Interestingly, the number of professionals in the Black community was relatively large, according to Reid, "more favorable in Baltimore than in the United States as a whole." The city then boasted approximately 3,000 African American teachers, clergymen, physicians, dentists, journalists, lawyers, social workers, and other professionals. Together they formed a salaried petty bourgeoisie, a middle-class intelligentsia, which included significant numbers of women, as well as men, and had a great impact on the community's culture and politics.[37]

Reid estimated that 400 social clubs existed in the community, and his qualifying statement that "bridge, five hundred and whist are the 'raison d'etre' for more than half" of them does nothing to diminish the perception that the community was a web of organization. This web included institutions devoted to "high" culture, such as the Baltimore City Colored Orchestra and Chorus and a variety of "clubs devoted to interpretation of the arts, literature and music." It included establishments of "popular" culture including the large theaters and dancehalls of upper Pennsylvania Avenue—a major center of the national "Negro Renaissance" of the interwar era—and neighborhood cabarets and poolhalls. The community also supported a professional baseball team, the Baltimore Black Sox, which won the American Negro League pennant in 1929 and soundly thrashed a team of White major and minor league players in an exhibition series that year.[38]

The institutional web also included twenty-odd fraternal organizations, including lodges of the Improved Benevolent Protective Order of the Elks of the World, the Grand Order of Odd Fellows, the Colored Knights of Pythias, and the Order of the Masons. A number of important institutions for social welfare and recreation, such as the Druid Hill YMCA and YWCA and the Sharp Street Community House, existed along with a string of active Parent–Teacher Associations. Both the Republican and Democratic parties had Black ward clubs. The community also maintained a series of women's organizations, including chapters of the Women's Christian Temperance Union, the National Association of College Women, the Maryland Association of Colored Women, the Cooperative Women's Civic League, and the Housewives League.[39]

Many institutions crossed social strata, but some were explicitly tied to particular classes and groups, such as the Baltimore Branch of the Maryland Medical, Dental, and Pharmaceutical Association, the Medical Forum, the Schoolmasters' Association, and the Social Workers' Roundtable. Students at the predominantly Black Morgan College had fraternities and sororities. The Association for the Promotion of Negro Business actively encouraged African American enterprise through a variety of activities, including Negro Trade Week, an event that drew tens of thousands of onlookers each year, while Black trade unionists, as noted above, carried forward a long tradition of African American working-class struggle.[40]

By the early 1930s, Baltimore's Black community was effectively co-opting segregated municipal institutions for its own purposes. For example, the Division of Recreation for Colored People of the Board of Education, with its all-Black staff, organized seventy-one neighborhood clubs with more than 5,000 members that sponsored dramatic, musical, and "Social-Civic" activities that attracted a total of 87,097 people. The "colored schools" were an even better example of such community organization. Starting in the immediate post–Civil War era, Baltimore's Black community fought a protracted battle for public schooling for its children (achieved in 1867), for Black teachers (fully achieved by 1904), and for community influence over Black schools. Two of the biggest victories also resulted from community agitation: in 1925, Black teachers won substantial salary equality with White teachers in the city's public schools, and in 1927 Francis Wood was appointed the first African American director of colored schools. Between 1900 and 1933, as the Black population in the city increased by 93 percent and the Black school population increased by 170 percent, educational facilities for Blacks greatly expanded. The Division of Colored Schools oversaw thirty-eight Black public schools, including elementary and junior high schools, Frederick Douglass High School (the pride of many in the community), the Colored Vocational School, and Coppin Normal School for teachers. As Reid explained, "With the possible exception of Washington, DC, Baltimore has the most elaborate public school set-up for the Negro population to be found in the United States." In addition, Morgan College, run by the Methodist church, was located in the community and offered four years of unaccredited higher education. However, the all-White Board of Education retained ultimate control over all schools, and in the early 1930s, $67.61 per year was spent on each White student, but only $48.01 on each Black student. Despite this inequality, overall illiteracy in the Black community fell from 25.7 percent in 1900 to 7 percent in 1930, and the educated stratum of the community increased. The Black schools, if still contested ground, were justifiably viewed as community institutions, inadvertently training a vigorous group of educated young people for the freedom struggle of the early 1930s.[41]

As in other urban African American communities, the main institutional and cultural cornerstone of Black Baltimore was the church—or, rather, the legion of Black churches. There were, in 1934, 216 Black Protestant churches in Baltimore, approximately one for every 425 African American adults. Of these, nine had regular memberships of more than 1,000; some were long established (five were more than a hundred years old); and a few had large, impressive houses of worship—notably the Sharp Street Methodist Episcopal church, with the oldest Black-built sanctuary in the city, and Bethel African Methodist Episcopal church. At the other end of the spectrum, more than one hundred churches were of recent origin, holding meetings in storefronts or houses, and many of these had congregations of fewer than fifty. Two-score Black pastors in the city claimed college and seminary degrees, but many more lacked any formal training.

The larger African Methodist Episcopal (AME) and Methodist Episcopal churches, located in less depressed neighborhoods in northwestern Baltimore, tended to minister disproportionately to more affluent urban Blacks, while the smaller churches, frequently Baptist in denomination and located in more depressed areas, attracted poor workers with recent rural backgrounds. The differences in social composition of these churches should not be overstated, though, for the Black community was so overwhelmingly poor and working class that all of the larger congregations had significant proletarian memberships; in the early 1930s, only one-fourth to one-third of the members of even the most affluent churches could afford to make regular financial contributions.[42]

An unusual feature of Black Christianity in Baltimore was that it included a large number of Black Catholics, estimated at more than 12,000 in the early 1930s. Most African American Catholics in Baltimore attended the city's four all-Black Catholic churches, and the rest sat in segregated pews of predominantly White churches. Significantly, none of the fourteen priests working with Black Catholics were themselves African American, although fifty of 161 nuns were. Beyond Christianity, there was a small movement of Muslims and another of Black Jews, but neither—nor in fact the Black Catholics—had much influence within the community. However, on the margins of Black Christianity were a number of so-called cult churches led by charismatic, millenarian figures and by self-defined bishops and archbishops, and they made more of an impact, especially in the early 1930s.[43] The religious ideology of the region's Black Protestant churches was, as in the United States as a whole, infused with images of resistance to oppression and the quest for freedom. More than simply religious institutions, many of these churches functioned as community centers with a wide range of activities specifically targeting young people, men, women, or families as a whole. Many became, to varying degrees, social welfare agencies for their congregations, providing numerous forms of relief to members in need, sometimes helping parishioners to find jobs, and, in a few cases, organizing sickness and death benefit societies. None of this meant that these churches or their clergy self-consciously viewed themselves as part of a social justice movement. Instead, they, like many of the other institutions of African American Baltimore, were shaped by the long struggle to create a culture under conditions of racist oppression and thereby carried within them traditions of resistance.

In addition, the churches represented a political reserve that could be tapped by the freedom movement when needed.[44]

In discussing the organizations of the Baltimore freedom movement proper, it is helpful to distinguish between those mainly oriented toward economic betterment and self-help and those that pursued political-juridical change. The most prominent organizations on the economic front were the Black trade unions, two organizations of Black women, and the local branch of the Urban League. The Black trade unions were reviewed earlier, but two additional points should be made here. First, they represented the only segment of the freedom movement that was openly led by working-class elements. Second, because they focused on the workplace, not the neighborhood or public realm, as other freedom organizations did, they were the segment least integrated into the freedom movement's core.

The Cooperative Women's Civic League (CWCL) and the Housewives League (HL) were both expressions of activism among African American women in Baltimore that, according to the historian Cynthia Neverton-Morton, is "often ignored by historians." As Neverton-Morton has shown, the CWCL was well known for its Annual Flower Mart and art contests but was also deeply involved in the fight for neighborhood and residential improvement, advocating both self-help and protest. In addition, the CWCL, which claimed 300 members on the eve of the Depression, played an important role in the struggles over Black schools during the 1920s. The CWCL was an outgrowth of the Women's Civic League, a White organization formed in 1911 as a part of the Progressive Movement and affiliated with the State Federation of Women's Clubs. White leaders of the Women's Civic League encouraged the formation of the CWCL in 1913 under the leadership of the African American social worker Sarah Fernandis. An integrated advisory committee composed of equal numbers of leading members from both leagues helped to guide the CWCL during the 1930s. Since the memberships of the two organizations seldom mixed, and there was no advisory committee including Black members for the Women's Civic League, the two bodies were not only separate but also *unequal*.[45]

While the CWCL focused on neighborhood and educational improvement, the HL sought to build a consumers' movement among African American women. Reporting a membership of 2,000 women organized into eighteen branches in Baltimore in the early 1930s, the HL encouraged the patronage of Black-owned businesses as a strategy to build community self-sufficiency and provide job opportunities for Black youth. Nationally, the HL had been established by the Colored Merchants Association, which was founded by the National Negro Business League in 1928. While the HL's advocacy that

Black consumers "buy only where you can work"—that is in stores with Black employees—had little practical effect, it prepared the ground for a watershed struggle of the Black freedom movement in the first half of the 1930s.[46]

The Baltimore branch of the Urban League (BUL), founded in 1924, was the most nationally connected of the local organizations involved in economic betterment. The BUL was heir to the Progressive era belief that by "scientifically" investigating social problems and publicizing them, remedial action could be stimulated. Its strategy was to work in concert with other community forces every step of the way. During its most successful campaign of the 1920s, the "Lung Block" campaign, the BUL studied the conditions in a particularly tuberculosis-ridden section of northwestern Baltimore, published its report in the *Afro-American* newspaper, and enlisted a series of community organizations (including the CWCL) to press for renewal of the area. The BUL used similar methods during the 1920s to expose the plight of Blacks in Baltimore's industries and to press for more jobs; to improve medical care at Provident Hospital, which served the African American community; and to win better recreational facilities for Black youth. The BUL, however, was not a mass-membership organization, and it was not capable of, nor oriented toward mounting popular campaigns to achieve its ends. A paid staff of one or two social workers largely carried out its activities, working with a small core of volunteer activists and occasionally with personnel from the national staff. In the words of Reid, himself a national staff member, the BUL functioned as the "electric eye of social organizations in the Negro community" and "sought . . . to utilize the available community resources in effecting the adjustments." Its executive board included some of the most prominent African Americans in Baltimore, as well as a number of leading White academics, religious figures, professionals, and businessmen. The Baltimore Community Chest, perhaps the most established White philanthropy in the city, provided the bulk of the BUL's funding.[47]

The Baltimore branch of the NAACP was from its founding in 1912—as the second local branch in the country—through the 1920s the leading freedom movement organization active in the political-juridical arena. Like the BUL, the NAACP was a product of the Progressive era, but unlike the BUL, it was a membership organization and had no paid staff, and nearly all of its members and leaders were Black. The Baltimore NAACP was heir to a local tradition of protest extending back to the Mutual United Brotherhood of Liberty, organized in 1885, which worked successfully to overturn "Black Laws," admit Black lawyers to the bar, and open Black schools to Black teachers. In 1904, the Brotherhood sent a delegate to the founding meeting of the Niagara

Movement. In the early 1900s, the Colored Men's Suffrage League (another NAACP precursor) allied with White immigrants and Republicans to stop attempts by the Maryland state government to ban party symbols on the ballot (making voting difficult for the illiterate) and to institute property requirements, literacy tests, and grandfather clauses. During the same period, the Black community of Baltimore lobbied actively against a state bill to segregate railroads and steamships in Maryland; as a result, Baltimore was exempted. Then, between 1910 and 1913, the city government passed four residential segregation ordinances to prohibit Blacks from living in White neighborhoods. Black activists challenged these ordinances in the courts, got the first three overturned, and in the process formed the Baltimore NAACP branch. Its immediate popularity was demonstrated in 1913, when 1,500 people assembled at Bethel AME church to hear the national NAACP leader Oswald Garrison Villard speak. The fourth ordinance was finally struck down in 1917 as a result of local and national NAACP litigation. Throughout the late 1910s and the 1920s, the Baltimore NAACP fought for improvements to Black education, aided the campaigns of the BUL and other freedom organizations, and provided a base of support for African American electoral campaigns. Harry S. Cummings, Warner T. McGuinn, Walter Emerson, and William Fitzgerald—all of whom served on the City Council at various points between 1915 and 1930—were affiliated with the NAACP, as was George McMechen, who ran unsuccessfully for the City Council in 1915. It is however important to note, that while the Baltimore NAACP and its precursors engaged in popular education around key issues, and became involved in electoral campaigns, they never really attempted popular mobilizations like those that became increasingly common in the 1930s.[48]

While the NAACP was the most important political *organization* in the community, its ally, the *Afro-American* newspaper was the center of the community's political culture. The *Afro*, founded in 1892, reported on religion, sports, all types of community activities, entertainment and culture, and "society" (meaning the activities of the Black community's upper crust). It combined lurid reporting of sex and violence with serious and sometimes moralistic editorials; it published stories of special interest to women and poems and fiction by Black authors. It had a magazine section, a regular person-on-the-street column, and a lively letters to the editor section. As the historian Hayward Farrar has pointed out, the diversity of the paper's features, including its infamous sensationalism, made it truly community oriented, with something for almost everyone. However, for all the variety of the *Afro*'s articles, editorials, and features, a consistent political advocacy permeated the newspaper. Important stories about the Black freedom movement, especially in Baltimore, invariably got prominent billing. Editorials and opinion columns, more extensive than those in many major African American newspapers, ruminated on the character of racism and the fight against it. Coverage of national and international events often had the purpose of educating the readership on Black culture, social reality, and history worldwide. Reviews of movies, plays, music, and art exhibitions often served to expose White racist stereotypes or to promote African American traditions. Especially during the Harlem Renaissance years, in Farrar's words, the "*Afro*'s feature pages were dotted with the poems and essays of Langston Hughes, Countee Cullen, and Claude McKay" and other racial/ethnically conscious writers. Even sports reporting became a celebration of African American identity, with this trend hitting its peak during the 1930s in the *Afro*'s abundant coverage of the fights, opinions, and romantic life of the heavyweight boxing champion Joe Louis. Moreover, the very language of the *Afro* served to positively reinforce African American identity. In a reversal of the practice of the White press, Whites in the *Afro* were routinely identified by race (e.g., "John Doe [White] was arrested"), while African Americans were not, and Whites viewed unsympathetically were frequently referred to with pejorative slang ("ofay" being common). In fact, the name of the newspaper itself was part of this language-conscious tradition: "Afro-American" was intentionally chosen because it was seen as a positive alternative to "Negro."[49]

In every issue at the top of the editorial page, the *Afro* reminded all of its readers of what might be called the traditional agenda of the local freedom movement. Under the title "What the 'AFRO' Stands For," seven points were listed:

1. Colored policemen, policewomen and firemen.
2. Colored representatives on city, county and State boards of education.
3. Equal salaries for equal work for schoolteachers without regard to color or sex.
4. Colored members of boards of State institutions where inmates are colored.
5. The organization of labor unions among all groups of colored workers.
6. A university and agricultural college for colored people supported by the State.
7. Closer co-operation between farmers and the State and Federal farm agents.

While hardly comprehensive, these points represent a broad set of cross-class demands for the African American community in the metropolis of Baltimore.[50]

By the early 1930s, the reach of the *Afro* had extended throughout the

5. Carl Murphy, publisher and president of the *Afro-American*. *Courtesy of the Afro-American Newspapers Archives and Research Center.*

metropolitan regions and well into its hinterlands. In addition to two weekly issues focusing mainly on Baltimore and Maryland, the *Afro* published a Washington, D.C., edition, and a national edition that had special news pages for Richmond, Philadelphia, and other nearby cities. Its total circulation rose from 20,149 in 1920 to 40,432 in 1930; in 1935, circulation reached 58,978, making it the third largest Black newspaper in the country after the *Pittsburgh Courier* and the *Chicago Defender*. Moreover, the *Afro* was one of the largest, most profitable, and fastest growing Black-owned businesses in Baltimore, expanding from fourteen employees in 1922 to seventy-six in 1933 and 118 in 1938. The paper made a profit during every Depression year but two: 1932 and 1938.[51]

Carl Murphy, publisher and president of the *Afro*, was one of African American Baltimore's most prominent figures (see figure 5). Murphy was the son of the newspaper's founder, held bachelor's and master's degrees in German from Harvard, did postgraduate study at Jena University in Germany, and was a veteran of the First World War. Before returning to Baltimore to take over the *Afro* in 1922, he was a professor of German at Howard University. From the early 1930s until his death in 1968, Murphy was at the center of the freedom movement, both locally and nationally, serving as a member of the executive board of the BUL, as chair of the legal committee of the Baltimore NAACP, as a member of the Maryland Interracial Commission, and as a national board member of the NAACP.[52]

One of the great strengths of the *Afro*'s political advocacy under Murphy's leadership was that it was not monolithic, and it made no attempt to promote a single viewpoint or strategy. This approach started under his father, John H. Murphy, who covered both sides of the debates between W. E. B. Du Bois and Booker T. Washington sympathetically but endorsed neither. As Farrar has shown, Carl Murphy's editorials extolling family, school, and motherhood, would appear side by side with columns by the *Afro* regular Ralph Matthews satirizing the same subjects. More generally, the *Afro* combined secularism with religiosity and pro-nationalist sentiments (praise for Marcus Garvey, advocacy of Black economic independence) with pro-integrationist views. By the end of the 1920s, the *Afro-American* was the most important bearer and propagator of the traditions, history, and agenda of the whole Black freedom struggle in Baltimore.[53]

Finally, a few words are needed on the overall social character of Baltimore's freedom movement on the eve of the Depression. Some, in analyzing such movements, follow the tradition of the sociologist E. Franklin Frazier and characterize them as products of the "Black bourgeoisie." However, if one takes the term "bourgeoisie" seriously to refer to the tiny Black capitalist class, it is clear that it did not and could not have dominated the movement in Baltimore of the late 1920s. Rather, it seems more useful to think of this freedom movement—its membership, its leadership, and the interests represented in its programs and activities—as a cross-class alliance within Black Baltimore. It represented a *social bloc* spanning the class hierarchy from the capitalist elite to the middle classes, including a small segment of the upper working class, and this bloc attempted with some success to speak for the overwhelmingly working-class African American community as a whole. The freedom movement was, however, not really a mass movement before the Crash. Its key organizations did not attempt to recruit a mass membership or to mobilize a mass base; the Black labor unions, which did to varying degrees make such attempts, were on its periphery. The real center of gravity, the activists at the core, were drawn from the ranks of teachers, lawyers, social workers, journalists, ministers, doctors, and members of the salaried and small-property-owning middle classes. It was an expression of the "premodern" freedom movement, and it provided the preconditions for the emergence of the transformed "modern" long freedom movement in Baltimore in the first years of the Depression.[54]

The 1920s End

After the school struggles of the mid-1920s, the Black freedom movement in Baltimore slid into a decline. The *Afro-American*, as it often did at such times, reminded the inactive freedom organizations of their responsibilities, but to little effect. As if in frustration, the *Afro* staff in July 1929 took an unusual step into the political arena by initiating a struggle themselves against Jim Crow in public transport, thereby anticipating the direct action tactics that later would become common. The only part of Baltimore's transportation system that was segregated in 1929 was the United Railways bus system. This was de facto segregation; White bus drivers would often refuse to pick up Black passengers or would harass them if they managed to get on board. Blacks felt these discriminatory actions were a matter of company policy, which, of course, the company denied. So the *Afro* sent a team of light-skinned and dark-skinned reporters out with a photographer to test and document the discrimination. The *Afro* published the resulting evidence of discrimination and called on Black Baltimoreans to go out and make their own tests. In addition, the *Afro* contacted the bus company, the Public Service Commission, and the mayor about the situation and published the results of those contacts. An ad hoc group of Black Baptist ministers answered the *Afro*'s call and began to test the bus company's policy for itself.[55]

Within a month, harassment of Blacks on the buses had ended, and the White president of United Railways assured the ministers that there would be no more racial discrimination. "We are all brothers," he told them. It was a victory, but an ambiguous one. No similar activity followed the United Railways bus actions, and the freedom movement continued to ebb, but the *Afro*'s campaign was a harbinger of the future.[56]

II. Emergences, 1930–1934

2

Disrupting the Calm

The Communist Party in Baltimore, 1930–1933

Reds as courageous as the Minute Men or the volunteer firemen seem
everywhere ready for a demonstration against race prejudice.
—CARL MURPHY, Publisher, Baltimore *Afro-American*, May 9, 1931

Although economic stagnation hit Baltimore as early as 1927, the Great Depression settled more slowly into this metropolitan region than others.[1]
About six months after the Crash, the U.S. Census Bureau recorded unemployment levels at 9.8 percent in Boston, 9.6 percent in New Orleans, 9.5
percent in Philadelphia, 9.4 percent in Pittsburgh, and 8.3 percent in New
York, but only 5.7 percent in Baltimore. Baltimore's diversified industrial sector, plus its strategic trading position internationally and vis-à-vis the South
and West, initially cushioned the blow. However, unemployment for Blacks
was, as it had been for a number of years, at least one and a half times that of
Whites. But despite the growing hardship, a tense calm prevailed for a time.[2]

The response of the city government and economic elites to the growing
misery was a combination of denial and malign neglect, mixed with only a
smattering of charity. On the other end of the spectrum, the crisis provoked
not rebellion but further demoralization among the already stagnating social movements of the region. In a mild stirring of the Black freedom movement, the local NAACP and the *Afro-American* newspaper announced a voter
registration drive, and the BUL called for a jobs campaign, but little resulted.
Spontaneous struggle occurred as yet another Black family fought its White
neighbors in an attempt to retain its home on an otherwise all-White block.
More dramatically, 2,000 African Americans protested the closing of a bank
that held their deposits, and sixty-four were arrested. Spontaneous popular
actions were infrequent and isolated, however, and although they indicated
impulses toward broader resistance, they had little immediate impact. At
the beginning of 1931, the *Afro* issued one of its periodic calls to arms, berat-

ing the NAACP, the BUL, and the Cooperative Women's Civic League for in-
action.[3]

The state of the workers' movement was little better. The overall strike
rate was down and continued to drop every year through 1933. Four hundred and fifty members of the Painters, Decorators, and Paperhangers Union
won a rare victory for the skilled trades in 1930 when they put down their
tools, demanded a pay increase, and prevailed. The drivers at Sun Cab who
walked out and the thousands of garment workers who struck twenty-four
clothing shops were far less successful. The Baltimore Federation of Labor
(BFL) went about business as usual by protesting Prohibition, ceremoniously
announcing plans to organize barbers, proposing concrete seats for the new
stadium, and discussing electoral endorsements. During a BFL debate on
daylight savings time, representatives of the White unions insisted on segregated seating, and the Black representatives of the mainly African American
Local 858 of the International Longshoremen's Association (ILA) walked out
of both the meeting and the BFL. White ILA representatives followed them
in solidarity. In response to growing unemployment, the BFL—imbued with
the "voluntarism" and hostility toward government social programs that was
the hallmark of AFL craft unionism—simply dithered.[4]

As the crisis deepened through the first years of the Depression, tensions
rose in the Baltimore metropolitan region, and new leadership emerged, in-
stituting new forms for struggle. It is notable that these new struggles were
often led by self-described radicals of various sorts, who sought fundamental change and were committed—whether their activities concerned the
workers' movement, the freedom movement, or both—to opposing racism.
Moreover, these new forms of struggle between 1930 and mid-1933 were
located almost entirely in the neighborhood and public spheres, although an
undercurrent of unorthodox workplace struggle surfaced during the period.
As the new forms of struggle proved more and more effective, a few of the
older local organizations were re-energized, but most continued to stumble
along toward the middle of the decade.

The Communist Party

The Baltimore section of the Communist Party (CP) was the first group decisively to disrupt the tense calm in post-Crash Baltimore. From 1930 to
1933, it launched a series of militant campaigns and developed a novel set of
organizational forms in both the workers' movement and the Black freedom
movement, based at first at the neighborhood level, then increasingly in the
workplace. The Baltimore CP insisted, as no predominantly White organiza-

tion in the region had ever done before, that antiracism had to be integral to every struggle. The CP was, of course, a national, internationally linked organization, but in these years there was something profoundly local about party initiatives, which often responded creatively to local conditions and opportunities. Moreover, the Baltimore CP got results (although not always the ones it desired): while historians have often missed the fact, it played a significant role in catalyzing and shaping the subsequent social movements in the region.[5]

It must be emphasized that the Baltimore CP was always a small organization, smaller than party sections located in a number of other large cities and industrial regions to the North and West. Indeed, its diminutive size has probably led many historians and observers to assume that it was of marginal importance. It appeared publicly in the region around 1926, and, by the end of the decade, its core membership probably numbered only in the dozens. Organizationally, the Baltimore party was a section of the CP's District Three, headquartered in Philadelphia. Through the early 1930s, membership in the Baltimore CP and Young Communist League (YCL) grew in a fluctuating manner, with much turnover in the ranks. But by mid-decade, a new party district was formed based in Baltimore, covering Maryland and the District of Columbia. At that point, CP membership in the city ranged in the low hundreds. The party, however, always had a periphery of close supporters that was several times larger than its actual membership. As early as 1927, a reported crowd of 1,500 came out to hear the national party leader Jay Lovestone speak in Baltimore, and in 1933, 800–1,000 people attended the party-sponsored celebration of the sixteenth anniversary of the Bolshevik Revolution.[6]

The evidence suggests that, during the early 1930s, the Baltimore CP was largely working-class in composition. Ethnically, the party membership was drawn heavily from recent European immigrant communities, especially Eastern European Jews, Finns, Lithuanians, and Russians. Toward mid-decade, more intellectuals and "Americans" (as party literature sometimes called them) gravitated toward the Baltimore party section, and increasing numbers of the Americans were Black. One military intelligence report in 1932 put the Black membership of the Baltimore CP at 60 percent of the total—surely an overestimation, but an indication of a significant African American presence.[7]

Despite their limited numbers, Communists in Baltimore were remarkably optimistic and energetic in the wake of the Crash, drawing strength from an ideological outlook that, in a sense, was millenarian. They saw the Depression simply not as a great disaster but also as an enormous opportunity.

Like their comrades throughout the United States and the world, Baltimore Communists were inspired by the "Third Period" position of the Comintern, the international organization of Communist parties, that world revolution was imminent. They believed that successful socialist construction was accelerating in the Soviet Union, thereby illuminating the road to the future, while international capitalism was in final collapse, and social unrest of explosive dimensions was simmering just under the surface. Bold actions by Communist militants, with guidance from the national Communist parties and the Comintern, could spark revolutionary upsurges everywhere. While this approach might be criticized as anarchistic in its belief in spontaneous rebellion, it gave the Communists of the time a confidence that their actions would matter, while many non-Communist activists in Baltimore were still overcome with pessimism. In addition, cadres in places like Baltimore viewed themselves not as a handful of revolutionaries lost in a vast, dispirited population, but as members of an international revolutionary army whose time was approaching. In a practical sense, their national and international network was of great importance to them, for militants in isolated locales could always look to the larger party for strategic direction, tactical ideas, and other resources that simply were unavailable locally. But the ideological dimension of the national and international movement was probably most important to local Communists, for the Third Period line gave them the faith to take bold initiatives against what seemed to most people overwhelming odds.[8]

The Third Period line also fostered the belief that the struggle against racism was absolutely central to all Communist practices. Adopted in 1928 by the Comintern, the Communist position on "the Negro Question" proposed that Black Americans were a distinct people, an oppressed *nation*, not a biologically defined race. Communists held that the struggle for "Negro liberation" was therefore a *national* struggle that could not be reduced to or subsumed under the class struggle, as socialist movements in the United States traditionally had done. Since the Black freedom struggle was seen as crucial to the coming socialist revolution, all Communists, regardless of their racial/ethnic identity, had a revolutionary duty to participate in struggles against all forms of racism. Indeed, this doctrine took the peoplehood of African Americans so seriously that it proposed (echoing Garveyites and post-Garvey Black nationalists) that Black Americans had the right to self-determination, including the right to establish a separate nation-state in the contiguous areas of Black majority in the South.[9]

Empowered by their belief in the Third Period line on revolution and race, and undeterred by their small numbers, Baltimore Communists in the early 1930s involved themselves in a dizzying range of activities similar to those initiated by their counterparts in other urban areas around the United States. They launched protest after protest; ran candidates in numerous local and national elections; distributed massive amounts of literature; sent soapbox speakers to street corners all over the city; commemorated revolutionary occasions from May Day to Lenin's death; and created a plethora of mass and party organizations, some of which never really got off the ground. Within all of this sometimes frenetic activity, however, there were priorities. Following the national strategy, the main goal of the Baltimore CP was to build a multiracial revolutionary workers' movement by focusing on neighborhood-based organizing of the unemployed and industrial unionism in the workplace. In Baltimore, conditions determined that the unemployed work would be far more important than union organizing during the first years of the Depression.

Organizing the Unemployed

For nearly three years after the Crash, Baltimore Communists had the field of organizing the unemployed virtually to themselves. Like Communists around the world, the Baltimore party section kicked off its unemployment campaign with a call for a demonstration on March 6, 1930, the day designated by the Comintern as International Unemployment Day. For weeks, the Baltimore Communists agitated for this demonstration with leaflets, meetings, speeches, and small-scale direct actions. Reflecting national party demands, they called for direct government emergency relief for the unemployed, administration of all relief by workers, national unemployment insurance with benefits equal to full wages, a mandatory seven-hour workday to provide more jobs, and U.S. recognition of the Soviet Union. The International Unemployment Day march in Baltimore was modest, drawing 300–500 demonstrators, compared with 40,000 (Associated Press estimate) to 110,000 (CP estimate) in New York and 5,000 (Associated Press) to 100,000 (CP) in Detroit. Nevertheless, this was Jim Crow Baltimore, a city very unfriendly to such radical demonstrations, and even a small march such as this one attracted a great deal of attention. In the aftermath of the demonstration, the CP began building Unemployed Councils, challenging political authorities, demanding government aid, and mobilizing on an interracial basis all over town.[10]

Over the next years, the party-initiated Baltimore Unemployed Councils led mass actions on both a neighborhood and a regional basis. As with the International Unemployment Day demonstration, some of the regional actions were nationally mandated, such as the mobilizations for the Bonus

6. Unemployed Hunger Marchers in Baltimore traveling by truck to a demonstration in Washington, D.C., December 7, 1931. *Courtesy of the Albin O. Kuhn Library and Gallery, University of Maryland, Baltimore County. Reused with permission of the Baltimore Sun Media Group. All rights reserved.*

March in 1932 and the three National Hunger Marches that passed through Baltimore en route to Washington, D.C., in 1931, 1932, and 1933. Such mobilizations were sometimes quite large: the column of Hunger Marchers that arrived in Baltimore in 1932 numbered 2,000, and 400 Baltimoreans joined the march as it left for Washington (see figure 6). Local actions, usually targeting City Hall or the State Capitol in Annapolis, numbered in the low hundreds but were militant, dramatic, and headline grabbing. For example, the seventy-five-person delegation from the Baltimore Unemployed Councils to the state legislature in March 1931 forced its way into the House of Delegates after being denied entry, halting the legislative session. Despite arrests, one of the marchers managed to testify before the Ways and Means Committee, and a delegation of the marchers was allowed to present demands for emergency state relief for the unemployed to Governor Albert C. Ritchie and other state officials (albeit while the dignitaries were surrounded by a detail of police). The *Baltimore Sun* announced in a banner headline that the legislature had been "invaded."[11]

As much as the regional mobilizations grabbed public attention, the real substance of the CP's unemployment work in Baltimore was ongoing, day to day work at the neighborhood level. "Every day, representatives of the neighborhood relief councils escorted dozens of people up to the relief agencies, demanding immediate relief," Bill Bailey, a Baltimore party activist in the early 1930s, has written. Most relief office actions were quite small, although others involved "a small parade of 100 or more," which occasionally grew larger. In early 1934, as the first federal unemployment relief of the New Deal began arriving, demonstrators besieged the Baltimore Emergency Relief office in the northwest for two days, and several details of police were needed to evict successive waves of protesters from the office's entrance area. Neighborhood-level actions were also mounted to stop evictions. Demonstrators blockaded the entrances to homes of families faced with eviction, or the belongings of the families were taken back inside as soon as the authorities left. Arrests often occurred during such actions, and those who were arrested typically demanded jury trials to use as a forum for popular political education.[12]

True to the Third Period line, these unemployment actions on behalf of the unemployed, whether citywide or more localized, were antiracist and interracial in character. Frequently, African Americans were on the soapbox or the podium, served as members and spokespeople of delegations, and were among those arrested. Antiracist demands were regularly and conspicuously raised, even when these demands—such as calls for the repeal of Maryland's Jim Crow laws or freedom for the Scottsboro Boys—were not directly related to the unemployment action at hand. Newspaper accounts of the demonstrations always commented on the prominence or "high percentage" of African American participants, often highlighting luridly that Black men and White women were in contact at an event. The *Baltimore Evening Sun* introduced its story on the unemployment demonstration in Annapolis by announcing "Assembly Chamber Invaded by Whites and Negroes."[13]

The Unemployed Councils invariably routed their larger demonstrations through both African American and White working-class neighborhoods. The citywide hunger march in January 1931, for example, arrived at City Hall in two columns from two staging areas: one in largely White working-class

East Baltimore and one in the predominantly Black northwest. Clarence Mitchell, then an emerging young activist in the city's freedom movement, later recalled that a relief office near his home "was a favorite place for Communist orators, and they would always show up there haranguing people." Moreover, many—perhaps most—anti-eviction actions occurred in Black neighborhoods.[14]

How did the CP's unemployment offensive affect Baltimore? At a minimum, it showed the thousands who encountered the many CP-led actions that resistance to unemployment was feasible and could yield occasional victories. It also introduced new forms of struggle and organization, adapted from the international Communist movement. The existing labor and freedom movements in Baltimore for the most part were tactically conservative and narrowly reformist in their goals and often conciliatory toward authority. To most in these movements, the idea of direct action, radical demands, and revolutionary vision was, in the early 1930s, quite foreign. In the face of the Depression, the newer forms of struggle initiated by the CP, at the very least, must have opened some space for working people to consider alternative ways to resist. Furthermore, as we have seen, the existing labor movement was essentially oriented toward trade unions and the workplace, and the existing freedom movement was neighborhood-based. The Baltimore CP challenged these separations by organizing the unemployed into neighborhood-based forms like the Unemployed Councils and by treating them as an integral part of the workers' movement. Indeed, the party affiliated the neighborhood-based Unemployed Councils to the Trade Union Unity League (TUUL), the new labor federation of Communist-led, workplace-based industrial unions.[15] Finally, the highly visible antiracism and interracialism of the party's unemployed campaign demonstrated the possibility of an integrated mass movement, something largely unknown in Jim Crow Baltimore. It also raised the prospect of cooperation, even alliance, between the freedom movement and the workers' movement.

The impact of the Baltimore CP's unemployment practice, however, was limited by its inability to create enduring organizational forms for the unemployed—a national failing of the Unemployed Councils movement. Aside from the Waterfront Unemployed Council, to which I will return later, there is no evidence that the Baltimore councils developed real, sustained institutional lives. The particular organizational weakness of the Unemployed Councils in Baltimore was probably worsened by the relatively small number of party members in the region and by the uphill battle they fought against the stifling conservatism of the region's segregationist culture. While Baltimore of the era was not Birmingham, where racist terror virtually drove the party underground, Jim Crow racism posed a powerful obstacle to any form of interracial activity. Still, the accomplishments of the Communist-led unemployed movement in Baltimore in the early 1930s were significant in terms of catalyzing social struggle, suggesting new directions to emerging activists, and taking a very public stand against the hegemonic mores of Jim Crow.[16]

From Neighborhood to Workplace

During the latter part of 1932 and the early part of 1933, the center of gravity of the CP's working-class activity in Baltimore began to shift, as it did across the country, away from the neighborhood-based unemployment movement toward the workplace-based union movement. The party felt that the class struggle was about to re-ignite at the point of production, and it wanted to be in a position to take advantage of the upsurge. The Third Period line on labor unions called for Communists to create new revolutionary industrial unions, embracing workers of all races and ethnicities, and both genders, affiliated nationally in the TUUL. Often criticized as "dual unionist" for creating new unions where older ones already existed, Communists rejected the charge, claiming that their line mandated them to work within already-existing non-TUUL unions whenever possible. In reality, though, in Baltimore and elsewhere, almost all the party's energies went into building new TUUL unions, since the racism, craft exclusivity, and anticommunism of many of the dominant AFL unions left little room for Communist activity.[17]

The preferred targets for Communist union organizing during this period were the great mass-production industries where large numbers of workers labored in highly concentrated, highly socialized labor processes. In the Baltimore region, the most desirable objective was the gigantic Bethlehem Steel complex at Sparrows Point (see figure 7), which employed 18,000 workers, 6,000 of whom were African American. Al Richmond, who arrived in Baltimore as a YCL section organizer in 1932, reflected the sense of awe and foreboding he and other Communist organizers felt when approaching Sparrows Point: "At the entrance you used, Bear Creek seemed like a moat and the bridge a single link with the rest of the world. Instead of turrets and spires, however, blast furnaces and smoking chimneys stood tall on the other side of the moat. . . . You approach the massive array of furnaces and mills and you thought: what a fantastic locale for a feudal castle, water on three sides and a narrow strip of land on the fourth." Unfortunately, Richmond found that only twenty-four Communists were organizing the TUUL's Steel and Metal Workers Industrial Union at Sparrows Point, not enough even to fantasize about seizing the "castle." The repressive, anti-union policies of the manage-

7. Bethlehem Steel's Sparrows Point mill. *Courtesy of Legacy Web, Baltimore County Public Library.*

ment, both in the plant and in the company town, and the spatial separation of Sparrows Point from the Baltimore City's working-class districts, made advances all but impossible. Any worker who showed union sympathies was immediately fired; the Communist TUUL leader Carl Bradley had been identified by company spies and ejected shortly before Richmond's arrival. The CP's attempts to build contacts with Black workers through actions such as agitation around the death of a Black worker in an accident at the plant were largely thwarted. Outside the steel plant, some Baltimore Communists were organizing unions in smaller-scale industries in the region, including the TUUL-affiliated Furniture Workers Industrial Union and the garment unions, but the CP had little apparent impact in either case.[18]

The union work of Baltimore Communists during this period was more successful among seamen, a marginalized group within the industrial working class. The seamen, who were few in number and worked in small gangs in isolated settings, were multiracial and multinational in composition. According to the census, there were 2,367 sailors and deck hands in Baltimore in 1930, 21 percent of whom were Black and 23 percent of whom were foreign-born. Of course, these numbers fluctuated with the comings and goings of ships. On the ships, seamen worked in truly wretched conditions, and on shore they were restricted to the harbor areas, where they were preyed on by shipping agents they called "crimps," boardinghouse managers, tavernkeepers, and criminals. According to the seaman H. L. Alexander, "Of all these parasites the shipping agent is the most ruthless. He does not even go aboard the ships, he knows that the seamen will eventually come to him to look for a job. These shipping agents . . . are given power by the ship owners to dictate to the seamen as to who is to go to a certain job." The authorities and many citizens in Baltimore viewed the seamen, even those who claimed the city as their homeport, as transients and pariahs. When unemployed and destitute, the seamen had nowhere to turn but to the charities, usually run by religious organizations such as the YMCA, which many seamen referred to as the "Holy Racket." The social world of seamen, then, was a shifting, overwhelmingly male, interracial milieu of cramped ship quarters and rundown waterfront districts in port cities around the country and the world. The seamen were among the least rooted, most fitfully employed, and most oppressed of all workers in Baltimore. However, their very rootlessness, relative lack of personal obligations, marginality, multiculturalism, and broad international experience gave rise to profoundly radical tendencies.[19]

The main vehicle for the Communist-led organizing among the seamen was the Marine Workers Industrial Union (MWIU) of the TUUL, and by late 1933, Baltimore-based Communists had built one of the most powerful locals in the country. In a sense, the MWIU existed in Baltimore before it was founded. Its predecessor, the Marine Workers League (MWL), according to its newspaper the *Marine Workers Voice*, had been quite active in the city in 1929, when MWL delegates visited 123 ships during one month. Also in 1929, the seaman Roy Hudson, then a member of the Industrial Workers of the World (IWW), first encountered MWL activists in Baltimore and was impressed with their work. Hudson subsequently attended the founding convention of the MWIU in April 1930 and, along with the rest of the sizable contingent of Wobblies and ex-Wobblies present, joined. He later became a key leader of the Baltimore MWIU.[20]

Like the IWW, the MWIU aspired to organize industry-wide, was aggressively antiracist and revolutionary, and was quite openly dual-unionist. The MWIU justified its dual unionism by arguing that its established rival, the International Seamen's Union (ISU), was a hopelessly ineffective, racist, anticommunist craft union. The ISU was at a nadir in both the size of its membership and the level of its activity in the early 1930s, and it had a very uncertain future. However, the MWIU intended to become an industrial union of all waterfront workers, not just seamen, and its efforts in this regard faced a much more formidable challenge on the docks than the ISU in the ILA.[21]

The MWIU was sporadically active in Baltimore through 1930 and 1931, but its organizing really picked up momentum in 1932. Agitation and strike activity by the MWIU during the summer of that year was dramatic enough to be reported in the mainstream press and to meet with swift repression and arrests. The Baltimore CP as a whole began to take more notice, and the local YCL decided for the first time to devote much of its energy to the waterfront struggle. The terrain was evidently fertile, for Richmond remembers that it was "heady stuff" to recruit seventeen seamen to the YCL in a single day.[22]

In February 1933, a strike led by the MWIU on the Munson Line's SS *Munmystic* won all the crew's demands; Anton Becker, the branch secretary in Baltimore, later called this a "turning point in winning the confidence of the seamen in the program of the MWIU." The *Munmystic* victory was followed up with the successful strike against the SS *Diamond Cement* in August of the same year. During that strike, the MWIU secretly infiltrated the ship; led the whole crew in a walk out; mounted a support picket line of 150 unemployed seamen; persuaded ILA longshoremen (most of whom were Black) over the objections of their union leadership to strike in solidarity with the MWIU; talked eighteen of twenty-one scabs sent from New York into joining the strike; held a mass rally of 400 people to welcome the former scabs; and, after the undermanned ship limped out of the harbor, sent a carload of pickets to Philadelphia to join the MWIU members in that port in giving the ship a warm welcome. The shipping company relented; wages were raised by $15; the fo'c'sle (or forecastle, the location of the crew's living quarters) of the *Diamond Cement* was cleaned up and painted; and the food was improved. In the immediate wake of this victory, seamen struck the SS *Cornore* with similar demands, and its owners readily capitulated.[23]

By the second half of 1933, the CP-led MWIU had established a revolutionary industrial unionist beachhead in what might seem to be a marginal corner of Baltimore's gigantic industrial-commercial complex. However, the MWIU was building foundations for the industrial unionist upsurge of the late 1930s, during which its successor, the National Maritime Union, would set the pace for both working-class militancy and antiracist workplace struggle.

The Euel Lee Defense Campaign

By applying the Third Period line and thereby breaking with the "workerism" of earlier U.S. socialist parties, the CP extended its revolutionary, antiracist, interventions beyond the workers' movement into the African American freedom struggle itself. In Baltimore of the early 1930s, the local branch of the CP-led International Labor Defense (ILD) was the main vehicle for this work. From mid-1931 on, before any organization in the local freedom movement had recovered from the effects of the Crash, the Baltimore ILD was in motion, focusing its energy on anti-lynching and legal defense work. In the process, it did much to revive the local freedom struggle and offer some new directions.

The Workers Party of America, predecessor to the CP, formed the ILD in 1925 as a national legal defense organization for radical and labor victims of oppression. In December 1929, the ILD, responding to the changing CP strategy on racism, made "the struggle for Negro rights its central priority," in the words of the historian Mark Naison. In Alabama in mid-1931, the ILD became involved in the famous Scottsboro Boys case, in which eight Black youths had been sentenced to death and one to life imprisonment for allegedly raping two White women. By October, the ILD had blocked the initial attempt by the authorities to carry out the executions, and the case was well on its way to becoming an international cause célèbre. Both the ILD and the party saw this intervention in the Scottsboro Boys case as a great success and a model for antiracist work elsewhere. Also during October, the Baltimore ILD began to investigate the case of Euel Lee to see whether racism was involved.[24]

Lee, a fifty-eight-year-old African American itinerant laborer, had been charged with murder on the Maryland's Eastern Shore, part of Baltimore's "Southern" hinterland. On October 11, four members of a White farm family in Worcester County—the mother, father, and two daughters age thirteen and fifteen—had been brutally shotgunned and perhaps bludgeoned in their sleep. Lee, who had worked as a hand on the farm, was subsequently arrested, beaten, and induced to confess to the crime. A quiet man, Lee was known as Orphan Jones because he had lost his parents when he was eleven; he had subsequently lived with the Joneses, a White family in Virginia. After his arrest, he became the object of intense White hatred. Throughout the day of October 13, crowds of White men gathered in the vicinity of Lee's jail cell in Snow Hill. At 4:30 in the afternoon, fearing a lynching attempt, the sheriff acted. Accompanied by his deputies, a Baltimore police detective, and a carload of state patrolmen, he transported Lee across the Chesapeake Bay to jail in Baltimore (see figure 8). In Baltimore, Bernard Ades, a twenty-eight-year old White ILD lawyer, was thwarted in his attempts to meet with Lee to explore his case. By October 18, Lee had been returned to Snow Hill for arraignment, and Ades, along with his ILD colleague Louis Berger, followed his prospective client to the Eastern Shore. During a recess in the court proceedings, Ades was finally allowed to meet with Lee, and Lee agreed to ILD representation. The murder trial was to begin the following Thursday in that

8. Euel Lee being removed from jail in Snow Hill to be transported to Baltimore to avoid a lynch mob. *Courtesy of Joseph E. Moore. Reused with permission of the Baltimore Sun Media Group. All rights reserved.*

courtroom, but news of another potential lynch mob arrived. Lee was again spirited, with a State Police escort, back to Baltimore, and the trial was postponed. On November 4, Ades, despite warnings that he might be exposing himself to danger, traveled from Baltimore to Snow Hill with two other White ILD members. His purpose was to confirm his status as Lee's lawyer and to petition the local court for a change of venue for Lee's trial because of the lynching threat on the Eastern Shore. The court rebuffed him on both counts. Outside the courthouse, crowds of Whites twice attacked the ILD representatives and vandalized their car. The authorities rescued the ILD delegation, then arrested the ILD member Helen Mays for carrying a concealed pistol ("Jones' Lawyer, Armed Woman Arouse Crowd," the *Baltimore Evening Sun* blared). Finally, the sheriff, accompanied by a State Police escort, drove the ILD representatives across the state line into Delaware. The Baltimore ILD decided to concentrate its resources on a defense campaign for Euel Lee.[25]

As was typical of Communist defense work during the Third Period, the Euel Lee campaign was fought on two interrelated fronts: a legal front and a mass-action front. The Communist outlook was that litigation in the "bourgeois courts" was most successful when it was backed by popular protest and that such litigation, especially when it was widely publicized, was in turn an excellent means to build the broader struggle. There was a long tradition in the Baltimore freedom movement of challenging Jim Crow through the courts, but there was little history of backing litigation up with mass action; indeed, there was no real tradition of mass mobilization in the local movement at all. Therefore, the ILD's mass organizing during the Euel Lee defense case introduced an important new strategic perspective into the movement. On the legal front, the Baltimore ILD's strategy was to focus not on the judicial question of Lee's guilt or innocence, but on the political reality that he could not get a fair trial because of racial discrimination. Therefore, while the ILD continued to press for a change of venue for the trial, it also demanded that African Americans be included on Lee's jury and that the Jim Crow jury system be abolished. The ILD widely publicized the facts of the case, the threat of racist terror, and the Jim Crow character of the legal system, thereby attracting the attention of the powerful *Afro-American* newspaper. And the ILD threatened to march on Snow Hill to publicize the attack. The town's mayor, revealing something of the nature of "law and order" on the Eastern Shore, replied that he would raise a mob if the ILD appeared. The ILD did not follow through on its threat to march on Snow Hill but a few weeks later mounted a demonstration at the posh University Club in Baltimore to protest the refusal by Governor Albert Ritchie to guarantee Lee's legal rights. The police dispersed the demonstration before the governor arrived; there were several arrests; and publicity resulted.[26]

Then on December 4, 1931, the Eastern Shore became the site of a lynching. Matthew Williams was a thirty-five-year-old Black laborer who had been accused of murdering his White employer, the box manufacturer and lumberyard owner Daniel J. Elliot. Allegedly, Williams shot his boss in the head because Elliot repeatedly refused to raise Williams's 15 cents an hour wage. Williams then reportedly attempted suicide by shooting himself in the head and was subsequently shot in the chest and leg by Elliot's son, James, who reportedly rushed into his father's office when he heard the first shots. This account of the shooting made little sense to some local people, and, accord-

ing to the historian Sherrilyn Ifill, an alternative account that James shot his
father over a financial dispute, then shot Williams to cover up his crime,
gained a wide following among both Whites and Blacks in the region. Nonetheless, Elliot was dead, and Williams, seriously injured, was held under
guard in the hospital in Salisbury. Subsequently, lynchers invaded the hospital, meeting only token resistance from the chief of police and a deputy sheriff; dragged Williams from his hospital bed and through the streets; stabbed
him with an ice pick; and then hoisted his body up and down from a tree on
the courthouse green several times before leaving it there to hang. The lynching became a White community festival: the crowd numbered about 2,000,
including, according to Sheriff Phillips, "a lot of women." It was reported
that three uniformed policemen directed traffic on the crowd's periphery.
To underline the fact that the lynching was meant as a terroristic warning
to the local Black population as a whole, Williams's body was finally cut
down, carried by a procession to a vacant lot in the Black community, soaked
with gasoline, and burned. Still not satisfied, the mob later carried Williams's
charred corpse back to the center of town and hanged it again.[27]

The news of this horrendous lynching was met with a wave of revulsion
nationally and in parts of the state of Maryland. The Baltimore ILD joined
African American community leaders, including the editors of the *Afro-
American*, and White progressives to condemn the lynchers and demanding vigorous state action to find and prosecute Williams's murderers. H. L.
Mencken, who wrote regularly for the *Baltimore Sun* papers, took his invec-
tive to an extreme with the front-page article "The Eastern Shore Kultur," in
which he excoriated what he considered the backward, degenerate, and mo-
ronic character of much of the shore's White community. Beyond Baltimore,
the local ILD used national networks to catalyze protests around the country,
continually linking the Euel Lee case with the Williams lynching. Without a
change of venue, they argued, Lee would suffer the same fate as Williams. In
response to these demands, and to avoid further outrage that a second lynching would bring, the courts finally moved Lee's trial to Baltimore County
but adamantly refused to integrate the jury rolls. As for Williams's lynching,
the protests, which were never very widespread, ebbed, and there was little
official follow-up, except for a few vague promises from the governor. No
one was ever arrested or even detained for the murder. Ominously, however,
some state officials began echoing the charge of the Eastern Shore racists that
the ILD was to blame for the Williams murder, ostensibly because the "Communists" had frustrated justice through their defense of Lee, thereby forcing
the White community to turn to vigilantism.[28]

The ILD's role in the protests after Williams's death, and its insistence on

9. Euel Lee's International Labor Defense (ILD) lawyers, David Levinson and Bernard Ades (*front, left to right*); the person in the back is probably Louis Berger, secretary of the ILD. *Courtesy of the Afro-American Newspapers Archives and Research Center.*

placing the Euel Lee campaign squarely within the freedom movement's tradition of anti-lynching campaigning, revived that tradition in the Baltimore region. In the early 1920s, anti-lynching activity had declined both in Baltimore and the country after the defeat of the Dyer Anti-Lynching Bill in the U.S. Senate. With the Euel Lee and Williams protests, anti-lynching work reappeared as a priority on the regional freedom agenda, where it remained throughout the 1930s.

The relocated murder trial of Euel Lee began on January 20, 1932, in Towson, just north of Baltimore City, with the ILD lawyers Bernard Ades of Baltimore and David Levinson of Philadelphia as the defense team (see figure 9). Two days later, despite contradictory testimony by key prosecution witnesses, and despite the fact that the prosecution decided not to enter Lee's coerced confessions, the all-White jury took only thirty minutes to find the defendant guilty. Lee was sentenced to death. The ILD immediately appealed the verdict, claiming again that the jury-selection process was discriminatory and unconstitutional, and launched another round of agitation. Then, to the astonishment of many, on July 5, 1932, the Maryland Court of Appeals ruled for Lee and the ILD. Lee got a new trial, and the jury rolls throughout Maryland were desegregated, scoring an important victory over Jim Crow and setting a legal precedent with national ramifications. In a period during which the aspirations of freedom movement were usually confined for tactical reasons to winning better conditions for Blacks without directly confronting Jim Crow, the ILD and the CP had launched a frontal attack on segregation in the judicial system in Baltimore County and won.[29]

On September 26, 1932, Euel Lee's second murder trial opened, and the ILD attorneys continued to defend him by attacking Jim Crow. Ades and Levinson pointed out that, although African Americans had now been included on the jury list, the jury itself was again all White; they also argued that the segregated seating arrangements in the courtroom prejudiced Lee's case. The three-judge panel rejected the defense's arguments for a change to a non-segregated venue or a postponement of the trial until segregation in Maryland was ended. Three days later, Euel Lee was again convicted of murder and sentenced to death. Again the ILD appealed.[30]

Throughout 1932, the activities of the ILD and the CP attracted increasing attention in Black Baltimore. The *Afro-American* reflected growing Black support for the Lee defense campaign and for the CP's other activities with a series of editorials, columns, and news stories that praised the party's work. During Lee's first trial in Towson, the *Afro-American* editorialized at length on what "two Jewish lawyers, backed by the Communist Party" had accomplished in moving the case from the Eastern Shore of Maryland, suppressing Lee's forced confession, and challenging the all-White jury rolls of Baltimore County. The editorial ended with these words: "This has been done by the International Labor Defense—the 'dangerous' Communists, the radical Reds. . . . These Reds, supposed enemies of the Bible and the United States Constitution, have contended for the right of a humble black citizen to a fair, orderly, and impartial trial before a jury of his peers. If that be dangerous, Communistic and radical, it is nevertheless patriotic Americanism to which all thinking citizens can well subscribe."[31]

Carl Murphy, the publisher of the paper and author of its main editorials, proclaimed his favorable assessment of the CP in the national Black media, as well. In April and May 1932, the NAACP's *Crisis*, edited by W. E. B. Du Bois, ran "Negro Editors on Communism: A Symposium of the American Negro Press" and included remarks from sixteen editors. Of the group, the *Afro*'s Murphy was by far the most enthusiastic: "The Communist[s] appear to be the only party going our way. They are as radical as the N.A.A.C.P. was twenty years ago. Since the abolitionists passed off the scene, no white group of national prominence has openly advocated the economic, political and social equality of black folks."[32] William N. Jones, managing editor of the *Afro-American*, in a column titled, "Worried about the NAACP," went as far as to hold the ILD up as a model to the freedom movement. At the same time, he criticized the NAACP for its lack of action in the Euel Lee case, wondering about the "flabby, . . . pink tea and caviar leadership" of that organization. An outraged Walter White, the NAACP's national executive secretary, responded to Jones with an angry two-and-a-half-page letter.[33]

After Lee's second conviction in September 1932, the ILD gained another group of important allies when the City-Wide Young People's Forum (the Forum) joined the Euel Lee campaign. The Forum had been founded by African American youth in late 1931, and, as chapter 3 will show, by late 1932 it was drawing thousands of African Americans of all ages to its educational meetings on Friday nights. In October 1932, the Forum invited Bernard Ades of the ILD to speak at a Friday night meeting. Following his presentation, the Forum plunged headlong into the Lee campaign, providing a corps of energetic organizers and raising the visibility of the ILD and CP in the Black community. Along with the Forum and other allies, the ILD then escalated its mass organizing with an ambitious statewide drive to get 100,000 signatures on a petition to support Lee and to abolish segregation in Maryland's courts and public utilities. In addition, it threatened a test case on bus lines that refused to serve Blacks. From this point on, the ILD increasingly made the Lee campaign a staging ground for a broadening attack on Jim Crow.[34]

Despite the efforts of the Euel Lee defense campaign, on April 6, 1933, the Court of Appeals denied the ILD's petitions and affirmed Lee's second conviction. An emergency mass-protest meeting was called for May 5; this meeting revealed much both about the depth of support for Lee in Black Baltimore and about the ILD's skillful joining of national and local issues. A Scottsboro Boys protest procession of 700 marchers led by the ILD, on its way from New York to Washington, D.C., arrived in Baltimore on May 5. It participated in an emergency meeting, billed as a protest of both the Lee and Scottsboro cases, at the Sharp Street Methodist Episcopal church. The turnout was so large that additional meetings were quickly organized at the Union Baptist church and the Metropolitan AME church, also eminent Black religious and community centers. Even this was not enough, for at both Union Baptist and Metropolitan AME, simultaneous meetings had to be held in the Sunday schools as well.[35]

At these meetings, Ades of the Baltimore ILD and Richard B. Moore, an African American member of the ILD's national executive committee, spoke to overflow crowds. Also featured was Ruby Bates, one of the alleged Scotts-

boro rape victims, who had recanted her earlier accusations and joined the
Scottsboro Boys campaign. Reverend C. Y. Trigg, a leading Black minister
and president of the largely inactive Baltimore NAACP, delivered the prayer.
The next day, more than 1,000 Baltimoreans joined the protest march to
Washington. Before the procession left Baltimore, a number of the demonstrators from New York caused a minor sensation and triggered a police
response by refusing water served to them in paper cups at a restaurant, demanding instead glasses like those given to White customers.[36]

Despite the protests, on May 11, Governor Ritchie signed Lee's death war-
rant; the execution was stayed, however, as Lee's lawyers took the case to the
U.S. Supreme Court. Months passed without word. Finally, on October 9,
with ninety demonstrators from Baltimore outside, the Supreme Court refused to consider Euel Lee's appeal; his execution was scheduled for October 27. Then, on October 18, about a week before Lee was to die, an Eastern
Shore lynch mob struck again. A crowd of thousands of Whites tortured,
mutilated, and murdered George Armwood, a twenty-eight-year-old Black
laborer, in Princess Anne.[37]

The lynching of Armwood and the outrage that followed became a watershed for the freedom movement in Baltimore and Maryland. As I will show
in chapter 5, these protests were far broader and more sustained than those
two years earlier following the lynching of Matthew Williams. The ILD's long
campaign to defend Euel Lee had created the conditions for the new, mass-
based anti-lynching movement in Baltimore that emerged following Armwood's murder. Nevertheless, the attempt to defend Lee failed, and he was
executed in the midst of this mobilization.

Red Dances

While organizing in the neighborhood and workplace around issues of
class and race, Baltimore's Third Period Communists also (and perhaps surprisingly) organized a series of dances and socials. As Bill Bailey, a former
Communist seaman, remembered it, "Every week, a social event of some
kind occurred either in the city, or in an outer community like Highlandtown. . . . Only on Saturday or Sunday was there a chance to relax, either by
attending some politicized social or dance gathering." These dances were
always interracial and multiethnic and were held in both African American and White working-class neighborhoods. As the Black freedom movement leader Juanita Jackson Mitchell recalled decades later, "The Communists came into the community and had these interracial dances down at the
New Albert Auditorium on Pennsylvania Avenue"; they also held them at the

African American Elks Hall. Mitchell never attended, she said, "because we were Methodists" and did not dance, but a number of other African Americans did.[38]

Dances and socials were a part of the CP's attempt to devise cultural forms to attract workers and youth to its movement and simultaneously to give overworked party activists a recreational break. They were also conscious interventions into working-class culture at the neighborhood level to build interracial solidarity, challenge Jim Crow, and fight racist attitudes in party and movement ranks. As such, they were an expression of the Third Period "Campaign against White Chauvinism," which held that Communists were duty-bound to challenge racist attitudes and actions whenever and wherever they were encountered, including in Communist circles. This campaign held that White Communists had a special responsibility to take the lead in confronting racism.[39]

Nationally, the flagship event of the Campaign against White Chauvinism grew out of events at a dance at the Finnish Workers Hall in Harlem in early 1931. During this dance, some White workers, including the Communist caretaker August Yokenin, objected to the presence of Black workers and ejected them. As an object lesson, the party publicly tried Yokenin for White chauvinism before a workers' court in Harlem. The event was widely publicized, and the press, including establishment newspapers, was invited. The prosecution, led by a White attorney, called for Yokenin's expulsion from the party, and the defense, led by an African American lawyer, countered that Yokenin's admission of guilt and his self-criticism for his racist behavior should earn him forgiveness. In the end, Yokenin was provisionally expelled from the party, to be readmitted if he proved himself by taking leadership in antiracist activities, which he subsequently did with reported enthusiasm. While the trial was clearly political theater, the spectacle of a predominantly White radical organization publicly trying a White member for discrimination against Blacks at a dance was quite startling to many at the time. While some found it bizarre or even frightening, it was widely covered in African American newspapers, and many Blacks welcomed it. In addition, many Communists, of various racial backgrounds, took the lesson to heart.[40]

The interracial dances, sponsored by Communist-led organizations in Baltimore from at least 1930, violated one of the most sensitive taboos of Jim Crow culture: socializing between men and women across racial lines. In late 1930, Mrs. Reuben Ross Holloway of Baltimore, a member of both the Daughters of the American Revolution and the Daughters of the Confederacy, proclaimed her fear of Communist "race mingling" during testimony before Hamilton Fish Jr.'s congressional investigating committee, announcing, "It's high time for Americans to wake up, when you find young people holding interracial dances, as these Communists do." Indeed, Communists charged that the police frequently harassed interracial dances and raided an integrated social in a private home in 1931. Then, on Sunday, January 8, 1933, the CP-initiated Workers International Relief sponsored a dance at the Polish American Hall in East Baltimore. Held in a largely White, predominantly Polish neighborhood four blocks from the Fells Point waterfront, close to the racially mixed Oldtown area, the dance attracted about 300 African Americans and Whites. According to a report in the *Afro-American*, a crowd of 150 White men gathered on the street outside, and as the dancers began to leave, a White youth walked up and slapped a White woman who was walking beside a Black man. The crowd of Whites then attacked, and a "free-for-all" broke out, resulting in several injuries. After a while, the police arrived and arrested four of the dance participants but none of the attackers.[41]

Far from being intimidated, Communists in Baltimore reacted with determination. Paul Cline, a White CP organizer, told the press that during the dance at the Polish American Hall on New Year's Eve the week before, a group of Whites had entered the hall and ordered an end to interracial dancing, only to be expelled by those in attendance. Cline contended that local business interests, to defend the "prejudiced and jim-crow" character of the area, had incited local White youth, telling them that the Black men were the White women's lovers and plying them with whisky. Cline also accused law enforcement of collusion in the attack, pointing out that the police took an exceptionally long time to arrive; that they had done nothing to protect those attending the dance; and that Captain Kahler of the Eastern Division was well known for his opposition to integrated social events. Then the CP and its allies announced another dance at the Polish American Hall for the next Saturday.[42]

A few days later, as if to validate many of Cline's accusations, a local weekly, the *Baltimore World*, published an inflammatory article about the dance and the ensuing disturbances. It included a poem containing lurid images of interracial sexuality, mixed with animalistic portrayals of Black men: "A thick Black hand on a slim, white back. . . . Black paws fondle the white girl's charms." The members of the attacking crowd, depicted sympathetically, were quoted as saying, "We are proud of our ancestry and our American citizenship," implying that African Americans were foreigners—an interesting twist, given that many of the attackers were probably first- or second-generation immigrants. Communism and radicalism were not only depicted as foreign, but were vividly racialized: "The red of Russia, the black of the Congo, and the white of European nationals will not mix." And the article raised the specter of lynching by claiming that the police saved an African American dance attendee "just as the mob was threatening an Eastern shore necktie party." It even contained an explicit warning: "If they try to repeat these dances, there will be trouble."[43]

Nonetheless, the dance on the following Saturday was held without incident, perhaps because of the preparatory work by Communists during the week before and at the event itself. According to Louis Berger of the Communist Party, the speeches at the dance convinced the "Polish and American young workers who were present . . . that they had been duped into making the attack last week" and that workers of "all nationalities and colors" must unite. While Berger's account may be somewhat idealized, it does indicate something of the party's approach to racism in the White working class. And the *Afro-American* gave lengthy, sympathetic coverage to the CP's response to the dance controversy.[44]

The city government, however, was becoming increasingly uncomfortable with the interracial dances and the publicity they were generating. Hoping to put an end to these events, the city declared Mooney Hall, the site of a CP-related dance scheduled for Saturday, January 21, to be unsafe, and the police turned guests away at the door. A few days later, the ILD won an injunction against the city's condemnation of the hall and held a protest rally on the premises. At this point, the city evidently gave up trying to block the party's integrated cultural activities, and a subsequent dance on September 28 came off without incident.[45]

The East Baltimore dance controversy was by no means a major historical event. But it did demonstrate that the CP and its allies were eager to take the struggle for a unified workers' movement into realms of community life often labeled "non-political," and that they would stand their ground when attacks and threats from racist Whites, the local press, and city government resulted. It also demonstrated that they could win — that there was room to defeat Jim Crow, even on issues involving interracial sexuality. In addition, this incident indicates something about the complicated character of segregationism in Baltimore at the time. Clearly violently racist forces were present, both in the neighborhood and in the power structure. But there were also community people of both racial backgrounds who were willing to defy racist mores to engage in interracial socializing. And while the city government was officially committed to Jim Crow, under conditions of militant mass agitation, it was more interested in making the issue of interracial dances (which were not technically illegal) disappear than in standing on principle against them. Then there was the judge who granted the ILD's injunction and the editor of the *Evening Sun* who wrote that the dances were constitutionally protected and that Communists should be able to "have their fun." A section of the establishment was apparently unwilling to defend Jim Crow customs when they came under serious fire, at least in the "petty" realm of interpersonal relations—something hardly conceivable in, say, Birmingham of the era. Ultimately, within all of these border-city contradictions, the CP showed that antiracist forces could maneuver, press forward, and sometimes prevail.[46]

3

The City-Wide Young People's
Forum, 1931–1933

The City-Wide Young People's Forum of Baltimore is the best, most
progressive and analytical organization of Negro young people in America.
—NANNIE BURROUGHS, National Training School for Girls

There is no doubt that the City-Wide Young People's Forum is
the most aggressive social organization in the city.
—IRA DE A. REID, National Urban League

In late 1933, the reviving Baltimore freedom movement was about to take a
leap forward, with the City-Wide Young People's Forum as its leading force.
From modest beginnings, the Forum, as it came to be called, had in two short
years become the most active and effective freedom organization based in
the African American community of Baltimore.

In the summer of 1931, Juanita and Virginia Jackson returned to their home
in the Black neighborhoods of northwestern Baltimore after graduating from
colleges in Philadelphia. The sisters found themselves in familiar but increasingly dismal surroundings. Unemployment in the community was growing
rapidly. Jobs for college-educated Black youth were nearly impossible to find.
And in contrast to the more flexible, northern-style Jim Crow of Philadelphia, the Jackson sisters found that Baltimore's system of sharp racial segregation was still in place and had further rigidified under the impact of economic crisis. Baltimore in 1931 was, as Juanita Jackson Mitchell later recalled,
a "nasty, demeaning place for Blacks."[1]

The Jackson sisters resolved to do something about their plight and that
of their peers. They found, however, that the local freedom movement was
in such disarray as to offer them little opportunity to work for change. Of
course, the Baltimore section of the Communist Party (CP) had been stirring
things up since early 1930, and its aggressive antiracist organizing attracted

the attention of Black Baltimore's more activist-oriented youth. But as appealing as its militancy might be, the CP's outspoken hostility to religion had put off religiously inclined young people like the Jackson sisters. It became clear to the sisters that something new was needed and that they would have to take matters into their own hands. "So," Juanita Jackson Mitchell later reported, "we organized a group of young people, both high school and college graduates who couldn't get jobs either. We started meeting at the Sharp Street Methodist Episcopal church, and we called it the City-Wide Young People's Forum."[2]

On October 2, 1931, a few days before Euel Lee was first charged with murder, the Jackson sisters and a small group of African American youth put on their first public program at the Sharp Street Methodist Episcopal church, with Juanita Jackson presiding. Three weeks later, on October 24, as news of repeated lynching attempts on Maryland's Eastern Shore enraged much of Baltimore's Black community, a larger group of African American youth "from all over the City of Baltimore" held a follow-up meeting. There they formally constituted themselves as the Forum. When on December 4, Matthew Williams was lynched in Salisbury, Maryland, the newly organized Forum responded with a militancy that scared the trustees of Sharp Street Memorial. After a meeting where, according to Juanita Jackson Mitchell, "we started talking about we weren't going to stand for lynching," and where the young people present chanted angry slogans, the church trustees tried to take over the Forum. The youth defended their independence and moved their base of operations to Bethel African Methodist Episcopal (AME) church, and the Forum grew with striking speed.[3]

Although the Forum is all but forgotten today, its importance to the freedom movement in Baltimore in the 1930s can hardly be overstated. The Forum organized a vital Black youth movement in Depression-ridden Baltimore, involving itself in a remarkably wide variety of activities, and affecting ever larger portions of Baltimore's African American community. By mid-decade, the Forum's influence had extended across the country, and over the ensuing years it contributed a surprising number of leaders to the Baltimore and national freedom movements. Like the local CP that influenced it, the Forum was an important innovator of new forms of struggle during the dormant period of the early 1930s, but unlike the Baltimore CP, the Forum was home-grown, unique, and completely African American. It developed organically out of the community structures and traditions of Black Baltimore—especially out of the experiences of the educated young Black people who formed its core—while avidly adopting a wide range of ideas and practices from social and intellectual movements across the country. According to later testimony, the Forum youth considered themselves, and were considered by others, to be radicals, although their radicalism was unorthodox, rapidly evolving, and eclectic. The Forum was, in short, sui generis, or as W. E. B. Du Bois remarked, it was an "unusual organization." And as it turned out, it became the main founding organization of the modern freedom movement in Baltimore and Maryland.[4]

The Jackson Sisters and the Forum Leadership

The youth who founded and shaped the Forum were firmly grounded in the institutions and traditions of Baltimore's African American community, although many of them had wider experience. They were the heirs to the expanding, though still limited, educational opportunities of the city in the 1920s. They came mainly from the middle and upper strata of that community—from the upper working class, the small property-holding and professional middle classes, and, occasionally, the small Black capitalist class. In some ways, they reflected the particular interests and aspirations of these strata, and they frequently saw their own class aspirations thwarted by Jim Crow and the Depression. Nonetheless, or perhaps as a consequence, a broad community pride and racial/ethnic consciousness permeated their outlook, and they tended to view themselves as representatives of the whole community. In other words, the leading core of the Forum represented the youthful wing of the social bloc that had led the Baltimore freedom movement throughout the early twentieth century. From the beginning, however, the Forum's leadership wanted to be more than an elite that spoke for, and acted in place of, the community as a whole.[5]

  Something of the character and consciousness of the Forum leadership core can be explored by reviewing the backgrounds of the Jackson sisters. They are, of course, more than random examples, for they conceived and founded the Forum, and Juanita Jackson was its president and most important leader through at least its first half of the decade (see figure 10). Their mother, Lillie Jackson, exercised a profound influence over the organization as its adult adviser, and their younger sister, Marion, was a Forum stalwart. Virginia and Juanita Jackson, born in 1911 and 1913, respectively, came from a family that traced its roots back through several generations in Maryland on their mother's side; their father's forebears had been sharecropping people in Mississippi. The family, although by no means rich, was part of Black Baltimore's established small propertied class, and they lived on Druid Hill Avenue, which Du Bois once described as "one of the best colored streets in the world." Lillie Jackson, who was trained as a teacher, ran a real estate business.

10. A portrait of Juanita
Jackson in the early 1930s
labeled "Founder of the
City-Wide Young People's
Forum" that appeared
in Forum publications
throughout the decade.
*Courtesy of Juanita
Jackson Mitchell.*

Her husband, Keiffer Jackson, when he was not helping with rental building maintenance, showed evangelical religious films at churches in the Baltimore region and its hinterlands. Earlier, he and Lillie Jackson had traveled though the South doing evangelical programs and film showings, and several of their children were born in various southern locations during their travels.[6]

According to oral history testimony, the sisters and their younger siblings, Marion and Bowen Keiffer, grew up in a religious, family-centered environment that the sisters characterized as close, loving, and strict. Their parents, for example, took a dim view of such activities as dancing, and they raised the girls to protect their virtue by not speaking to boys. Juanita Jackson Mitchell later recalled that she was still scared to talk to boys in high school. The Sharp Street Methodist Episcopal church became a center of family activities, not just on Sundays, but all week long. Virginia and Juanita Jackson graduated from Frederick Douglass High School in 1926 and 1927, respectively, but were barred by segregationist policies from the best institution of higher education in Maryland. In response, Lillie Jackson enrolled Virginia, an aspiring artist, in the Philadelphia Museum and School of Art, and Juanita, after a year at Morgan College in Baltimore (then an unaccredited Methodist Episcopal college), in the University of Pennsylvania, severely straining the family's resources in the process.

At a glance, the Jacksons' tradition of family, religion, education, and property seems almost prototypically middle class. But in their case, these values were infused with, and overdetermined by, a powerful racial/ethnic consciousness and a deep sense that living morally meant resisting racist oppression. The family proudly traced its lineage on Lillie Jackson's side back to an African chief, John Bowen, who, according to family lore, had come to Maryland generations before but was never enslaved. (Lillie Jackson also claimed Charles Carroll, the White slaveowner and signer of the Declaration of Independence, as an ancestor.) The family also took great pride in the fact that Keiffer Jackson, who physically appeared to be White, always affirmed his African American identity and refused to pass. Moreover, according to Juanita Jackson Mitchell's later testimony, for three generations her mother's family held firm to the belief that property and education were crucial for Black people, not as means to individual wealth and status, but as ways to attain some independence from segregation and to serve the community. For example, Lillie Jackson chose to rent houses and apartments to poor Blacks rather than to speculate; she "would not buy and sell, but buy and provide," while church was not solely about individual faith, but also a collective affirmation of ethnic beliefs and aspirations. For the Jacksons, racial pride produced a sense of identity with the overall African American community. Lillie Jackson repeatedly warned her children "not to segregate off into an intelligentsia few," apart from those in the community who were less educated or less affluent.

It is important to emphasize that the Jackson sisters grew up with examples of strong women in their mother and grandmother. Their grandmother Amanda Bowen Carroll had been a schoolteacher, the successful proprietor of a boardinghouse and ice cream parlor, and a well-known community figure. Lillie Jackson, by all accounts, was a particularly powerful personality. The sisters watched at close range as she recovered from a botched operation that disfigured the right side of her face; she built a real estate business and overcame resistance from men to become the first female trustee of her church. They also watched as she assertively and successfully reformed their father, Keiffer Jackson, a rather traditional and autocratic man who refused to allow his wife to drive. According to testimony, Lillie Jackson bought an old car when he was away and learned to operate it, facing down her husband's wrath when he returned home. Although neither parent nor relatives were known to be particularly politically active, the sisters' early experiences in their family and community did much to create the ideological basis for their later activism. But it was their college years in Philadelphia that fully politicized them.[7]

In an interview, Juanita Jackson Mitchell later referred to their time in Philadelphia as "our years abroad," then caught herself and explained: "Well, it almost was like abroad from Maryland." The more subtle forms of racism in Philadelphia proved to her that life could be different from the unrelenting oppression of Jim Crow Baltimore. In Philadelphia, she and her sister could go to restaurants, stores, concerts, plays, and museums with little care. "When I went up there, I was afraid of White people. [In Baltimore], everything I had been in interracially was formal. You didn't make friends. But there I began to make friends among White students. In Baltimore, you know, you waited for a rebuff: 'We don't take niggers here.' The main thing is I made friends among White students and learned and *competed* with the best [in Philadelphia]. I was a high-ranking scholar up there. I could compete. They might say I was inferior, but I knew I was equal." Growing up in a border city, with access to the North, made a big difference in both sisters' lives.[8]

In Philadelphia, the Jackson sisters became involved with the cultural and political renaissance of the New Negro movement of the 1920s, and they connected with the rising spirit of rebellion among Black college students that was most clearly manifested in the wave of campus revolts that hit as many as half of the predominantly Black colleges in the country between 1925 and 1928. While majoring in education at the university, Juanita Jackson became involved in racial advancement activities with her sorority, Alpha Kappa Alpha, and she helped to organize concerts by Marian Anderson and Paul Robeson at the Philadelphia Academy of Music. She also participated in interracial civil rights work with the Christian Association at the university and the Interracial Commission of the American Friends Service Committee in the city. Decades later, Virginia Jackson Kiah claimed that the idea behind the Forum was originally hers, inspired by an Epworth League Institute at Morgan College in Baltimore, sponsored by the Methodist church, that she attended. But, she, the artist, added, "I didn't have the training [to lead the Forum]. My sister had, and after we got started on this Forum, it was my sister, who was much better equipped than I, who carried it on successfully." Juanita Jackson's "training" came from her movement activities in Philadelphia.[9]

When the Jacksons came home from "abroad" after graduation, they were primed to initiate the Forum, and the Forum very much bore the stamp of the sisters' political-cultural formation. The other Black youth who formed the Forum's core and shaped the organization during the early 1930s had broadly similar backgrounds to the Jackson sisters. Most were firmly grounded in the broad religious-cultural traditions and institutions of the middle layers of

Black Baltimore, on the one hand, and had been strongly influenced by the New Negro movement and rebelliousness among Black college students, on the other. For example, Clarence Mitchell Jr., probably the most influential Forum leader after Juanita Jackson, was born in Baltimore in 1911 to a deeply religious Episcopalian family with paternal roots in Maryland going back several generations. The whole family was involved with fraternal organizations: his father was a Mason; his mother, a member of the Mason's Women's Lodge; and the children, Lilies of the Valley.

Although they came from the community's middle strata, the Mitchell family was poorer and more working-class than the Jacksons. Clarence Mitchell's father was a musician who often had to work at proletarian jobs in the service sector, such as cook or waiter, to get by. His mother, whose strength Mitchell much admired, ran the home and raised eight children, two of whom died young. Mitchell himself found employment in working-class jobs after school and during the summer. Like the Jacksons, the Mitchells believed deeply in the importance of education. After graduating with honors from Frederick Douglass High School, Mitchell went to Lincoln University in Pennsylvania, a historically Black school, at great financial sacrifice to the family. Lincoln, the scene of a Black student revolt the year before he arrived, changed Mitchell. He studied Greek and Latin, was one of the strongest students in his class, and hoped to enter medical school but had no money to do so. In fact, he owed money for his tuition and was unable to participate in graduation exercises or receive his diploma after he finished his coursework. He returned penniless and jobless to Baltimore in 1932 and got a job at the *Afro-American* newspapers. He encountered the Forum, joined immediately, and rose rapidly to become its leading vice-president.[10]

Undoubtedly, the member of the Forum who achieved the most illustrious standing later in life was Thurgood Marshall. The son of an established working-class-professional family—his father was a Pullman porter, and his mother was a teacher. Marshall also went north to college. He graduated from Lincoln University in Pennsylvania, where he and Clarence Mitchell became close friends. After being denied admission to the University of Maryland Law School (a racist affront that he never forgot), he earned his law degree at Howard University, at the time a center of the African American renaissance. Marshall came under the tutelage of Charles Hamilton Houston, who was reconstructing Howard's law school as a training ground for freedom movement lawyers. After graduating, Marshall returned to Baltimore in 1933 to set up a law practice and immediately became an activist in the Forum and its legal counsel.[11]

Other Forumites had middling backgrounds and similar trajectories to

Marshall's, Mitchell's, and the Jackson sisters'. Elsie Bevans grew up in a religious family on middle-class Druid Hill Avenue, across the street from the
Jacksons. When Bevans was barred from college in Maryland, her parents
sent her to the University of Pennsylvania. Like her counterparts, she returned committed to serving the community, became an early vice-president
of the Forum, and in 1934 became Baltimore's first Black social worker, a
position won as a result of Forum protests.[12]

Some important Forum activists came from more elite backgrounds in the
Black community. W. A. C. Hughes Jr., the son of a Methodist bishop and also
a graduate of Lincoln University, went on to graduate with distinction from
Boston University Law School. A long-time legal adviser and key leader of
the Forum, Hughes, unlike most Forumites, had particularly strong ties to
the traditional freedom movement in Baltimore. His father had long been an
activist minister who rose to become a Methodist bishop, and his law partner, Robert P. McGuinn, was a member of the well-known McGuinn family
of freedom movement activists. Like Hughes, Elmer Henderson Jr., a long-
time vice-president of the Forum, was the son of a well-known community
leader; his father, Elmer Henderson Sr., was the director of colored schools
in Baltimore. At Douglass High School, where he was a classmate of Clarence
Mitchell's, Henderson won numerous victories in oratorical contests and became known as the "boy elocutioner," a talent he put to good use with the
Forum after returning from college. Donald Gaines Murray, the grandson of
a famous AME bishop, came from a family that highly valued education and,
unlike most, had the means to pay for it. After a year at Lincoln University, he
went on to graduate from the overwhelmingly White and highly prestigious
Amherst College. His involvement with the Forum began later than that of
some of the others, but he rose to prominence when he became the plaintiff
in a major desegregation lawsuit in 1934.[13]

Finally some core Forum activists, such as Evelyn Smith, hailed from the
poorer sections of Baltimore's Black working class and had less exposure to
national cultural and political trends. Later known by her married name,
Evelyn Burrell, she was brought up by a single mother and her grandparents; her grandmother, mother, and sisters were domestic workers, and her
grandfather was a porter. Smith was probably the youngest person to join the
Forum during its early years when she became active in 1933 as a fourteen-
year-old high school student. Nonetheless her background contained important similarities to that of other Forum activists. Her family was deeply
religious and emphasized the importance of education. While a member of
the Forum, she completed her high school education at Frederick Douglass
High and graduated from Morgan College.[14]

These brief sketches of some key members of the leadership core of the Forum give a sense of what Juanita Jackson Mitchell later called the "uniting tie" of their similar community and educational experiences. The Forum transformed many of its leading activists into long-term freedom movement leaders, some of whom became important at the national level. Thurgood Marshall, of course, went on to become the most prominent civil rights lawyer in the United States and the first African American Supreme Court justice. Clarence Mitchell and Juanita Jackson were married in 1938 and became the central link of the "Mitchell–Jackson dynasty" within the Maryland freedom movement (sometimes referred to as Maryland's "Black Kennedys"). Clarence Mitchell himself became a national freedom movement leader of great stature, most famously for his work as the director of the Washington Bureau of the NAACP from 1950 to 1978, where he earned the unofficial title of the "101st Senator" for his successful civil rights lobbying. Juanita Jackson Mitchell, although in many respects a national leader, as well, focused her work in Baltimore. There, she held a number of top positions with the NAACP branch, was a leading civil rights lawyer (the first Black woman admitted to the Maryland bar), and was ultimately described as the "matriarch" of the region's freedom movement.[15]

Of the other Forum leaders sketched above, only Elmer Henderson became a truly national figure. He received a law degree in Chicago, directed Region VI (Illinois, Indiana, and Wisconsin) of the Fair Employment Practices Committee during the Second World War, became an aide to a leading Black congressman, served as lawyer to the House Appropriations Committee, and was the plaintiff in the famous *Henderson v. United States* lawsuit that resulted in a U.S. Supreme Court decision in 1950 desegregating railroad dining cars in interstate travel. But the other Forum leaders discussed — Bevans, Hughes, Murray, and Burrell — remained prominent activists in the cause of freedom in the Baltimore region well into their advanced years, as did many other Forumites. Virginia Jackson, who married Calvin Kiah in 1933 and left Baltimore, returning during the Second World War, also participated in the freedom movement throughout her life. However, her first love was always art; she became a well-known painter, portraitist, and museum director, remaining active until her death at age ninety.[16]

The Friday Night Community Meetings

In late 1931 and early 1932, drawing on the traditions and experiences that they broadly shared and on their understandings of the situation they faced, the Forum core developed a list of the goals for the new organization. Their ultimate goal was to build "youth consciousness" and a youth movement to serve the community: "To establish an intelligent, trained young people's leadership engaged in a constructive program with city-wide community influence." To build this movement, the Forum planned to "create opportunities of employment" for qualified youth and "to discover and develop the talent and rare ability" of young people who needed help. This was not, however, a youth movement driven by what would later be called a generation gap in the community; it was, rather, a movement that sought to overcome a gap that already existed by "convert[ing] many of the older people to an interest in and love for young people." Also, it was to be an African American youth movement that promoted racial understanding by "making . . . fruitful inter-racial contacts on a ground of mutual interest." And the Forum sought to stimulate a consciousness of spiritual values. But most fundamentally, at least in its first months, the Forum wanted to educate the Black community: "To afford the people of Baltimore information by experts in the various fields concerning the variety of problems that confront them! To provide a place where they might pour out their difficulties and conflicts, and by discussing them be led to form safe, practical solutions and conclusions." The Forum's open, community-wide Friday night meetings, held from October through April, were the main venue for its educational project. In the words of one Forumite, the meetings were "a popular university." Starting with 1932–33, each meeting focused on a social, artistic, or moral question and featured a presentation by a speaker or, less often, a panel of speakers. Sometimes locally based but more often from out of town, speakers received only travel expenses, raised by passing the hat at the end of the meeting, for their efforts.[17]

The Forum's popular university was undeniably very popular. The Friday night meetings were regularly held in "the largest meeting place in the Black community," the Bethel AME church, with its 2,000 person capacity sometimes filled to overflowing. When Mary McLeod Bethune spoke at the Forum in October 1932, an "immense crowd jammed the auditorium of Bethel Church," according to the *Afro-American*, "and hundreds were reported turned away." Similarly, attendance for Nannie Burroughs in 1933 and for James Weldon Johnson in 1935 exceeded the available seating. Overwhelmingly African American, with only a scattering of Whites, audiences were drawn from all age groups with roughly equal numbers of males and females. Juanita Jackson Mitchell later recalled that the Forum strove to attract working-class and poor, as well as middle-class and more affluent, Black people, and it apparently succeeded. The size of these audiences testifies to a deep, cross-class desire for knowledge, as well as to the shrewd tactics of the organizers. "People did not have any jobs," Juanita Jackson Mitchell later recalled. "They had no place to go. They had no money to go. And ours was a Friday night social event. 'Go to the Forum!' And we had activities!" The Forum leadership charged no admission and made all of the meetings into cultural events. As Juanita Jackson Mitchell recalled, "We had a large group in the choir." The Forum's organist, Luther C. Mitchell, would often play a musical piece, sometimes with accompaniment. The Forum Trio, featuring the youngest Jackson sister, Marion, would often sing. To make everybody feel at home, and to overcome any unease the older people might feel toward the younger generation, there was a "corps of trained young ushers and a courtesy committee [to] greet, welcome, and take care of the comforts of the visitors."[18]

The Friday meetings rapidly became a community institution; the speakers' presentations were the most important part of the meetings. The greatest number of these presentations, more than one-third during the Forum's first years, focused on the culture, history, and current plight of the African American community. Many of these programs concentrated on the Black freedom movement itself: developments in racial consciousness, Black labor and radicalism, the history of the NAACP, strategies for attacking discrimination in education, Black candidates for office, the Black press. Others dealt with current issues facing Baltimore's African American community, such as lynching, migration from the southern countryside, and discrimination in relief. Still others took up diverse topics such as the African origins of Black Americans, the "New Negro," and the nature of Black business. And a number of the Forum's programs discussed African American art, music, and literature.[19]

By 1935, the Forum had been addressed at least once by W. E. B. Du Bois, James Weldon Johnson, Nannie Burroughs, Charles Houston (who returned almost yearly throughout the 1930s), Walter White, William Pickens, Mary White Ovington, Mary McLeod Bethune, Ira De A. Reid, Roy Wilkins, E. Franklin Frazier, George Schuyler, Joel E. Spingarn, Ralph Bunche, William Hastie, and the poet Sterling Brown. Together, these speakers represented a significant section of the national African American intelligentsia and of the leadership of the national freedom movement. In recruiting speakers, the Forum drew heavily on the intellectual resources of Howard University in nearby Washington, D.C., as well as on other Black colleges and universities, and on the leading circles of the NAACP (although the Forum in the beginning had no formal relationship to that organization).[20]

Reflecting the importance of religious faith to the Forum youth, about one-sixth of the Friday night meetings during the early years addressed specific questions of religion. The titles of religious presentations indicated that the Forumites were interested in an activist view of religion, one that informed both personal moral decisions and collective social action. Those meetings that dealt with theology or the institutional church often had decidedly political overtones—for example, "The Fruits of Living the Principles of Jesus Christ in Times Like These," "The Light That Christmas Throws on the Problems of the Hour," "The Church—An Asset or a Liability?" Religiously oriented meetings also emphasized individual moral questions such as marriage and divorce, self-respect, and conscience. Both Black and White religious speakers addressed the Forum; the Whites were often Quakers and, sometimes, Jewish rabbis.[21]

Finally, the meetings considered a potpourri of issues that the Forum leadership believed to be important for general community education. Political radicalism was a live issue for Forumites, who hosted both Communists (Euel Lee's lawyer, Bernard Ades; the national CP leaders William Patterson and Angelo Herndon) and Socialists (Broadus Mitchell and Frank Trager). Panels addressed national politics, such as a symposium on the National Recovery Act featuring the New Dealer Clark Foreman, and local politics, including panels of major and minor party candidates for city and state offices. Eyewitness accounts of other countries and cultures were included when the opportunity arose. One Forum supporter recounted his travels to the Soviet Union, and another recounted his travels to Cuba, while a participant on a goodwill tour from Haiti discussed "Haiti and Voodooism." There were occasional programs on women's issues, such as the debate titled "Resolved That a Woman's Place Is in the Home," with Howard Cornish, a mathematics professor at Morgan College and a vice-president of the Forum, taking the negative position and Frances Williams from the national office of the YWCA the affirmative position. There was at least one program on love, sexuality, and dating, which had to be handled carefully, given the intergenerational audience. ("We were starved for information [on such topics]," Juanita Jackson Mitchell later observed.) Since the Forum prided itself on the range of topics and opinions, it occasionally included some fairly conservative presenters, such as Judge T. Bayard Williams of Baltimore, who advocated the forced return of Black immigrants from southern rural areas. Furthermore, the Forum did not shrink from controversy, inviting Clark Foreman while the national freedom movement was protesting his appointment as a White by President Franklin D. Roosevelt to the position of National Advisor on the Economic Status of the Negro.[22]

Most significantly, the educational process at the Friday night meetings was not a passive one; increasingly, the meetings became a springboard for social action. After each presentation, the floor was opened to discussion, and the discussions were frequently lively. At a reunion of Forum veterans in 1987, Juanita Jackson Mitchell reminisced about William Dorsey, who read constantly and was "a walking encyclopedia." Dorsey, she recalled, loved to put "trick" questions to speakers, including questions that "deemed him an atheist" to some in the audience. Dorsey, who was also present at the reunion, recalled the time he upbraided W. E. B. Du Bois for "talking down to these church people" and even "talking a whole lot of nonsense." Dorsey also recalled how, when Baltimore's Mayor Howard Jackson spoke, Clarence Mitchell asked him how he stood on certain issues. Mayor "went on, he rambled, and he didn't ever answer the question. And Clarence got up and said, 'I've made up my mind that on my next birthday, which will be my 21st birthday, I will never vote for anybody who doesn't answer a question' . . . and Jackson got red in the face." "He used to get red in the face all of the time!," others at the reunion added among laughter. In fact, one of the purposes of the discussions was to give the speakers, in the Forum's own words, "the opportunity to learn what the Negro is thinking socially and economically." The Forum youth were not shy about challenging their "expert" speakers, White or Black.[23]

The Forum's community meetings were more than opportunities to learn and debate. As Virginia Jackson Kiah put it years later, they became "a town hall meeting every Friday night." As in any good "town hall" meeting, a vote was often taken at the end to express a majority opinion and, increasingly, to choose a course of action. The resolutions that were passed might simply register the opinion of the group as a public statement, such as whether or not the audience agreed that woman's place was in the home. At other times, the action taken included fund raising to aid the Friday meeting speaker's cause. Collections were frequently taken for Black educational institutions: $50 each for Bethune-Cookman College and for Bennett College for Women, $30 for Palmer Memorial Institute, and $85 for the National Training School for Girls—all significant amounts for Depression-era Black Baltimore. Forum participants contributed directly to political causes, such as the defense of Euel Lee, and passed resolutions at Friday night meetings to become involved in social justice campaigns.[24]

Finally, the Friday night meetings were used to encourage the development of youth leadership in all fields through "Talent Nights," concerts, piano recitals, and debates. At such events, the Forum awarded scholarships for enrollment at various African American colleges and vocational training schools.

For the final Friday night program of every season, the Forum held its Annual Intercollegiate Oratorical, Vocal, and Instrument Contest, involving musicians, singers, and orators from a number of predominantly Black colleges, including Howard, Morgan, Hampton Institute, Virginia Union, and, occasionally, Cheyney State College. Self-help and social uplift activities such as these, which focused on changing people rather than society, drew on traditions central to African American culture and were promoted historically by figures as diverse as Booker T. Washington and Marcus Garvey. As paradoxical as it might seem in retrospect, from the point of view of Forumites, such activities were consistent with the Forum's growing social radicalism.[25]

Social Base and Organization

By 1934, the Forum claimed in an official publication "a membership of five hundred young people, representing thirty-six churches and nine denominations," with a following significantly bigger than its membership. Clearly, the Forum was becoming a large neighborhood-based, cross-class, mass-membership organization, something quite unusual in the history of the Baltimore freedom movement. In an oral history interview, Juanita Jackson Mitchell stressed that the "Forum had no class," and that members came from many strata of the community. "Most of them came out of the churches, and a lot of them came from the street," she said. "They weren't in any formal churches, but they just had this fire in them." Most members, she added, lacked any college education. Unlike the leadership, the Forum's rank-and-file was increasingly reaching into the working class, and its membership was growing beyond the traditional social bloc of the freedom movement into a broader cross-class alliance.[26]

The Forum developed a rather complex structure and division of responsibility, one that mirrored organizational features of the Black churches, colleges, and community organizations from which its founders were drawn. The top office was that of president, held by Juanita Jackson during the Forum's first seven years, and by the Reverend Howard L. Cornish for the subsequent four. Other officers included a half-dozen or so vice-presidents, whose duties included chairing the Friday night meetings on a rotating basis; recording, corresponding, and financial secretaries; and a treasurer and assistant treasurer (see figure 11). This core of about fifty people met weekly. In addition, there was a large array of standing committees, each with its own chair or director, including the ushers, the chorus, the dramatic unit, the social committee, the sick committee, the publicity committee, the auditing committee, the research

OFFICERS OF THE CITY-WIDE YOUNG PEOPLE'S FORUM,
JUANITA E. JACKSON, President, 1933

11. From a Forum publication, 1933. *Photograph by Paul Henderson.*

committee, the civic committee, and the ways and means committee, some of
which functioned more consistently than others. The variety of the committees
testifies to the range of interests the Forum attempted to incorporate and to the
importance of culture and sociability to Forumites.[27]

A review of the names of the Forum's officers and chairpersons in its early
years reveals another interesting fact: women played a strikingly important
role in the top leadership. Juanita Jackson above all epitomized the female
leadership of the Forum. She not only dominated during its first four years
but also remained the president and key leader between late 1935 and 1938
while she lived in Harlem and worked at the NAACP's national office. Indeed, Forum minutes indicate that through 1936 she regularly traveled back
to Baltimore from New York City, apparently at the Forum's expense, to preside over executive committee meetings and to participate in Friday night
meetings; she continued to make this trek periodically until 1938, when she
married and left for Minneapolis. As late as 1941, her name still topped the

list of officers as "Founder," and a portrait of her alone was printed on the first page of the Forum's annual pamphlet, even though she was living a thousand miles away.[28]

But Juanita Jackson was by no means alone. Although her sister and Forum co-founder, Virginia Jackson, married and left Baltimore in 1933, many other women stepped forward. In 1934, ten of the fifteen executive committee members, including three of six vice-presidents, were women; eight of eleven heads of standing committees or bodies were likewise women. The year 1934 may have represented a high-water mark in terms of female leadership, for by 1935 all of the vice-presidents (four that year) were men, but women still held the majority of the executive committee positions. Evelyn Burrell, speaking years later of the Baltimore freedom movement of the era, remarked, "You know, it's been the women, usually, who have been at the top of this. So many of us in the movement were females, although there were males. But the push came from the females." As discussed in chapter 1, a tradition of women's leadership in the Baltimore freedom movement predated the Forum, and the Forum enhanced this tradition. Unlike earlier women's organizations, such as the Cooperative Women's Civic League, the Forum represented a breakthrough of sorts—an important community organization comprising both men and women, with women predominating in the leadership.[29]

While the Forum was an organization of Black youth, some older adults also played important leadership roles in the grouping. Not surprisingly, the adult participants came from the same social strata as the Forum's leadership. Most prominent among these older adults was Lillie Jackson, main adviser to the Forum, who supported the organization in part, Juanita Jackson Mitchell recalled, because "at that time the Communists were active here and she didn't want us to be Communists." A very active adviser, Lillie Jackson regularly attended the Forum executive committee's weekly meetings and looked after the group's finances. Katrine White, another key adult participant, was probably in her forties when she became corresponding secretary during the Forum's first year, a position she held until the organization's demise. White, a trained typist and a skilled correspondent, was the widow of a doctor who co-founded the Black community's Provident Hospital. Fannie Johnson, a member of the Sharp Street church's women's club with Lillie Jackson, and the wife of a successful physician, was the organization's treasurer in its first years. Sarah F. Diggs, who was married to the theater owner Josiah Diggs, was the adviser to the Forum's ushers for a decade. Notably, most of the adult advisers who worked directly with the youth were women, with the exception of Luther C. Mitchell, the Forum organist.[30]

Juanita Jackson Mitchell later recalled that her mother organized an advisory committee of older Forum supporters: "Because of my mother's far-sighted leadership, she got an adult advisory committee that included Carl Murphy of the *Afro-American*, the businessmen, and all of the heads of the fraternal organizations. In those days the fraternal organizations were some of the biggest institutions in the community. She got the women's organizations, and mother also got the churches." In addition to offering advice, the committee functioned as a buffer between the Forum youth and those community leaders, including some of the clergy, who feared the "radicalism" of the organization. As Juanita Jackson Mitchell later remarked, critics of the Forum "couldn't call us Communists because of this committee of notables." Furthermore, with the disarray in the local freedom movement, many adults on the advisory committee did not know how else to respond to the crisis of the times, and in Mitchell's words, "the City-Wide Young People's Forum became their channel of protest." Hence, the advisory committee came to embody a growing alliance between the Forum youth and a section of the Black community's leadership, including some of the most formidable elements of Baltimore's adult civil rights establishment. Carl Murphy, publisher of the *Afro-American* and a member of the advisory committee, was key to this alliance. Murphy published long articles on Forum meetings and activities, and he ran a regular column by Forum Vice-President Clarence Mitchell (who landed a job at the *Afro* through the New Deal's Blue Eagle program). He also assigned the *Afro*'s most radical editor, William N. Jones, to see that the Forum was covered and, according to Juanita Jackson Mitchell, to "take care of these young people."[31]

Beyond the advisory committee (and partly because of its activities), support for the Forum among adults grew over time, especially, as Genna Rae McNeil has pointed out, in terms of funding and material backing. The list of advertisers in Forum publications reads like a directory of Baltimore's Black businesses, and the long lists of individual sponsors and patrons in Forum publications include a virtual *Who's Who* of the progressive section of the city's African American elite, along with many working adults of more modest circumstances. On these lists were also a number of White supporters, including, not surprisingly, socialists and radicals such as Elisabeth Gilman, Broadus Mitchell, and A. E. O. Munsell, as well as a few White establishment figures, including Mayor Howard Jackson of Baltimore. Juanita Jackson Mitchell was asked in an interview many years later whether Mayor Jackson had been an ally of the Forum, and she replied, "Oh, no, he was an enemy." And she was right. But he was the kind of enemy whose ostensible "support" could be accepted to better position the Forum to do the work it wanted to do. In addition, some other conservative figures, mainly from the Black community, also found it expedient to identify themselves as supposed supporters of the Forum as its prestige rose. For better or worse, the Forum was willing to accept the tradeoff.[32]

Social Action

Promoting racial integration was one of the Forum's goals from the start. As a Forum publication put it, "Church, college and labor groups of young white people have visited the Forum," and the "officers of the [Forum] are frequently invited to address white youth and adult gatherings." Beginning in 1932, the Forum conducted what it called Good Will Tours, during which "an equal number of white and colored young people spent a day together." As Juanita Jackson Mitchell later described the tours: "We would go to their church. We would take a program, and my [future] husband [Clarence Mitchell] was one of the speakers. We had someone who would read James Weldon Johnson's 'Creation,' and the [Forum] Trio would sing, and my husband would speak. Oh, he could speak! Then we would appeal for interracial fellowship. Then we would invite them back to Sharp Street Methodist church. We would take them first to the Black businesses, the Black newspaper, the *Afro-American*, to see the Black churches, and where we lived. Then we would go to dinner, take fellowship together."[33]

While the attempts of the Forum to build interracial understanding probably affected the thinking of a number of White young people, no ongoing, integrated church-related youth grouping emerged. In fact, sometimes the Forum's efforts at interracial understanding received rude rebuffs. On one occasion, according to Juanita Jackson Mitchell, White young people of the Epworth League of the McKendree Methodist Episcopal church invited the Forum to conduct a Good Will Tour with them. However, on the Friday before the scheduled tour, the pastor of the church, Reverend Asbury Smith (a well-known White opponent of segregation), called the Forum's leaders to apologize and ask them not to come. The trustees of the church had met and nullified the Epworth League's invitation, threatening to bar the church doors if the delegation showed up. Subsequent attempts by Smith and allies in his congregation to change the mind of the church's board of trustees failed.[34]

The Forum's social activism had the most impact, however, in the political struggle for social justice, in the beginning by supporting and joining efforts led by other forces. The Forum's first real involvement in political action was inspired by the Baltimore CP and followed the appearance of the attorney Bernard Ades of the International Labor Defense (ILD) at a Friday night meeting in October 1932. The meeting passed a support resolution for the Euel Lee defense campaign and raised $73.60 for the cause; then the Forum itself jumped into the campaign. As Juanita Jackson Mitchell remarked, "The City-Wide Young People's Forum was a religious-oriented organization, but we cooperated with the Communists." The former Forum activist Eleanor Burrell spoke of the Forum's involvement in the Euel Lee campaign when she later remarked that the Communists "were the ones who got the attorney, and we were the ones that got petitions." Burrell's comment vastly under-states the CP's role but accurately indicates the Forum's immersion in the Euel Lee campaign. This was the Forum's first real involvement with mass mobilization, and after the Lee campaign, its political engagements multi-plied rapidly.[35]

In late 1932 and 1933, the activity of the freedom movement was picking up in Baltimore and in Maryland, and the Forum became involved with the unsuccessful Committee to Repeal the Maryland Jim Crow Law. During the same period, Forum members and supporters canvassed from door to door during the voter-registration campaign that was initiated by the *Afro-American* and led by an ad hoc group called the Good Citizens' League. Also, in early 1933, the Forum got involved in a question that was being debated across the United States: should married female teachers, with employed husbands to support them, keep their jobs? After a Friday night meeting discussion, the Forum decided that the answer was no. Forumites plunged into a petition campaign during which they canvassed community meet-ings, churches, and homes. Eventually, 2,150 people in the African Ameri-can community signed the petition asking the school board to "remedy" the situation. The Forum's petition argued that, under circumstances of high un-employment, married female teachers with working husbands represented an unfair "distribution of employment" and "an especial hardship on quali-fied people" who could not find work. "It is for the ultimate moral, civic, and physical advancement of any community to provide employment for its qualified and efficient youth." This rationale was, of course, a common one in the United States in those years, and it was in line with the Forum's stated desire to expand employment opportunities for its youthful base.[36]

But why did an organization with strong female leadership not demand that *either* the man or the woman in such two-job couples surrender a job? Juanita Jackson Mitchell later suggested an answer. She reminisced a bit ruefully that, "back in those days," the woman was the one who quit work when there was a marriage—"it was a different conception" from today. She seemed to look back on the controversy over married teachers with some regret, referring to it as "a big hullabaloo [that] tore this community apart."

Evidently so, because of all the organization's early involvements, only this one goes unmentioned in the official summaries of its history.[37]

By March 1933, the Forum had gained enough confidence to initiate its own protest activities. "In an effort to open up avenues of employment for eligible qualified youth," the Forum announced three campaigns for:

1. Permission to qualify for positions on the staff of the Enoch Pratt Free Library, a tax-supported institution.
2. Equitable distribution of positions in the public school system.
3. Increase in the number of colored Welfare Workers employed by the Family Welfare Association.

The campaigns to open the library training programs and to employ Black social workers took off rapidly. By April 19, more than 6,000 signatures had been gathered, and the Forum sent a delegation led by its attorney, W. A. C. Hughes Jr., to the Board of Estimate to present the petitions. For the first time, the *Baltimore Sun* and *Baltimore Evening Sun* — papers well practiced at ignoring Black protest activities — took notice of the Forum. Mayor Howard Jackson solemnly swore to study the issues, then quickly referred the petitions to the trustees of the library and the administrators of the Family Welfare Association.[38]

The Forum, however, in alliance with Baltimore Urban League (BUL), which was then reviving under its new executive director, Edward Lewis, followed up with further efforts on the social worker issue. Victory came in September and October 1933, when the Baltimore Emergency Relief Commission (BERC), the New Deal agency that had just taken over welfare administration in Baltimore, hired five Black social workers. Juanita Jackson Mitchell remembered the campaign as relatively effortless; the Forum directly pressured the head of the BERC, the municipal reformer Anna Ward, and "she broke easily, without even a picket line." By 1934, a total of eighteen Black welfare workers had been hired.[39]

The Enoch Pratt Free Library, with its lily-white staff, was harder to crack. The Forum demanded only that African Americans be admitted to the training program for the Pitcher Street branch, which was located in the Black community. Library administrators, while "expressing sympathy with this desire," demurred, and the city government claimed that despite its annual budgetary support, the library was a private corporation beyond city control. Integrating the library's staff became a protracted struggle that was not won until years later.[40]

Therefore, by late 1933, the Forum had worked successfully in alliance with both the CP and the BUL, had initiated its own social justice campaigns, and had tasted victory with the hiring of the Black social workers. However, some tensions developed in its alliance with the BUL when the first Black social workers hired came from outside the city. According to Juanita Jackson Mitchell, "The Urban League said, 'Well, you can't argue about the fact that they are getting those who were trained in social work.' But we had a lot of college graduates who could have done the social work they were doing. When it came to us, they had to be so overly well trained. We were kind of disappointed."[41] The Forum also found that its alliance with the BUL was less than satisfactory in another way. Clarence Mitchell remarked years later that he and other Forum members were irritated that some of the press credited the BUL for the victory and ignored the Forum. These tensions indicated contradictions between generations of the freedom movement, and between fundamentally different kinds of organizations. One was an upstart local youth organization with a mass membership and growing mass base, and the other was a branch of a venerable national organization with a respectable older adult constituency and a small paid staff. These relatively minor problems aside, the protests initiated in March 1933 represented an important evolution for the Forum and a step in the reactivation of the local freedom movement. Even the leadership of the national freedom movement was beginning to notice. In mid-1933, the NAACP invited Juanita Jackson, as president of the Forum, to the Second Amenia Conference.[42]

The conference was held on August 18–24, 1933, on the estate of the NAACP's president, Joel Spingarn, in upstate New York. The NAACP organized the conference in response to increasing criticism that the organization was out of touch with the needs of most African Americans—similar to the criticism raised in Baltimore around the lack of involvement by the local NAACP in the Euel Lee campaign. Echoing the purpose of the first NAACP conference at Amenia in 1916, the second conference aimed to develop a new agenda for the national freedom movement through a process of open, no-holds-barred discussion among the attendees. Only forty-three Black intellectuals and activists, most of them young, were invited, and thirty-three attended. Juanita Jackson was one of eleven women at the conference and probably the youngest person present. Those attending included the strongest proponents of the various trends of thought in the freedom movement, including Abram Harris, Ralph Bunche, E. Franklin Frazier, Charles Houston, Sterling Brown, Ira De A. Reid, and other soon-to-be luminaries of the movement. W. E. B. Du Bois, Walter White, and Roy Wilkins represented the NAACP establishment. Only a few Whites were present, mostly for short periods;

12. As he rose to national prominence in the NAACP during the early 1930s, Charles Houston greatly influenced the City-Wide Young People's Forum and the Baltimore freedom movement. *Courtesy of the Library of Congress.*

they included Spingarn himself; his wife, Amy Einstein Spingarn; the long-time NAACP leader Mary White Ovington; and Lewis Mumford and his wife, Sophia.[43]

The discussion at the conference was wide ranging. While no unanimity was achieved, most present proposed that action around economic as well as political questions was essential. Many advocated a semi-nationalistic reliance on Black community power. Some questioned whether a social system based on private ownership and private profit could ever produce social equality for Black people. And a number argued that it was necessary to organize the African American working class in unity with White workers. For some participants, such as Charles Houston (see figure 12), dean of Howard University Law School, the conference did not live up to expectations because it failed to develop a new program for the movement; he called it "the anemic conference of Amenia." Du Bois, too, was "not satisfied," especially because so few young people were invited. Juanita Jackson, however, found the conference extremely stimulating, and, by her own account, it greatly broadened her sense of political possibilities.[44]

Juanita Jackson was not the only Forumite to encounter freedom politics outside the confines of Baltimore in 1933. In his position as columnist and reporter for the *Afro*, Clarence Mitchell was exposed to a wide range of ideas and experiences and was even sent to Alabama to cover the Scottsboro Boys case. And Thurgood Marshall continued to participate in the main political debates in the national freedom movement of the day, centered at Howard University. Such experiences outside Baltimore helped to shape and reshape the direction of the Forum in increasingly activist and radical directions. Moreover, the character of the social struggle was changing in the Baltimore region in 1933, especially in the progressive sectors of the union movement, and with an emerging, neighborhood-based mass organization, the People's Unemployment League, that would soon influence the direction of the Forum.

4

Garment Workers, Socialists, and the People's Unemployment League, 1932–1934

We pledge our loyalty to the People's Unemployment League of
Maryland in its struggle for justice. We promise to work in the spirit
of brotherhood to help the oppressed of every race and creed. We will
work to build a new workers' world of peace and plenty, beauty and
freedom for all the people.
—"Initiation Procedure and Pledge of Loyalty," PUL

In late 1932 and early 1933, Baltimore, like the country as a whole, was heading into the trough of the Great Depression. Joblessness in the region was
estimated at 16 percent but was undoubtedly much higher; it was higher
yet for African Americans—and rising. The financial system seemed to be
collapsing, and a period of further steep economic decline appeared to be
ahead. The prospect for a major outbreak of working-class protest looked
dim; indeed, in the Baltimore region in 1932, the number of strikes had been
even lower than in the previous year. Then two important breakthroughs
occurred in the region's workers' movement. The ACW, the city's most established progressive industrial union, sprang back to life with a massive walkout in the men's clothing industry, and the People's Unemployment League
(PUL) appeared and swept through the neighborhoods of the region, building a new movement of the unemployed with amazing speed. Like other
struggles in the region early in the Depression era, both of these were concerned with racial/ethnic justice, and both were largely led by radicals, this
time affiliated with the Socialist Party of America. With the ACW strike and
the emergence of the PUL, the prospects for the Baltimore workers' movement began to brighten.[1]

The ACW Strike of 1932

On September 13, 1932, workers in the men's garment industry of Baltimore, led by the ACW, walked out en masse, demanding pay raises, improved working conditions, and, most important of all, union recognition. As the historian Jo Ann Argersinger has written, "The strike was at once a bold and a desperate move for the ACW, whose ranks had been decimated by the anti-unionism of the 1920s." During its "golden age" of 1916–1920, the Baltimore ACW had 10,000 members and dominated the regional men's clothing industry, the fourth largest in the nation. However, by the early 1930s, the output of the region's industry had dropped to fifth place in the country, and the dues-paying membership in Baltimore ACW was down to fewer than 1,000, barely 10 percent of the remaining labor force in the region's men's garments industry. Its much vaunted social, educational, and cultural programs had all but ceased to function; the electricity to the union hall had been turned off for nonpayment of bills. "The union was at rock bottom," Argersinger remarked, and the national ACW had come to view the Baltimore situation as a "danger" to the union as a whole.[2]

During the 1920s, the structure of the garment industry in Baltimore, unlike other industry centers where large factories or "inside shops" continued to prevail, had been transformed by the proliferation of small shops that contracted production out from the larger firms. The growing numbers of these "contract shops" weakened the union's authority in the industry, undermined the conditions for worker solidarity, and gave employers the leverage to reduce wages and working conditions to levels approaching those of the sweat shop era at the turn of the century. In addition, the decline in wages and union power in Baltimore prompted clothing companies in other cities to transfer production to non-union Baltimore-based shops, thereby weakening the position of ACW workers in these other cities. The national leadership decided that it was in the vital interest of the union as a whole to address its problem in Baltimore by helping to resurrect the region's ACW. But the tactic they chose, an industry-wide general strike, was risky. For eight weeks in the summer of 1932, the leadership and staff of the national ACW, including the former Baltimore leaders Dorothy Jacobs Bellanca and Hyman Blumberg, worked with the local leadership in agitating and organizing at the grassroots. Then the general strike was called.[3]

As it turned out, the ACW's "bold and desperate move" worked, much to the amazement of local and national leaders. Five thousand mostly female workers, mainly of Jewish but also of Italian, Lithuanian, Polish, Bohemian, and other European ethnic backgrounds, struck more than 200 men's clothing shops in the Baltimore area. They even walked out of factories that the union had not targeted. Sara Barron, an important Baltimore ACW leader, recalled decades later that when the ACW's national president, Sidney Hillman, came to Baltimore to speak at a mass meeting on the eve of the strike, he "was surprised when he got to the Fourth Regiment Armory and not only was the place inside packed, there were hundreds and hundreds of people outside trying to come in." An estimated 4,000–5,000 attended. Without electricity at the union headquarters, and despite a greatly diminished roll of dues payers, the Baltimore ACW, with its progressive industrial unionism, had clearly retained the allegiance of its broad, multiethnic, multiskilled, majority female base.[4]

After the initial walkout, the strikers picketed enthusiastically and continuously in large numbers, participated in frequent mass meetings, and endured large-scale police harassment that sent hundreds of strikers to jail. When Schoeneman's, one of the largest clothing manufacturers in the city, got an injunction limiting the number of pickets at its establishment, the workers defiantly mounted a massive picket line, and mass arrests followed. Despite the repression, unity among the ethnically diverse strikers not only held but also deepened, and support for the strike grew. Female workers of different ethnicities proved to be the backbone of the strike and were prominent among the strike's organizers and leadership. Sara Barron led fifty female activists in the militant "Activity Group," which was particularly important to the struggle, and was herself arrested thirteen times during this strike.

From its beginnings, the Baltimore ACW—a union imbued with various forms of radicalism—had had strong supporters in socialist and progressive circles in Baltimore. Once the 1932 strike was on, solidarity networks rapidly developed. A high-profile citizens' committee led by Rabbi Edward Israel formed and, while bemoaning the strike as tragedy for the city, pressured the authorities to intervene on the strikers' behalf. In mid-November, a group of sixty—including, according to the *Baltimore Sun*, "private school instructors, college professors, Catholic, Protestant, and Jewish clergy men, welfare workers, and women political leaders"—called on the mayor to bring the workers and employers together in arbitration (which the employers rejected). Key movers in the support networks included the socialist intellectuals Broadus Mitchell and Frank Trager of Johns Hopkins University, Elinor Pancoast and Naomi Riches of Goucher College, and Elisabeth Gilman, all of whom had been involved with the ACW in various ways. Ethnic, religious, and civic organizations such as the Workmen's Circle, the YMCA, the YWCA, and the League of Women's Voters pitched in. The mainstream newspapers reported strike activities almost daily, and as the weeks rolled by, sympathy for the strikers grew across the social spectrum.

In response to mounting pressure, Mayor Howard Jackson appointed an investigating commission chaired by an esteemed professor of political economy, Jacob Hollander of Johns Hopkins University. An old-time Progressive (with a capital "P"), Hollander led his commission with vigor. The garment manufacturers refused to cooperate with the commission, but the union and the workers did so very willingly. The general public learned in firsthand detail from the testimony of worker after worker—mostly women—about the terrible working conditions, meager wages, and despotic management that prevailed in the industry. Many Baltimoreans were shocked, and a public clamor against the garment companies grew.

As a result of the militancy and solidarity of the strikers and the growing public sympathy for the strike, clothing manufacturers began to settle with the union. By the end of the year, the strikers had won. According to Argersinger, "The ACW had unionized 133 contract shops, 61 inside shops, and it celebrated with a Victory Mass Meeting," addressed by local and national ACW leaders, and by New York Congressman Fiorello LaGuardia. In just a few months, the ACW had put approximately 70 percent of the Baltimore men's garment industry under contract, and the workers involved had received wage increases of as much as 30 percent. Nonetheless, the two largest men's clothing manufacturers, Greif's and Schoeneman's, resisted unionization, and during the strike Schoeneman's moved its plant out of town to a non-union location in rural Pennsylvania.

The Baltimore local received a great deal of support from the national ACW during the strike; in all, the national office spent some $12,000 on the struggle. ACW workers in other regions, including Chicago, New York City, Rochester, and New Jersey also raised funds, sent organizers, and threatened action against local garment companies whose Baltimore branches were being struck. From the national ACW's point of view, its aid to the strikers was more than worth the effort, for the strike substantially solved its Baltimore problem and mobilized sections of the still lethargic national union toward greater activity. However, in spite of important national support, the strike in 1932 succeeded because the leadership on all levels was largely local. By the end of the strike, the Baltimore Joint Board had reconstituted itself as an effective, militant leadership body for the ACW locals in the region, and Ulisse De Dominicis, an ACW activist in Baltimore known for his socialist, class-struggle orientation, had become its president. As an indicator of consolidated cross-ethnic cooperation during the strike, it should be noted that De Dominicis, an Italian, was now the main leader of a largely Jewish union.

Although the ACW continued to agitate and organize, the Depression deepened in the months after the strike, and some of the gains were erased. As the New Deal emerged during the first one hundred days of Franklin D. Roosevelt's presidency in early 1933, the ACW leadership realized that, whatever the pro-business bias of legislation like the National Industrial Recovery Act (NIRA), the union needed to intervene immediately to ensure its membership's interests. National and local ACW leaders became involved in the drafting of the National Recovery Administration (NRA) codes for the men's garment industry, then in compelling employers to comply with the code's provisions. They rallied their rank-and-file to support their positions on the men's garment codes, resorting to strikes when they felt strikes were necessary. By early 1934, the dues-paying membership of the Baltimore ACW, which had numbered about 1,000 before the strike, had grown to 6,000.

African American workers had little involvement with the 1932 strike, but in its wake, as the sociologist Ira De A. Reid of the National Urban League observed in his study of Black Baltimore in 1934, the ACW "made a determined effort to unionize . . . Negro workers in the garment industry." Interracial working-class unity was, of course, the official position of the ACW, but it appears that in Baltimore, despite attempts, the union had organized few Black workers. The union's successful effort to maintain unity among strikers across White ethnic lines during the strike must have strengthened the hand of those in the union leadership who wanted to organize across racial-ethnic lines, as well; after the strike, interracialism became an increasingly important part of the ACW's approach. In mid-1933, during the negotiations over the NRA codes, the ACW publicly insisted that the men's clothing codes for Baltimore bar racial discrimination. When a number of Black female workers organized by the ACW went on strike in Baltimore in August 1933, the union held a meeting in the African American community, co-sponsored by the Baltimore Urban League (BUL), to build support for the strike and recruit more African American workers to the union. The meeting was entitled "Should Our Workers Join the Unions Now?" and the answer given by the interracial group of speakers was a resounding yes. The meeting's participants voted to create the Negro Labor Committee (NLC) as an ongoing body dedicated to organizing Black workers into the ACW and other unions, then followed up with additional recruiting meetings in other parts of the city. By year's end, the ACW, BUL, and NLC announced plans to hire a Black organizer. Hence, in the wake of the 1932 strike, the ACW not only increased its interracial organizing but also entered into an alliance to recruit more Black workers with the BUL, a freedom movement organization that, under its new executive secretary, Edward S. Lewis, was growing in importance.[5]

Moreover, the 1932 ACW general strike and its aftermath represented something of a turning point for organized labor locally and nationally. It was one of only a few major strikes called at the time by an established union; one of even fewer that was offensive, not defensive (reacting directly to wage cuts or layoffs); and one of very few that largely succeeded. While it anticipated the national strike wave that began in the second half of 1933, its greatest impact was on the workers' movement in Baltimore. There it demonstrated that, even under dire economic conditions, an aggressive, unified mass strike could win, and that multi-ethnic industrial unionism could triumph in a region dominated by craft unionism and Jim Crow. As the future would demonstrate, the ACW in the men's clothing industry, like the MWIU on the waterfront, was establishing the regional foundations for the wave of industrial unionism that would roll across Baltimore during the second half of the decade.[6]

The People's Unemployment League

In the wake of the ACW strike, another mass campaign developed in the Baltimore workers' movement, this time on the neighborhood level and this time creating something new both in scale and form. Voters in Baltimore in November 1932 had joined citizens across the country in turning out Herbert Hoover, despite the fact that his Democratic challenger, Franklin D. Roosevelt, was largely an unknown quantity. These voters also gave the Democrats a local victory, even though the re-elected mayor, Howard Jackson, lacked any apparent will or ability to alleviate popular suffering. But Roosevelt's election, and the New Deal programs that followed, brought a sea change in the political-psychological environment, encouraging both hope and activity among the masses. In this context, the PUL was born.[7]

In 1928, Frank Trager moved from New York to Baltimore to become a graduate student and an instructor in philosophy at Johns Hopkins University. Nearly fifty years later, he recalled that "in 1929 a number of us at Hopkins and at Goucher College and in the city joined and became active in the League for Industrial Democracy. We began to get more and more concerned about the immediate plight of the unemployed, and we organized what came to be called the People's Unemployment League of Maryland." The League for Industrial Democracy (LID), the organization that Trager and his colleagues joined, was a nationwide left-progressive organization founded as the Intercollegiate Socialist Society in 1905 by Upton Sinclair, Jack London, and a number of leading socialists. In 1921, it changed its name to the League for Industrial Democracy and began recruiting beyond student ranks, attracting educators, intellectuals, and professionals, many of whom also belonged to the Socialist Party of America. By the early 1930s, Trager and his LID group were members of the Maryland branch of the Socialist Party (SP). In late 1932, the group was deeply involved in support work for the ACW strike and, immediately afterward, the presidential campaign of the SP candidate Norman Thomas, who was also the national co-director of LID. Both the strike and the campaign fired the imaginations of LID group members about the possibilities for social action, and they turned their attention to organizing the unemployed in the Baltimore region.[8]

The national SP gave the LID group very little guidance for their unemployment work. During the first years of the Depression, the SP's program called for "Emergency Conferences" (not organizations) to educate (not to organize) around unemployment, all with little effect. In frustration, younger, more militant Socialists began in a few locales to organize the unemployed on their own. The most successful of these efforts to that point was the Chicago Workers' Committee, which in the course of one year recruited 25,000 members into sixty locals. The Baltimore LID activists were inspired by the Chicago committee and took it as a model for their work. The LID group also had another source of inspiration: Trager later recalled that he and his comrades were motivated by a desire to confront "the challenge of the Communist Party's Unemployment Councils."[9]

In early January 1933, after weeks of preparatory work, the LID activists in Baltimore and their allies hosted the founding meeting of the Maryland PUL at the Christian Temple in Baltimore. The meeting was lively and well attended, and it was addressed by a star-studded group of, as the *Baltimore Sun* put it, "Labor leaders, clergymen, educators and manufacturers." It was a success. During the two years following the meeting, the PUL grew rapidly and, as Jo Ann Argersinger has written, "became one of the strongest such organizations in the country." Within two weeks of the founding meeting, ten neighborhood-based PUL locals with a total of 1,750 members had formed. In four months, twenty locals with more than 7,000 members were functioning, and in eighteen months, the PUL had thirty-three locals with some 18,000–20,000 members. While 1934–35 was the apparent high point for PUL membership, the organization continued to claim 8,000–12,000 members throughout much of the decade. Although it called itself the People's Unemployed League *of Maryland*, in March 1934 all but six of its locals were in Baltimore City, and five of those were in adjacent Baltimore County. The

PUL, therefore, was a creature of the city and industrial areas of the Baltimore metropolitan region, where it swiftly became a powerful presence. Even though Trager, PUL's vice-president, estimated in January 1934 that only 1,200–1,500 of the total membership of 12,000 were active in an ongoing manner, this was still an impressive number.[10]

As its membership grew, the PUL developed an elaborate, yet effective organizational structure, broadly similar to that of a democratically organized labor union, which attempted to balance localized decision making with centralization. The neighborhood-based locals, situated so all members were able to walk to meetings from their homes, elected their own leaders, organized their own activities, and operated with a good deal of autonomy. Each local sent representatives on a proportional basis to the General Council of Delegates, which, in the words of the PUL constitution, was "the Supreme law-making body." An Executive Committee was composed of the PUL's officers and the chairs of its organization-wide committees, who oversaw the day-to-day functioning of the PUL as a whole. There were committees for advocacy with relief agencies, legislation, mutual aid, education, finance, membership, and protest. In addition, there was an advisory committee composed, in the words of the *Monthly Labor Review*, of "the original sponsors of the league and other prominent citizens."[11]

With the exception of its organizers from LID who were professionals, the PUL's membership was drawn almost entirely from the unemployed ranks of the working class, including a few from the skilled crafts and many from the ranks of the semi-skilled and unskilled. The PUL was remarkably successful recruiting across racial lines; by mid-1933, about a fourth of the PUL's membership was African American, and by mid-1934, almost one-third of its locals were predominantly Black. Since the locals reflected the racial-ethnic composition of the neighborhoods in which they were based, and given the sharp residential segregation in Baltimore, only a few of the PUL locals were truly interracial, but, by accounts, its committees and leadership bodies were more integrated.[12]

Programmatically, in its first years the PUL called for financial relief and medical care for the unemployed, large-scale public works projects, massive construction of low-cost housing, unemployment insurance, public employment bureaus, and a mandatory thirty-hour maximum work week. From its beginnings, the PUL actively promoted its program. In mid-February 1933, the PUL announced that it was sponsoring unemployment legislation in Maryland's state legislature. In mid-March, less than two weeks after Roosevelt's inauguration, it sent a delegation to the White House with mass petitions demanding greater relief for the jobless. In late March, it forwarded suggestions on bond issues for relief to Baltimore's Mayor Jackson. And in early April, it held its first march to Annapolis to confront Governor Albert Ritchie and the legislature over the need for rapid passage of legislation for the unemployed. The PUL continued activities of these types throughout its first years.[13]

Although the PUL sent a telegram to Roosevelt at the end of July 1933 endorsing the NIRA, the leadership remained skeptical of the New Deal, fearing, in the words of the PUL chair that the "trend of federal relief policy shows plainly that the first consideration is for the protection and extension of private profit." Similar to the way the Baltimore ACW worked to shape the NRA codes for the men's garment industry, the PUL acted to influence the implementation of the New Deal on the local and state levels. During 1934, the organization amplified its support for full federal unemployment insurance; it pressed for higher wages for Civil Works Administration jobs and then vigorously opposed the termination of the program in late March; and it opposed the imposition of a state sales tax, calling instead for a graduated income tax. The PUL also conducted a drive to oppose a series of attempted reductions in relief by the BERC with delegations, petitions, picket lines (sometimes resulting in arrests), and mass meetings (often drawing as many as 800 people and sometimes as many as 1,200). As a result, BERC retracted at least one major reduction.[14]

While challenging the existing relief system through collective action, the PUL advocated for individual unemployed workers to ensure that they got the benefits they deserved. By the end of its first year, the PUL had reportedly appealed just over 600 rejected claims to the social agencies in Baltimore and had received adjustments on 542. In early 1934, PUL delegates were appointed to the Committee on Standards of the Council of Social Agencies to represent the "radical viewpoint" and thereby influence relief eligibility requirements.[15] Because many of its members received little or no relief even after the early New Deal programs were fully functioning, the PUL devised ways for the unemployed to provide for some of their own most basic needs. Using a donated truck, PUL members picked up surplus foodstuffs from central marketplaces and various food-processing concerns and took the food to a previously vacant warehouse lent to the PUL by Johns Hopkins University. Food was then sent to the PUL locals, and the locals in turn distributed it to unemployed workers throughout the city. By the end of November 1933, food valued at $5,060.22 had been dispensed. In addition, the PUL took possession of several vacant houses owned by the Pennsylvania Railroad. PUL members renovated these houses themselves, and the PUL then offered them as homes to unemployed families. By the end of April, the PUL had received eighteen houses: nine for Black families and nine for White families. Seven months later, it had acquired fifty houses, twenty-five of which were already reconditioned and occupied by thirty-one families, a total of 119 people. The PUL's self-help efforts were so successful that, at the end of December 1933, the organization claimed that it had returned $9.85 in donated labor and goods to the general community for every $1 in cash donations that it received.[16]

The PUL also sought to meet the educational and cultural, as well as the economic, needs of jobless workers. It demanded that the government set up adult recreational and educational facilities, and it instituted its own cultural programming. Throughout 1933 and 1934, it provided speakers on economics and current affairs to its locals, sponsored performances by the Labor Chautauqua of Brookwood Labor College, organized a ten-day Street Carnival, and held a series of smaller social events and picnics. The PUL also encouraged its members to take advantage of educational opportunities at such progressive community institutions as the Baltimore Open Forum and the Workmen's Circle. Finally, in the words of its chairperson, Reverend Clarence W. Whitmore, the PUL aimed "to cooperate with other community forces in promoting all constructive measures to restore and safeguard the economic security, health and general welfare of all the people of the State of Maryland." The PUL sent delegates to the Continental Congress for Economic Reconstruction, initiated by the Socialist Party, and later joined with a number of groups in Maryland to sponsor the Maryland Convention of the Continental Congress of Farmers and Workers. But the PUL's first real regional coalition work began in October 1933, when it joined the widespread protests in Baltimore in response to the lynching of George Armwood. During those protests (described in chapter 5), the PUL extended its range of activities beyond the workers' movement by joining forces for the first time with leading groups in the Black freedom movement.[17]

Like the other efforts to resurrect social movements in the Baltimore region during the years after the Crash, a commitment to antiracism and interracialism was central to the PUL's program and outlook. Stated frequently in the PUL's publications and public announcements, and contained in its membership oath (as reproduced at the beginning of this chapter), its antiracist commitment was also integral to its day-to-day practice. Many years later, Trager, who was White, recalled his work with an African American colleague in the PUL: "He wasn't a bodyguard, since we didn't need one, but he was burly enough. I had been a wrestler, so that together we could handle the produce and distribute it with no difficulty. He accompanied me on street corner talks, which I used to give from the back of the truck. We had a slogan at that time that we used as an opening and closing signature—'Black and white, unite and fight.' My Negro companion . . . would walk through the area and yell out the slogan to drum up an audience."[18] The high priority that PUL organizers gave to interracialism is evident in a letter Trager wrote to the national SP leader Norman Thomas in 1934 stating that the PUL's greatest achievement had been "to get white men and women to work with and under Negro men and women." And while the PUL's highest leadership was largely White, at least one African American, Reynaldo Waters, was among the top leaders in its early years. Ira De A. Reid of the National Urban League wrote in 1934 that the PUL "is accomplishing the very thing that has troubled inter-racial organizations, that is, getting the common white man to work with the Negro." As Edward Lewis of the BUL (and a frequent participant in PUL activities) wrote in the *African-American* in 1935, "The history of this group of white and colored workers in a Southern city is unique."[19]

In early 1935, the character of both the regional and national social struggle again was shifting, and the first phase of the PUL's history was coming to a close. About that time, Joel Seidman, a member of LID, summed up the re-lationship of the PUL and the workers' struggle during the former's first two years when he wrote in the *Maryland Leader* that one of the "most encour-aging features of the labor movement in Baltimore is the steady growth of the People's Unemployment League in numbers and influence. . . . Whatever improvements in relief conditions have been effected in the last two years can be largely traced to the activities of the League."[20]

Organizing the PUL

The obvious question to ask is: how did a remarkable organization like the PUL develop so quickly and become so effective in just two years? Part of the answer is that the economic, political, and ideological situation in the Baltimore region was changing throughout 1933 and 1934, providing the PUL organizers with new opportunities that they successfully exploited. Presi-dent Roosevelt, elected with majority support in Baltimore shortly before the PUL's founding, was proving to be a master of winning the confidence of ever larger sections of the population. The one hundred days following his inauguration in March 1933 produced, with great drama, the emergency legislation of the first New Deal, raising popular hopes that things were be-ginning to change. In fact, to some, the Roosevelt administration, with its rhetorical affirmation of the right to organize, in Section 7a of the NIRA, and its Blue Eagle campaign, seemed to be encouraging the population to par-ticipate actively in making change happen. By the last months of 1933, New Deal agencies were beginning to function, and federal relief was beginning to appear in Baltimore and elsewhere. After the trauma of the long economic slide after the stock market crash of 1929, and the severe financial crisis of early 1933, people were becoming more optimistic and more willing to engage in popular action. As a result, by the end of 1933 and the beginning of 1934, the tempo of social struggle was quickening almost everywhere, and the growth of the PUL was a part of this process.

The PUL grew because its organizers followed a strategy that addressed the concrete, rapidly changing conditions of Baltimore and the nation during this period, demonstrating their ability to connect with unemployed workers and to draw them into the ranks *and* the leadership of the new organization, and mobilizing a wide array of social forces to support the new organization with both material and human resources. But how did they do it? They were, after all, only a handful of White professors, teachers, and intellectuals. Although they are sometimes depicted as youthful militants at the time the PUL was founded, they actually represented quite an age range: Joel Seidman and Frank Trager were twenty-six; Naomi Riches, Elinor Pancoast, and Broadus Mitchell were between thirty-seven and forty; and Gilman, very much the elder of the group, was sixty-five. How did this rather elite, racially homogenous group manage to initiate a large mass organization made up mostly of unskilled and semiskilled unemployed workers of diverse racial and ethnic backgrounds?[21]

Ultimately, the LID activists' participation in the Socialist Party is key to answering these questions, but not in an obvious way. The SP in 1933 was not, in the Baltimore region or in the county as a whole, a particularly impressive organization. Its national membership had declined from about 100,000 in 1919 to 10,000 in 1934. In Maryland, it attracted only 4,178 votes in the 1930 gubernatorial election and had only 375 members in 1934. As with SP across the country, many of the members in Maryland represented an "old guard," inclined toward neither active militancy nor new organizing approaches. They tended, as the historian Roy Rosenzweig notes, to nourish their "Fabian faith in the 'inevitability of gradualism.'" In great contrast to the Baltimore Communist Party, Maryland's SP did not really function as a unified, coherent, energetic political organization; nor did it promote a strong antiracist platform. The national election platform in 1930, for instance, never even mentioned Black Americans or their needs, and the organization, as far as can be determined, had no Black members.[22]

The LID militants in Baltimore sometimes became frustrated with the lack of activism among the old guard SP members. Thirteen months after the PUL's founding, Trager complained in the local socialist press that a public meeting on the Civil Works Administration had been organized by the

PUL only because the SP, after promising to initiate it, had failed to do so. Shortly after, in a letter to Norman Thomas, Trager wrote in exasperation that only twenty or so SP members were active in the PUL, which by then was 15,000-strong.

However, while old guard Socialists were, by and large, not much help to the Baltimore LID group in terms of strategic or tactical guidance, or in the process of actual, day-to-day neighborhood organizing, and while the regional SP was unwilling or unable to throw the bulk of its energy into the PUL, they were willing to help in other important ways. The SP was in fact the main heir to, and carrier of, socialist traditions in Maryland, and it was deeply embedded in the modest but important progressive networks and institutions of the region. The SP was *connected*, and it helped the LID militants to become connected. In fact, some of the core LID group members—particularly, Broadus Mitchell and Elisabeth Gilman—were themselves deeply embedded in the region's progressive networks, while others, such as Trager and Joel Seidman, were relatively recent arrivals in the area. But whatever the individual situations of the LID militants, the SP as an organization effectively facilitated their connection as a group to key regional networks and institutions, gave them entree to building alliances with a range of important individuals and groupings, and helped them gain access to the masses of the unemployed. In a sense, the SP functioned as the PUL's midwife and in this role facilitated the connections of the PUL organizers to three overlapping progressive networks in the region that existed within the labor movement, among social liberals, and within the Black freedom struggle.[23]

Three Progressive Networks

By 1933, the Baltimore SP 1933 had long-term, important links to a number of labor unions and labor-oriented ethnic institutions. It had especially strong ties to the leadership of the ACW. Consequently, the ACW, which had helped to prepare the political and ideological groundwork for the PUL with its strike in 1932, became the strongest, most consistent union supporter of the league from its very beginning. Hyman Blumberg, national vice-president of the ACW and previous leader of the ACW's Baltimore Joint Council, formally endorsed the PUL's founding meeting, and Ulisse De Dominicis, the new head of the ACW's Baltimore Joint Council, spoke frequently at PUL events. ACW leaders, as well as some other industrial unionists, provided PUL organizers with material support, gave them legitimacy in the eyes of portions of organized labor, and offered them connections to large sections of the multi-ethnic White working class, especially its unemployed sector. Trager later remembered, "Those of us who were active in the PUL were also teaching for the trade unions, and those of us who were teaching for the trade unions were also active as more or less unofficial and sometimes official trade union organizers for the textile workers, the clothing workers, the needle trades."[24] The ACW leader and socialist Sara Barron recalled that Joel Seidman, Naomi Riches, and Elinor Pancoast traveled with her and other ACW organizers to Westminster, Maryland, to distribute leaflets among workers on their rights under the NRA. And she remembered that Broadus Mitchell, Elinor Pancoast, and other professors from Johns Hopkins and Goucher were her teachers at union-sponsored classes. Speaking of Mitchell in particular, Barron remembered, "We paid him a quarter a week for class; the union did not have any money."[25]

Socialist Party connections also helped the PUL develop relations with the BFL, despite the fact that the federation was dominated by conservative craft unions and deeply compromised by segregationist ideology. The BFL itself was moving toward greater popular engagement in the changing context of early 1933; it had, for example, finally overcome its voluntarist resistance to government relief and officially called for government unemployment insurance. Under these circumstances, the federation was willing to support, legitimate, and provide resources to the PUL in a number of ways. Henry Broening, then head of the BFL, addressed the founding meeting of the PUL, and in July 1933, he co-sponsored the Maryland Convention of the Continental Congress of Farmers and Workers, which was initiated by the SP and supported by the PUL. Broening's successor, Joseph McCurdy, whose relationship with the PUL organizers was sometimes tense, also appeared at PUL rallies and events. In mid-1934, McCurdy went as far as to defend the PUL publicly from a redbaiting attack shortly after he had launched a similar attack on the Communist-led seamen's movement. "The PUL are often called communists and radicals. . . . So were our forefathers at Boston Commons, but now as then, right will prevail," McCurdy declared. In addition, PUL organizers gained access to the SP's connections with socialist-oriented institutions in the European ethnic working-class communities—especially the Jewish community—including Der Arbeiterring (the Workmen's Circle) with its Labor Lyceum; its Yiddish and Russian library; its lecture, dance, theater, and concert programming; and its Yiddish classes for children and adults. The Labor Zionist organization, the Histadrut, also became a PUL ally.[26]

The second SP network the PUL organizers used was that of reformist professionals and educators, socially conscious religious leaders, and upper-class philanthropists, including Judge Thomas J. S. Waxter; Elmer V. McCollum, a

13. Elisabeth Gilman in the late 1910s. *Courtesy of the Ferdinand Hamburger Archives, Johns Hopkins University.*

professor of biochemistry at Johns Hopkins; Reverend Peter Ainslie; Rabbi Edward L. Israel; the manufacturer Sidney Hollander; the radical philanthropist A. E. O. Munsell; and Paul T. Beisser, president of the Maryland Conference of Social Work. The first chairperson of the PUL, Reverend Clarence W. Whitmore, an Episcopal clergyman, came from the social Christian segment of this network. These figures, and the circles within which they functioned, were heir to the leftist tradition of the old Progressive Movement, characterized by the historian Norman Markowitz as "social liberalism." In the early 1900s—in Baltimore, as in the country as a whole—the Socialist Party and left-wing Progressivism had overlapped, and in the early 1930s, the more middle- and upper-class members of the Maryland SP were still deeply imbued with the social liberal ethos and maintained social liberal contacts.[27]

While the SP was tied to social liberal circles through many of its members, one member, Elisabeth Gilman, stands out because of her role as a leading member of the LID group that initiated the PUL, and because of her exceptionally strong relationship to the Progressive tradition (see figure 13). Born on Christmas day in 1867, Gilman was the second daughter of Mary Ketchum Gilman and Daniel Coit Gilman, the first president of Johns Hopkins University. She literally grew up at Hopkins, in an atmosphere of wealth, high culture, and liberal thought. As a child, she joined Baltimore's oldest Episcopalian church, St. Paul's, and remained a devout Episcopalian throughout her life. Beginning at age nine, she began to travel internationally, and she continued to make regular trips to Europe throughout her life. Educated at Miss Comegys's School in Chestnut Hill near Philadelphia, she did not, as a youth, attend college but became increasingly involved with Progressive-era social work and settlement houses, developing personal relationships with many of the national leaders of the movement including Jane Addams. Family friends included members of the region's capitalist elite, such as Daniel Willard, the president of the Baltimore and Ohio Railroad, as well as prominent thinkers of the day in the region and the nation; her fellow socialist Broadus Mitchell later observed that Gilman's father "was the center of intellectual life in more than Baltimore." By the early 1910s, Gilman worked with the Baltimore Charity Organization Society over which her father presided, founded both the St. Paul's Boys Club for poor boys and an emergency workshop for the unemployed, and was on the governing board of the Baltimore Family Welfare Association. Also, during this period she became friendly with Vida Scudder, a professor at Wellesley and a well-known Socialist, and she began to work with the Intercollegiate Socialist Society.[28]

It was, however, the First World War that fully transformed Gilman's philanthropic Progressivism into radicalism, pacifism, and socialism. Despite her opposition to the war, she served in Europe in 1917–19 with the Surgical Dressing Society and in soldiers' canteens, returning to Baltimore shaken by what she experienced and wholly committed to fundamental social change. She revived the Baltimore Open Forum, a social liberal institution that had been founded in 1914, and turned it into the center of liberal and leftist debate in Baltimore, bringing in a stream of radical speakers of national and international renown. She also became involved in labor causes, traveling to coalfields to support striking miners. In 1924, she served as the Maryland chair of the women's division of Robert La Follette's Progressive Party presidential bid. Also during this period, she decided to go to college, and at fifty-seven she received a bachelor's degree from Johns Hopkins; her comrade Broadus Mitchell was one of her professors.[29]

Although she had been long involved with the Intercollegiate Socialist Society, had served on the national LID board, knew socialists across Europe, and had visited the Soviet Union, she did not formally join the Maryland Socialist Party until 1929. Nevertheless, by 1930, when she ran for governor of Maryland on the SP ticket (the first of her many SP candidacies), she had become the most famous Socialist *and* Progressive in Baltimore. Her home was a stopover point for Socialist leaders from all over the United States and the world, including her friends Norman Thomas, Morris Hillquit, and Harry Laidler, and she frequently entertained rank-and-file social activists and grassroots organizers, sometimes giving them a place to live for extended periods. Very much a Christian socialist, she organized the Christian Social Justice Fund and helped to finance a variety of social liberal causes in the Baltimore area. Moreover, as the historian Janice C. H. Kim has argued, while not a feminist in organizational affiliation, Gilman's outlook was feministic in that she entirely ignored the prevailing restrictions on women's behavior in her own life (for one thing, she never married) and she interacted with the female activists of her day. To again quote Mitchell, "Elisabeth Gilman was the center of liberal thought and all sorts of welfare movements which were either organized in her home, or she nursed along the committees, or she proposed." With Gilman, the "matriarch of Baltimore Socialism," among the leaders of the PUL organizing effort, it was able to attract broad social liberal support.[30]

Social liberal assistance to the PUL took a number of forms, from supplying material support to providing links to segments of the region's establishment, to giving a façade of respectability to the organization in middle- and upper-class circles. Social liberal backers of the PUL prevailed on Johns Hopkins University to donate a truck and the use of a warehouse for its food bank, convinced the Pennsylvania Railroad to donate vacant housing, and secured substantial financial contributions to the organization from wealthy supporters, such as A. E. O. Munsell and Sidney Hollander. In addition, on a more day-to-day level, liberal White ministers frequently worked with PUL locals and allowed their churches to be used for meetings. According to Naomi Riches, a former vice-president of the PUL, the league "made a rule that the treasurers of all locals must be clergymen" in the hope of avoiding problems with corruption. Also, liberal social workers mediated the relationship between PUL protesters and relief authorities; liberal journalists gave the organization good press; and liberal students, often at their liberal and socialist professors' behest, participated in PUL activities. "The PUL was not a pariah organization," Trager remarked years later. "We were . . . respectable citizens of Baltimore as well as respected citizens of Baltimore."[31]

The third progressive network accessed by PUL organizers was composed of people active with the Black freedom struggle. Although the Socialist Party itself had a very weak record of antiracist activism, a few SP members and close supporters had long been involved in freedom movement circles, especially through the BUL. A product of the Progressive era and a prototypically Progressive organization, with its commitment to social investigation as a key to progress, the National Urban League, nationally and in various locales, attracted social liberals and socialists across the country. In Baltimore, a few White and Black socialists and social liberals were the main

14. Broadus Mitchell, 1939. *Courtesy of the Ferdinand Hamburger Archives, Johns Hopkins University.*

founders of the BUL in the early 1920s, and continued to work with the organization into the early 1930s. Of this group, Broadus Mitchell was the most
important (see figure 14).

Mitchell was born in 1892 into a White southern academic family. His
mother, Alice Broadus Mitchell, was the daughter of the president of the
Southern Baptist Seminary in Louisville, and his father, Samuel Chiles
Mitchell, was a professor at Richmond College and, for four years, the president of the University of South Carolina. The Mitchell family was politically
liberal and, in the words of the historian Jacqueline Dowd Hall, "devoted to
the 'New South' panaceas of industrialization, education, and racial uplift."
The family was antiracist in its philosophy and its practices. Samuel Chiles
Mitchell, for example, lost his job as the president of University of South
Carolina after being attacked by the state's governor for favoring "blacks over
white womanhood" because he advised that a Peabody Fund gift go to a
Black college rather than to one for elite White women.[32]

Broadus Mitchell began his long residence in Baltimore in 1914 as a graduate student in political economy at Johns Hopkins University, earning his
doctorate in 1918. After a short absence to work on a newspaper in Richmond
and to serve in the U.S. Army during the last days of the First World War,

Mitchell returned to Johns Hopkins, where he taught political science from 1919 to 1939. A very successful and popular teacher, he frequently took his students off campus to learn about the neighborhoods and communities of the Baltimore region. Mitchell was also a rising scholar, publishing his classic study, *The Rise of Cotton Mills in the South*, in 1921. Politically active both on and off campus, he participated from the mid-1910s in regional organizations including the Open Forum, the Family Welfare Association, the Christian Social Welfare Fund (despite his own secular orientation), and the LID. In the process, he met Elisabeth Gilman and drew closer to socialism. During the early 1920s, he founded the BUL, along with the social liberals Reverend Peter Ainslie and the Quaker businessman John R. Carey, who were White, and Dr. B. M. Rhetta, who was Black.[33]

The BUL, with Broadus Mitchell as the chair of its first executive committee, formed on May 9, 1924. In preparation for its founding, Charles S. Johnson, director of the National Urban League's Department of Research, plus Mitchell and Rhetta, as chairman and vice-chairman, respectively, of the Industrial Committee of the Inter-Racial Conference, all worked on a three-month study of African Americans in industry in Baltimore. Mitchell's work on the industrial survey and on founding the BUL brought him into close contact with the political, religious, and educational leaders of the Black community of Baltimore, and many of these leaders joined the BUL's advisory board. His relationship with Carl Murphy of the *Afro-American* was strengthened later in 1924 when Murphy endorsed the Progressive Party's presidential candidate, Robert La Follette, and joined Mitchell and Elisabeth Gilman to work on La Follette's campaign in Maryland.[34]

Throughout the second half of the 1920s, Mitchell rose in the professorial ranks at Johns Hopkins, published three more major books, and worked closely with R. Maurice Moss, the executive director of the BUL, on several neighborhood-based campaigns. The most notable was the long struggle to renovate the "Lung Block," an exceptionally depressed section in northwestern Baltimore's Black community that got its name from its astronomically high tuberculosis rate. In late 1931, when Matthew Williams was lynched in Salisbury, on Maryland's Eastern Shore, Mitchell became one of the most vocal White critics of the murder, the authorities, and the legal system, publishing an exposé of official misconduct around the lynching for the National Council of Churches, which appeared in the *Baltimore Sun*. By this time, Mitchell was undoubtedly the best-known White activist in the African American community. As the freedom movement began to revive in the early 1930s, Mitchell became involved with the young African American activists of the City-Wide Young People's Forum, spoke at their Friday night

15. Edward S. Lewis, circa 1931.
*Courtesy of the Afro-American
Newspapers Archives and
Research Center.*

meetings a number of times, and, according to the later testimony of Juanita
Jackson Mitchell, was one of the few Whites who frequently attended and
consistently supported the Forum. As the PUL emerged, Mitchell was well
placed to facilitate the relationship between its White SP–LID organizers and
the Black freedom movement.[35]

The links between the freedom movement and the LID group organizing
the PUL strengthened in 1931 when Edward S. Lewis came to town as the
BUL's new executive director (see figure 15). A remarkably energetic Black
activist with a background in Progressivism, direct experience in labor
unions, a bachelor's degree from the University of Chicago, and a strong
socialistic bent, Lewis pushed for interracial cooperation among Baltimore's
activists. While still in high school, he had joined the Musician's Union, and
while working as a meat cutter in Kansas City, he became a charter member
of a Butcher's Union local. Upon arriving in Baltimore, he immersed himself in the regenerating freedom movement, rapidly developing relationships
with key movement forces, including the Forum and the *Afro-American*.
He sought out activists in the Baltimore workers' movement, both African American and White, who supported interracial organizing. He built

a strong working relationship with militant ACW leaders, and, after the 1932 strike, founded the Negro Labor Committee in alliance with them. Also in this period, he began to collaborate with the LID circle, became active in the PUL from its beginning, and worked to bring this organization to Black Baltimore. He officially endorsed the PUL's founding meeting, sponsored the first organizing gathering of a PUL local in the African American community, and became a major promoter of the PUL through his regular column in the *Afro*. Over time, Trager and Lewis became especially close, speaking as a team at Black community forums, co-authoring articles for the *Afro-American*, and developing personal ties so close that Trager became godfather to Edward and Mary Lewis's daughter. Because of Lewis, Broadus Mitchell, and a few others, the PUL was quickly able to obtain regular coverage in the Black press, endorsements from a range of Black community leaders, meeting places in Black churches, and a growing base among unemployed Black workers.[36]

The PUL and the Unemployed Councils

A comparison of the first years of the Socialist-led PUL with the Communist-led Baltimore Unemployed Councils throws additional light on both organizational efforts, on the radicals that led them, and on the whole process of reconstructing the workers' movement in the Baltimore region during the early 1930s. Given the amazing accomplishments of the PUL, it is tempting simply to conclude that the councils and the PUL were opposites and that the PUL's approach was far superior in almost every way. It is further tempting to attribute the apparent superiority of the PUL to the pragmatic moderation of the Socialists, which contrasted dramatically with the sometimes dogmatic revolutionary zeal of the Communist Party (CP). However, these conclusions oversimplify history and obscure the debt that the PUL owed to the Unemployed Councils. It is important to remember, when comparing the PUL and the councils, that before the PUL emerged, the CP-led movement in Baltimore had fought unemployment almost alone for nearly three years. From 1930 to 1933, the CP demonstrated, quite dramatically at times, that the unemployed could be mobilized, directly inspiring the founders of the PUL in the process and unwittingly preparing the ground for the PUL's later success. Moreover, breaking with the main traditional approach of the U.S. labor movement, the CP organized the unemployed by neighborhoods, separate from particular unions. The PUL followed suit with great success, at times encountering friction with some trade unions. Most important, the vigorous antiracism and interracialism in the CP-led movement was unprecedented, especially in Jim Crow Baltimore, and it deeply influenced the PUL organizers. Furthermore, the CP's antiracism may have begun to loosen the grip of White supremacy on some sectors of the White unemployed and opened some Black unemployed to the possibility of interracial organizing, all to the later advantage of the PUL.[37]

However, there were important differences of organization, tactics, and political stance between the two unemployed movements. The Baltimore councils were organizationally underdeveloped, with activists' energy largely devoted to sometimes frenetic direct action, while the PUL organizers paid much more attention to developing stable, participatory organizational processes, thereby giving the organization an institutional coherence and consistency that the Unemployed Councils never achieved. Tactically, the CP-led movement was oriented toward confronting injustice head on, wherever or whenever it occurred, resulting in a good deal of spontaneity and an anarchist-like "propaganda of the deed" mentality. While the PUL also involved itself in protest and direct action, including confrontations with authority, it employed a wider range of tactics—including such activities as "self-help" projects, which the CP disdained—with greater flexibility and more planning. Politically, the CP-led movement was self-consciously revolutionary, stressing an uncompromising, Third Period "class against class" approach, even when the immediate objectives (such as unemployment insurance or adjustment of relief benefits) were really quite reformist. And the CP began its work with far lesser connections to traditional activist circles in Baltimore and was reluctant to develop strategic alliances with less revolutionary progressive forces. The PUL by contrast, often appeared reformist and "respectable." It was the product of an intricate set of alliances emerging organically from several progressive circles, and it continually sought coalitions with other forces.[38]

Too much, however, can be made of the differences between the Unemployed Councils and the PUL as the explanation for their different histories. It is very unlikely that the PUL as it developed in 1933 could have succeeded in 1930 or 1931 or even 1932 under the prevailing conditions of economic free fall and popular demoralization. Arguably, those conditions demanded something like the brasher, more confrontational strategy employed by the Communists to catalyze resistance. Moreover, by late 1933 and early 1934, the Baltimore CP was broadening its approach to alliances, and something of a strategic convergence was occurring between Communists and PUL Socialists in Baltimore, although by this time the CP was shifting its focus in the workers' movement from the neighborhood to the shop floor.[39]

It is also necessary to underscore the radicalism of the PUL in the context of the early 1930s because it is, in hindsight, easily underestimated. Even former PUL leaders, in their reminiscences occasionally have overstated the organization's respectability or reduced its politics to a struggle for "liberal welfare programs." In fact, the PUL's program was first formulated before FDR's inauguration and amounted to a series of demands for radical structural reform. At every step of the way through its first years, the PUL kept well ahead of the New Deal by demanding more than the Roosevelt administration was prepared to offer, and by attempting to hold the president to his promises. In fact, the PUL leadership continued its running public critique of the New Deal throughout the 1930s, even declaring in 1939 that the "New Deal has tried and failed."[40]

Also, it is important to note that the PUL's self-help projects were not simply liberal welfare projects—or, worse, charity. Frank Trager remarked in an oral history interview that "self-help" was a misleading label, because "we didn't go around collecting old clothes," as the Salvation Army did. Rather, these self-help projects represented, as the PUL's chairman Clarence Whitmore wrote, "the exchange of services between the members, through the formation of unemployed workers' *cooperatives*." The PUL later formed a cooperative store and experimented with labor accounting in the distribution of goods. Ultimately, however, it had to drop its plans for developing a labor scrip because Maryland law forbade money to be issued by private parties. The cooperative impulse in the PUL was the legacy of many socialist traditions.[41]

Finally, the fundamental radicalism of the PUL is expressed in the fact that many of its leaders were open and outspoken Socialists. Despite the fact that the PUL was officially nonpartisan, the leadership introduced a significant amount of explicitly socialist education into organizational activities. Internal education in PUL was explicitly designed to teach the "fundamentals of economics" (in a letter, Trager referred to this as "socialist economics") and "political science" to "lead our people to criticize against the mayor, against the governor, and against the President and his policy." The well-known local Socialists Elisabeth Gilman, Broadus Mitchell, and Frank Trager spoke frequently at events sponsored by the PUL. Periodically, national SP leaders including Frank Crosswaith and Norman Thomas addressed the PUL's rank-and-file, and socialistic institutions such as the Brookwood Labor College (with which Joel Seidman was affiliated and which he would later direct) made presentations. And as mentioned earlier, official PUL delegates attended a number of SP events, including the Continental Congress for Economic Reconstruction, and PUL members were urged to participate in party-related institutions such as the Workmen's Circle and the Open Forum. All of these educational efforts had an effect on PUL members. Trager wrote in

1934, for example, that at a PUL meeting to protest the termination of the New Deal's Civil Works Administration in February of that year, "The membership spontaneously cheered the assertion by Broadus Mitchell that socialization offers the only solution." PUL locals on occasion endorsed SP candidates for local office.[42]

In early March 1934, some of the young SP militants proposed that the PUL move in a more radical direction by taking up "independent political action" and, with the backing of the ACW and groups in the Black freedom movement, offer an independent slate of local candidates with a socialist program in the 1934 election. The plan was short-lived, for Norman Thomas discouraged it, and local SP leaders, according to Trager, were "unsympathetic." The old guard evidently felt threatened.[43]

So if the PUL was essentially a radical organization, and if there was some political convergence between the PUL's militant socialists and the CP in 1933 and 1934, the question arises: what was the actual relationship between the PUL and the CP-led unemployed movements in those years? Indications are that contact was minimal and that the two operated largely in parallel. For as the PUL emerged in 1933, the CP was de-emphasizing its general unemployment work and focusing its energy more on union organizing on the waterfront and elsewhere. There were, though, a few Communists active in the PUL. Naomi Riches remembered one in particular: "We did have one active C.P.[arty] member—very active in a cooperative way with P.U.L. He died after a short illness at local hospital, and he asked to be buried with a C.P.[party] flag—and I saw to it that this was done. I had to make several visits to our large financial backers to explain the situation after the publicity in the papers." She was probably referring to Nicola Ceattei, also known as Nicolas Chatty, a cobbler and longtime labor radical in the Baltimore area who died in February 1936. Dorothy Dare, a leader in his PUL local and a Communist, and James Blackwell, then chairman of the PUL, spoke at his funeral.[44]

As it turns out, in the late 1930s the unemployment movements led by the SP and by the CP did end up in the same national unemployment organization, the Workers' Alliance of America (WAA). As will be discussed later, the WAA was formed in March 1935 from SP-led and independent—but not CP-led—organizations across the country; subsequently, in March 1936, the Unemployed Councils joined the WAA. In Baltimore, the PUL and the remnants of the Unemployment Councils were finally allied under the local WAA banner. However, the context and direction of the struggle by then had changed significantly.

III. Transitions, 1933–1936

5

The Lynching of
George Armwood, 1933

They lynched a man on Eastern Shore,
Lynchland, that's Maryland
That's twice, they did it once before
Lynchland, that's Maryland
They beat and strung up the poor frail,
Five thousand strong they stormed the jail,
Where law has crumbled, died and failed
Lynchland, that's Maryland. . . .

Our race must now retaliate
Lynchland, that's Maryland.
And teach our children they should hate
Lynchland, that's Maryland.
If they must lynch, let us lynch too
And burn our victims as they do
We'll give the state the name its due
Lynchland, that's Maryland.
—DONALD SMITH, *Afro-American*, October 28, 1933

On October 18, 1933, George Armwood, a twenty-two-year-old African American laborer, was lynched by a White mob in Princess Anne, Somerset County, on the Eastern Shore of Maryland. Racialized lynching, which had been epidemic in the U.S. South since the end of Reconstruction, remained common during the first quarter of the twentieth century, only to decline during the 1920s. Then the rate of lynchings rebounded during the early 1930s; according to the *Afro-American*, Armwood was the thirty-fourth Black victim of U.S. lynch mobs in 1933. In Maryland, where the last pre-Depression lynching had occurred in 1911, Armwood was the second lynching victim in fewer than two years. There were, however, repeated outbreaks of lynch fever in the eastern and southern sections of the state; at least twice in the three months before Armwood's murder, White mobs had set out in search of African American men accused of crimes.[1]

In the metropolis of Baltimore, African Americans quickly learned the details of the sadistic lynching of George Armwood in the hinterlands of the Eastern Shore. The dimensions of their horror and outrage were expressed in Donald Smith's "Lynchland, That's Maryland," a bitter parody of Maryland's unofficial state anthem, "Maryland, That's Maryland," that was published in the *Afro-American*, along with many other expressions of anger from members of the Black community. Regardless of the second verse of the poem, few in the African American community of Baltimore—including, most likely, Donald Smith himself—advocated violent, in-kind retaliation, but sentiments such as those of Marse Calloway, a moderate Black Republican Party politician with connections to White machine politics, were not unusual: "We have kept quiet too long about the unjust laws and unjust treatment meted us by the other race. Cowards never win any victories or wear any crowns. We must protect ourselves as the white man protects himself. If we find it is necessary to protect ourselves with guns and the like, then let us do it wholeheartedly." The Baltimore community had strong ties of kinship, interaction, and history with the Black communities of the Eastern Shore, and the wave of racist attacks and murders occurring across the Chesapeake Bay and in the U.S. South bespoke a threatening resurgence of terroristic segregationism.[2]

The broadest spectrum of Black community forces in decades, joined by significant numbers of progressive and radical Whites, mobilized to protest the lynching and to demand that the murderers be brought to justice. Far larger, more inclusive, and more effective than those following the lynching of Matthew Williams in 1931, the protests provided a gauge of how much the Baltimore freedom movement had revived in two short years. In many ways, the protests of the Armwood lynching were a culmination of the long campaign led by the International Labor Defense to save Euel Lee. They also built on the political and educational work of the City-Wide Young People's Forum (Forum), and the interracial gains of the Unemployed Councils and the PUL. The anti-lynching protests consolidated the gains of the movement of the early Depression years, reconfigured the forces involved, and took the movement to a higher level. In a sentence, these protests represented the end of the initial phase of movement building in the 1930s and the beginning of a new phase.

Finally, the Armwood lynching protests of late 1933 began to transform the relationship of the re-emerging freedom movement in Baltimore to the national freedom movement. Even before the lynching of George Armwood, the Baltimore movement had been attracting the attention of the national office of the NAACP; this attention grew qualitatively during the anti-lynching protests. Although the national NAACP had, since its earliest days, been in the leadership of the campaign against racialized lynching, during the decade after the congressional defeat of the Dyer Anti-Lynching Bill, which the NAACP had strongly supported, the national organization's involvement in anti-lynching work declined. And during the first years of the Depression, the national NAACP was in too much financial and organizational crisis to respond effectively to the rising rate of lynchings in the United States; the Baltimore branch, for its part, was all but moribund. Then in late 1933, in part because of the lynching of George Armwood, and the protests in Baltimore that followed, the national office of the NAACP moved to renew its anti-lynching campaign and to revive its branch in Baltimore.[3]

The Lynching

In mid-October 1933, George Armwood, who apparently had mental disabilities, was accused of assaulting Mary Denston, an elderly White woman. Hundreds of White vigilantes went in search of him, but the authorities found him first, beat him, and jailed him in Salisbury. A lynch mob immediately began to gather outside his cell, on the very lawn where Matthew Williams had been lynched two years earlier. Alarmed, the sheriff hustled Armwood out the back and drove him to Baltimore, where he was put in the city jail. A cry of protest went up on the Eastern Shore, and State's Attorney John B. Robins, who was based in Princess Anne, called for Armwood's return. Circuit Court Judge Robert Duer of Somerset County, who had been involved in the Euel Lee case, complied. Just over twenty-four hours after being removed from the Eastern Shore, Armwood was sent back despite fears that he faced certain lynching.[4]

Beginning at about noon on October 18, a White crowd began to assemble noisily in Princess Anne near the jail in which George Armwood was awaiting arraignment. Frank Spencer, a White native of California and a resident of Washington, D.C., who was visiting the town, observed a young White woman, evidently a relative of Denston, "inciting the mob on to lynch Armwood." Spencer later testified, "everyone" in Princess Anne knew Armwood was to be murdered that night. The pending lynching was even common knowledge across the Chesapeake Bay in Baltimore. Juanita Jackson Mitchell remembered listening to radio reports in Baltimore of the mob gathering in

Princess Anne, and Clarence Mitchell recalled that these broadcasts were like announcements for the coming lynching.[5]

As evening fell, the crowd grew, and a steady stream of cars arrived in town. Judge Robert Duer, on his way to a dinner engagement, stopped to urge the crowd to disperse. When rebuffed, he continued on to dinner. At about 8:30, fifty to seventy-five White men moved toward the jail. A short skirmish ensued with the twenty-five State Police officers guarding the jail, during which the overwhelmed police fired their tear gas canisters and then fell back without drawing their firearms. The mob broke the jailhouse doors open with a battering ram and violently pulled Armwood from his cell. As the town's fire siren blared, he was displayed with a rope around his neck before a crowd of an estimated 2,000–5,000 Whites, including women and children. Initial chants of "lynch him" were replaced with chants of "don't kill him yet," and he was savagely beaten. Several men jumped full force on his body as he lay on the ground, and he was repeatedly slashed with knives. A White man of about eighteen cut off his ear. The mob then dragged Armwood, who was grievously wounded, through the streets past the house of Judge Duer, who was scheduled to preside over his grand jury hearing the next day. Despite Armwood's desperate pleas for his life, he was stripped naked and hanged by the neck from a tree. After about half an hour, the mob again dragged the body through the streets to the courthouse, briefly hanged him again, then dropped the corpse to the ground, setting it on fire in the middle of a main street. After the fire burned out, the charred remains were discarded in a lumberyard where Black schoolchildren and adults had to pass it on their way to school and work the next morning.[6]

As observers noted, the whole lynching process took place in an atmosphere of festivity among the White community, and those involved sought souvenirs after it ended. Lynchers stole gold fillings from the teeth of the smoldering corpse. The hanging rope was cut up, and pieces were passed out with the ends carefully tied to prevent unraveling. The empty tear gas canisters became highly prized items. When more mementos of the occasion were demanded, the wooden pole that had served as a battering ram at the jail was sawed into six-inch sections and distributed.[7]

William Denston, a motorcycle policeman in Pennsylvania and the thirty-five-year-old son of Mary Denston, Armwood's alleged victim, was present at the lynching. After returning home from Baltimore, the *Philadelphia Inquirer* interviewed him, and he articulated some of the lynchers' justifications for their actions. "I'm satisfied," he said. "My mother is revenged. He deserved every bit of it." He added, "That'll be a lesson to them not to go fooling around with our women." An *Evening Sun* reporter talked to a number of White men in Princess Anne the day after the murder, and one offered another popular rationale for the lynching: blaming the communists. "If it wasn't for the [Euel] Lee affair," he remarked, "this wouldn't ever have happened." In reference to the town's African American community, another White man remarked ominously to the reporter, "The colored population haven't got anything to be afraid of. . . . But they're not making any mistakes." When reporters asked who had participated in the lynch mob, the Whites who had been on the scene—including Judge Duer, the jailer, the sheriff, the coroner, William Denston, and people on the street—claimed they recognized no one. Some suggested the mob must have come from Virginia.[8]

Some Eastern Shore Whites did oppose the lynching, including John Richardson, Armwood's employer, who tried to hide him and was arrested for his efforts. Some White law enforcement officials appealed to the state government right before the lynching to remove Armwood again from Princess Anne, but to no avail. The State Police officers who were guarding the Princess Anne jail did resist the mob, although they were unwilling to use their guns; they received injuries for their trouble. Some of these police, quite remarkably, proved willing to identify lynchers. Nonetheless, a very large portion of the region's White community and its officials clearly supported the lynching. Reverend Asbury Smith, a progressive minister in Baltimore, remarked: "I have lived on the Eastern Shore the greater part of my life. My family and friends are there. To know that these people whom I love almost without exception approved of the brutal lynching of Armwood grieves me deeply. I feel ashamed of being an Eastern Shore man. I feel ashamed of being a white man."[9]

Governor Albert Ritchie, stung by accusations that he shared responsibility for the lynching, denied that he had been involved in Armwood's return to the Eastern Shore, maintaining that he had learned of the prisoner's removal from Baltimore only after the fact. He claimed that he had failed to bring Armwood back again to Baltimore in the hours before the lynching because, despite requests, he lacked the power to do so as long as Judge Duer and State's Attorney Robins continued to assure him that Armwood was safe. In Ritchie's words, "responsibility rested . . . squarely on the shoulders" of Duer and Robins. Paradoxically, though, Ritchie gave these two officials the responsibility for apprehending the lynch mob's leaders. Shamefully, the governor even joined the Eastern Shore chorus in attempting to place the responsibility for Armwood's death on the Communist Party's Euel Lee defense campaign, claiming that resulting sluggishness in the justice system in the Lee case was a major cause of the lynching. Subsequently, Ritchie hastily set up a judicial committee to study ways to speed up trials. One of the first recommendations of the committee was to prohibit "outside" organizations such as the International Labor Defense (ILD) from involving themselves in cases like Euel Lee's.[10]

Tragically, as scholars since Ida B. Wells-Barnett have indicated, there was little that was unique about the lynching of George Armwood. The hysterical response to an alleged attack on White womanhood; the public preparations for the event; the massive size of the White mob; the participation of men, women, and children; the highly ritualized torture murder; the continued mutilation of the body after the victim's death; the carnival-like atmosphere; the grisly souvenir seeking; the collusion of officials—all of this characterized hundreds of what the historian W. Fitzhugh Brundage has called "mass mob" lynchings that occurred during the half-century after the end of Reconstruction. Moreover, historians, activists, and observers have all rightly argued that such racialized lynchings were an institution deeply implanted in Jim Crow culture. Even the Eastern Shore's weekly, the *Transcript*, stated, "Lynching has been the method of dealing with perpetrators . . . for generations," and the murder of Armwood "was the carrying out of a tradition."[11] Mass mob lynchings functioned, on the one hand, to terrorize the African American population, to discourage resistance, and thereby to facilitate the reproduction of the segregation system. On the other hand, they were a grisly affirmation of absolute White supremacy and of White community identity. Lynching was, in a sense, the ultimate assertion of Whiteness in the segregated South. And during periods like the early Depression, racialized lynching displaced the anger and distress felt by the general White population over deteriorating conditions away from ruling White elites, and, in a violent spasm of White solidarity, toward the Black population.

As the crowd gathered outside Armwood's cell on October 18, Clarence Mitchell, two other *Afro-American* reporters, and a photographer—all African Americans—raced their car around the Chesapeake Bay to the Eastern Shore. They arrived in Princess Anne while Armwood's body was still smoldering, and, showing remarkable courage, immediately began interviewing local White residents and officials. They also forced their way into the coroner's secret inquest on the lynching. It fell to them to break the news of Armwood's death to his mother, who had not been informed of what happened, and they helped to bury his body. Upon returning to Baltimore, Mitchell went home, sat down at the family dinner table, looked at the food, got up, and left the room. Forty-three years later, Parren Mitchell, Clarence's younger brother, vividly remembered the moment: "I love my brother very much, as most people know, and to see him that evening at supper that my whole family ate together, to see him not be able to eat because of that—And the thing, I guess, that upset me most was, really, I didn't know what a lynching was. I was a little child. But whatever the thing was that had hurt him so badly, the fact that he was hurt, I guess, really started sparking my interest in [civil rights]." Juanita Jackson Mitchell later recalled that the Armwood lynching caused Clarence Mitchell to abandon his lingering desire to go to medical school and to dedicate his life to the struggle for freedom. Armwood's death deeply affected many people in Baltimore. But many of them were not terrorized; they saw his murder as a call to arms.[12]

Protests in Baltimore

Protests in Baltimore began almost as soon as the news reached the city. Within days, the Communist Party (CP), the ILD, the Forum, the BUL, the Socialist Party of Maryland, and the PUL issued strong protest statements. Normally nonpolitical groups in the African American community, including the Chi Delta Mu medical fraternity, the Ministers Wives' Association of the South Baltimore District of the Washington Annual Conference of the Methodist Episcopal Church, and the African Methodist Episcopal (AME) Preachers' Meeting, joined the chorus of protests. At the AME Preachers' Meeting, Reverend John Colbert, a grandson of the abolitionist Henry Highland Garnet, declared, "I have never approved of ministers engaging in politics, but from now on I recognize that such indulgence is desirable." The ILD blamed Governor Ritchie for the lynching, demanded the arrest of Judge Duer and State's Attorney Robins, and proposed the death penalty for lynchers. The Socialist Party (SP) called for Ritchie's impeachment, the prosecution of Duer and Robins for second-degree manslaughter, and full prosecution of lynchers. The BUL, echoing the most common demands from religious and community organizations, demanded that all those responsible be brought to justice and called for state anti-lynching legislation.[13]

On the day after the lynching, the lawyers Bernard Ades and Henry Williams of the ILD turned a previously scheduled Euel Lee clemency hearing with Ritchie into a hostile interrogation of the governor over his actions in both the Lee case and the Armwood murder. Shortly thereafter, Judge Joseph Ulman, president of the BUL, led an interracial Urban League delegation of thirty "notables"—including representatives of the NAACP, the Housewives League, the Cooperative Women's Civic League, Provident Hospital, Morgan College, the Colored Bar Association of Baltimore, and several fraternal organizations—to the governor's office to press for state anti-lynching legislation. This delegation also contained a number of important White social liberals who were affiliated with the BUL, including Reverend Asbury Smith and the industrialist Sidney Hollander.[14]

The growing politicization of the Black religious community was confirmed a few days later when a delegation of forty-five Baptist ministers and officials met with the governor. Claiming to represent 50,000 Black Baptists and "the whole body of the Negro population of Maryland," the ministers delivered a resolution that asked God to condemn all officials implicated in the lynching and all the members of the mob. They also demanded that all responsible for the lynching be prosecuted, that every state official involved in returning Armwood to the Eastern Shore be impeached, and that state law be changed to ensure that a lynching never happen in Maryland again; they also demanded that the State Police, at that time totally Jim Crow, be required to recruit Black officers. The ministers told Ritchie, "Your explanation in the press as to your position and power in the matter is not savory, to say the least." According to the *Afro*, Ritchie was visibly shaken and took an hour to defend himself. Those few ministers whom the governor was able to convince were roundly and publicly criticized afterward.[15]

Protestors arrived from out of state as well. Led by National Secretary William L. Patterson, the ILD assembled a delegation from Trade Union Unity League unions and CP-related organizations in Boston, New York, Philadelphia, and Baltimore. This interracial group of about thirty, armed with the names of four alleged lynchers that had recently been published in the CP's *Daily Worker*, marched from the ILD office in northwestern Baltimore, through the Black community, to the governor's downtown office. Since the ILD-led delegation had no appointment and arrived at the same time as the Urban League delegation, the police ejected the ILD marchers and ushered in the Urban League group. In addition, a delegation of nine Black lawyers from Baltimore, the District of Columbia, and Virginia handed the governor a detailed proposal for a Maryland anti-lynching law to submit to the legislature, called on him to support federal anti-lynching legislation, and challenged him to mount an internal investigation of the State Police's role in the Armwood murder. Josiah F. Henry, the exalted leader of the Monumental Lodge of Elks in Baltimore, introduced the lawyers' group to the governor. Charles Houston, dean of Howard University Law School, who was becoming increasingly involved in the Maryland freedom movement, led the delegation, which included Thurgood Marshall and the movement veteran Robert McGuinn among the Baltimore delegates. Reportedly, Ritchie was nonplused. After the meeting with the governor, Houston sent telegrams protesting the Armwood lynching to the American Bar Association, the Maryland Bar Association, and the American Legion (which had refused a request by the State Police to help them defend Armwood as the lynch crowd was assembling). Along with two other lawyers from Washington, he then filed a brief with the federal government, arguing that the U.S. military should be called out to apprehend local officials who allowed the lynching of prisoners in their care.[16]

The *Afro-American*, confirming the newspaper's central role in the city's Black community, assembled a broad interracial delegation composed of the most activist forces in the emerging Baltimore protest movement, including both Communist- and Socialist-led groups, the Forum, the NAACP, the BUL, two Black lawyers' groups, the Young Negroes Progressive League, the AME Preachers' Meeting, the Women's International League for Peace and Freedom, a Black veterans' group, and several other community organizations. As the main spokesperson, Broadus Mitchell of the SP and the PUL lectured Ritchie vigorously on his failures, a performance sufficiently effective to earn the ire of the liberal Judge Eugene O'Dunne, who later denounced the delegation in general and Broadus Mitchell in particular. Indeed, the *Afro*-led delegation had been unwelcome from the beginning. When it arrived at the governor's office, the police saw that Bernard Ades was present, blocked the hall, and called in reinforcements. The delegation was finally allowed to see the governor an hour later, with more than thirty police lining the walls.[17]

On October 9, more than a week before the Armwood lynching, the U.S. Supreme Court had turned down Euel Lee's last appeal; sixty-five or so mainly African American demonstrators from Baltimore, led by the ILD, marched outside. Euel Lee was scheduled for execution on October 28, ten days after George Armwood was murdered, and the ILD hoped that the wave of anti-lynching protests after Armwood's death would stall the execution. The link between the Armwood and Euel Lee cases was central to Bernard Ades's and the ILD attorney Henry Williams's final appeal for clemency to Governor Ritchie. No appeal, not even a request from Howard University officials representing prominent African Americans in three cities or the 10,000 signatures from Lee's supporters, was sufficient to sway the governor. Euel Lee, protesting his innocence to the end, was hanged at Maryland Penitentiary in Baltimore after midnight on October 28. Outside the penitentiary, 200 police waited nervously for an expected onslaught of violent Communist demonstrators that never came. A small interracial group of Euel Lee supporters stood quietly by, and White revelers, some from the Eastern Shore, made "merry."[18]

According to an *Afro-American* editorial, "Euel Lee was a mirror which the director of our destiny held up to reflect the corruption in our legal practices which denied justice to a large portion of the citizenry because of the color of their skin. . . . Euel Lee did not live in vain." Once again, the *Afro* highlighted the role of the ILD. In turning down Lee's final appeal, the White liberal Judge Morris Soper had celebrated the fact that Lee's case showed "that no one in this country is so poor and friendless that he cannot have the benefit of the best counsel and admission to every court in the land." The *Afro* rejected Soper's thinking by reminding him who was really responsible for what little justice Lee got: "Neither the money nor the friends which kept Euel Lee alive for two years was the willing gift of America. To the ILD, an international organization which is looked upon as an alien body within our gates, is due the credit for the saving of America's face." But perhaps the most powerful statement on the ILD's campaign to defend Lee was the fact that a reported 4,000 mourners, overwhelmingly African American, viewed Lee's body as it lay for one night in a funeral parlor.[19]

Mass Mobilization

The anti-lynching movement intensified after the execution of Euel Lee, and protest resolutions and delegations to the governor were increasingly eclipsed by popular mobilization. However, apart from a Communist-led demonstration of more than a hundred militants at City Hall Plaza the day after the Armwood lynching (with speakers addressing the crowd from the back of a truck mounted with a gibbet and noose) and the ILD march through the northwestern section to City Hall, protest meetings, not demonstrations, were the main forms of mass mobilization (see figure 16). These meetings were many and varied, and together they indicate much about trends in the growing movement, emerging alliances within it, and the contradictions among its forces.[20]

An unknown number of protest meetings were spontaneous and went un-recorded—regular gatherings of Black community institutions that shifted their attention from their planned business to the lynching of Armwood. One of these that did leave a record was the regular Friday night meeting of the City-Wide Young People's Forum, where the scheduled speaker, the White Baltimore clergyman Reverend T. Guthrie Speers, prefaced his presentation, "Educate Your Conscience," with remarks on the lynching. Then, after Speers finished his prepared talk, the room erupted in a spontaneous discussion of Armwood's death. In another example, the Maryland Federation of Women's Clubs added Armwood's murder to its yearly meeting agenda and passed a resolution condemning the "breakdown of law" on the East-

16. J. Green speaking at an anti-lynching protest led by the Communist Party at Baltimore City Hall, October 21, 1933. *Courtesy of Joseph E. Moore. Reused with permission of the Baltimore Sun Media Group. All rights reserved.*

ern Shore. As one member put it, the "group must be missionaries . . . in this fight." In churches on the Sundays following the lynching, Black ministers made Armwood's murder the subject of angry sermons, while at professional societies, fraternal organizations, card clubs, and taverns, attention turned to the question of the lynching of George Armwood.[21]

Protest meetings with both African American and White speakers attracted thousands of African Americans. The participation of Whites, while an important development, was limited to a modest number of leading progressives and radicals. A particularly striking feature of the larger protest meetings was that they revealed the extent to which national figures from the freedom movement and radical circles were becoming involved in the increasingly important struggle in Baltimore. A "committee of prominent and interested citizens," many with clear CP links, sponsored an "indignation meeting" on Sunday, October 22, four days after Armwood's death. Angry and militant speakers, mostly African American from both the national and local levels of the movement, included William Patterson and James Ford from the national ILD; Gough McDaniels, a teacher at Douglass High School who was involved with the local ILD; Linwood Koger, past president of the

17. Clarence Mitchell of the Forum became a prominent leader of the movement protesting the lynching of George Armwood in late 1933. *Courtesy of the Library of Congress.*

Baltimore branch of the NAACP, now affiliated with the Young Negroes' Progressive League and the Walter Green Post of the American Legion; and Clarence Mitchell of the *Afro* and the Forum.[22]

The following Friday, a larger and more diverse group, including a cross-section of social liberals and socialists, sponsored a mass meeting at Lehman Auditorium. The meeting featured an integrated grouping of national and local speakers, including the ubiquitous Clarence Mitchell (see figure 17), Roy Wilkins from the national NAACP office, and Roger Baldwin of the national American Civil Liberties Union (ACLU). As evidence of the growing prominence of the PUL Socialists in the anti-lynching protests, Frank Trager served as the event's secretary. At the meeting, the ACLU offered a reward of $1,000 for information leading to the conviction of any of the murderers of George Armwood, and it was announced that the NAACP, the ILD, and the ACLU were acting jointly to call for a federal investigation of the lynching.[23]

The most significant result of the meeting at Lehman Auditorium was the founding of the Maryland Anti-Lynching Federation, a coalition devoted to securing state and federal anti-lynching legislation. Organized as an interracial center-left coalition, the Anti-Lynching Federation linked the most active leadership of the freedom movement—especially the Forum—with one of the most dynamic sectors of the workers' movement, the PUL Socialists. In fact, the planning meetings for the federation had been held in the home of the Socialist leader Elisabeth Gilman. With a leadership balanced between old and young, Black and White, and liberal and radical, Reverend Peter Ainslie was the honorary chair, and Reverend Asbury Smith was the acting chair. The vice-chairmen were George Murphy of the *Afro*'s Murphy clan and the prominent social liberal Rabbi Edward Israel. The absence of the ILD and activists affiliated with the CP from the mass meeting and the coalition is striking. The new federation represented, in effect, a competing center to the ILD in the anti-lynching struggle.[24]

Shortly after the meeting at Lehman Auditorium, a more politically moderate meeting was held at the Sharp Street Memorial Methodist Episcopal church, with the objective of alleviating emerging tensions in the movement by "burying the hatchet" among the various White and Black forces opposed to lynching. A number of White clergy, including Asbury Smith and Guthrie Speers, and Black clergy, including C. Y. Trigg and R. F. Coates of Sharp Street Methodist, were featured speakers. Marie Bauernschmidt, a prominent, wealthy White civic leader, and the former state's attorney (and future governor) Harry Nice, sought to steer the movement in very moderate directions. In addition, one Black politician, unnamed in the *Afro* news article, caused some controversy by railing against clergy in politics and by complaining that few ministers had supported him in his last electoral bid.[25]

Then, on November 18–19, the ILD and the League of Struggle for Negro Rights, initiated by the CP, sponsored their Eastern Conference against Lynching in Baltimore's New Albert Auditorium, a conference they had previously announced on the day after Armwood died. The purpose of the conference was to build a militant anti-lynching movement throughout the northeast, to link the struggle against lynching to the general struggle against Jim Crow, and to work toward a national conference to be held the next year. Approximately 1,500 people attended, including (unlike the other anti-lynching meetings) a large minority of Whites. Leading figures from national Communist-led organizations attended, including James Ford, Robert Minor, William L. Patterson, Benjamin Davis Jr., Richard B. Moore, and a number of representatives of the revolutionary industrial unions. From militant but non-Communist sectors of the freedom movement came Dean Charles Houston (see figure 18), along with a number of other figures from Howard University; Mary Church Terrell of the National Federation of Colored Women's Clubs; W. T. Clark of the Hodcarriers Union; and repre-

18. The protests in Baltimore after Armwood's death revitalized the national anti-lynching movement. Here Charles Houston, who participated in the protests, demonstrates with Virginia McGuire, president of the District of Columbia branch of the NAACP in Washington, D.C., in 1934. *Courtesy of the Afro-American Newspapers Archives and Research Center.*

sentatives of the New Negro Alliance, an organization based in Washington with close ties to the Forum. Walter White, executive director of the NAACP, refused the invitation, but a number of figures who were affiliated with the NAACP participated, including Charles Houston.[26]

Several important literary and artistic figures were also involved, including Countee Cullen, Grace Lumpkin, F. E. Brown, Barbara Alexander, and Eugene Gordon. Leading participants in the conference from Baltimore included the ILD-related activists Linwood Koger, J. Howard Payne, Gough McDaniels, Bernard Ades, and Albert Blumberg, a White professor of philosophy at Johns Hopkins University. W. A. C. Hughes of the Forum and Ralph Matthews of the *Afro* were billed as speakers and were representative of a number of more militant, non-ILD freedom movement activists in Baltimore who participated; the Forum sent an official delegation. The main event of the conference was a tribunal of inquiry, chaired by Dr. Harry F. Ward of Union Theological Seminary, that heard testimony on the Armwood murder and other recent lynchings. The conference attracted a great deal of attention and gave the struggle in Baltimore its broadest national visibility to date. Indeed, the participation of so many high-profile national and regional figures—Black and White; political, cultural, and religious—in this Left-led anti-lynching conference was striking.[27]

Finally, a special anti-lynching meeting was scheduled for November 18 in an attempt to resuscitate the local NAACP branch. Although Reverend Trigg, president of the Baltimore NAACP, was much in evidence during the protests after Armwood's death, his organization remained little more than a shell. The main speaker at the reorganization meeting was Walter White, who criticized the Baltimore branch as "lethargic" and called for its reconstruction. Despite good attendance at the meeting, no rebuilding followed, and it would be nearly two years before the Baltimore branch was to be transformed into an effective chapter of the NAACP.[28]

Inevitably as a movement expands, political contradictions arise among its participants, and various trends within the movement emerge, reposition, and redefine themselves. Such was the case with the anti-lynching movement that followed George Armwood's murder. The contradictions that surfaced were seldom terribly disruptive to protest activities, but they reveal something of the ideological struggles and potential future directions of Baltimore's reviving freedom movement. These contradictions were complex but largely fell along two axes: between more radical and more moderate currents of the movement and within the radical current itself.

Tensions between the militant Black activists and elite White centrists were revealed in Clarence Mitchell's column in the *Afro* discussing the moderate anti-lynching meeting at the Sharp Street Memorial church. Mitchell noted the "sound advice" given by the two White clergymen, Reverend Asbury Smith and Reverend Guthrie Speers, who spoke at the meeting, then he took aim at the "deluge of 'heartthrob' oratory from Mrs. Marie Bauernschmidt who told her hearers that she was praying for them in their hour of need with hope that they would remain level headed and do nothing rash." Mitchell continued by lampooning the "assemblage," which, he wrote, "swayed to her way of thinking like a reed in a hurricane, and as the last echoes of the applause died down she departed as suddenly as she arrived, leaving in her wake many foolish people who believed that they were getting a lot of much-needed consolation." Mitchell believed differently: "When a man or a race is ready to right a wrong already done, no condescending messages of consolation are welcome." Patronizing advice from White elite figures to go slow was not needed, and those of whatever race who listened were being misled.[29]

An *Afro* editorial, probably written by Carl Murphy, also criticized aspects of the meeting at the Sharp Street church but targeted the speech by the liberal White clergyman Asbury Smith, who was involved in the effort to build the Maryland Anti-Lynching Federation and who had earlier written about his "shame" over being White and from the Eastern shore. Rather paradoxically, at this meeting Smith took "colored people [in Baltimore] to task for their political backwardness," comparing them unfavorably with African Americans in Chicago. The *Afro* retorted that the main difference between Baltimore and Chicago was not the "backwardness" of Baltimore's Blacks but the "hostility" of local Whites, who were "a different species" from Whites in Chicago. Bringing the argument all the way back home, the *Afro* proposed that the next greatest handicap facing the Black freedom movement was the "acquiescence of the white Christian church" to segregationism. The more militant forces in the movement were glad to have progressive White allies, but they were not about to let those allies set the agenda, or define the character, of the Black community. Contradictions between militants and moderates did not, however, always have a cross-racial character. At the protest meeting with an all-Black roster of speakers, organized by Linwood Koger at the Gospel Temple, Reverend C. H. Harge "flayed" those "turncoats" who, after the meeting of Baptist preachers with the governor, called Ritchie a "nice man."[30]

Nonetheless, the harshest conflicts between militants and moderates involved the Communists and a number of Black preachers. During the "indignation meeting" at Union Baptist church right after the Armwood lynching, a sharp exchange took place between Bernard Ades of the ILD and Reverend C. Y. Trigg of the NAACP. According to Clarence Mitchell, Ades attacked Trigg as a "false leader" because Trigg "had chosen to use tact rather than bullying during an interview with Governor Ritchie." Both Mitchell's column and an editorial in the *Afro* (again, probably written by Carl Murphy) called in effect for center-left unity, asking that the NAACP and the ILD unite against "the enemy at the gate" and respect each other's different approaches.[31]

Despite such calls for reconciliation, controversy between the ILD and more conservative Black religious forces arose again two weeks later when the Bethel AME church barred a scheduled anti-lynching protest meeting sponsored by the ILD. Reverend Peter Ainslie, the venerable White progressive, was scheduled to speak, as were Ades and several others. Bethel AME's pastor, Reverend C. C. Ferguson, specifically objected to Ades because he "was too closely allied with a program that was not in keeping with the best interests of the race" and because he made "unnecessary attacks on the clergy and the church." However, Gough McDaniels, a Black organizer of the meeting and a scheduled speaker, accused Ferguson and the board of trustees of Bethel AME of playing "peanut politics." And C. C. Owens, the African American chair of the meeting, claimed that Ferguson and the board rejected Ades, who was Jewish, because he was "of a different faith." The protest meeting, however, went off as planned. It simply moved a few blocks to Cosmopolitan church, indicating that not all African American religious leaders had problems with Ades's speaking in church.[32]

Contradictions also emerged in the more radical wing of the anti-lynching movement. The Baltimore CP and the ILD were not ones to shrink from intra-movement struggle, and at the northeastern ILD regional conference, the Baltimore ILD escalated its conflict with the more centrist forces in the movement. For the tribunal on lynching, the ILD had "subpoenaed" local and state officials who were implicated in Armwood's murder. To no one's surprise, the officials declined to attend, but their alleged crimes were exposed anyway. However, in a spate of Third Period sectarianism, summonses were also sent to figures in the Baltimore anti-lynching movement who crossed swords with the local ILD at some point. They included Judge Joseph Ulman of the BUL, Reverend C. C. Ferguson of Bethel AME church, and (most surprising) Edward Lewis, executive secretary of the BUL.[33]

Differences also arose between Communist-led and militant non-Communist forces in the anti-lynching protests. For example, Clarence Mitchell, who just a few days earlier had counseled reconciliation in the rift between Reverend Trigg and Bernard Ades, became angry with the Com-

munists over an incident at the ILD regional conference. As he recalled in an
oral history interview conducted many years later,

> One of the things that I was so disgusted with them about was, they brought
> up a number of people from the Eastern Shore of Maryland. There was one
> poor old gentleman about 80 years old, I guess, who got to describing the con-
> ditions, and he said, "And there's nothing we can do about that." . . . Well, this
> crowd just tore into him and did all sorts of insulting things. And the poor old
> man was up there trying to explain, and he said, "Well, what can we do?" And
> somebody yelled out in back, "You can fight!" I thought this was so bad—80
> years old, what could he do against that crowd?

The gentleman in question was Reverend William C. Jason, former head of
Dover College. Ralph Matthews of the *Afro* was also incensed over this incident. Scheduled to speak right after Jason at the ILD conference, he threw
away his prepared speech and lectured the crowd on its behavior, a summary
of which he published in his *Afro* column under the title, "Anti-Lynch Conference, Bunk vs. Common Sense." The rift between Matthews and the Communists over this incident should not be overstated, however, for two weeks
later, Matthews opened his column to Richard B. Moore of the Communist-
led League of Struggle for Negro Rights to state his side of the story.[34]

The CP also got embroiled in disagreements with the local Black left, including the *Afro*, one of its staunchest friends. First, there was contention between the CP and the *Afro* over the origin of the names of the four lynchers
that the ILD had delivered to the governor. In its November 4 issue, the *Afro*
published an editorial claiming that, despite several promises to the contrary,
the CP's *Daily Worker* had again taken credit for discovering and first publicizing the names of four of Armwood's murderers. According to the *Afro*, it,
not the CP paper, was responsible for this disclosure. With some disdain, the
Afro editorial remarked that any claims to the contrary were "not only misleading, but downright dishonest."[35]

Second, there was the embarrassing dispute over Euel Lee's body. Ades had
obtained Lee's permission to take possession of his corpse after his execution, and the ILD planned to make Lee's body the center of an anti-lynching
protest in New York. Judge Eugene O'Dunne, however, blocked the plan.
Lee was quickly buried, and his grave was guarded for several days by armed
police. This controversy led to a rare editorial criticism of the ILD in the *Afro*
and to tension with some of its younger allies in the Black freedom movement. Five decades later, Juanita Jackson Mitchell remembered how the CP
plan to parade Lee's body through the streets incensed her and her comrades
in the Forum. In this case, the CP's sense of political morality came into con-

flict with the moral and religious sensibilities of important segments of the Black community.[36]

Again, the tensions between the Communists and other militants in the freedom movement should not be exaggerated. In a short time, the *Afro* was again praising both the ILD and Ades himself. And Communists continued to work with Forumites, although the relationship was beginning to turn frosty. Probably the most important result of these tensions at the time, though, was the ILD's absence from the coalition that formed the Maryland Anti-Lynching Federation.

Lynchers' Arrests

In late November, with the clamor over Armwood's murder fading, the immediate political impact of the protests became evident. The Ritchie administration, bowing to public pressure, announced that it was seeking indictments of nine alleged leaders of the lynch mob that had been identified by State Police officers who were present at the Armwood lynching. However, State's Attorney Robins and Eastern Shore justices Duer, Bailey, and Pattison refused to arrest the suspects. Caught between the angry anti-lynching protests in Baltimore and the embarrassing defiance of the Jim Crow extremists on the Eastern Shore, Ritchie and his attorney-general, William Preston Lane Jr., finally took decisive—and, for Jim Crow Maryland, astounding—action.[37]

The governor declared martial law in Somerset County and cut off phone lines. At 2:30 AM, State Police, reinforced by 300 National Guardsmen in full combat dress with bayonets set, moved into Salisbury while squads were dispatched to Princess Anne and surrounding areas to arrest the suspects. Although only four of the nine suspects were caught and transported to Salisbury, the local White community erupted, and Whites from surrounding towns poured into Salisbury. A mob of 1,000 battled the troops and attempted several times to free the four suspects. When dispersed by tear gas, the mob turned on the reporters present, attacked the car of Attorney-General Lane, and rampaged through the Black community, forcing residents to flee. Finally, still under mob pressure, the troops withdrew, and the four arrested men were moved to Baltimore. As the *Afro* put it, "The lawless Eastern Shore is in full rebellion against the governor and the constituted authorities of the state."[38]

At this point, the state's attempt to punish the lynchers began to collapse. Ritchie—under attack in the state legislature, with calls to lynch him and Attorney-General Lane reverberating across the Eastern Shore, and with potential rivals in the next election maneuvering for advantage—vacillated again. He allowed the four arrested men to return to Princess Anne, where Judge Robert Duer, in a courtroom filled with 2,000 cheering spectators, released them for alleged lack of evidence after an eight-minute hearing. A White crowd then attacked the local Black community, driving many from their homes and, according to Clarence Mitchell, the mob besieged the White out-of-town press in a hotel. In 1934, in the aftermath of this aborted attempt at justice, Albert Ritchie, a potential Democratic Party presidential candidate not long before, lost the gubernatorial election to the Republican Harry Nice, partly because his short-lived attempt to prosecute the lynchers had alienated White segregationists, and partly because his vacillations and his acquiescence to the lynching of Armwood had infuriated Black and progressive White voters.[39]

As was usually the case with racialized lynchings, no one was ever punished for George Armwood's murder. But change had begun. In early December 1933, three fearful Eastern Shore African American leaders, probably at the behest of prominent local Whites, published a letter in two Eastern Shore newspapers blaming Ades and the Communists for Armwood's lynching. Across the Chesapeake Bay in Black Baltimore, coverage of the letter in the *Afro* appeared under the ridiculing headlines "Three Uncle Jameses Speak" and "Three Jimmies Glorify Lynching." Then, in a break with precedent, sharp criticism of the letter was raised at home. Nineteen Eastern Shore Black leaders, at considerable risk to themselves, published a sharp rebuttal in the *Afro* to the three leaders' letter, denying that sentiments in the letter represented those of the local African American community and endorsing federal anti-lynching legislation. Such assertiveness shattered what Sherrilyn Ifill has described as the silence with which Black communities often responded to the terror of lynching. The struggle in the metropolis of Baltimore opened space for the struggle in the hinterlands to emerge.[40]

Another change was evident, as well. When Sam Jones was arrested in Somerset County on New Year's Eve of 1933 for the murder of a White woman, he was immediately transferred to Baltimore to obviate any possibility of a lynching. The Forum, the local NAACP branch, the PUL, and the national office of the NAACP intervened, and after a month, Jones was released. "When one remembers the Euel Lee case," Walter White wrote to Juanita Jackson, "this is indeed a miracle." Several months later, again in Somerset County, Howard McClellan, a Black man, allegedly stabbed a White police officer to death, and the sheriff sent McClellan to Baltimore as soon as he was apprehended. While the threat of a lynching did materialize on the Eastern Shore several more times in the 1930s and '40s, the movement based in Baltimore remained vigilant, and its reaction was always swift. As it turned out, George Armwood was the last recorded African American victim of a mass mob lynching in Maryland to the present day. The Baltimore anti-lynching movement gave a major boost to the national anti-lynching movement, and subsequently, the two worked in close coordination. Moreover, the Baltimore freedom movement that emerged from the protests of George Armwood's murder was fundamentally changed and strengthened, and it was immediately swept into the Buy Where You Can Work campaign's Pennsylvania Avenue boycott.[41]

6

Buy Where You Can Work, 1933–1934

Right across the street from where I lived at 1216 Druid Hill Avenue there was this A&P Store with all White sales clerks, and in those days they didn't employ women. And all over this Northwest ghetto, and all over the city, we had just White employees in Black communities. They wouldn't let us have jobs.

—JUANITA JACKSON MITCHELL

The protest campaign that followed the lynching of George Armwood was not the only mobilization to transform Baltimore's fledging Black freedom movement in late 1933 and early 1934. "The Buy Where You Can Work" campaign, a jobs boycott of White-owned stores in the Black community to force the hiring of Black clerks, was equally transformative. In fact, the two campaigns formed a continuum: the first phase of the jobs boycott ended when activists were diverted to the protests following the murder of George Armwood; the second phase began as anti-lynching activities passed their peak. These two campaigns together defined the Baltimore freedom movement's watershed in 1933–34. Surprisingly, the originator of the first of these campaigns, the jobs boycott, was an enigmatic figure who first arrived in the city in mid-1933.

The First Phase of the Campaign

In early June 1933, a reporter with the *Afro-American* announced that Prophet Kiowa Costonie, the "New Messiah" to his followers, had come to town (see figure 19): "Discovered here about four weeks ago when tall stories of miraculous healings and divine cures drifted to the *Afro-American*, the writer investigated and found the healer besieged by hundreds in the base-

19. Prophet Kiowa Costonie, from a photograph taken in the 1940s. *Used by permission of Toni Costonie.*

ment of Shiloh Baptist Church where, amid demonstrations of religious frenzy, the man whom thousands were following from church to church made cripples walk, deaf hear, blind see simply by the laying on of his long tapering hands." The "thousands . . . following from church to church" may have been an overestimate, but the twenty-eight-year-old Prophet Costonie was obviously a man of great religious charisma. Described as "suave" and "immaculately dressed," he was, in Juanita Jackson Mitchell's words, "a handsome man. He said his mother was Indian. He had these beautiful eyes that were a bit slanted. And he put a beautiful turban, with gold in it, on his head."[1]

While Baltimore at the time had nowhere near as many charismatic revivalists or (in the poet Claude McKay's words) "cultists" and "occultists" as Harlem or Chicago, it had its share. Eleanor Burrell, who was fourteen when Costonie appeared in Baltimore, recalled that mystics and revivalists were increasingly common in the city's African American community during the early Depression years: "All these Prophets and all of these holy-rolly or whatever you call them, they would come here and get rich. They had the ability and faith to heal people. And people really believed all of this, you know. There were loads of them. They had tents all over Baltimore city." In his column for the *Afro-American*, Clarence Mitchell periodically derided "our many religious fanatics," such as "the New Christ," Robert Peeks, who wandered around displaying what he claimed were stigmata on the palms of his hands. In mid-1933, Father Divine had established a "kingdom" in Baltimore and was preaching to hundreds at the New Albert Auditorium. And later that year, Prophet John Means was put on trial for taking children into his cult.[2]

However, it quickly became evident that Prophet Costonie was different. First, Costonie's revivalism, unlike that of some other mystical figures of the time, did not alienate the religious establishment of African American Baltimore. Rather than setting up a rival organization, Costonie cultivated relationships with the preachers in the community, and, shortly after his arrival, he was conducting revivals at some of the most important Black Baptist churches in town. If some local ministers and lay people were suspicious of Costonie's preaching and healing, many others were not, feeling instead that he was theologically compatible with the existing churches and, if not a benefit, at least not a threat. Moreover, cash-strapped churches were aware that revivals could relieve financial distress during the Depression.[3]

Second, Costonie differed from the other mystics in that, despite his phenomenal ability to move the faithful, he often displayed an unusual modesty about his religious powers. This humility made him more acceptable to those Christians and secularists who were distrustful of extreme evangelical fervor. As Mitchell wrote in an *Afro-American* column, "His common sense really is above the average. He doesn't pretend to be divine or superhuman and frankly admits that he has his limitations." Costonie repeatedly admitted that he had no idea of the source of his own faith-healing ability.[4]

Finally, unlike other spiritualists of the time, Costonie had an interest in African American identity and politics. In Juanita Jackson Mitchell's words, he "had this racial advancement emphasis." At his revival meetings in May and June 1933, he championed a "new racial consciousness," and was even quoted as saying that his "power to heal the sick by touch is merely used as an attraction to draw crowds so he can promulgate his ideas of racial betterment." He advocated the development of Black enterprises built on Black patronage as the path to progress, opposed the color bar in municipal jobs, and called on his audiences to "unseat your underworld political leaders" because "Baltimore has to be shaken to its foundations." Costonie was emphatically not an integrationist; rather, he was one of a wide variety of spiritually oriented figures across the country associated with the amorphous post–Marcus Garvey Black nationalism of the time. Unlike Garvey, some of these figures focused their energy on social protest.[5]

Costonie related his mystical-political ideological outlook to his adventure-filled life story. While the accuracy of his exotic personal narrative cannot be fully ascertained, it is worth reviewing because it reveals much about the image he wanted to project. He was born, he said, on a Ute Indian Reservation in Utah to a well-known Native American faith healer who died when he was four. A Black woman named Mrs. Green adopted him from the Catholic orphanage in which he had been placed, renamed him Tony Green (the name he later used in vaudeville), and, according to Costonie's daughter, "promoted him as a child prodigy at local clubs and honky tonks." Mrs. Green became increasingly abusive toward him and the adoption failed, as subsequently did two more, leaving Costonie on his own and on the road when he was ten years old. Becoming a "happy-go-lucky" wanderer, he worked on ships and railroads throughout the United States, Canada, England, the Caribbean, and Latin America, sometimes taking a Spanish identity. During his travels, however, he discovered racial oppression and, as he stated it, "I was disgusted with my own people" for not resisting their oppression. Disgust aside, he began to "dream that if a man had enough courage, he really could do something for his people." Reportedly, during these travels he inadvertently discovered his faith-healing abilities when he cured a sick shipmate. Thrilled by this discovery, he began to experiment with it as a hobby.[6]

Costonie forged a "career" alternating among politics, the entertainment business, and faith healing that took him across the country. He claimed that he became a political leader in Boston and the vice-president of the Massachusetts State League of Colored Political Clubs while he was still too young to vote, ran a recreation parlor for awhile, and subsequently lost all his money in real estate speculation. In New York, he invested in a show called "A Manhattan Cocktail" that failed in two weeks, and he ended up in Washington, D.C., as a part of the Ziegfeld Follies' production "Hot Chops." He worked for a period on the railroads, joined the Butter Beans and Susie comedy act, engaged in some faith healing on the side, and in 1928 became involved in Herbert Hoover's presidential campaign. For his political efforts, Costonie was rewarded with a patronage job and access to the highest circles of African American society in the capital, through which he met his wife, Emma Stewart, the daughter of an "aristocratic" Black family in Washington. The marriage was short-lived, he explained to the *Afro-American*, because his humble background (something he frequently stressed) left him ill-suited to the "continual rounds of gay festivities" demanded by society life and, conversely, because his new wife could not adjust to his faith healing, as well as to his long-standing "friendship" with an actress. In 1931, Costonie left Emma Stewart and began his travels again, for the first time devoting his full energy to faith healing. Some two years later, he showed up in Baltimore.[7]

In the weeks after his first appearance in Baltimore, Costonie seems to have restricted his activities to revivals, despite his nationalistic political rhetoric. In mid-June 1933, he moved to Philadelphia but did not remain long, despite his contacts in the African American clerical establishment and a following in the community. He was apparently put off by what the *Afro-American* called an unending "stream" of faith healers through that city. Sometime in the late summer, he resumed his revivals in Baltimore, where his activities took an increasingly political turn. Costonie declared that one of his "ideals" was to "teach the Negro to vote. The ballot is the greatest weapon they have." From a base at the Perkins Baptist church, he launched a registration campaign, financed with his own funds, through which he transported carload after carload of voters to the courthouse downtown to declare their intention to vote. When critics charged that his campaign was designed to augment the Republican vote, he reacted angrily, contending that "the masses of Baltimore" had no "faith in our supposed political leaders"; he told politicians of both parties to stay away. By early October, he claimed to have registered some 200 people and to have stimulated others, including several clergymen and the Fourth District Republican Club, to begin their own registration drives.[8]

The *Afro-American*'s publisher, Carl Murphy, who had previously shown interest in Costonie as a religious figure, now held him up as a political model: "Costonie, unhampered by the inhibitions, obligations and fears of retribution, which cause many of our old residents and leaders to refrain from taking these forward steps, is also entitled to our encouragement and support. May his work continue." Meanwhile, Costonie began promoting education, focusing initially on schoolchildren but also proposing to teach "old people how to read and write." At the Perkins Square and Bethlehem Baptist churches, he organized free classes for some 330 students designed to strengthen their basic academic skills and to teach them African American history.

In the midst of all this activity, Costonie and a committee of three surveyed the White-owned stores on Pennsylvania Avenue, the commercial heart of the Black community in northwestern Baltimore. Finding an overwhelmingly White sales force, Costonie demanded that the stores begin hiring African Americans immediately or face a community boycott. In September,

Costonie initiated what would become the Buy Where You Can Work movement.[9]

The call for a jobs boycott was not a new tactic, either in Baltimore or elsewhere. By 1933, boycotts of White-owned stores to increase the hiring of Black clerks had been attempted in several cities, with varying success. The Chicago boycott of 1929 and 1930 was the most famous and successful at the time, but there had also been smaller campaigns in Toledo (1930, 1932), Cleveland (1931), Detroit (1932), and New York (1932). Eventually, jobs boycotts would become, in the words of the historians August Meier and Elliot Rudwick, the "most important and sustained of the black direct-action demonstrations during the 1930s," with at least forty-six such boycotts occurring in thirty-six cities during the decade. The conditions in the Black community in Baltimore were definitely ripe for a jobs boycott. With many people unemployed, including many who qualified for "white collar" occupations such as sales clerks, African Americans encountered all-White sales staffs in White-owned stores in a community with very few Black-owned stores. Two years earlier, the Baltimore Urban League (BUL) had made launching a jobs boycott a major strategic goal for the year. However, since the BUL, then in a state of decline, was unwilling to picket, the campaign went nowhere. In January 1931, the *Afro-American*, under the headline "Don't Spend Your Money Where You Can't Work," called on the community to "prod its Urban League and affiliated agencies into a campaign to have these neighborhood stores employ colored girls and boys as clerks, deliverymen, and managers." Nine months later, the *Afro* was more militant: "We are supporting a Women's Civic League, a Baltimore branch of the Urban League and a Baltimore branch of the National Association for the Advancement of Colored People. They cannot justify their existence if Baltimore taxpayers must continue to spend money where they cannot work." Nearly two years after this, in an editorial published on August 12, 1933, on the eve of Costonie's campaign, the *Afro-American* again advocated boycotting and picketing, this time against businesses that fired Blacks and hired Whites at the higher wages mandated by the National Recovery Act. Naturally, when Costonie threatened the merchants on Pennsylvania Avenue with a boycott, the *Afro* took notice.[10]

For a while after Costonie issued his threat in late September, it appeared that a boycott might not be necessary. Tommy Tucker's Five-and-Dime store, Goodman's Five-and-Dime, and Max Meyers' shoe store all agreed to hire Black clerks. Howard Cleaners and Dyers announced a new branch on Pennsylvania Avenue with a Black manager and all-Black staff, and the Atlantic and Pacific Tea (A&P) stores, a frequent target of Black boycotts elsewhere, claimed that it had hired a Morgan College graduate as a clerk. The shoe-store owner Max Meyers even appeared at Costonie's mass meeting at the Perkins Square Baptist church when these apparent victories were announced, and before 450 people made, as the *Afro-American* put it, "a speech of thanks." Costonie, however, reported that other White merchants were noncommittal, and he announced that managers of the A&P and the American Stores Company (ASCO) had until October 15 to hire Black employees or face picket lines. He then thanked his supporters, including "Shiloh Baptist Church and several local ministers who were urging their congregations to back him up." Characteristically, he ended the meeting with faith healing.[11]

By October 7, both ASCO and A&P had agreed to start hiring Black male clerks from job seekers sent to them by Costonie. For this purpose, he carefully screened and recruited a group of young men who became known as the Opportunity Makers Club. Subsequently, Costonie told a meeting of AME preachers that his next campaign would target the remaining White-owned stores on Pennsylvania Avenue, involving some 600 jobs. By this time, Costonie had started to build a coalition to support his efforts, including the Monumental and Pride of Baltimore lodges of the Elks, the Knights of Pythias, and (somewhat surprisingly) the Challenger and Baltimore auto clubs. This was, however, a rudimentary coalition, one that would have been hard pressed to pull off the kind of boycott Costonie threatened. Nevertheless, with very little more than the prestige he brought from his revival meetings, he had given the incipient Buy Where You Can Work movement its first victories. In mid-October, the boycott hit a rough patch, as the A&P market in northwestern Baltimore charging that its new Black clerks were "inefficient," fired them and hired White clerks. At the same time, it became clear that most small businesses on Pennsylvania Avenue were not honoring their pledges to hire African Americans.[12]

At this conjuncture, Costonie made contact with the activists of the City-Wide Young People's Forum, who, interestingly, had toyed with the idea of a jobs boycott the previous spring but were unable to carry through because of their other projects. As Maceo Howard, then a vice-president of the Forum, remembered decades later, he was having his hair cut when the barber introduced him to the man in the next chair who was interested in getting "some civil rights action going." It turned out to be Costonie. Howard arranged a meeting with the Forumites. Juanita Jackson Mitchell later recalled:

> When I first saw him, and he proposed this boycott, he was at Perkins Square Baptist church. He came to us and asked us to support it. We had him speak at the Forum. He said why not go after the A&P stores, so we said fine. . . . He took the initiative. He brought us the plan. . . . We voted to support the boycott,

and with it we took all the preachers we had and the *Afro*—everything. . . . He never had any big organization. It was our army of freedom fighters that was the bodies for his program, really. And we supported him 100 percent.

Although Costonie and the Forum intended to launch a direct action campaign immediately on Pennsylvania Avenue, the murder of George Armwood on October 18 intervened, and the activists shifted their attention to protesting the lynching outrage.[13]

The Second Phase of the Campaign

By the beginning of November 1933, as the anti-lynching protests were entering their third week, boycott activities restarted in an atmosphere of greatly heightened awareness and mobilization in the Black community. Prophet Costonie, who played a minor role in the anti-lynching upsurge, continued as the undisputed leader of the jobs boycott coalition, with the Forum as his main ally. But the coalition was broadening—most significantly, the Housewives League, with its official membership of several hundred, came aboard—and a Citizens' Committee that included Costonie and representatives from the different allied groups was formed to direct the struggle. Lillie Jackson, who served on the committee because of her role with the Forum, quickly became a key leader. On November 2, 1933, the Citizens' Committee called on the A&P markets and the stores on Pennsylvania Avenue to employ Black staffs immediately, to hire Black managers by January 1, and to dismiss recently hired White clerks. If the demands were not met, the committee threatened mass picket lines. At a meeting sponsored by the Forum, A. C. MacNeal of the *Chicago Whip*, a leader of the pioneering jobs boycott movement in Chicago, urged those present to "create jobs for Negro youth by militantly organizing and using your buying power." The A&Ps stonewalled, and Prophet Costonie called for 2,000 people to pledge to boycott the stores. On November 18, the picket lines went up.[14]

When the call went out to picket A&P, the community, especially its youth, was ready as never before. In an interview conducted years later, Evelyn Burrell told how she and her friend Elva, then both schoolgirls, responded so enthusiastically that they began picketing by themselves one day early:

We were coming down from school one day. We saw some young men that we knew with [Costonie], and he turns around and says to the [A&P] manager, "Well, if you feel that, there will be pickets here in the morning."

We were children, twelve years old, and didn't know that [Costonie] was in the city organizing. But we approached the fellows who were with him. We asked them what was going on. They fully acquainted us and introduced us to Mr. Costonie. We assured them that there would be pickets as soon as we could get to my girlfriend's father's house and make the signs. We were out there picketing by four o'clock.

A White policeman—"Sergeant Buster, who was the favorite policeman in the community," according to Burrell—stopped the two girls, who were picketing alone, and escorted them home, dropping Burrell off at the house she shared with her grandparents and mother. Her grandfather was sympathetic to the boycott and to what she had done, but her mother and grandmother were upset; she was "greatly chastised and reprimanded" and told "not to go back." But, Burrell recalled, "The next morning, the boys were there. And, honey child, we couldn't wait for the next morning! We were there, too!" She remembered that the boycott took hold quickly, and, "On Tuesday, November 21, the stores were practically closed down, because, believe it or not, we had young people going from door to door, acquainting people. We had trucks and loudspeakers going all around the neighborhood. People really were not going in the stores. Consequently, the stores were hurting. I mean, hurting."[15]

The community mobilization shook A&P's management, and the corporate offices dispatched William Scrimger, the eastern regional director, to meet with the Citizens' Committee at the Sharp Street Methodist church. Rebuffed in his initial offer, Scrimger soon surrendered and agreed to hire twenty-one Black clerks within two weeks, to continue hiring Blacks until "every boy is colored," and to have three Black managers in place by March 1, 1934. This promise was largely kept, and by April 1934 A&P had at least thirty-eight African American employees, including two assistant managers. At the meeting called to announce the victory, Prophet Costonie "declared that 4,200 persons had been behind him in the effort along with the heads of many organizations." Commenting on the capitulation of A&P, Juanita Jackson Mitchell recalled that the victorious campaign "liberated the people. It gave them a sense of power. It was a tremendous victory; for the churches, too. And then we were ready to go on to Pennsylvania Avenue." The Buy Where You Can Work campaign had had its first successful experience with mass direct action, and it was ready to do it again.[16]

To concentrate their forces, the Citizen's Committee targeted stores on only the 1700 block of Pennsylvania Avenue. Aaron Samuelson, owner of the Tommy Tucker's Five-and-Dime and several other stores, reportedly responded to the boycott threat by declaring, "You couldn't pay these Negroes to stay out of my store." The picketing began at noon on Friday, December 8,

20. Boycott pickets on Pennsylvania Avenue in front of Tommy Tucker's Five-and-Dime store. *Courtesy of the Afro-American Newspapers Archives and Research Center.*

as the Christmas shopping season was moving into full swing. In a characteristically colorful report in the *Afro-American*, Ralph Matthews described the picket line several days later:

> With gloveless fingers, cold and numb, faces bleached and blistered by the cutting winds, feet frost-bitten through none-to-sturdy shoes, and clothes that to the zero weather were but a mockery, 200 boys and girls went into the fourth day of their boycott march. . . . Back and forth they marched, huddled together in little groups to ward off the cold. Sometimes in pairs—sweethearts perhaps—locked arm in arm; sometimes dwindling to only a score as the ranks are thinned to recoup from the cold and get a bite to eat—and suddenly the mass swells again. Marching slowly, silently, back and forth, as a policeman stationed along the way utters a gruff "keep moving."

Picketing started at 9 AM each day, with one-hour shifts, and ended when the stores closed well after dark (see figure 20). At times as many as eighteen police were assigned to oversee the demonstration, and each weekday, when students got out of a nearby school, the picket line expanded. At least two food stations and three physicians, aided by "several drug stores," provided support for the demonstrators. Several Black-owned restaurants served the pickets hot drinks, and local residents spontaneously offered nourishment and places to rest. Picketing and boycotting were publicized in the *Afro-American*, through thousands of handbills and circulars, and at mass boycott meetings held at the Cosmopolitan Community church. In Juanita Jackson Mitchell's words, "It became a kind of religion, Don't Buy Where You Can't Work!"[17]

The Northwest Businessmen's Association represented the merchants in opposing the boycott's demands and attempted to maintain a unified front in the face of drastically declining business. The merchant Aaron Samuelson later admitted a 60 percent drop in business at Tommy Tucker's during the weekend after the picketing started. By the middle of the following week, business had "practically disappeared," as an investigating judge later put it, and cracks in the store owners' unity began to appear. Some merchants made false claims that they were hiring Black employees, only to be confronted and exposed. Others may have hired a few Black workers, but this did not satisfy the pickets. The A&P, whose store on the 1700 block was not being picketed because it had already hired Black clerks, was reportedly asked to support the Northwest Businessmen's Association, but it declined.[18]

Although there were some indications that the merchants might be willing to negotiate, the situation grew increasingly tense. Claiming threats against his life from gunmen rumored to have been "imported from New York to wipe [him] out," Costonie moved around with five young male activists serving as bodyguards. With frustration mounting, pickets aggressively confronted storeowners and prospective shoppers, occasionally blocking stores' entrances; one storeowner charged that the boycott leaders Costonie, Lillie Jackson, and Elvira Bond had threatened him physically. Max Meyers of Meyers Shoes had Jacob Baggett arrested for causing a disturbance, although Baggett protested that he was just a shopper. The Forum raised the bail, the Forum attorney W. A. C. Hughes defended Baggett, and the court dismissed charges. Also, several light-skinned African American activists, apparently acting on their own initiative, impersonated White businesspeople and slipped into a Northwest Businessmen's Association meeting. While three of the infiltrators were discovered and evicted, a fourth managed to stay for the duration and report the proceedings to the boycott's leadership.[19]

Finally, some merchants mobilized counter-pickets, and violent incidents occurred as the picket lines were harassed. Evelyn Burrell later remembered one such incident involving a gang of thugs from the "sporting world" led by a woman named Salina, who was "rough and strong as any man you could name." At the time, Burrell recounted that she was on the picket line with Vivian Marshall (known as "Buster"), the future wife of Thurgood Marshall: "Buster and I were walking down the street. Well, Buster looked like she was White. So one of Salina's henchmen busted her head. She had to have some four or five stitches put in her head. A couple of the pickets were actually knifed. And, of course, you know the policemen were there. Well, the picket line was [temporarily] broken up as a result of Salina's activities." [20]

Beyond the picket line, there was also tension among older adult community leaders who were reluctant to get involved but were pressured to choose sides. Some established members of the community moved into stubborn public opposition to the boycott. Reverend Beale Elliot objected to the boycott because, as he explained to the *Afro-American*, "You make it by the sweat of your brow and your own effort in life," apparently seeing the boycott as a demand for a handout. "Yes, I'm an Uncle Tom," he added. However, many among the Black elite supported the boycott. For example, Reverend C. Y. Trigg of the NAACP and Josiah Diggs, owner of the Dunbar Theater, were both on the Citizens' Committee and active participants. [21]

Another complication revolved around Costonie himself. About a month before the final campaign against the A&P stores began, a number of his supporters among the Baptist clergy broke with him, claiming that he was "putting on a program of false faith healing." In retaliation, during the days following the victory over A&P, Costonie announced that he had "a list of names of persons who were traitors" to the cause of freedom. "The Ark is about to leave, and I am giving all the backsliders a last chance to get on," he declared. Whatever the backsliders thought of Costonie's statement, some of his allies were skeptical; in his *Afro-American* column, Clarence Mitchell even questioned the existence of Costonie's list. Nevertheless, as the campaign approached the one-week point, fear of treachery grew within the ranks of the boycotters; alleged traitors to the cause, including several ministers, were publicly denounced not only by Costonie but also by Josiah Diggs; and suspected "stoolpigeons" were interrogated at length during at least one boycott meeting. [22]

At one point, the contradiction between Costonie's clerical critics and his young supporters threatened to become violent. Costonie's Opportunity Makers Club, whose spokesperson was Thurgood Marshall, asked an interdenominational meeting of ministers to support the boycott and allow boycott activists to speak at Sunday services. In the words of the *Afro-American*, the meeting "nearly precipitated a free-for-all fight" over the accusations by several Baptist ministers that Costonie had sold "healing handkerchiefs." Later in the meeting, stink bombs were set off with the apparent purpose of disrupting the meeting, allegedly by members of the Opportunity Makers Club. Amid threatening chaos, Thurgood Marshall was called on to dispel rumors circulating among the clergy that White-owned businesses downtown were about to fire all of their Black employees in retaliation for the boycott. Finally, Trigg calmed the meeting down, and an ambiguous decision was made "that the ministers would give the movement their whole-hearted support," although "they did not . . . approve of the boycott." While contention among community forces did not significantly weaken the boycott, it did undermine Costonie's leadership position relative to that of other forces on the Citizen's Committee.[23]

On Friday, December 15, some three carloads of police pulled up in front of the Bethel AME church during a City-Wide Young People's Forum meeting. Clarence Mitchell later recalled that he and his compatriots thought they were all going to be arrested, and a rumor that they had been taken to jail subsequently swept the Black community. Instead, this intimidating show of police force was an attempt to serve Costonie, as boycott leader, with a temporary injunction ordering an immediate cessation of the picketing. In the short term, the police did not succeed. Reverend W. H. Baker stood in the doorway and ordered the police to leave; in the subsequent confusion, Costonie, who had been speaking to the crowd inside when the police arrived, snuck out the back and went into hiding. Reportedly, the humiliated police "roundly denounced colored people in general when they got back to the station house." Although the Forum leadership protested the disruption of the meeting by the police, and picket lines went back up, they were soon recalled. Faced with arrest and a $1,000 bond for release, the boycott leadership decided it had no choice but to comply with the injunction. The Pennsylvania Avenue picketing was called off a little more than a week after it began.[24]

The injunction of December 16 broke the momentum of the boycott struggle at a time when hopes were high that segregated employment was about to be swept from the stores in Baltimore's Black neighborhoods. Demoralized but not broken, the boycott's leadership embarked on a new strategy. The wording of the temporary injunction prohibited all boycott agitation against the stores on the 1700 block, so activists relied on word of mouth and telephone networks, supplemented by the letters and editorial columns of the *Afro-American* — and on one occasion, by some stink bombs — to continue the boycott activity. The Forum clearly believed that jobs as store clerks would soon open to Black youth, and mounted a successful petition campaign for a "training course in salesmanship" at the evening school of Frederick Douglass High; eighty-five youths signed up. In February, in office space donated by Lillie Jackson, the Forum began "to provide an employment service for trained young people."[25]

Overturning the temporary injunction through litigation became a top priority for the boycott movement. The Forum's legal adviser, W. A. C. Hughes, and his partner, the former City Council member Walter T. McGuinn, took the case, with advice and support from the national NAACP. Although the freedom movement had a long history, dating from the late nineteenth century, of taking battles to court, the only important recent legal action had concerned the defense of Euel Lee, during which the ILD combined legal maneuvers with mass protest. The legal fight against the injunction echoed the ILD's approach, with litigation supplemented by mass meetings and demonstrations. Repeatedly, starting with the trial of Jacob Baggett for allegedly causing a disturbance during the picketing, supporters packed court proceedings and, although generally disciplined and proper, made their sympathies obvious.[26]

Contrary to expectations that the injunction would be quickly dismissed, the case dragged on for months, with postponement following postponement. First, Judge Stump, then Walter McGuinn, then the storeowner Aaron Samuelson became ill, each for several weeks. Then Judge Stump died, and the case was passed back to Judge Albert S. J. Owens, who had issued the injunction in the first place. Faced with postponement after postponement, popular interest began to wane, as the freedom movement became involved in other activities. W. A. C. Hughes, reflecting the boycott leadership's uneasiness, publicly complained about the postponements.[27]

Finally, on May 24, 1934, the judge rendered his decision. The main legal issue involved was whether the Buy Where You Can Work picketing was an economic dispute, like a workers' strike, and thus legal under the recently passed Norris-LaGuardia Act, or whether it was a racial dispute, which was not protected by law. The movement's lawyers claimed the former; the merchants' lawyers claimed the latter. In addition, the merchants' lawyers argued that the pickets had used force and intimidation; the movement's lawyers denied these charges. The judge agreed with the merchants and made the injunction permanent. He lectured the defendants before a courthouse packed with their supporters, calling them "colored persons of the highest types, well educated and essentially religious," and feigning astonishment that they "could have been misled into believing that any cause . . . could justify their action." He stated that the police should have arrested the pickets for disorderly conduct and asserted that they were guilty of "criminal conspiracy." In response to the judge's decision, the movement reignited.[28]

To build public support and raise money for an appeal, the Citizens' Committee held a series of three "monster mass meetings" during the month of June, with attendance in the thousands, where moderate pastors reportedly spoke out like raging militants. Organizers distributed hundreds of placards and thousands of handbills, and they coordinated an extensive fundraising and educational drive through a network that included community organizations ranging from the churches to the Lucky Strike Pleasure Club and Maxine's Whist Club. The reviving Urban League and the still stumbling NAACP branch joined the City-Wide Young People's Forum in making financial donations, and the NAACP voted to become a co-litigant with the Citizens' Committee. Juanita Jackson made an appeal directly to Walter White for support from the financially strapped national NAACP and received a pledge of $100 for every $400 raised locally. The boycott raised more than $1,500 in less than a month, a very large sum for the Depression-bound Black community.[29]

The evolution of the social base of the boycott movement, from its origins as a localized, largely spontaneous grouping of youth and churchgoers led by a charismatic individual to a broad, multigenerational movement embracing many sectors and organizations of the African American community, was complete. Indeed, the change went even further, for in the months following the injunction, Prophet Costonie became alienated from the rest of the leadership of the movement, and authority became concentrated in the Citizens' Committee presided over by Lillie Jackson. Shortly after the injunction was made permanent, Costonie disappeared from Baltimore.[30]

Tension between Costonie and the forces grouped around Lillie Jackson had grown for some time. Earlier concerns about "fake faith-healing" had joined concerns about Costonie's means of support, and some boycott leaders wanted to keep him away from the fundraising, fearing he would use the money for his own purposes. As early as January, the Young Negroes Progressive League, which had previously sponsored Costonie at meetings, held a forum to discuss "Is Prophet K. Costonie a False Messiah?" As the police patrolled outside, Costonie, who had been in hiding, made a surprise appearance at the forum and joined the debate on his leadership of the boycott movement. Some of the younger militants grew tired of what they considered his political theatrics. Clarence Mitchell wrote in his *Afro* column on July 7, 1934, that he had long thought Costonie "had something up his sleeve, and most of it was cheap melodrama which involved bodyguards and harrowing tales of threats the Prophet had received from various merchants. . . . He could tell his audiences how squad cars were following him, and that people were plotting against his life." Decades later, Juanita Jackson Mitchell recalled another dimension of the split with Costonie: "[He] and my mother matched up, except when he got to fooling around with the girls. . . . The real downfall of Costonie was when the preachers turned against him, because they had so many complaints about how fast and loose he was with young women, and the parents were complaining." To the surprise of the Forum's leadership, when Costonie left Baltimore, several Forum women, including the sister of one of the leaders, went with him.[31]

Finally, a key difference between Costonie and much of the boycott leadership was related to Costonie's Black nationalist outlook: he argued that the money being raised for the appeal could be better spent setting up Black businesses. He received little support for this idea, for even the Opportunity Makers Club, the organization that he had created, decided to donate its money to the appeal fund. Costonie, however, had defenders, as reflected in the letters column of the *Afro-American*. But among the community's leading intellectual and political figures, only Ralph Matthews of the *Afro* publicly defended him. After Costonie left town, Matthews lashed out at the ingratitude of the "old Baltimoreans" who, he felt, had allowed Costonie to take all the risks of building the movement, then took it over when it was successful and kicked the Prophet out.[32]

The mobilization for funds to appeal the permanent injunction was the last and broadest mass activity of the Buy Where You Can Work campaign in Baltimore. The attorneys for the Citizens' Committee filed the appeal, and the process continued for another year until, on April 10, 1935, the Court of Appeals affirmed the lower court's ruling and continued the injunction against picketing, although on a narrower legal basis. By this time, there was no money for further appeals, and the attention of the Baltimore movement had shifted elsewhere. Ralph Matthews, who bemoaned the treatment Costonie received before he left Baltimore, had warned nearly a year before in the *Afro-American* that the appeal would come to nothing and that the movement should have worked to continue the boycott by other means instead. But in fact, the boycott was carried on spontaneously to a considerable degree, and employment at many stores in northwestern Baltimore, especially the chain stores, had been substantially desegregated (see figure 21). The Forum's board, for example, sent a "letter of appreciation" in May 1934 to the local Brill Five and Ten Cents store for "help in relieving the unemployment situation by hiring colored sales girls." Nonetheless, there was considerable backsliding in the employment practices of the White-owned stores of the northwest during the late 1930s; activists had to launch another jobs boycott in 1941 to regain lost ground, which they successfully did under very different conditions.[33]

21. Earl Parker (*middle*) and Milton Robinson (*right*) were two of the Black youth who got jobs in White-owned stores as a result of the Buy Where You Can Work campaign. *Courtesy of the Afro-American Newspapers Archives and Research Center.*

As it turned out, the New Negro Alliance (NNA) of Washington, D.C., which was in frequent communication with the Forum, had mounted a jobs boycott of its own in 1933 and had also been served with an injunction. The NNA was able to pursue its appeal all the way to the U.S. Supreme Court under the direction of Charles Houston, by then the leading national attorney of the NAACP, and the NNA's lawyer, William Hastie. In 1938, the Supreme Court reversed the injunction, ruling that picketing in support of a consumer boycott was legal under the Norris–LaGuardia Act. Former participants in the Baltimore boycott movement celebrated this victory as their own.[34]

Thoughts about the Watershed Protests

By mid-1934, the wave of protests over George Armwood's murder and the Buy Where You Can Work campaign—the watershed struggles of the Baltimore freedom movement in the early 1930s—had receded, but the movement had been changed. These two struggles, with their sometimes divergent tendencies, reshaped the movement in ways that would do much to determine its future course. Together, the anti-lynching protests and the jobs boycott created probably the broadest coalition of Black community forces ever achieved in the region, and mobilizing large numbers of people in the process. Moreover, the jobs boycott, with its mass picket lines and its use of confrontation, made direct mass action a key part of the revitalized freedom movement's arsenal. While the Communists had employed direct action during the early 1930s, by 1934 the new freedom movement came to fully embrace this tactic as its own and, in so doing, took another step toward re-defining itself as a true mass movement. In addition, the anti-lynching protests in Baltimore made the horrific practice of Jim Crow lynching, a long-term grievance of African Americans in Maryland, a central focus of the new movement; lynching and racist violence—including police brutality— against Blacks would remain so throughout the 1930s into the 1940s. The jobs boycott challenged Jim Crow around another traditional grievance, the color bar in employment, and it did so in direct relationship to the needs of young Blacks for jobs in the midst of the Depression. In the aftermath of the Buy Where You Can Work campaign, the question of the racial division of labor became increasingly important to the Black freedom movement during the rest of the 1930s, and a major movement-wide preoccupation with the onset of the Second World War.[35]

Studies of the jobs boycotts across the country in the 1930s have raised the question of the movement's class character, often arguing that these were middle-class or petty bourgeois movements in their aims, leadership, and, to a large extent, social base. As Gunnar Myrdal, who examined the boy-cott movements for his seminal *An American Dilemma*, asserted, "It runs on a petty middle class racial basis." According to August Meier and Elliot Rudwick, the boycotts were "imbued with a petit-bourgeois Black business philosophy." In fact, to this day, the Black freedom movement of the 1930s and 1940s across the United States, except for the "labor-based civil rights movement" that emerged in the industrial union movement during the late Depression and Second World War years, has been seen as middle class. The problem with this analysis is that it is far too simplistic, at least as far as Balti-more is concerned. It is true that both the youthful and older adult leader-ships of the two watershed campaigns of 1933–34 were largely drawn from the educated, professional, and small-property-owning strata of the community, although it is likely that a significant portion of the activist youth came from families that contained at least some wage-workers. It is not true, though, that there was anything intrinsically petty bourgeois about the main goals and outlooks of these two campaigns. The jobs campaign may have been demanding "white collar" employment for Black youth, but the jobs sought were in reality thoroughly working-class, service-sector positions. Moreover, while some movement leaders, especially Prophet Costonie and occasion-ally Carl Murphy of the *Afro*, linked the jobs boycott to the need to build Black-owned businesses, participants more commonly saw the campaign as an attack on racism in the labor market and on the indignities that Black customers, many of them working class, suffered at the hands of White clerks in their own neighborhoods. Likewise, it is hard to see how the anti-lynching campaign was especially petty bourgeois or served particularly middle-class Black interests. The victims of lynching were drawn from all strata of the African American community, but they tended to come disproportionately from the working poor, as George Armwood and Matthew Williams did. Moreover, racialized lynching aimed to terrorize the whole community, not just its more elite strata. Finally, given the extent of the mass mobilizations of both campaigns, it is likely that the majority of the active participants were working-class African Americans fighting for what they rightly saw as their own interests. Describing these campaigns as running "on a petty middle class racial basis" is neither accurate nor helpful.[36]

Previously, when discussing the class character of the traditional Baltimore freedom movement, I argued that it was composed of a social bloc made up of sections of the upper working class, the petty bourgeoisie, and the bourgeoisie of the Black community; while this social bloc attempted to speak for the community as a whole, it was dominated by the middle class, with little participation from working-class elements. Later, when discussing the Forum in 1932 and early 1933, I argued that as the organization drew more and more of the community into its sphere and its activities, it came to represent a real, if incipient, alliance between the working class and petty bourgeoisie. The two watershed struggles of late 1933 and early 1934 deepened this process of alliance. In the wake of these struggles, the Baltimore freedom movement constituted a social bloc that, while continuing to have mainly middle-class leadership, had developed a greatly enhanced and more fully participatory working-class constituency, pursuing cross-class (and sometimes specifically working-class) demands.

While the anti-lynching and jobs campaigns were similar in class character, they differed somewhat in their racial/ethnic makeup and orientation. The anti-lynching protests brought a significant number of social liberal and radical Whites into active alliance with the freedom movement for the first time in many years and produced a promising interracial united front organization, the Maryland Anti-Lynching Federation. The Buy Where You Can Work campaign, by contrast, was an almost entirely African American affair that gained few White allies, even in its second, mass action phase. The exception to this was the rather modest support offered by the interracial Baltimore Communist Party, which, reflecting the concerns of the national party, feared that such jobs boycotts might divide Black and White workers. When Bernard Ades spoke at a mass rally during the Pennsylvania Avenue boycott, he offered solidarity and support to the boycotters but also asked that the White workers in the Pennsylvania Avenue stores not be antagonized; he proposed that the boycotters fight for shorter hours at full pay for all workers in the stores, thereby opening jobs for Black clerks without firing any White clerks. The *Afro-American* reported, "Although the audience applauded, many murmurs could be heard against his proposal."[37]

Apart from the Communist Party, only the Socialist Party leadership of the interracial PUL offered assistance to the Buy Where You Can Work campaign, and it only did so very late in the game. After Judge Owens made the picketing injunction permanent on May 24, 1934, the PUL, which had been working with the Forum for some months in the Maryland Anti-Lynching Federation, passed a strong resolution in support of the boycott movement. Submitted by Frank Trager and published in the *Afro*, the resolution contained scathing criticism of the permanent injunction and urged that the judge's decision be appealed in the name of both the boycott movement and the working-class movement. The resolution introduced a strong sense of class into the jobs boycott by declaring, "There is nothing new in the sustaining of injunctions which deprive workers, *who are also consumers*, of their civil and legal right to picket and boycott." In addition, the Eleventh Ward Socialist Club, meeting at Elisabeth Gilman's house, resolved to support the appeal and made a modest donation to the effort. Since the ban on picketing in disputes other than strikes by employees restricted the PUL's own tactical options in its unemployment work, the league mounted a picket line on August 22 at the offices of the Baltimore Emergency Relief Commission as a test case. With *Afro-American* reporters looking on, twenty PUL pickets, six of whom were African American women, were arrested. The White leader of the demonstration was the Socialist Adelaide Mitchell, whose husband was Broadus Mitchell. The grand jury refused to indict the pickets; the PUL kept picketing; and the police decided to look the other way.[38]

The only other known example of significant White support for the boycott campaign was by an unnamed White philanthropist, probably A. E. O. Munsell, a well-known backer of liberal causes, who matched every $1.50 raised by the anti-injunction campaign with a dollar of his own. All in all, the contrast between White progressive support for the anti-lynching protests and the relative dearth of such support for the jobs boycott is revealing. It most likely stemmed from White social liberal misgivings over African American direct action, which may have been perceived as anti-White. Also, it is possible that some of the White storeowners traveled in circles close to those of some of the social liberals. The boycott crossed a line uncomfortably close to home.[39]

So what happened to Kiowa Costonie, and what was his legacy? It appears that, as his charismatic mixture of post-Garveyite Black nationalism and Christian spiritualism lost resonance in Baltimore and as support for his leadership eroded, he left in search of greener ideological fields. The greener fields he found led him deeper and deeper into the spiritualist wing of post-Garvey Black nationalism. In 1935, the *Afro* described Costonie as the "youthful invader of Father Devine's Brooklyn territory" and as an organizer of a group called the League of the Darker Races of the World. Also in 1935, according to his daughter, Toni Costonie, he petitioned the U.S. government to create a separate state for African Americans: "His idea was that if we were not wanted here or in Africa, then give us our own land and let us be." Kiowa Costonie later relocated to Harlem and established the Interdenominational Temple, which had "a food pantry [and] free legal and medical clinics." He also counseled women on romance and marriage, as he had done in Baltimore, and in 1945 he published the book *How to Win and Hold a Husband*. He left New York in 1950, and his daughter writes that from 1950 to 1959, "He was an itinerant faith healing preacher who traveled from coast-to-coast spreading his message of self-determination, entrepreneurship, and wholesome living. He was vehemently opposed to integration, he believed that it would be the demise of African-American entrepreneurs. In 1959 he moved us to Chicago where he worked exclusively as a renowned faith healer and entrepreneur until his death in 1971." It seems that the Prophet Costonie continued to pursue many of the same nationalistic-spiritualistic interests that he was developing in Baltimore for the rest of his life. However, Costonie's nationalist legacy in Baltimore was in this regard weak. After he left in 1934, explicit, culturally oriented Black nationalism largely disappeared as a social force in the city until the post–Second World War period. This is not to argue that integrationism in some simple sense emerged victorious in mid-1934. There was an old tradition in the Baltimore freedom movement that put the African American community and its interests first, no matter how much erstwhile White allies objected. If Costonie did in fact leave a legacy, perhaps it was in successfully reactivating that old tradition.[40]

Another tension that was exposed during the watershed campaigns of 1933–34—one that would reappear through the 1930s and 1940s—was the antipathy between some African Americans and some Jews. As we have seen, during the anti-lynching campaign, some of the moderate Black preachers rejected Bernard Ades's participation in protest meetings because he was Jewish. In the Pennsylvania Avenue phase of the boycott movement, anti-Jewish sentiment was even more visible because the great majority of the White storeowners in the Black community of northwestern Baltimore were Jews. In the stories, columns, and editorials of the *Afro-American*, the storeowners on Pennsylvania Avenue were frequently identified as Jews or "Hebrews" rather than as Whites (one columnist even wrote of "Jooish" merchants). After the Northwest Businessmen's Association stopped the mass picketing with their injunction, a wave of anti-Jewish feeling broke out in the movement. Subsequently, when the hearing on the temporary injunction was postponed until after Passover by a Jewish judge, anti-Jewish remarks were again heard in the movement.[41]

The issue here is complicated. In some cases, statements identifying Jews were simply descriptive, referring more or less neutrally to the ethnicity of those concerned. In other cases, there was a strong sense that being Jewish was related to discriminatory behavior against Blacks. Of course, Jews, like other Whites, did practice discrimination against Blacks. Henry Louis Gates has written that the anti-Jewish sentiment "common among African-American communities in the 1930s and 1940s . . . followed in many ways a familiar pattern of clientelistic hostility toward the neighborhood vendor or landlord." That certainly was true in Baltimore, but there was still more to it. In the Ades case or in the reaction to the postponed hearing, the hostility was expressed toward Jews as part of an "alien" group, hostility with strong overtones of classical Christian anti-Semitism. But whatever the combination of factors behind it, the anti-Jewish sentiments that appeared during the jobs boycott would reappear again in the new freedom movement in the near future.[42]

A word should also be said here about the contrasting gender relations and gender politics revealed in the anti-lynching and boycott campaigns. While many women were active in the anti-lynching movement, the movement's leadership was overwhelmingly male. By contrast, a list of Citizens' Committee members in early December 1933 indicates that 25 percent of the membership of that body was female, and that of the twenty-six individuals specifically named in the injunction against picketing, eighteen were women. Then, as Costonie's power ebbed in early 1934, he was displaced as the top leader by the mother-and-daughter team of Lillie and Juanita Jackson. The prominence of women in the leadership of the boycott may have been partly due to the role played by the Housewives League after it joined, but mostly it was due to the influence of the City-Wide Young People's Forum, with its large contingent of female leaders. Whereas Costonie was training eighty men for jobs, the Forum, according to Juanita Jackson Mitchell, was demanding jobs for "*salesgirls*." In addition, Costonie's "womanizing" was as much an affront to the gender-consciousness of the female leaders as it was to their religious morality. To repeat Juanita Jackson Mitchell's observation, "The women got him run out of Baltimore."[43]

Finally, the anti-lynching protests and the jobs boycott intensified the frustration of the national NAACP leadership and of activists in Baltimore with the moribund state of the city's NAACP branch. During these protests, Walter White, executive director of the NAACP, began to correspond with Juanita Jackson of the Forum about resuscitating the Baltimore branch. On December 7, one day before the beginning of the picketing on Pennsylvania Avenue, the "NAACP Boosters," as Jackson and her circle chose to call themselves, met and signed up sixty-seven new NAACP members, including many Forum activists, adult advisers of the Forum, and activists from the boycott movement—including Prophet Costonie. Although the effort to reactivate the branch failed in the short term, the relationship of the Forum leadership circle with the NAACP national office continued to develop through 1934, and the rebuilding of Baltimore's NAACP branch became a top priority of both.[44]

7

The Baltimore Soviet, the ACW,
and the PUL, 1933–1935

We laid it down on them how important it is that this ship has to be struck
in Baltimore. . . . The reason why we should strike in Baltimore is because
there the Marine Workers Industrial Union was in charge of relief and
housing, and they had a strong branch—stronger than anywhere else
in the United States. They called it the Baltimore Soviet.
—BILL BAILEY, former Communist seaman

As with the African American freedom movement, the workers' movement
in the Baltimore metropolitan region showed definite signs of revival from
late 1933 through 1935. During this period, the working-class struggle grew
broadly, if fitfully, across the region, and while the unemployed movement
led by the People's Unemployment League (PUL) remained strong, the locus
of the workers' struggle began shifting decisively from the neighborhood
back to the workplace.

Nationally, the early or "first" New Deal period, which extended from
the passage of FDR's emergency legislation in mid-1933 to the series of U.S.
Supreme Court decisions beginning in mid-1935 that nullified much of this
legislation, was a time of escalating workplace mobilization. The legislation
of the first New Deal, which gave workers hope that the Depression would
soon end, and the belief that they had the legal right to organize, helped to
unleash a wave of strikes and industrial union activity. The wave grew mod-
erately at first, then rapidly, spreading into many sectors of the economy and
peaking in mid- and late 1934 with the monumental "eruptions" of the Auto-
Lite workers in Toledo, the Teamsters in Minneapolis, the longshoremen in
San Francisco and along the Pacific coast, and the cotton-textile workers in
the eastern United States.[1]

The first New Deal industrial organizing wave occurred in the Baltimore
metropolitan region as well, and was indicated in the strike statistics. Ac-

cording to the monthly reports of the Baltimore Labor Relations Panel, the number of reported strikes between late 1933 and September 1934 rose 60 percent over the previous year. Between 1934 and 1935, the number of workdays absorbed by strikes in Baltimore grew by 91 percent, and the average numbers of strikers per strike increased from 144 in 1934 to 300 in 1935, suggesting that more and larger, industrial concerns were involved. In 1935, Baltimore ranked third among the ten largest cities in the country in the number of strikes.[2]

The changes that occurred between late 1933 and mid-1935 in the Baltimore workers' movement can be symbolized by two large, public events that bracketed the period. The first was a parade in August 1933 that officially kicked off the National Recovery Administration (NRA) and the New Deal in Baltimore. The purpose of the parade was to build popular support for the NRA and to begin the drive to get businesses to sign a Blue Eagle pledge to abide by NRA codes, including the labor codes. Although initiated by government and establishment forces, the planning for the parade and the ensuing NRA campaign enlisted the leadership of popular organizations and institutions throughout the city. Organized labor played an important role, and Henry Broening, president of the Baltimore Federation of Labor (BFL), was a member of the Baltimore City NRA Steering Committee. The parade involved participants from many sectors of the population, especially from the working class. Twenty bands and 7,000 marchers wound their way from Mount Royal Avenue in north-central Baltimore past City Hall as an estimated 250,000 Baltimoreans watched and cheered.[3]

If the NRA parade in 1933 revealed White Baltimore's initial optimism over the New Deal, preparations for the event also revealed the optimism in the Black community over the possible benefits of FDR's programs. African American leaders saw the NRA parade as a means by which to participate in and influence the New Deal in Maryland. Carl Murphy of the *Afro-American* accepted an appointment to head the Colored Division of the state's NRA organization, and Howard H. Murphy of the Negro Business League (who was also a member of the *Afro*'s Murphy clan) joined the Baltimore City NRA Steering Committee. Under the Murphys, many notables and organizations from Black Baltimore were drawn into NRA support work. Howard Murphy used his position on the steering committee to publicly advocate for Black community interests, arguing, for example, for a wages and hours standard for the domestic service workers the New Deal had ignored. He also held a special conference with his fellow committee member Henry Broening of the BFL on the question of opening all of the unions affiliated with the federation to African American workers; the *Afro* remarked that "this question is bound to become one of importance as the [NRA] program proceeds." As the date of the NRA parade approached, the organized contingent of 400 Black marchers received the news that it was to be placed, Jim Crow-style, at the very end of the parade. The Colored Division lodged a strong protest, asking that the contingent be moved to the middle of the march. NRA officials then decided to place one truck behind the Black marchers. Angrily, the Murphys announced that the African American unit was withdrawing from the parade. Coming on the eve of the Buy Where You Can Work campaign and the anti-lynching mobilization, the disastrous experience with the NRA parade strengthened the feeling of many African American people in Baltimore—like that of many Black people around the country—that the New Deal might be a "raw deal" for them and that "NRA" might stand for "Negro Run Around." The prospects of working cooperatively with established White labor, which gave no evident support to the Colored Division in its dispute over the NRA parade, must have seemed dim.[4]

The second event was quite different. On May 29, 1935, some twenty-one months after the NRA parade and in the immediate aftermath of the Supreme Court's decision nullifying the NRA, the Baltimore labor movement protested with a massive demonstration. A reported 10,000 workers, including many members of the ACW and the ILGWU who walked off their jobs, marched through the city in what the *Maryland Leader* headlined "The Greatest Turnout of Organized Labor in the History of Baltimore." Some 4,000 labor unionists and unemployed workers packed the Lyric Theater, with the remainder spilling into the street, and listened to Congressman Vito Marcantonio of New York and Joseph McCurdy, head of the BFL, denounce the Supreme Court's ruling. The assembled body passed a series of militant resolutions offered by Frank Trager of the PUL and others, then joined together in singing "The Star-Spangled Banner," "Solidarity Forever," and "The Internationale" to the accompaniment of a marching band. For many in the working class, the hope of 1933 had turned into the fury of 1935.[5]

Between the NRA parade of 1933 and the demonstrations against the Supreme Court's rulings in 1935, the workers' movement had burgeoned in Baltimore, and the antiracist struggle both within this movement and within the neighborhoods of the region had greatly advanced.

The Harbor and the Baltimore Soviet

In each industrial region across the country, the first New Deal wave broke out in forms that reflected the local socioeconomic context, character of the working class, and history of the class struggle. Particular sectors of the working class took the lead in particular places, giving the emerging union movement distinctive regional characteristics. In Detroit, for example, auto-workers dominated the organizing wave, and the ensuing regional labor movement was made much in their image, while in Pittsburgh, miners and steelworkers took the lead in fundamentally shaping the movement. In Baltimore, with its broad, diversified industrial economy and its large port, no one or two sectors of the class strongly predominated; however, for historical reasons, the seamen and the garment workers emerged as the leading centers of the upsurge.

In late 1933, the struggle in Baltimore harbor, led by the seamen of the Marine Workers Industrial Union (MWIU), an organization initiated by Communists, expanded dramatically. In December, *Marine Workers Voice*, the monthly newspaper of the MWIU, announced that more ships had been struck in the previous month than in the previous decade. Nationally, the MWIU was concentrating its energy on organizing the weak shipping companies before proceeding to the strong ones, and the Munson Line was the current target. According to the former seaman Bill Bailey, Munson crews were frequently not paid for months, and onboard conditions were the most demeaning in the shipping industry: "Occasionally the engineer would leave his work clothes outside your room, and it was intended that you were supposed to wash them on your time off." The Baltimore MWIU went after the Munson line with a vengeance. Starting in October 1933, the union struck a series of Munson ships, including the *Munorleans*, the *Munloyal*, the *Munindies*, and the *Munlisto*. By December, five Munson ships in Baltimore harbor had been forced to pay back wages to their crews, sign articles guaranteeing improved conditions, and promise not to fire strikers. According to *Marine Workers Voice*, "Baltimore is becoming known as the pay-off port for Munson ships." The only weakness the Baltimore MWIU saw in its Munson campaign was that it frequently was unable to persuade Munson crews to stay with the ship and fight for further gains; crewmen often wanted to get the money owed them and get off.[6]

As the Munson Line campaign proceeded, the Baltimore MWIU and the affiliated Waterfront Unemployed Council (WUC) were also agitating and organizing for seamen's unemployment and relief. Meetings on these and other issues were frequently held on the waterfront, often at the MWIU union hall. (Bailey recalled that Baltimore "had a beautiful hall, a big storefront hall that held maybe a hundred guys.") By the end of the year, the MWIU and the WUC—probably the only organizationally stable Unemployed Council in Baltimore—had established a serious presence in both the workplaces and the neighborhoods of the harbor district. Hence, these organizations were well positioned when the New Deal took over local seamen's relief from the private charities, precipitating one of the most remarkable struggles of the first New Deal period. At the end of 1933, the New Deal's Federal Emergency Relief Administration (FERA), working with the Maryland Transient Bureau, began to send federal relief to unemployed seamen in Baltimore. The Transit Bureau and FERA planned to rent the Anchorage, a seamen's center and boardinghouse run by the YMCA, and to hire Anchorage personnel to manage the distribution of federal relief funds. When it was made public that the "Holy Racket," as the seamen referred to the unpopular Anchorage, was to administer the new relief effort, the seamen rebelled. The MWIU and the WUC immediately advanced another plan, proposing that an elected committee of seamen administer federal relief. A series of packed meetings took place on the waterfront in support of the MWIU-WUC plan. A petition circulated among the seamen, and many signed; local small merchants signed, too, because Anchorage officials had frequently demanded payoffs from storekeepers and boardinghouse owners for any business that the officials sent their way.[7]

In early January 1934, the MWIU and the WUC called an open hearing on the federal relief situation, but none of the invited relief officials showed up. A delegation was then chosen to take the seamen's demands directly to the Anchorage officials and to relief officials in Washington. The Anchorage officials refused to consider the demands, so after another mass meeting, the delegation headed for the FERA offices in Washington. Concurrently, the seamen residing in the Anchorage struck against the new rules imposed by the management and then insisted that the officials continue to serve them meals while they were on strike. The threat of police action grew.[8]

When the delegates returned from Washington, they reported that progress had been made during the conference with FERA and that another conference, with both federal and local relief officials, was scheduled for the next day in Baltimore. During the second conference, federal relief officials, to the surprise of many, agreed to most of the seamen's demands, including improved relief benefits, three meals a day, clean bedding, clean clothes, clean quarters, and paid cooks and maintenance personnel. They also guaranteed free speech, unrestricted distribution of literature, and the right of assembly on all federal relief premises. Amazingly, they also agreed to a committee elected by the seamen to administer the federal relief funds themselves. In effect, the Anchorage management had been fired, and the Holy Racket was out. Ecstatic local seamen met en masse the next morning to elect their committee, officially named the Seamen's Subcommittee. The police were removed, and shortly thereafter, the YMCA officials withdrew. Through a campaign that actively involved, by one estimate, more than 1,000 participants, the Baltimore seamen's movement had won an unprecedented victory.[9]

As impressive as the mass mobilization was, the victory was also the result of the movement's ability to maneuver in special circumstances. Like other New Deal agencies, FERA had to implement its programs very quickly and looked initially to traditional charity-based relief institutions, such as the YMCA Anchorage, to administer relief. The FERA officials undoubtedly knew, though, that the local charity officials were often inefficient, corrupt, and opposed to the New Deal. With chaos threatening on the Baltimore waterfront, with the YMCA officials unable to handle the situation, and with the whole relief operation thereby imperiled, FERA officials may have seen the subcommittee's offer as the best available option. Progressives within the FERA bureaucracy may secretly have liked the idea of democratic control of relief funds; however, their immediate concern was to distribute relief competently. It turned out that FERA made the right decision. Three months later, after an investigation by its own examiner, FERA gave the subcommittee high marks for efficiency, effectiveness, and honesty in managing waterfront relief in Baltimore. Surprisingly, FERA officials were initially unconcerned about the possibility that they might have been dealing with radicals or Communists on the subcommittee. A FERA participant in the Washington meeting with the Baltimore seamen's delegation in January later reported, "While their terminology and temper were obviously radical, no information was requested or volunteered regarding their political or trade-union affiliations."[10]

As the subcommittee consolidated its control over seamen's relief, the MWIU escalated its organizing campaign, focusing once again on the ships of the Munson Line, and also on Bethlehem Steel's notorious Ore Steamship Company. Unemployed seamen supported the campaign by participating on picket lines and refusing to scab, and the subcommittee made relief readily available to striking seamen. *Marine Workers Voice* observed that workers on board ships increasingly "hold back strikes till they get to Baltimore, because they know they will have shore support in that port," which, in fact, was the intent of the MWIU and the subcommittee. By April, the MWIU was claiming that the Munson Line was "100% organized with ship's committees on all ships," and, as Bailey later wrote, "Conditions on the fifteen Ore ships improved tremendously." All told, the MWIU claimed fifty strikes in Baltimore's harbors in fewer than two months—a maritime strike wave in one port (see figure 22). In addition to taking charge of relief and unleashing a strike wave, the MWIU-led movement successfully forced the shipping companies to accept an employment system, referred to as the Centralized Shipping Bureau (CSB), that rotated work equally among seamen thereby bypassing the hated

22. The MWIU and Baltimore Soviet activist Bill Bailey (*right*) photo-
graphed with two other seamen during a waterfront strike in 1936.
Courtesy of Lynn Damme, Larkspring Productions.

crimps and corrupt private shipping agents. As with the relief system, a body
of elected seamen, the United Front Shipping Committee, ran the CSB, winning in Baltimore a demand that had been an important objective of casual
maritime workers nationwide. Taken together, the victories of the seamen
during the first months of 1934—management of hiring and of relief distribution by elected committees—amounted to a remarkable degree of worker
control over the country's third largest port. It was something unique in U.S.
maritime history, and the radicals and seamen in Baltimore called the whole
experience (a bit romantically) the "Baltimore Soviet."[11]

True to the Communist Party's Third Period line, the MWIU attempted to
make anti-racism integral to the life of the Soviet, as it had to its earlier union
organizing. The sociologist and National Urban League leader Ira De A. Reid
wrote that in mid-1934 "about one-fourth" of the Baltimore MWIU local's

"500 members are colored." The leadership bodies and committees of the union, the Unemployed Council, and the Seamen's Subcommittee were all integrated, and workers from all racial/ethnic backgrounds reportedly had the same access to benefits, to decision-making processes, to living facilities including sleeping and dining quarters and even to the barber shop. Furthermore, the MWIU and the CSB opposed both racially discriminatory hiring practices and the segregated division of labor, forcing shippers to accept integrated crews and to distribute work equally to White and Black seamen. Finally, to strengthen racial-ethnic solidarity and to build class-consciousness, the MWIU carried out antiracist political education and encouraged seamen to participate in interracial activities elsewhere in the city.[12]

White seamen largely accepted the Soviet's challenge to Jim Crow, although there were exceptions. A distressed member of the International Seamen's Union (ISU) wrote to the federal government to complain that "there were signs about the 'Scottsboro martyrs' and pleas for racial equality" all over the relief facilities in Baltimore. He also objected to the fact that Black seamen felt comfortable expressing their own opinions: "One 'fellow worker' a darky . . . should have been flogged [for referring to President Roosevelt as] 'Rosie.'" Another White seaman wrote to complain about integrated crews. Not surprisingly, the shipping companies, the Baltimore Association of Commerce, the city government, the ISU, and even the BFL mixed racism with anticommunism in their attempts to divide the seamen from the MWIU, but with little initial success.[13]

The MWIU had always aspired to organize all maritime workers, not just seamen, and, from its earliest days in Baltimore, it had attempted to build a base among longshoremen, especially among the African American longshoremen majority. However, most of Baltimore's longshoremen, White and Black, remained loyal to the International Longshoremen's Association (ILA). Even if the ILA was compromised by White supremacy, African American workers—and especially their leaders—had a lot to lose by forsaking the ILA, particularly Local 858, a union they had created and now dominated, for a fledgling, Communist-led revolutionary union, however antiracist that union might be. Moreover, many Black ILA members no doubt were wary of the MWIU's revolutionary industrial unionism, as were many White workers. Hence, despite the MWIU's efforts, most Black longshoremen generally kept their distance, although in late 1933, as the MWIU's influence on the waterfront grew, a few Black ILA longshoremen spontaneously supported MWIU actions. Then, on the eve of the Baltimore Soviet, ILA longshoremen and MWIU seamen united and won two strikes against the shipping companies, with lower-level ILA leaders joining, not opposing, the struggles. They formed joint ILA-MWIU strike committees and mounted joint picket lines; during the second strike, the MWIU borrowed a launch from local ILA leaders for water picketing, and the ILA requested legal-defense assistance from the CP International Labor Defense.[14]

The national MWIU heralded these successes in *Marine Workers Voice* and called for similar efforts everywhere to build the "united front from below." An editorial titled "United Front Wins" pointed to these coalitions and proclaimed: "This shows that while difference exist[s] in the programs of various organizations, it is possible for workers[,] regardless of their affiliation, to act jointly." Still suspicious that the ILA leadership had joined the united front in the Baltimore struggle "to disrupt and betray it," the MWIU nevertheless used the struggle as an example to promote coalitions nationally with more conservative union forces. The collaboration between the Baltimore MWIU and the ILA longshoremen, and the national MWIU's enthusiastic response to it, was clearly a step away from the more sectarian aspects of the Third Period line and toward the emerging Popular Front strategy that historians have noted in CP-led organizations as early as 1933.[15]

To build support among longshoremen, the MWIU encouraged the formation of a "Central Shapeup, run by the elected committees of longshoremen, on a strict rotary basis," similar to the seamen's CSB, but to no avail. However, solidarity actions between MWIU seamen and ILA longshoremen continued, and the MWIU developed a small base among some unorganized Black longshoremen. The Baltimore CP itself attracted a small but important following among African American longshoremen, who were frequent, energetic participants in activities sponsored by the party around the city. And in 1934, two African American maritime workers appeared on the CP's election ticket: the longshoreman Samuel Gates ran for the U.S. Senate, and the seaman Bruce Parker ran for clerk of the Court of Appeals; the *Afro-American* endorsed them both. But the hoped-for radical interracial alliance between seamen and longshoremen did not progress any further during the Soviet.[16]

Ultimately, the government, corporate, and craft union forces opposing the Baltimore seamen's movement regrouped and worked with increasing diligence to undermine the Soviet, often by means of police and goon violence. Under pressure, FERA reneged on its earlier agreement to allow the Seamen's Subcommittee to distribute unemployed relief, and shippers increasingly rebuffed the CSB. Because of the spatial segmentation, craft unionist mentality, and anticommunism of the region's working class, the emerging workers' movement elsewhere in the region provided the Soviet with little support. Most strikingly, the PUL, which was growing rapidly and organizing aggressively during the period of the Baltimore Soviet—and which seemed so similar to the seamen's movement in its interracialism, industrial union-ism, and radical leadership—never, as far as can be determined, worked with or extended support to the Soviet. Then from early May, the West Coast dock strike, which culminated in the general strike in San Francisco in July, eclipsed the Baltimore Soviet nationally and diverted the attention of the nation-wide maritime workers' movement away from Baltimore. During the summer of 1934, the seamen's unity weakened, and the Baltimore Soviet de-clined, then collapsed.[17]

Nonetheless, the MWIU continued its agitation in the city's harbor areas, with a few successes. For a brief moment in late October 1934, a surprising united front strike of all seamen, regardless of union affiliation, appeared to be possible on the Atlantic and Gulf coasts. But the MWIU's rival, the ISU, pulled out, and made a separate peace with the shippers. The MWIU struck the coasts anyway, and the seamen in Baltimore walked out, but the strike failed to gain sufficient momentum. In addition, the MWIU continued to par-ticipate in actions with the largely Black longshoremen concentrated on the Pratt Street docks. The struggle around relief continued, as the seamen main-tained their resistance to the forced work requirements, until mid-1935, when the federal government phased out its transient relief program.[18]

In the meantime, the international Communist movement was involved in a programmatic re-evaluation that ended up later that year with a shift from the sometimes ultra-revolutionary Third Period line to the more mod-erate United Front against Fascism, or Popular Front line. During this re-evaluation, the CP abandoned dual unionism and in February 1935 abolished the MWIU, despite the objections of much of its rank-and-file. Former MWIU members joined the ISU to transform it from within, and by mid-1935, they had established a fledgling ISU rank-and-file movement in the port of Balti-more. When Charles Rubin, a veteran of the MWIU, arrived in Baltimore in 1935 to take over the editorship of the local rank-and-file newspaper, the ISU *Pilot*, the repression against the dissident movement was heavy. However, in a short period he and his comrades rallied Baltimore seamen to challenge the refusal of the ISU's leadership to support a strike by the American Radio Telegraphists Association on the West Coast. According to Rubin, when a top ISU leader known as the "Crown Prince" moved to expel Rubin as a dual-unionist, a body of rank-and-filers invaded the trial committee meeting and forced the Crown Prince to withdraw his charges.[19]

During 1935, there was only sporadic activity in the harbor: a tugboat and barge strike in February that tied up the whole port for a few days; a ships radio operators' strike later the same month; a scattering of job actions throughout the rest of the year. But there was nothing to match the struggles of the year before. Eventually, the ISU rank-and-file movement led to the founding of the National Maritime Union (NMU), the lineal descendant of the MWIU, which became a cornerstone of the industrial union movement in the Baltimore region during the late 1930s. Through the NMU, the MWIU bequeathed to the industrial unions of Baltimore a tradition of militant, socially conscious, and—this would become crucial as the decade preceded— aggressively *interracial* industrial unionism. From a broader historical point of view, though, the Baltimore MWIU, the Seamen's Subcommittee, and the CSB were important examples of short-lived, innovative forms of struggle that experimented with multicultural workers' control and that indicated some of the possibilities of what working-class democracy might achieve.[20]

The Garment Unions during the Early New Deal

Throughout the first New Deal period, the Amalgamated Clothing Workers (ACW) maintained the momentum it achieved with its general strike in 1932 in the men's garment industry in Baltimore, continuing, along with the seamen, to shape the region's new industrial unionism in the process. The ACW intervened to shape the NRA codes for the men's garment industry as they were being written, then fought a series of battles to ensure that the codes were implemented. On July 7, 1933, for example, the ACW called a one-day strike of all of its members to demand that the NRA force code compliance on defiant manufacturers in the region. In addition, the ACW organized shop after shop (some more than once); called strikes when necessary to force recognition, restore wage cuts, or protest contract violations; and continued, without success, its assault on the anti-union bastion of the Greif clothing company. Following the lead of the national, the Baltimore ACW began targeting cotton-goods shops, which were largely unorganized, and began organizing in Baltimore's hinterlands in places such as Union Bridge, Maryland, fifty miles northeast of the city, and even in Alexandria, Virginia, where it chased down a runaway shop. After co-sponsoring the massive demonstration in Baltimore on May 29, 1935, protesting the Supreme Court's nullification of the NRA, the ACW fought to retain its NRA gains. In August 1935, it launched another industry-wide strike, involving 5,000 ACW workers in 160 factories (90% of the total) to enforce the thirty-six-hour week and the wage scale that had prevailed under the NRA and to establish a single agreement with the whole industry rather than on a shop-by-shop basis. The union succeeded in a few days. At this point, the Baltimore ACW claimed to represent 8,000 workers, 2,000 more than it had a year and a half before.[21]

The ILGWU, while smaller than the Baltimore ACW, also continued to develop as an effective model of industrial unionism during the early New Deal years. By 1936, it claimed nine locals in the women's clothing industry of the region. Like the ACW, the ILGWU organized and struck workplace after workplace and sent organizers into the hinterlands, including to the cotton-goods factories of the Eastern Shore. It mounted large actions, including a successful citywide strike in March 1935 to enforce the NRA garment codes. It won a ten-week strike against American Raincoat, one of the industry's most recalcitrant employers, employing both mass picketing and legal action. The ILGWU and the ACW also worked together, jointly shutting down twenty-five shops in the Baltimore cotton-goods industry in April 1934.[22]

The ACW and the ILGWU expanded their interracial organizing during the period, especially in the cotton-goods sector that contained more Black workers. Opportunities to organize Black garment workers were slowly growing as a few manufacturers began hiring African Americans in an effort to get around the NRA codes and pay lower wages; the unions opposed the attempt to pay Black workers less. The ACW continued its alliance with the Negro Labor Committee initiated by the Baltimore Urban League (BUL) and formed during the 1932 strike, organizing Black garment workers in highly segregated industries such as rag picking, as well as in more integrated workplaces. On occasion, White members resisted organizing African Americans, and the ACW Joint Board mounted educational efforts to change their minds. However, significant numbers of White ACW members supported interracialism. The English-language Local 70, known as the "American local," which was chartered with an all-female membership in the wake of the 1932 strike, was especially welcoming to Black workers.[23]

At the same time that the ACW and ILGWU became more active in interracial organizing, they also became more openly involved with the Socialist Party (SP). During the early New Deal years, publicly identified SP members and candidates frequently participated in picket lines and addressed meetings of both unions. In 1935, Norman Thomas, leader of the national SP, addressed 5,000 ACW members in Baltimore at their annual ball at the Lyric Auditorium, and in April 1935, Elisabeth Gilman opened her campaign as the SP's candidate for mayor of Baltimore by marching on a picket line with striking garment workers. In 1936, the SP, ILGWU, and ACW—along with the Cap and Millinery Workers, the Neckwear Makers, the Workmen's Circle, and the Jewish Socialist Verband—jointly sponsored a large May Day celebration. After the demise of the NRA, the Baltimore ACW and the ILGWU endorsed the sp's proposed workers' rights amendment to the U.S. Constitution, originally drafted by the Socialist Morris Hillquit in 1931; the amendment would have given the federal government the ultimate right to legislate on all matters of workers' rights, unrestricted by the question of states' rights.[24]

Therefore, despite differences between Baltimore's garment unions, on the one hand, and the MWIU, on the other, both were solidly industrial unionist; both were militant in their organizing; both were interracialist in approach; and both were led by socialist-oriented radicals (albeit of different types). Their successes in the first New Deal period constructed much of the framework within which the later explosion of industrial unionism would occur.

Beyond the Harbor and the Garment Industry

Apart from the waterfront and the garment factories, workplace struggles in the early New Deal years occurred in the large mass-production industries of Baltimore among the textile workers of Mount Vernon Mills, the steelworkers of Eastern Rolling Mills, the aircraft workers of General Aviation Manufacturing Company, the chemical workers of Davidson Company, and the workers in the meat-cutting industry. By early 1936, the Welders Union in the shipyards was beginning to organize, and management of both Crown, Cork, and Seal (the largest factory of its type in the world) and Bethlehem Steel at Sparrows Point were beefing up security in response to union "threats." In the smaller industries, workplace organizing and strikes took place among fur workers, boot and shoe workers, bakers, bookbinders, cigar makers, brewery workers, printers, painters, and furniture and upholstery workers. The building trades engaged in a number of actions, including an important strike of ironworkers and carpenters against non-union labor on a viaduct construction project. In the municipal sector, workers contracted to the city mounted a disruptive garbage strike, and a teachers' union emerged to protest inadequate funding of the schools. In the service sector, hotel and restaurant workers organized, as did bartenders, filling station attendants, cooks and waiters, motion picture operators, and newspaper reporters. Perhaps the widespread character of union activity in Baltimore during the first New Deal is best indicated by its reach into some of the least likely corners of the workforce. Members of an opera chorus, dental technicians, and the grooms and exercise boys at a racetrack all went on strike. Unlike most of the campaigns in the mass-production industries and the port, these small struggles often took place in a craft-union framework or in spontaneous or ambiguous forms, but they contributed breadth to the evolving union movement.[25]

In the transportation sector in September 1934, railroad, motormen, brakemen, and conductors, organized into the craft-unionist Railroad Brotherhoods and shut down the Washington, Baltimore, and Annapolis line for five days. But the most important mobilization of transportation workers occurred under the leadership of the International Brotherhood of Teamsters, Chauffeurs, and Stablemen of America—the Teamsters Union— whose struggles were the most militant of the BFL affiliates (the ILGWU excepted). The Teamsters Union mounted a series of large and small strikes, including one in mid-1934 against the three largest trucking companies in the region—a strike that lasted three weeks, threatened to shut down the whole Baltimore-based trucking industry, and brought the intervention of federal mediators. In a tumultuous strike that threatened to spread throughout the taxi industry, Teamster Union cab drivers struck the Diamond Cab Company in February 1935. Federal mediators brought in to quell the chaos imposed a settlement that left the drivers dissatisfied and led to subsequent job actions over the next few years. During these disputes, Harry Cohen, head of the Teamsters Union, emerged as a prominent militant leader in the region because of his willingness to confront the employers, the scabs, and the police, even at the risk of violence and arrest.[26]

The organizing activities and strikes in Baltimore of the early New Deal achieved uneven results. Some took place without sufficient organization or support, and they were crushed. Others took place within the framework of craft unionism, which often proved to be an inadequate framework for the new workplace rebellions. Some won gains for the workers involved, and some won nothing. And many took place without questioning or breaking with White supremacy. Others made a break, and African American workers were involved, often alongside Whites. In March 1934, the newly formed Hotel and Restaurant Employees Alliance No. 223 announced that "Negro cooks and waiters have . . . affiliated." Later that year, the predominantly White Moving Picture Operators Union claimed that all African American moving picture houses were organized, that the Black operators were a part of Local 181, and that all were "good union men." In addition, the Dental Technicians Association, which successfully organized its constituency that year, was integrated and, according to its organizer, was united in opposition to "race prejudice." In early 1935, at the founding meeting of the Tenth District of the Amalgamated Association of Iron, Steel, and Tin Workers (AAISTW), with four lodges in Baltimore and three in Pennsylvania, the delegates passed a resolution "against the practice of the steel trust of jim-crowism and discrimination." When, during a meeting, a local restaurant refused to serve one of the Black delegates, a "sharp protest was delivered to restaurant proprietor," and the entire AAISTW group went elsewhere. Perhaps most significant, the Teamsters Union's organizing campaign took an overtly integrationist approach. In a story about the truckers' strike of mid-1934, the *Maryland Leader* observed, "The spirit of the Negro workers in their loyalty to the union is gratifying. . . . [T]he Negro workers stand side by side with their White colleagues." Edward Lewis of the BUL later recalled that Cohen, who was Jewish, was a committed opponent of racism because of his own experiences with anti-Semitism.[27]

The wave of organizing during the early New Deal began to revitalize the nearly dormant BFL; by the end of 1935, an estimated 17 percent of the Baltimore labor force was in a BFL-affiliated union, up from 7–10 percent at the start of the decade. Of course, much of the new membership of the BFL essentially fell into its lap. The organizing gains of the industrial garment unions (the ACW, by the end of this period, had joined the federation) automatically became gains for the BFL. In addition, some workers essentially organized themselves, then asked for the federation's recognition. For example, in August 1935, one hundred women and girls struck National Wiping Cloth Company, then marched to BFL headquarters to ask to join. Still, times were changing, and the BFL organizing department—especially the organizer Anna Neary from the Bookbinders Union—was directly and effectively involved in a number of strikes and campaigns. The federation increasingly publicized the organizing efforts of member unions, called for solidarity with striking workers, promoted boycotts, supported labor legislation, and even created a solidarity committee for the labor victims of European fascism. Joseph McCurdy, president of the BFL, was the principal spokesperson for Baltimore labor and a member of the NRA Labor Board during these years, speaking at gigantic mass meetings such as the one after the Supreme Court's nullification of the NRA, as well as small events such as the celebration of the new charter for Dressmakers Local 106.[28]

As the BFL became more active, a part of the federation became friendlier to radicalism and interracialism. Whereas McCurdy and others from the BFL were happy to rail against Communists and workers led by the CP, as they did during the Baltimore Soviet, there was, according to Joel Seidman of the SP and PUL, "a growing cooperation between the PUL, the Baltimore Federation of Labor, and the SP, with party members exercising more and more influence in the ranks of the other two organizations." When the Amalgamated Meat Cutters and Butcher Workmen called 1,200 workers out in a general strike that shut down the meatpacking industry, the BFL dispatched Neary, and the SP sent Elisabeth Gilman and other well-known Socialists to help out. Likewise, when a local newspaper reporter was fired for union activity with the Newspaper Guild, the BFL and the SP both protested. Of course, a number of radicals had long worked within the BFL, and a few BFL leaders were socialists, including J. Fred Rausch, the well-known secretary of the BFL's influential Building Trades Council. Finally, BFL and SP officials, including SP candidates for office, frequently spoke from the same platforms; McCurdy and Broadus Mitchell, for instance, spoke together at a number of functions.[29]

Moreover, on several occasions the BFL worked programmatically with the SP. In early 1935, the SP, the BFL, and the railroad unions jointly presented draft labor legislation to the state legislature (and the SP added a few separate demands in its own addendum). Shortly thereafter, on the Socialists' initiative, the BFL officially opposed the pending adoption of "Maryland, My Maryland" as the state anthem because of its pro-Confederate imagery. The BFL also considered ratifying both the Socialist-backed "Hillquit" Workers' Rights Amendment and the SP's call for a labor party. While the BFL ultimately adopted neither (although the Printing Pressman's Union and the ILGWU did), McCurdy stated that he believed that a labor party would eventually emerge. Then, in March 1936, the BFL participated in a broad coalition, initiated by the SP and the PUL, that founded the Citizens' Alliance for Social Security for Maryland to fight attempts to levy a state sales tax and to deal with questions of relief. This coalition also included the Baltimore Urban League, the Association of Social Workers, and a number of social liberal ministers. As evidence that the Popular Front was fully functioning in this alliance, Albert Blumberg of the teachers' union, an emerging leader of the Baltimore section of the CP, was a vice-president of the alliance. But perhaps the most graphic display of the SP's influence in the BFL came in mid-1935 when, for three weeks running, the Socialist Naomi Riches presented lectures on labor history to the delegate meetings of the federation.[30]

In reality, though, the relationship between the Socialists and the BFL never really became intimate; this was a relationship of a different nature from that between the Socialists and the garment unions or the PUL. There were, in fact, definite political tensions between the SP and much of the BFL leadership, including its president. Speaking at a mass PUL meeting in early 1934, Broadus Mitchell supported the call by the BFL's President McCurdy to organize the unorganized but went on to wonder how far the BFL and its parent organization, the AFL, would actually implement the call. The BFL and AFL, Mitchell noted, "have been at it a long time and they have only organized a fraction of the American working class. They have been aristocratic. They have been unsympathetic with the problems of common labor. They have done little to organize women, to organize Negroes." Still, because of the BFL's greater openness to radicalism during the early New Deal upsurge, Mitchell and the Socialists continued to work with the federation for more than two years after this criticism was made. Eventually, in 1936, under the impact of national developments, disagreements over the points Mitchell raised tore the BFL in two and alienated most who remained in the federation from radicalism.[31]

The PUL and the Union Revival

The PUL consolidated as an organization as the organizing wave of the early New Deal began. Throughout 1934 and much of 1935, the PUL continued to organize the unemployed in the neighborhoods of Baltimore's metropolitan region, much as it had done during its first year of existence, generating an array of protest delegations, picket lines, open-air meetings, and mass actions, the largest of which drew crowds numbering in the thousands. The PUL protested the treatment of clients at relief offices, the scarcity of Civil Works Administration (CWA) employment, the end of the CWA, the "Pauper's Oath" (a demeaning relief application questionnaire), the differentials between city and county relief, the inadequacy of the BERC coal and food allowances, and so on. In late 1935, the PUL campaigned against both the demise of direct federal relief payments and the failure of the city and the state to fill the gap.[32]

The PUL also continued its cooperative work around food and housing and its educational and cultural activities. In addition, as the workplace-based struggle developed, the PUL's influence progressively extended beyond unemployed workers to the labor movement as a whole, supporting strikes and working in concert with labor unionists in various campaigns. At the same time, the PUL's involvement with the freedom movement deepened following its participation in the anti-lynching protests of late 1933. The PUL's vigorous advocacy of a state anti-lynching law became an important part of the legislative program it put forth in January 1935. The most comprehensive the PUL had yet offered, this program called not only for a state anti-lynching law but also for unemployment insurance, an old-age security system, a state income tax, and increased inheritance and gift taxes. Finally, the PUL maintained its practice of coalition work within the progressive spectrum of the region: in March 1936, it joined with the SP in initiating the Citizens' Alliance for Social Security for Maryland, the center-left coalition that drew in forces of the union movement, the freedom movement, and the social liberal community.[33]

However, starting in mid-1934, the PUL began taking a new direction. In an oral history interview, Frank Trager reminisced about the growing national involvement of the PUL: "During [the PUL's] first two years, it became clear that there were a variety of unemployed organizations of different political complexions in the country. I remember attending [national conferences] in order to coordinate national protests seeking national alleviation of the unemployed. From this emerged the first Workers' Alliance that amalgamated a variety of these non-Communist leagues under, at that time, Socialist leadership." By July 1934, PUL was part of the new Eastern Federation of Unemployed Movements. During its meeting that month, the Eastern Federation drew up a "National Demand," a proposal for a national unemployment organization. David Lasser of New York and James Blackwell of the PUL were selected to recruit other unemployment organizations to this proposal. Their efforts succeeded, and on Labor Day 1934, unemployment organizations from all over the country met in Chicago, formed a National Provisional Committee, and proclaimed November 24 as National Unemployment Day. On that day, an estimated 300,000–1 million people rallied in locales across the county. In Baltimore, the PUL held a large mass meeting, then sent sixteen delegates with the National Action Committee to Washington to present demands directly to Secretary of Labor Frances Perkins and FERA Administrator Harry Hopkins.[34]

By early 1935, seventy-seven unemployment organizations had signed the call for a national federation, and on March 2–4, the National Convention of the Unemployed met and founded the Workers' Alliance of America (WAA). James Blackwell led a large PUL group to the convention as part of the Eastern Federation delegation, and Trager was elected to the National Executive Board of the WAA. While the organizations that came together in the WAA were not all led by Socialists, Socialist militants from around the country, with politics similar to those of the militants of the SP and League for Industrial Democracy (LID) who had created and led the PUL, dominated the national leadership of the alliance. The PUL, which had played a central role in creating the WAA, immediately became the alliance's official Maryland affiliate. Initially, association with the WAA did not much change the character of the PUL or its day-to-day activities, and the PUL never changed its name. Then the national political context changed.[35]

Throughout 1935 and 1936, opposition from right-wing business elites, culminating in the Supreme Court's nullifications of New Deal programs, put heavy pressure on the Roosevelt administration. In response, FDR, to shore up his popular base for the election in 1936, moved to the left and supported a new spate of legislation that emphasized social relief and popular rights. On May 6, 1935, FDR created the Works Progress Administration (WPA) by presidential order, signaling not only an enhanced commitment to alleviate

23. The WPA employed thousands of White and Black workers in Baltimore, many of whom became involved in PUL and WAA organizing campaigns. *Courtesy of Legacy Web, Baltimore County Public Library.*

suffering, but also a move away from direct relief to work relief (see figure 23). On July 5, the president signed the National Labor Relations Act (Wagner Act), which guaranteed the right to organize unions, as the NIRA had, but this time provided means of enforcement. On August 14, Roosevelt signed the Social Security Act, which created a national pension system and national unemployment insurance, thereby answering key demands that had been raised by the unemployment movement since 1930. As the second New Deal implemented these legislative acts, the conditions of the social struggle in general, and of the unemployment struggle in particular, shifted significantly.

With the right to organize strengthened and unemployed workers increasingly channeled into WPA projects, the PUL and other alliance affiliates across the nation began organizing WPA workers, thereby redirecting part of their attention from the neighborhood to the workplace. The thirty-odd affiliates of the alliance took up WPA organizing with some militancy, calling for strikes on public works projects that paid "scab wages." The WAA called a second National Unemployment Day for August 17, 1935, under the slogan "Trade Union Wages and Conditions to Prevail!" on WPA projects. In Baltimore, the PUL added its own demands over the rent allowance policies of the BERC to the demands of the national WAA, and the Baltimore Unemployment Day demonstration at City Hall Plaza, according to the *Maryland Leader*, drew the largest crowd ever to attend a PUL event. By October, the PUL was distributing leaflets and agitating among the 4,000 WPA workers in Baltimore, protesting their "insecurity wages" (a play on the WPA's term "security wages"), and urging them to organize. In addition to PUL activists, the BFL and the Building Trades Council (BTC) called for wage and hour changes on WPA projects and threatened work stoppages.[36]

Less than a month later, in Cumberland, in western Maryland, seventy-five WPA workers struck with the support of the Western Maryland Unemployed League (an ally of the PUL), the Allegany Trades Council, the mayor, and the City Council of Cumberland. When the state WPA officials refused to meet the strikers' demands, the PUL, BFL, and BTC called a mass protest meeting of WPA workers on November 9. On December 6, 350 workers walked off the job on two WPA projects in Baltimore, and one hundred strikers marched to the PUL's headquarters. Shortly after, a magistrate, who publicly advocated harassing relief workers by arresting them on technicalities, fined a Black WPA worker $25 for driving without a license; the PUL denounced the magistrate, calling his action "fascist." The struggle of the WPA workers in Maryland was on in earnest.[37]

The PUL threw itself into WPA organizing, using the same mass-oriented, antiracist approach it had developed in its community work. Authorities with the WPA attempted to limit the PUL's influence, and by late January 1936, WPA workers in Baltimore reported suffering harassment and firing for distributing or reading PUL literature. The PUL countered with protests to the WPA authorities and by distributing leaflets describing the workers' right to organize. In the fall of 1936, in response to the alliance's successes nationally among WPA workers, Aubrey Williams, assistant director of the WPA, recognized the WAA as the collective-bargaining agent for the WPA workers throughout the United States. This recognition strengthened the position of the PUL in Baltimore and signaled that the PUL was now both a neighborhood-based unemployment organization and a workplace-based labor union. In addition, it was now both a locally generated, grassroots, regionally based group and an affiliate of a national organization in the midst of a nationally coordinated campaign.[38]

The PUL's role in the WPA organizing campaign gave it a preview of the

24. Despite discrimination within the New Deal, Black working-class youth in Baltimore became involved in programs such as the National Youth Administration Project, depicted here in a photograph by a WPA worker. *Courtesy of the Enoch Pratt Free Library, Baltimore.*

looming collision between industrial and craft unionism in Baltimore. Although the BFL, the BTC, and the PUL successfully worked at first as allies in organizing the WPA projects — the *Maryland Leader* even complimented them at one point on their cooperation — tension rapidly developed between them over who should be in control. In late 1935, President Joseph McCurdy of the BFL attempted to assert traditional craft-unionist jurisdictional prerogatives by demanding that any WPA strike be called by the BFL. Unfortunately for the BFL, the PUL was doing most of the actual organizing, and the WPA workers knew it. As far as can be determined, McCurdy's demand came to nothing. The PUL and the WAA organized, of course, on an industrial union basis, and when they gained official recognition from the WPA a year later, the tension with the BFL sharpened.[39]

There is disagreement among historians about how, and how much, the PUL and other locally based unemployed organizations were changed by their involvement in the WAA. Roy Rosenzweig and Irene Oppenheimer have

argued that the PUL and similar organizations experienced a "gradual evolution from the position of a purely conflict group to an organized and responsible relationship with the authorities." Frances Fox Piven and Richard
Cloward put it in somewhat more abrasive (and strangely gendered) language when they wrote that groups like the PUL "forfeited local disruption
and became, however inadvertently, collaborators in the process that emas-
culated the movement." However, Jo Ann Argersinger has argued that "most
PUL leaders held firm to their difficult position of calling for a new social
system while working to improve the conditions of the jobless." Rosenzweig
appears to be right when he suggests that the WAA from the start submerged
the radicalism and Socialist politics of its leadership far more than the PUL
had done. But Argersinger seems right in claiming that the PUL guarded its
distinct radical identity while it was part of the WAA. The PUL continued to
criticize the New Deal, sometimes quite harshly, throughout the 1930s; it
continued to engage in a range of protest activities, including direct action
demonstrations; it continued to respond to the local demands and needs of
the Baltimore region; and it continued socialist education among its rank-
and-file. This is not to say that being a part of a national organization had
no effect on the PUL. All of the groups in Baltimore that developed in the
early Depression years changed as they became increasingly connected to
the national struggle of the late 1930s. And this is not to say that WAA was of
marginal importance to the PUL or that the PUL failed to participate fully in
the national organization's actions. But when it did participate in such actions—as, for example, in 1937 when it twice provided a staging ground for
a national WAA march on Washington—it did so very openly and distinctly
as the PUL. While the PUL changed over the years, the change was not simply
a declension from grassroots, localized radicalism to institutionalized, national moderation. To the contrary, it appears that the PUL was able to maintain much of its original vision through the twists and turns of the second
half of the decade.[40]

Freedom Movement Interventions

During the first New Deal period, the center of gravity of the developing
workers' movement in Baltimore shifted away from the neighborhood sphere,
where unemployment organizing had been focused, toward the workplace.
Conversely, after the fiasco surrounding the African American contingent to
the NRA parade in 1933, and after the lynching protests and the Buy Where
You Can Work campaign, the mainstream of the reviving freedom movement increasingly channeled its energy into the neighborhood and public

spheres. The strategic-geographic focuses of the workers' and freedom movements were diverging, and this reduced the opportunities for the two growing movements to "run into" each other and to collaborate in the same social space. There were, though, two key groups within the freedom movement that considered workplace-based organizing a priority and that continually attempted to link the larger movement in work-related struggles.

The first was the *Afro-American*, the ideological center of Black Baltimore. After the NRA parade, the *Afro*'s publisher, Carl Murphy, intensified the paper's coverage of issues concerning Black workers, New Deal policies toward workers, and labor unions. The *Afro* regularly exposed racial discrimination in the relief system and publicized the actions of those who fought it. It reported on firms such as the Swindell Company of Baltimore, which replaced Black workers with White workers to avoid paying Black workers NRA code wages. It editorialized against the federal government's violation of the spirit of its own NRA codes through its discriminatory firing of Black customs workers; called for an NRA code to cover domestic work; railed against the racist practices of local and national AFL unions; and closely followed the struggle within the national AFL over the role of Black workers. On one occasion, the *Afro* even proposed an organizing drive across the country by African Americans *against* the AFL. It reported on the activities of predominantly Black unions such as ILA Local 858 and on integrated unions such as the MWIU and the ACW, and it approvingly covered the interracial activities of labor radicals and industrial unionists. At the very least, the *Afro* offered its readers important information about the reactivating workers' movement and the role of Black workers and antiracism within it. At most, it influenced community activists to see the new labor movement as a potential ally and as a possible area for their involvement, and it alerted and reminded antiracist labor activists that they had potential allies in the freedom movement.[41]

The other key group, the BUL under the leadership of Executive Secretary Edward Lewis, complemented the *Afro*'s educational work around the workers' movement with organizational work. As the National Urban League shifted its attention toward Black workers during the early New Deal, Lewis, a former worker and trade unionist, moved to Baltimore and rapidly became the leading freedom movement advocate for Black workers in the city. Lewis and his close colleagues were probably way ahead of the BUL as a whole in this regard, for he later revealed that he started organizing Black workers in Baltimore without the knowledge of the BUL's executive board. As we have seen, Lewis was integrally involved in launching the PUL in 1933, and he continued to work closely with that organization in the ensuing years, appearing as a speaker at innumerable mass meetings and demonstrations. As we have also seen, Lewis and his circle were also largely responsible for the BUL–ACW meetings for Black garment workers in early 1933 and the creation of the Negro Labor Committee (NLC). His work and that of the NLC with the garment unions; the Amalgamated Iron, Steel, and Tin Workers; and other unions continued throughout the early New Deal. The ACW found Lewis so effective that it invited him to Norfolk, Virginia, to help it organize Black workers there. In addition, in March 1936, Lewis brought the BUL into the broad, labor-centered Citizens' Alliance for Social Security for Maryland, initiated by the SP. The work of Lewis and his colleagues in Baltimore was linked to the National Urban League's Negro Workers' Councils campaign that attempted to organize Black workers and to break the hold of Jim Crow on the existing labor movement across the United States. Lewis quite effectively adapted the thrust of this campaign to the conditions of the Baltimore metropolitan region.[42]

In late 1935, Lewis and two Urban League leaders from New York and Philadelphia joined Lester Granger, head of the National Urban League Workers' Councils, in a special delegation to the national convention of the AFL in Atlantic City. This delegation's purpose was to work with A. Philip Randolph, head of the Brotherhood of Sleeping Car Porters, and a number of other antiracist unionists in convincing White AFL delegates to support a resolution fighting racial discrimination in the federation. Lewis and his colleagues were hopeful because a special AFL committee had filed a report recommending major changes in the racial practices of the AFL and had drafted a resolution based on the report. However, William Green, president of the AFL, and his executive committee watered the resolution down, then buried it. The Urban League delegation and Randolph's forces were outraged. At the same convention, the conflict between the craft unionists led by Green and the industrial unionists came to a head, resulting in the formation of what would a few weeks later become the dissident Committee for Industrial Organization. The threat of a split in the U.S. labor movement loomed. In response to questions from an *Afro* reporter, Lewis stated that such a split, which he felt was inevitable, would be "the most encouraging news in ten years" for unorganized workers generally and for African American workers in particular. The ensuing history of both the Black freedom movement and the workers' movement in Baltimore would prove him right. And the militancy and antiracism of key sectors of the Baltimore workers' movement during the first New Deal had prepared the ground for the upsurge to come.[43]

8

Seeking Directions,
1934–1936

Baltimore became a proving ground because Charlie Houston was right over there in Washington, and he was testing some of his legal theories in our cases, because we were—in those days we were called militant although we weren't for violence, but we were standing up and speaking out—we were kind of a radical group.
—JUANITA JACKSON MITCHELL

The watershed protests of late 1933 fully re-established the Black freedom movement in Baltimore as a social force in the region, gave it new momentum, and moved it into a new phase of development. From early 1934 through early 1936, the freedom movement, like the workers' movement, grew considerably both in size and level of activity. During these early New Deal years, activists within the freedom movement addressed a variety of issues, positioned and repositioned themselves in coalitions, searched for effective organizational arrangements, and tested different political directions. Before 1934, nontraditional freedom movement organizational forms such as the Euel Lee defense campaign led by the International Labor Defense (ILD), the City-Wide Young People's Forum, the Citizens' Committee of the jobs boycott, and, more recently, the Maryland Anti-Lynching Federation guided much of the local movement's activity. This trend continued well into the 1934–36 period, resulting in a convergence between the youthful wing of the freedom movement led by the Forum and the Socialist militants of the PUL, which drew the growing workers' and freedom movements toward closer local alliance. However, countervailing tendencies developed, as well, as older local forms—most notably, the Baltimore branch of the NAACP—revived, and connections between the local and national freedom movements strengthened. The interplay between these tendencies defined much of the trajectory of the freedom movement in Baltimore in the 1934–36 period.

The Forum after the Watershed

Although older adult participation in Baltimore's Black freedom movement had grown considerably by the first half of 1934, the Forum was still very much at the movement's center. The Forum emerged from the anti-lynching struggle and the Buy Where You Can Work Campaign with enhanced prestige, with a more secure network of supporters throughout the city's Black neighborhoods, and with a great deal of energy. The Forum's Friday night meetings, which drew larger crowds than ever, continued to educate the community on a wide range of issues. As a direct legacy of the jobs boycott, the Forum continued to work for greater youth employment through advocacy and through its employment center. It also continued to participate in efforts to oppose segregation. For example, in early 1934 the Forum forwarded 1,000 letters to the Maryland representatives in Congress, calling on them to support Congressman Oscar De Priest's efforts to end Jim Crow in the restaurants in the House and Senate buildings. The Forum also worked with the National Urban League on a comprehensive survey of Baltimore's Black community. Directed by the sociologist Ira De A. Reid, the survey was a major event in the Black community; followed closely by the *Afro*, its results were published to acclaim in early 1935 under the title *The Negro Community of Baltimore*. To help gather data for the survey, the Forum sponsored and conducted a public Court of Social Justice in April 1934, during which thirty African Americans testified on the problems of Black Baltimore in a "mock trial" before a panel of seven judges and a large audience."[1]

Reflecting the powerful impact of the Armwood protests on Baltimore's Black community, the main emphasis of the Forum's political work in 1934 and early 1935 was the anti-lynching struggle. The Forum, as a part of the Maryland Anti-Lynching Federation, urged the passage of state anti-lynching legislation through mass agitation and delegations to Annapolis. Also, because of strengthened ties to the national NAACP, the Forum became deeply involved in the national campaign for federal anti-lynching legislation. In 1934 and 1935, Forumites began an extensive letter-writing campaign in support of the Costigan-Wagner Anti-Lynching Bill, which was then before the U.S. Congress. Forum activists visited business owners and prominent individuals to persuade them to write personal letters in support of the bill, and they collected thousands of signatures on form letters to congressmen and on petitions to President Roosevelt. It also sent a delegation accompanied by Charles Houston to meet with Senator Millard Tydings of Maryland to lobby for Costigan-Wagner.[2]

For the Forum leadership, the high point of this anti-lynching work came on February 21, 1934, when the Forum's president, Juanita Jackson, and vice-president, Clarence Mitchell, joined a delegation from the Maryland Anti-Lynching Federation that traveled to Washington to testify at the Senate subcommittee hearings for the Costigan-Wagner Bill. The delegation, which included Reverend Asbury Smith, Rabbi Edward L. Israel, and Elisabeth Gilman, presented a petition with 6,000 signatures favoring the bill to the subcommittee, and each delegation member testified about the lynching of George Armwood and how it demonstrated the need for federal legislation. More than a half-century later, Juanita Jackson Mitchell remembered the brief testimony that she, then twenty-one years old, and Clarence Mitchell, then twenty-three, gave at these hearings as one of the most moving and exciting events of their lives. For the first time, they had offered their views to reasonably sympathetic forces in the national power structure, and they felt that they had been heard.[3]

While the Forum continued to function at the center of the reviving freedom struggle, the Forum youth, as self-defined radicals, increasingly experimented with other political issues traditionally beyond the main concerns of the Baltimore movement. Reid observed in the study for the Urban League, "The problems of peace, economic reconstruction, and public discussion offer the most fertile field for true interracial activity. Yet the extreme race-consciousness of the Negro group has tended to prevent its active interest in matters of public import other than racial adjustment." From 1934 through 1936, the Forum proved to be an important exception to this observation by Reid. Working closely with the League for Industrial Democracy (LID) and the PUL-oriented Socialists, the Forum became a constituent part of the emerging interracial peace movement in the city.[4]

In early May 1934, the Women's International League for Peace and Freedom announced that a delegation from Baltimore would participate in the mass meeting and disarmament demonstration to be held in Washington, D.C., on May 18, World Goodwill Day. The Forum, the Maryland Anti-Lynching Federation, and the PUL officially took part. Other African American groups that participated included the LID at Morgan College, representatives from Coppin Normal School (both of which probably had links to the Forum), and the Negro Labor Committee. The predominantly White groups included the Liberal Club of Johns Hopkins, the Goucher College LID, and the Young People's Socialist League (all of which were close to the Socialist Party [SP]), as well as the Society of Friends, the Baltimore Council of Churches, the YMCA, and representatives from the University of Baltimore. The chairman of the Baltimore delegation was none other than Frank Trager of Johns Hopkins, the PUL, the LID, and the SP. Six months later, the

Forum participated in the Interracial Peace Parade sponsored by the Baltimore Peace Conference, held on November 10 in the city. More than 1,000
young people, including a contingent of fifty from the Forum, marched,
rallied, and listened as the African American Socialist Frank Crosswaith addressed the crowd. The Forum also entered a float titled "The Unknown Soldier" in the parade. As Juanita Jackson Mitchell remembered the float, it was
a "white tomb, and here was this Black man with his hands lifted—he was
the Unknown Soldier!" In Jim Crow Baltimore, both the integrated peace
march and the Forum's float must have caused some sensation. Sometime
during this period, "Study War No More" joined the "Negro National Anthem," "America the Beautiful," and several spirituals on the Forum's song
card.[5]

The Forum became involved with the peace movement more than a year
and a half before fascist-ruled Italy invaded Ethiopia in October 1935, precipitating a sharp rise in antiwar and anticolonial consciousness in African
American communities around the United States. The historian Lawrence
Wittner has argued that women, peace-oriented Protestants, and young
people on and off the college campuses were the backbone of the movement
in these years, so in a sense, the Forum fit in well with the movement's demo-
graphics, with the exception that there was little apparent African American participation. The Forum was again the youthful vanguard of the African American community in Baltimore, combining its pro-peace stand with
antifascism. Progressives in the workers' movement were also increasingly
involved in the Baltimore peace movement, including not only the PUL socialists, but also locals of the ACW and the ILGWU. Even Joseph McCurdy of
the BFL spoke at least once at a large peace meeting. Then, at the end of 1935,
the Forum was invited to join the League against War and Fascism, initiated by the Communist Party (CP). The Forum sent its vice-president, Elmer
Henderson, to the league's national conference as a part of an interracial
Baltimore delegation of thirty-two people. On January 18, 1936, Henderson
and Dr. Shapiro of Johns Hopkins University reported on the league's conference to a Forum Friday night meeting.[6]

In early 1936, when the Baltimore chapter of the League against War and
Fascism began to agitate against the planned visit of the German cruiser
Emden to Baltimore in late April of that year, the Forum executive committee joined in. Eventually, a grand coalition of more than thirty progressive,
religious (both Christian and Jewish), labor, and freedom organizations sent
letters of protest and delegations opposing the visit of the "Nazi ship" to the
mayor. When the *Emden* docked in Fells Point, some 2,000 demonstrators
from groups that included the PUL, the ACW, the ILGWU, the Forum, the BUL,

and the NAACP, met it. Thurgood Marshall, by then legal counsel to the Baltimore NAACP, gave the keynote address to the gathering. The *Emden* protests revealed a broad and growing antiwar, antifascist coalition in the region, and the Forum was in the middle of it. Moreover, at about this time, students at Morgan College joined a national student strike against war, indicating the spread of such sentiments among Black college youth; an *Afro* editorial bemoaned the fact that high school students did not do the same.[7]

The Forum, Socialism, and Communism

The Forum's antiwar activism was symptomatic of its further radicalization during the early New Deal period. While recalling her protest activities at National Methodist Youth Conference in 1934, Juanita Jackson Mitchell described the social Christian ethics that were also at the core of the Forum's outlook at the time: "Our whole thrust was, what would Christ do if he was here?" She recalled that their social Christianity tended toward Christian socialism: "We were going to change the world. Some said we were pro-socialist—we believed in the division of the wealth. . . . We were going back to Christ—sharing." And, she added, "We were antiwar. We were never going to have another war. We firmly believed that." The developing social Christianity of the Forum's leadership was quite compatible with the social message of the antiracist activists in Baltimore's SP, some of whom, including Elisabeth Gilman, combined their socialism with a deeply held Christianity.[8]

By late summer of 1934, the growing political ties between the Socialists and the Forum resulted in even closer public collaborations. The Maryland SP nominated Broadus Mitchell for governor, Elisabeth Gilman for senator, Naomi Riches of the PUL for Congress, *and* Clarence Mitchell of the Forum for the state's legislature. Juanita Jackson Mitchell later recalled the campaign. Speaking of Elisabeth Gilman and some of the other Socialist leaders, she remarked: "They fell in love with Clarence Mitchell. This is something that is not known. They had him come, and I went with him, to some of the meetings. And they persuaded him to get on the Socialist ticket in 1934. He ran for the legislature. The City-Wide Young People's Forum was his campaign committee."[9]

During the first years of the decade, electoral activity by the SP began to attract some attention in the Black community, especially among the youth. In October 1932, for example, a majority of the students at Morgan College who participated in a "mock election" sponsored by the YMCA elected the Socialist candidate over the Democratic, Republican, and Communist candidates. But only the emergence of the PUL-oriented Socialist candidates in 1934 infused the SP's election platform with a strong antiracist plank. Point seven of the platform, "For the Negro," demanded: "(A) Every form of economic and political justice and all civil rights and privileges guaranteed to him as citizen by the Constitution of the United States. (B) Laws against Jim-Crowism. Laws against the crime of lynching." During the campaign in 1934, Broadus Mitchell expanded the content of point seven to include much of the traditional agenda of the Baltimore freedom movement. At a PUL picnic in Druid Hill Park in July, he called for a state anti-lynching law; equal schools for Blacks; equal pay for Black teachers throughout the state; admission of Blacks to state-run graduate and professional schools; scholarships for Black students to study out of state if in-state programs were unavailable; an end to Jim Crow laws; and employment of Blacks on the police forces and in government departments throughout Maryland. There is little wonder that the Forum youth were willing to have one of their own run in such a campaign.[10]

Clarence Mitchell did not, however, run on the Socialist ticket solely because the party's platform gave him space to oppose racism, as Denton L. Watson, Mitchell's biographer, suggests. Watson's account of the campaign in 1934 depicts Mitchell as an "independent" who ran an antiracist campaign on the Socialist ticket as a protest against the Democratic and Republican parties. Watson is probably right that Mitchell was "never a Socialist" in the sense of being a party member, but his portrayal of Mitchell and, by extension, his supporters in the Forum as non-ideological opponents of segregation underestimates the extent to which socialistic ideas were present among the Forum leaders and in the freedom movement in the early 1930s, both in Baltimore and nationally. The Forumites may not have been official Socialists during the 1934 campaign, but there is reason to believe that they were investigating socialism as a valid political — and antiracist — outlook. Moreover, it is hardly credible that anyone as smart and savvy as Clarence Mitchell would fail to recognize that if he ran on the SP ticket, people would believe he was a socialist. The *Maryland Leader*'s account of Mitchell's speech at the ratification meeting for the SP candidates certainly indicates his interest in socialism: "Clarence Mitchell, candidate for the Legislature from the [Fifth] District, was also an electrifying influence on the ratification meeting. His prediction of the turn of the colored voters from the old parties to the SP was one of the important notes of the meeting. A good speaker, his plea for workers' solidarity met an instant and enduring response."[11]

The Fifth Legislative District where Clarence Mitchell ran had been gerrymandered in the 1920s, and it included few Black voters. Mitchell was the first African American to run for office there. Nevertheless, as Juanita Jackson Mitchell recalled, his campaign focused heavily on demands for anti-lynching legislation and equal rights for all. The Forum established a Civic Committee, with Vice-President Henderson as chairman and the Forum adviser Sarah Diggs as treasurer. The Civic Committee mobilized a squad of Forum members and supporters to raise money and to campaign door to door, on the streets, and from the back of a truck at street corners. The committee also used Mitchell's campaign to run a voter registration drive, and 700 people signed up. The *Afro* publicized Clarence Mitchell's campaign and, in the last issue before the election, endorsed him and the Socialist gubernatorial candidate Broadus Mitchell. Although, as expected, both candidates lost, they made surprisingly good showings. Broadus Mitchell received 6,787 votes across the state for governor, significantly more than earlier Socialist gubernatorial candidates, and Clarence Mitchell received more than 1,700 votes in the Fifth District. As Broadus Mitchell put it years later, "It wasn't politics, it was an educational propaganda thing." Furthermore, the militants of the Forum and the militants of the Baltimore SP had collaborated in an explicitly Socialist, antiracist electoral campaign. It seems possible that a radical interracial leadership core composed of leaders from the Forum, the most important mass organization of the freedom movement at the time, and from the PUL, a leading organization of the new workers' movement, might have emerged from the campaign, moving the two movements toward closer alliance. But this was not to happen.[12]

The campaign in 1934 was the high-water mark of collaboration between the Forum and the Socialists, and although the groups subsequently worked together on specific issues, they were only intermittently affiliated. Clarence Mitchell spoke at a National Unemployment Day event sponsored by the PUL at the end of 1934, and in April 1935, Frank Trager and Edward Lewis addressed a Forum Friday night meeting on the unemployment crisis. Trager became an official sponsor of the Forum, and he maintained a formal liaison with the PUL. And although no one from the Forum ran on the Socialist ticket in the municipal elections at the end of 1935, Elisabeth Gilman, the SP's candidate for mayor, put forward a program, prominently featured in the *Afro*, that included many of the demands for racial justice that Broadus Mitchell and Clarence Mitchell advanced in 1934. Nevertheless, nothing quite like Clarence Mitchell's Socialist candidacy happened again.[13]

Other forces were at work, pulling the Forumites and the PUL activists in different directions. For the PUL activists, helping to found and lead a national unemployment organization, the Workers' Alliance of America (WAA), and a shift of strategic focus toward union organizing among WPA workers, left less time and energy to explore cross-racial, labor-freedom movement unity.

And as the Forum drew closer to the NAACP locally and nationally it shifted away from the PUL's fields of activity. In addition, within eighteen months of the election campaign of 1934, Juanita Jackson, Frank Trager, and Joel Seidman all moved out of Baltimore to pursue responsibilities elsewhere, and Clarence Mitchell followed soon after, further weakening the possibility of long-term ties between the Forum's leadership and the Socialists of the PUL. Nonetheless, for a short period, the two groups of radicals converged ideologically and practically; under different historical conditions, their unity might have been more fully realized.[14]

Although the Communists had initially been the integrated radical group most involved with the re-emerging freedom movement and with the Forum itself, as the leaderships of the PUL and the Forum developed stronger ties, the CP's relationship to the Forum and the freedom movement became more tense and complicated. The contributions of the CP-led's ILD to the Euel Lee defense campaign and to the anti-lynching struggle were much appreciated by many freedom movement figures, but contentions between the Communists and some of the more moderate participants of the protests of late 1933 had negative repercussions for the CP. Still, when the ruling elites of Baltimore and Maryland retaliated against the ILD for its role in the Lee campaign by attempting to disbar Bernard Ades, freedom movement activists rallied to Ades's support.

State's Attorney Herbert O'Conor filed a complaint against Ades with the Maryland State Bar Association in July 1933, before the lynching of George Armwood. And on October 23, 1933, five days after Armwood's death and five days before the execution of Lee, Judge William C. Coleman suspended Ades from practicing in federal courts and started disbarment proceedings against him in the U.S. District Court. Ades was charged with forcing his way uninvited into cases that were in process, defaming court officials, inducing a government witness to perjure herself, lying to a court, and attempting to obtain Euel Lee's body for improper purposes. With remarkable hypocrisy, State's Attorney O'Conor expressed the fear that Ades's behavior had the "effect of engendering race prejudice." In an act of solidarity, Charles Houston and his protégé, Thurgood Marshall, agreed to defend Ades in court. As Houston put it, the "real basis for the attack on Ades [was] Ades' insistence on exposing officials with a dual standard of public morality—one for whites and one for blacks. . . . They cannot stand publicity and maintain their respectability therefore they want to remove Ades from the bar so they can rest in their hypocrisy." After two months of pretrial maneuvering, Ades's disbarment trial began on February 28, 1934, before Judge Morris O. Soper,

25. Euel Lee's attorney Bernard Ades (*center*) during his disbarment hearings, with his attorneys, Charles Houston (*left*) and Thurgood Marshall of the NAACP. *Courtesy of the Afro-American Newspapers Archives and Research Center.*

a White liberal (see figure 25). On March 20, Judge Soper sustained only two of the eight charges: attempting improperly to obtain Lee's body and slandering the prosecutors in another case. Because of the service Ades had rendered in defending poor Blacks and in establishing the right of Blacks to sit on juries in Maryland, Soper did not disbar him; he only reprimanded him "severely." The right of the ILD to intervene in cases without explicit prior invitation had been upheld, and Ades was again able to resume his practice of law. Nonetheless, he and the ILD were not happy with Soper's decision.[15]

The forces of law and order, however, were not finished with Ades. In mid-May, an investigation of Home Finance Company of Baltimore, of which Ades was an agent and his father, Harry Ades, was president, resulted in a restraining order issued by Maryland's Attorney-General Lane that froze the company's assets. This was probably simple harassment, for the press reports no ensuing legal action. Then, shortly after Soper's decision, the grievance committee of the Baltimore City Bar Association brought its own charges of misconduct against Ades. On May 8, Ades advised the City Bar Association that he was refusing to reply to its charges because it denied membership to African American lawyers and thereby forfeited "its right to act as representative of the entire bar" in the city. The City Bar Association's response to Ades's refusal was to file disbarment charges against him on June 25 with the Baltimore City Supreme Bench. Nearly six months later, on December 8, after a brief hearing, the Baltimore City Supreme Bench found Ades guilty of conduct unbecoming an attorney and of inciting racial prejudice and suspended him from practice for three months.[16]

The campaign against Ades diverted the Baltimore ILD from other work and appears to have drained its meager resources for most of 1934. Nevertheless, the ILD attempted to turn a bad thing into a good thing, with some success. It widely publicized the attempt to disbar Ades and included agitation around his case in its other activities. For example, in March, the ILD called a mass meeting to protest both a ruling in the Scottsboro Boys case and Ades's disbarment proceedings. In addition, the CP attempted to capitalize on Ades's notoriety by nominating him to run for governor at the head of its Maryland electoral ticket in 1934. However, during the same period, the ILD and the CP damaged their relationship with the freedom movement by accusing Charles Houston of selling Ades out by failing to get him acquitted of all eight state charges. Stunned, Houston protested to the ILD's national leadership, and Ades admitted that Houston and Marshall had provided him with a powerful defense, causing the ILD to back down. The historian Genna Rae McNeil, Houston's biographer, reports that "Houston was pleased" and offered to serve once more as Ades's counsel during the second set of disbarment proceedings. Although Houston did not in fact defend Ades again, the two did appear together a few months later to debate the Scottsboro Boys case, where, despite the fact that Houston was representing the NAACP and Ades was representing the CP, they found little to disagree about.[17]

The CP's standing was also damaged when, in early 1934, its relationship to its former ally, the Forum, began to turn sour. A day after the delegation from the Maryland Anti-Lynching Federation, including the Forum leaders, appeared at the Costigan-Wagner hearings in Washington, Ades, and the CP's vice-presidential candidate, James W. Ford also testified at the hearings. Neither was a scheduled witness, but both appeared unexpectedly and demanded the right to speak. In contrast with the federation delegates, who had strongly supported the Costigan-Wagner Bill, Ades and Ford criticized weaknesses in the proposed legislation, linked Jim Crow and lynching to capitalism, and denounced the authorities in Maryland as accomplices in Armwood's death. Both men were forcefully removed from the podium before they finished their statements. Despite the contrast between the federation's and the ILD delegates' approach to the hearings, Ades and Ford received support in Baltimore for their efforts in Washington. Clarence Mitchell, whose own earlier testimony at the hearings was quite different from theirs, wrote a positive news story for the *Afro* on Ades's and Ford's appearance, and an *Afro* editorial proclaimed, "Ades is right," and published his whole statement. Ades though, went ahead and attacked the testimony of the federation delegates, including that of Juanita Jackson. According to a report that appeared some months later in the *Afro*:

> Sometime ago, Mr. Ades is thought to have incurred the displeasure of the [F]orum group when he is said to have belittled the speech made by Miss Jackson, the president, during the Senate investigation of lynching.
>
> Mr. Ades is said to have remarked that Miss Jackson's address was too religious and that she reminded him of a "sanctified nun."
>
> Later, Mr. Ades, upon learning that Miss Jackson had taken offense to the criticism, is said to have sent Miss Jackson a box of candy as a peace offering.
>
> The candy was returned, unopened.[18]

Relations between the Forum and the CP deteriorated over the ensuing months. In late October 1934, the Forum announced the program for its Friday night meeting on the governor's race, inviting the candidates from the Republican, Democratic, and Socialist parties, but not from the CP. Ades, as the CP's gubernatorial candidate, immediately requested that he and his party be included in the program, but the Forum's executive committee failed to respond. Reached by an *Afro* reporter to explain the omission of the CP, Clarence Mitchell explained unconvincingly that time permitted presentations from only three candidacies. The dispute raged in the pages of the *Afro*, moving back and forth between the Forum's and the CP's points of view. Finally, and perhaps surprisingly, the *Afro* stood up for the CP and, in an unprecedented editorial, rejected the Forum's explanation for excluding Ades, scolded it for "muzzling" the Communists, and accused it of "making its name and purpose a misnomer." Furthermore, the SP's candidate, Broadus Mitchell, also took the CP's side and refused his invitation to speak to the Forum, stating that "he would not care to speak on a better social order for colored people on a platform from which Bernard Ades was excluded."[19]

This series of disputes between the CP and various movement forces complicated, and no doubt weakened, the party's position within the freedom struggle in Baltimore. By late 1934, the new freedom movement in the city had expanded greatly, in no small part due to the CP's work over the previous five years; however, the CP was less central to the movement than it had been a year before. This was partly because the CP was at the left pole of an expanding movement; more centrist forces disagreed with aspects of the party's program and approach; and some were influenced by anticommunist prejudice. The Communists' diminished position was also partly due to a re-curring pattern of sectarian excess on the part of the CP. Still, there was no decisive split between Communist-oriented and non-Communist freedom movement militants, and on the level of practical politics, they agreed much more than they disagreed. Moreover, as the editorials, columns, and letters in the *Afro* attested, many non-Communists continued to hold Communists, especially Ades, in high esteem.

Over the next year, the CP increasingly shifted away from its Third Period strategy to that of the Popular Front and a less sectarian style of work. The chapter of the League against War and Fascism in Baltimore by 1935 had be-come an exemplar of the emerging Popular Front approach, and it received support from the Forum and other forces in the freedom movement. Elmer Henderson, vice-president of the Forum, along with two other African American delegates from Baltimore—Mary Lewis of the BUL and William N. Jones of the *Afro*—were elected to the league's national executive board. However, the downside of the Popular Front approach, as it evolved during the late '30s in Baltimore and nationally, was that Communists increasingly underplayed much of the radicalism of their social critique and increasingly masked their political identities. As a result, the CP never again attained the open prominence and influence in the Baltimore freedom movement that it had in 1933 and 1934. As historians of the 1930s, including those sympathetic to the CP's overall role in those years, have stressed, there was a lot that was wrong with the ultra-leftism of the party's Third Period strategy and practice. However, there was much that was right, especially with the exceptional mili-tancy of its opposition to racism. Charles Houston's views of the Commu-nists and antiracism are relevant here, given his importance to the Baltimore freedom struggle in the early 1930s (and national freedom movement in the post-1935 years). In a speech to the National YWCA Convention in Philadel-phia in May 1934, Houston stated:

> The contribution of the Communists to the Negro has been to turn the race issue into a class issue. They have been the first, at least in recent times, to have appealed to the masses, as distinguished from the classes. Whereas all prior approaches to the masses had been paternalistic, the Communists came along and walked among them, like the disciples of old, and offered them full and complete brotherhood, without respect to race, creed or previous condition of

servitude. Finally the Communists have been the first to fire the masses with a sense of their raw, potential power, and the first openly to preach the doctrine of mass resistance and mass struggle: Unite and fight.

When we think about Houston and his many contributions to the freedom struggle, it would be useful to remember this quote.[20]

Suing the University of Maryland

In July 1935, while leading figures in the reviving Baltimore freedom movement were still seeking direction for their activities, Charles Houston began a leave of absence from his position as dean of Howard University Law School, relocating to New York City to become the full-time special counsel for the NAACP. Houston's move had far-reaching consequences in Baltimore and the nation, because his major responsibility was to launch a national legal campaign for African American rights, funded by a $10,000 grant from the American Fund for Public Service. This fund, also known as the Garland Fund, was a philanthropy based in New York with progressives and socialists, including Roger Baldwin, Norman Thomas, and James Weldon Johnson, on its board of directors.[21]

We have often met Houston before in these pages, but at this point it would be helpful to sketch his background. Charles Hamilton Houston was born in Washington, D.C., in 1895 to Charles Houston, a lawyer, and Mary Hamilton Houston, a hairdresser. Houston's mother and father cultivated a love of learning and culture in their young son and sent him to one of the foremost Black high schools in the country, from which he was admitted on scholarship to Amherst College. The only African American in his class at one of the country's most elite colleges, Houston graduated with high marks in 1915. After teaching English and literature at Howard University for two years, he enlisted in the Army to avoid being drafted as the United States entered the First World War, and he was accepted into the first Black officers' training camp at Fort Des Moines, Iowa. Subsequently, he served in France.[22]

Throughout his early life, his time at Amherst, and, especially, his time in the military, Houston became increasingly aware of racial ethnic discrimination. As he grew older, he began speaking out against it. His return home in 1919, in the midst of more than two dozen anti-Black race riots during the "red summer" of that year, crystallized his commitment to fight racism and bigotry, and partly influenced by his father, he decided to become a lawyer. He gained admission to Harvard Law School, where he again excelled and became the first African American on the editorial board of the *Harvard Law*

Review, graduating among the top 5 percent of his class. He went on to earn a doctorate in juridical science. In 1924, he returned to Howard University, this time to the law school, where as a professor then as vice-dean he renovated the whole course of study. His goal was to build an institution capable of producing a highly skilled, deeply committed cadre of Black civil rights lawyers. As Houston had written earlier, "There must be Negro lawyers in every community," and most of these "must come from Negro schools." By the early 1930s, Howard Law School was well on its way to becoming an institution that could perform such a task, and Houston himself, not yet forty, was becoming the most important legal activist in the freedom movement. It was during this period that he became involved with the movement in Baltimore. When, in 1935, he was offered the position as special counsel to the NAACP to lead the national campaign funded by the Garland Fund, he seized the opportunity.[23]

During the months before leaving for New York, Houston began to refine his strategy for the coming national campaign. As McNeil relates in her fine biography of Houston, he approached the campaign with a number of very definite ideas. First, he believed that this would be only the beginning of a larger, more protracted struggle against segregation. Second, given the limited initial funding, this campaign would have to be carefully planned and focused and could not spontaneously and randomly respond to instances of injustice, no matter how deserving each might be. Third, this was not simply a legal campaign, for in Houston's words, it would have "to arouse and strengthen the will of local communities to demand and fight for their rights." Indeed, it would have to provide local communities with models for how to mobilize themselves to carry out that fight, something that his speech to the YWCA in 1934 suggests he may have learned from the Communists. Houston and his colleagues decided to focus the campaign on racial discrimination in education. They believed that Jim Crow schooling was crucial to the reproduction of the segregation system, so an attack at this level could cripple the larger system. In addition, they felt that segregated education so angered Black communities that they would be willing to fight to overturn it. Moreover, White Jim Crow education in the South was so obviously superior to that provided to Blacks that it was patently illegal even by the "separate but equal" standard of the U.S. Supreme Court's decision in *Plessy v. Ferguson* in 1896. Houston's initial tactical targets included inequality in educational funding and infrastructure, disparities in teachers' salaries, and lack of access for Blacks to graduate and professional schools—problems the freedom movement in various locales had already intermittently targeted. Furthermore, Houston and his team felt that the border states, with their contradictory combinations of northern and southern features, would provide the best setting for the initial campaign. Because of his ties to the Baltimore freedom movement, and to the Forum in particular, Houston regarded Maryland as ideal for his plans. According to Juanita Jackson Mitchell, he came to refer to the state as his "legal laboratory." Therefore, in the months before he left for the NAACP's national office in New York, Houston approached freedom movement activists in Baltimore to discuss his legal strategy. As Mitchell remembered it,

> He said that while he was in the Army, taking all those insults and the like, he figured out that, with the 14th Amendment equal protection clause, we could start hammering away at this damnable segregation, especially state-supported segregation. His proposal was, when he first came and talked to us, that if a state is in the business of providing education for its citizens, and it excludes a group of citizens solely because of race, and it doesn't provide them a law school, then on its face, it has violated the Constitutional right to the equal protection of the law under the 14th Amendment. And that was so simple and so clear.

Activists in Baltimore, including the leadership of the Forum, were impressed with Houston's plans and leapt at the opportunity to participate in what became the first case of a long legal crusade against segregation: opening the University of Maryland Law School to Black students.[24]

Some activists questioned the rationale behind the plan to target a law school, given the serious educational deprivation for African Americans at the elementary and secondary levels. However, as Houston explained, graduate and professional schools such as the University of Maryland Law School were often the weakest links in the chain of segregated education, and it was relatively easy to demonstrate in courts that they were in violation of the U.S. Constitution. Frequently, as in Maryland, the issue in such cases was not unequal opportunity, but *no opportunity* at all, for only White institutions of this type existed, thereby contravening even the "separate but equal" doctrine established by *Plessy v. Ferguson*. If cases against institutions like the University of Maryland Law School were won in court, the states concerned would probably find it too expensive to provide segregated all-Black graduate and professional schools and would have no choice but to integrate the existing schools. Such strategic precedents in higher education could then be used to attack segregation in lower education, thereby chipping away at the foundations of the entire system.[25]

The focus on the University of Maryland pleased Baltimore's activists. Several of the Forum youth, including Juanita Jackson, had been refused entry to the University of Maryland because of racist barriers, and others had not even bothered to apply, knowing the inevitable outcome. Thurgood Marshall himself had been turned down by the University of Maryland Law School and was burning for revenge. Houston was known for his exacting requirements for test cases to ensure that they not fail due to technicalities. Even so, the attempt to sue the University of Maryland got off to a rocky start. On his own initiative, Clarence Mitchell hastily applied to graduate school at the university, planning to file suit; unfortunately, he applied to a nonexistent program. Houston and the NAACP team rejected several other potential applicants because their cases had possible complications. Finally, Thurgood Marshall, who although he was only twenty-seven was co-counsel with Houston on the case, ran into Donald Gaines Murray. A native of Baltimore and the son of a well-known African Methodist Episcopal bishop, Murray had just returned to the city after graduating with high marks from Amherst College (Houston's alma mater) and had been attracted to the Forum. He was, in Juanita Jackson Mitchell's words, part of the "most privileged group of Blacks" in the city, although according to his own later oral history, he returned to Depression-bound Baltimore because he had no money to go on to law school. Marshall and Houston agreed that Murray would be an excellent test applicant to the University of Maryland Law School, but before the process could get started, another glitch occurred. It turned out that a Black social fraternity, Alpha Phi Alpha, was also planning to use Murray's application for its own test case; the controversy was eventually settled in the NAACP's favor. Murray applied to the law school, he was summarily turned down, and a famous legal battle commenced.[26]

The NAACP team of Houston, Marshall, and the Forum's legal adviser W. A. C. Hughes carefully prepared Murray's case against the state of Maryland (see figure 26). The state argued that it had complied with the "separate but equal" doctrine with its scholarship fund for out-of-state education (which, the state failed to mention, had no money in it). Then the state and the university used every excuse possible to delay the proceedings while simultaneously appealing to White racist fears that the admission of African Americans would ruin the university's academic and financial standing, result in a mass exodus of White students and trigger race riots. Houston and his colleagues, also mindful of public opinion, publicized their arguments widely, relying on Black community institutions and networks, such as the *Afro*, which gave prominent coverage to every development. A number of allies in the White mainstream press emerged, including the famous journalists H. L. Mencken and Gerald Johnson, who in contrasting styles lambasted the pretensions of the state officials and argued the case for Murray's admission in the *Baltimore Sun* papers and elsewhere.[27]

26. Thurgood Marshall, Donald Gaines Murray, and Charles Houston preparing Murray's lawsuit against the University of Maryland Law School. *Courtesy of the Library of Congress.*

The Murray suit finally came to trial in Baltimore on June 18, 1935, before Judge Eugene O'Dunne, who, despite a mixed reputation, had been requested by the NAACP. Juanita Jackson Mitchell later remembered that, just prior to this date, "Charlie Houston said to my mother, 'Miss Lillie, I want you to pack the courtroom with people in their Sunday-go-to-meeting clothes. I want the court to see a solid, sober, intelligent group of Black citizens who want their freedom, want to be first class citizens, want their Constitutional rights.' And we did pack that courtroom." Juanita Jackson and other Forum activists were in court on June 18. A half-century later, her words testify to the exhilaration that she and others felt on that day:

> They predicted that the case was going to take two to three months at least. Charles Houston with just simple words presented that case. In one day, not having left the bench, Judge O'Dunne, a White Irish judge in a lynch state, got the court to order the Board of Regents of the University to process mandamus.
>
> Young Herbert O'Conor, the Attorney General—he later became governor and senator—had his assistant handling the case. When he heard what the judge had done, he came quickly, and he argued with the judge to stay the mandate until he could get it into the court of appeals.

And Judge O'Dunne said, "You know when I went to law school, they taught me that a constitutional right is like a cloak, you are enveloped in it. You either have it, or you don't have it. This young man's constitutional right to attend law school at the University of Maryland has been violated. And if I were to grant you a stay, that would be compounding the injury."

Freedom movement activists were surprised that O'Dunne ordered Murray's immediate admission with no further review of his credentials; this was more than Houston had asked. The O'Dunne decision was a big victory, and reaction in the Black community was immediate. "The colored people of Baltimore were on fire," Juanita Jackson Mitchell later observed. "They were euphoric with victory. . . . [Houston] brought us the Constitution as a document like Moses brought his people the Ten Commandments." The victory in the Murray case "energized the whole community very much like the breakthrough that came in the Buy Where You Can Work campaign."[28]

Obviously, state officials had not taken the case seriously, and now they were scrambling to make up for lost time. They made several attempts to stop Murray from entering law school that fall. First, they tried to get the appeal date moved up to the summer. That failed. Then they tried to force Murray to study at Howard University while awaiting an appeal decision, with Maryland paying the bills. That failed. When it became clear that Murray could not be kept out, the authorities attempted to institute Jim Crow inside the law school. According to Juanita Jackson Mitchell, "Dean Howell thought that Murray ought to sit two or three chairs away from the White students. Thurgood wouldn't agree to that. And Murray went in, no problem at all." A last-minute hitch developed when it turned out that Murray did not have the money for the tuition, and the NAACP, the *Afro*, and Alpha Phi Alpha had to rush around to raise the necessary funds.[29]

Murray began attending the law school, and the predicted riots, withdrawals from the university, financial crises, and educational strife failed to materialize. Murray, by his own account and the accounts of others, got along quite well with his classmates, although an *Afro* survey of a number of White law students showed that some harbored feelings of hostility toward him. The NAACP watched over Murray closely, and he received constant advice and occasional tutoring from everyone, including Houston. As they saw it, it was the movement's responsibility that he succeed. By the time the state's appeal of the case came to court in January 1936, Murray had successfully completed an uneventful semester of law school and the Appeals Court upheld Judge O'Dunne's decision. Somewhat to the disappointment of the NAACP, the state declined to take its appeal any further, ending the possibility that the U.S.

Supreme Court might set a national rather than state precedent. Nevertheless, the NAACP's legal campaign, under Houston's direction, had won its first victory. It is no exaggeration to say that, with the Murray case, the campaign had taken its first step toward the *Brown v. Board of Education* decision of 1954, the climax of Houston's strategy—sadly, he died of a heart attack four years before this decision.[30]

After the Murray Victory

The success of the Murray case had three main, interrelated consequences for the Baltimore movement. The first had to do with the use of the courts; the second, with the organizational structure of the movement; and the third, with national linkages. Whereas litigation as a tactic had a long history in the freedom movement in Baltimore and had played an important role in recent years with the Euel Lee case and the injunction against the jobs boycott, the Murray case was different because it was a really big win against segregationism. Integrating an important Jim Crow institution was an *offensive* victory, a planned attack against the racist regime, not a defensive action attempting to limit or reverse a racist intrusion. And it was part of a larger, planned strategy. In an editorial, the *Afro-American* offered its vision of what that strategy could mean for the state:

> There are other inequalities in educational opportunities in Maryland that are crying out for court action.
>   Suit must be filed to compel the State to give colored children a school term equal with white children.
>   Suit must be filed to compel the State and the counties to provide equality in school buildings and equipment.
>   Suit must be filed to compel the State to provide equal transportation facilities for colored children living long distances from rural schools.
>   And, finally suit must be filed to compel the State and the counties to give colored teachers equal salaries with white teachers.

By the time this editorial appeared, activists in the Baltimore freedom movement were already committing themselves to precisely such a campaign. As Juanita Jackson Mitchell explained, "Charles Houston taught us that we could sue Jim Crow out of Maryland with the 14th Amendment equal protection clause," and little time was wasted in applying this lesson.[31]

The second result of the Murray case was that it facilitated a dramatic turn of the Baltimore movement toward the national freedom movement. This reorientation to a degree had been in the works since the protests of late 1933, when national connections played an important role, but it was not consolidated until the Murray victory.

The third result of the Murray case was that its victory exacerbated existing organizational contradictions in the Baltimore freedom movement. When older activists finally emerged as a force in the rejuvenating freedom movement in late 1933 and 1934, there was no adequate organizational form for them. The Forum, as an organization of young people, was certainly not suitable. Consequently, with the Murray victory, Carl Murphy, the Forum leadership, and others in the movement, encouraged by the national office of the NAACP, redoubled their efforts to reorganize the local NAACP branch.

In September 1935, the NAACP announced that Juanita Jackson had joined the national staff. Her assignment was to build a NAACP youth movement nationally, modeled on the now famous Forum. At that time, "The branches were resistant to developing youth groups because they thought the Communists would get into the NAACP through the young people," Juanita Jackson Mitchell later remembered. With the founder and former leader of the Forum as the national youth organizer, the national leadership of the NAACP hoped that the resistance in the branches would dissipate. However, adding Jackson to the national office as a full-time staff member was a major commitment of resources, since the staff numbered only six people. Interestingly, Houston, Jackson's friend and mentor, had reservations about her appointment to the national staff because he felt that available resources should be used to build a Black working-class base. As Houston wrote to Walter White, "Personally . . . Juanita . . . is swell. But frankly what bothers me about your own set-up, and personal thinking, is it is too white collar. What you need now is some strength on the industrial side; and frankly, you don't get it with Juanita." Perhaps Houston was right, and a national NAACP staff member devoted to connecting the organization to the burgeoning union movement could have moved the freedom and workers' movements into a much closer alliance in the mid-1930s than actually happened. Nevertheless, over the next few years, Juanita Jackson successfully led in the establishment of a nationwide network of NAACP Youth Councils, the national legacy of the Forum. The Youth Councils helped to expand the NAACP's mass base into the Black working class, and some of the councils, such as the one in Detroit, had real impact on later industrial struggles. But the Youth Councils aside, Juanita Jackson's first assignment on the national staff was to work with Field Secretary Daisy Lampkin on a membership drive in support of a new effort to reorganize the Baltimore branch of the NAACP.[32]

Reorganizing the Baltimore NAACP

From the time of the Crash through the mid-1930s, the various attempts to rebuild the Baltimore NAACP yielded disappointing results. Lampkin led a drive in 1930 that contacted dozens of organizations and churches in the hope of drawing in members, with meager results. Subsequently, Reverend A. C. Clark replaced Linwood Koger as president of the Baltimore branch. (Carl Murphy turned down a suggestion from the national office that he take the job.) In mid-1931, a tardy request for another membership drive was sent to the NAACP's national office, but because of scheduling conflicts, the national office could not help. A member of the national staff complained, "They will not do anything without help from us."[33]

During 1932, Murphy, by then a member of the national board of the NAACP, became increasingly concerned about the dearth of NAACP involvement in the Euel Lee case and in other activities of the regenerating Baltimore movement. Murphy pushed for the reorganization of the Baltimore branch that year, but a leadership crisis interceded when, after a nervous breakdown and an indictment for grand larceny in Virginia, the branch's president, A. C. Clark, resigned. Murphy, casting about for a successor to Clark, finally suggested the young Forum legal adviser W. A. C. Hughes for the office, but the branch presidency went to the well-established pastor Reverend Charles Young Trigg. As an individual, Trigg had worked hard during the anti-lynching protests and the jobs boycott in 1933, but he was unable to build a functioning branch. To give the process of rebuilding the local branch a lift, the Forum helped to form an NAACP Boosters Club, but neither the Boosters' rallies with national speakers nor even a fleeting discussion of having a national NAACP convention in Baltimore did much to resuscitate the local branch.[34]

Finally, in 1935, with the victory in the Murray case and the growing prestige of the national NAACP, Baltimore appeared primed to give reorganization another try. To clear the way for new leadership, Reverend Trigg announced his resignation, and Carl Murphy asked Lillie Jackson to preside over the reorganization process. She accepted. Juanita Jackson was dispatched to the NAACP convention in 1935 with the assignment of convincing the organization to locate its convention in Baltimore in 1936. She was successful. The Baltimore membership drive was then scheduled for October 1935 under the joint direction of Daisy Lampkin and Juanita Jackson.[35]

To state the obvious, a major problem for the Baltimore branch throughout the early 1930s was the weakness of its leadership. As early as 1931, an NAACP field secretary wrote to Walter White that in Baltimore, "The trouble is those who can won't give the necessary time to leading [the process of rebuilding the branch]." Four years later, Lillie Jackson was emerging as the leading leadership candidate, but there was, on the face of it, no certainty that she was one of "those who can." Langston Hughes later referred to Jackson as "a Baltimore lady . . . small in stature, but a dynamo," but this was far from evident in 1935. At forty-six, Lillie Jackson, a Forum adviser and Citizens' Committee leader during the jobs boycott, had a relatively brief tenure in the freedom movement. She had served for a short time as branch vice-president in 1928 but had resigned, as the historian George Derek Musgrove put it, "in disgust, calling the branch 'non-functioning.'" Moreover, as Lillie Jackson had discovered years before at Sharp Street Methodist Episcopal church, male community leaders, including some from the clergy, were resistant to women in top leadership positions. Nevertheless, in the wake of the Murray decision, when Lillie Jackson joined Carl Murphy in agitating for the renewal of the Baltimore branch, Murphy decided—correctly, as it turned out—that his childhood friend was the person to bring the local NAACP out of its coma.[36]

The membership campaign that kicked off the reorganization of the NAACP's Baltimore branch was approached as a major community-wide mass mobilization. With Lillie Jackson presiding, Carl Murphy chaired the campaign's steering committee, which included Thurgood Marshall as legal adviser, Clarence Mitchell as head of publicity, the chairpersons of several committees, and the "generals" of several divisions, including the men's division and the youth division. Five thousand posters with pictures and slogans raising key issues—lynching, the absence of Black police and firefighters, Jim Crow in public accommodations, segregation at the University of Maryland, inequality in the schools, and so on—were distributed throughout Baltimore's African American neighborhoods. The *Afro-American*, of course, publicized the drive to the hilt. Predictably, the Forum activists played a prominent role everywhere in the drive. A flying squad of young orators, led by the teacher (and ILD activist) Gough McDaniels and the Forum's Evelyn Travers (later, Evelyn Burrell), soap-boxed on crowded street corners and spoke from the back of a borrowed truck. Announcements about the membership drive rang from Sunday pulpits. Ralph Matthews of the *Afro* produced a radio presentation of his play on the Ossian Sweet Case (in which a Black family in Detroit who resisted a White mob trying to evict them, killing a mob member in the process, was ultimately acquitted of murder) to be broadcast over the local CBS-affiliated radio station. The broadcast of the play was canceled at the last minute, however, because the station feared it would upset the Ku Klux Klan in Maryland. On October 10, as a wrap-up to the ten-day campaign, a parade featuring an African American company of the Maryland National Guard, the bugle corps of a Black American Legion Post, the marching clubs of the Knights of Pythias and the F. E. W. Harper Temple of the Elks, and a young people's contingent proceeded through the city, ending in a Victory Mass Meeting where hundreds finally heard Ralph Matthews's banned radio play, read from behind a partition through loudspeakers. The membership drive was an enormous success. Approximately 2,000 people joined the local NAACP branch, and $2,314 in membership fees was collected. According to the NAACP's national organ, *The Crisis*, "All groups, all classes, all types of people were reached in the membership solicitation. Trades and labor groups, fraternal groups, social, civic and educational organizations, churches, businesses, institutions—all were solicited in this drive."[37]

Afterward, Lillie Jackson, who had proved her considerable leadership skills during the membership drive, was unanimously elected president. The new branch officers reflected a range of prominent older adult community leaders, from the lawyer Robert A. McGuinn to the schoolteacher Gough McDaniels to Sarah Diggs. As in the Forum before it, women were a majority of the branch leadership group—six of ten. However, with the exception of Thurgood Marshall and W. A. C. Hughes as branch legal counsels, young activists were conspicuously absent from the NAACP leadership. In the evolving division of labor, the responsibility of young activists continued to lie with the Forum until the NAACP Youth Councils were established. With the membership drive over, the branch was well on the road to reorganization, and the new leadership turned toward its first big task: hosting the Twenty-Seventh Annual Conference of the NAACP, scheduled for June 29–July 5, 1936 (see figure 27).[38]

The Twenty-Seventh Annual Conference, according to *The Crisis*, was the best in years. Five hundred and thirty delegates from across the country discussed the major issues of the day, from the political questions of lynching, Jim Crow, and the New Deal to the economic topics of organizing tenant farmers, domestic workers, industrial workers, and cooperatives. Many important progressive intellectuals and political figures, White and Black, spoke at the convention, including Secretary of the Interior Harold Ickes (his presentation was broadcast over national radio), John Brophy of the United Mine Workers, the sociologist E. Franklin Frazier, Angelo Herndon, John P. Davis, Ralph Bunche, senators Robert Wagner and Edward Costigan, and, of course, a host of top NAACP leaders. Apart from the welcomes from Mayor Howard Jackson and Governor Harry W. Nice, figures from the local progressive community—Rabbi Edward L. Israel and Edward Lewis of the BUL; Lillie Jackson, Enolia Pettigen, and Thurgood Marshall of the

27. Delegates to the Twenty-Seventh Annual Conference of the NAACP at the Community House of the Sharp Street Memorial Methodist Episcopal church in Baltimore. Photograph by Paul Henderson. *Courtesy of the Library of Congress.*

Baltimore NAACP—appeared on the program. To initiate the national campaign for an NAACP Youth Movement, the convention for the first time had a special youth section. As *The Crisis* reported, "Baltimore was an ideal city for the initiation of this much needed and long awaited youth movement. It was in this city that the work of the now famous City-Wide Young People's Forum came into being and subsequently lent its influence and inspiration to youth of other sections of the country." The youth section met every morning, separately from the regular convention, then on Wednesday evening the entire conference program was turned over to the young activists for "Youth Night," featuring Baltimore's Clarence Mitchell chairing and Juanita Jackson offering the keynote address. The Youth Night program, the handiwork of Juanita Jackson, had the largest attendance of any event during the whole conference, and the youth section of the conference drew a total of 217 participants from across the United States, and 142 of them from the Baltimore region.[39]

The NAACP convention in 1936 was a national coming-out party for Baltimore's freedom movement, especially for its militant youth, who basked in a newly found visibility and self-confidence. With the convention, the second period of struggle for the Depression-era freedom movement in Baltimore — a period of seeking directions, consolidating gains, and making advances — came to an end, and a new period was beginning. While the various directions explored by the movement during the early 1930s continued to shape the freedom struggle for the next decade, the main direction was now irrevocably linked to the national NAACP.

IV. Risings, 1936–1941

9

The CIO and the First Wave,
1936–1937

For who will accept the stories—that Pat Whalen made union speeches
to the native shore-side workers along the African coast, including Cape
Town, Durban, Port Elizabeth; or that Pat, single-handed, organized
a strike of natives in Calcutta; or that Pat was once framed on a murder
charge in one of the big railroad strikes out West, and was freed with
the help of the great Clarence Darrow; or that he led the big 1936 strike
of the seamen in the port of Baltimore? . . . But the fact is that many
of the stories about him are true.
—I. DUKE AVNET, Baltimore CIO Lawyer

In mid-1936, the social movements in Baltimore entered a new phase that
continued until the U.S. entry into the Second World War. During this phase,
the slow, halting economic recovery continued, albeit with a major inter-
ruption in 1937–38; the social legislation of the second New Deal was implemented; and FDR won re-election by one of the biggest landslides in U.S.
history. As confidence spread fitfully that recovery and change were real possibilities, the struggles in the Baltimore metropolitan region, as in the United
States as a whole, greatly intensified.

The 1936–1941 Phase

The character of the two major movements of the Baltimore region changed
markedly during this phase in several ways. First, both the workers' movement and the Black freedom movement grew rapidly and enormously,
spreading throughout the region and into its hinterlands. The workers'
movement expanded throughout the factories, shops, and workplaces of
the Baltimore industrial region and the state, hooking up with the workers'
struggle in the District of Columbia. The freedom movement extended itself

into the African American neighborhoods of the metropolitan region and of the cities, towns, and countryside of Maryland. In the process, the mainstreams of these movements concentrated increasingly on relatively separate spheres of activity.

Second, the earlier regionally based initiatives and actions of both of these movements during the pre-1936 era were transformed, step by step, into broader, more nationally connected, and sometimes nationally directed, processes as national organizational forms came to predominate over more local ones. The most obvious example of this transformation of the late 1930s occurred in the workers' movement, with the rise to pre-eminence in the region of the nationally based unions of the CIO. In a parallel development in the freedom movement, the Baltimore branch of the NAACP reorganized and rose to regional ascendance as it developed strong connections to its national organization.

Third, as the workers' and freedom movements in Baltimore grew rapidly in their increasingly separate spheres and "nationalized" orientations, their relationship to each other changed. Most notably, there was less overlap and interaction between the two movements, which now often developed their distinct purposes and directions in parallel: the workers' movement led by the CIO concentrated largely on building class solidarity in the workplace, and the freedom movement led by the NAACP mainly organized in neighborhood and public spheres on the basis of racial-ethnic solidarity. Nonetheless, the two movements functioned in a broadly common milieu, each with the other in its background, each indirectly affected by the activities of the other; they also maintained a degree of interaction and cooperation, although less intensely and frequently than before. In addition, there were crucial underlying convergences. The workers' movement, as it broadened and became more industrial-unionist in nature, became more multiracial and multiethnic. Simultaneously, the expanding freedom movement, as it recruited a wider mass base, became increasingly working class in its composition and, to a significant degree, in its orientation.

Finally, political radicals continued, during the post-1936 era, to play crucial roles within both movements, and in bridging the two movements, although in different and less readily observable ways than in the pre-1936 era. Indeed, U.S. radicalism itself had entered a new phase by 1936, and the Popular Front in Baltimore and elsewhere had become the dominant framework for progressive activism. Under the Popular Front, radicals consciously cultivated left-wing unity to build broad center-left mass organizational forms and an increasingly populist (as distinct from socialist) political culture. This shift in leftist strategy had definite, and somewhat different, effects on the freedom and workers' movements. Drawing on this general sketch of the 1936–41 period, we can now turn to examine both movements in more detail, starting with the workers' movement.

The Baltimore CIO Emerges

The big story in the workers' movement in Baltimore, and across the nation, during the last half of the Depression decade was the industrial unionist-upsurge led by the CIO. More a mass social movement than a federation of trade unions in its early years, the CIO burst the organizational and ideological constraints of the craft unionism associated with the American Federation of Labor (AFL) nationally, and the Baltimore Federation of Labor (BFL) locally. It effectively appropriated and redefined the various mass-democratic and radical traditions of industrial unionism that had developed during the late nineteenth century and early twentieth century and combined them with the Popular Front mentality. Everywhere, it sought in principle to build a broad, multifaceted coalition of radicals and progressives across lines of political doctrine and of working people and their allies across lines of occupation, skill, race, ethnicity, and gender.

The CIO, on a national and local level, was a response to both the successes and the shortcomings of the many workers' struggles, large and small, of the early New Deal organizing wave that swept through communities across the country from late 1933 to mid-1935. Organizationally, the CIO emerged from a national split in the AFL and was shaped in part by the existing national structures of the unions that turned their backs on the AFL hierarchy to launch a new industrial-unionist effort. At the same time, the CIO's call for a nationwide industrial organizing campaign spoke to the pent-up frustrations and aspirations of large sections of the multiethnic, multiracial working class—male and female—in locales across the United States. In Baltimore and elsewhere, the CIO amplified and redirected the class struggle that was in motion and effectively absorbed most of the projects, groups, and activists from the workers' movement of the early '30s, redeploying them in a new surge of workplace-based activity. The particular nature of the locally based forces that flocked to the CIO and the trajectories of their localized struggles before 1936 gave the CIO in regions like Baltimore many of its specific characteristics and contours.

Especially in "middle-ground" Baltimore, interracialism and antiracism were key to the CIO's industrial-unionist strategy. Of course, the CIO's interracialism was everywhere uneven and contradictory: at one pole of the spectrum, CIO groupings became virtual vehicles for a freedom struggle within the workplace and the working class; at the other end, CIO units endorsed interracialism as a slogan, then all but ignored it in practice. In Baltimore—as, no doubt, elsewhere—the degree to which the CIO's practices approached the former pole often reflected the level of participation of African American workers in particular CIO units and the role that radicals, both Black and White, were playing. In addition, the influence of the separate, meteoric growth of the Black freedom movement in the neighborhoods of the Baltimore region, and the intermittent collaboration of CIO unions with some neighborhood-based activists in the freedom movement, enhanced the success of workplace interracialism. Despite sound criticisms by a number of observers of the Baltimore CIO for its shortcomings on the question of race, the basic truth is that the antiracism and interracialism of the struggles the CIO led during the 1936–41 phase quite often approached the first pole. Furthermore, as time passed and as the struggle deepened, CIO interracialism in Baltimore, and nationally, strengthened interracialist tendencies within a number of AFL and BFL affiliates.

The working-class struggle during the 1936–41 period, both nationally and in the Baltimore region, occurred in two distinct waves of organizing. Beginning in 1936 and intensifying the next year, more and more workers began challenging capital from the standpoint of industrial unionism, demonstrably breaking with craft unionism. From late 1937 through the first half of 1938, momentum slowed because a new economic crisis, often referred to as the "Roosevelt Recession," weakened the conditions for successful struggle. Nonetheless, the movement regrouped, and by the end of 1938 it was gaining ground, albeit unevenly at first, in what would become the second, ultimately larger organizing wave of the period. From late 1939 through 1941, as economic activity significantly picked up because of the on-again, off-again European war and growing war preparedness in the United States, industrial unionism developed momentum while simultaneously facing a growing counteroffensive from its enemies. In addition, during the second wave of industrial-unionism, affiliate unions of the AFL and the BFL, often borrowing strategy and tactics from the CIO, began increasing in size to challenge the CIO's rising predominance.

The Split

The appearance and initial development of the CIO in the Baltimore metropolitan region during the first organizing wave can be viewed from both the top and the bottom. While developments at the bottom—on the shop floor, in the streets, on the picket line, in the local unions—were the most fundamental and decisive, the processes at the top in the various regional and national organizational forms of the workers' movement were also crucially important. I will begin with a look at the process at the top to get a sense of the overall character and pace of the changes that took place and of the emerging industrial-unionist leadership.

In October 1935, the annual national convention of the AFL, meeting in Atlantic City, rejected an industrial-unionist resolution on organizing mass production and an antiracist resolution against trade union Jim Crow. A split in the federation appeared, punctuated by a fistfight between John L. Lewis of the United Mine Workers (UMW) and William Hutcheson of the Carpenters Union. A few weeks after the convention, the leaders of eight industrially oriented unions and divisions of the AFL met and decided to put an industrial-unionist strategy, with an interracialist approach, into practice. On November 9, 1935, they formed the CIO as a grouping within the AFL. In August 1936, with industrial-unionist activity erupting across the country, the executive committee of the AFL, which had resisted and attempted to marginalize the CIO for months, finally rejected the CIO's strategy and suspended the CIO unions from the federation. These unions were formally expelled at the AFL convention in Tampa, Florida, the following November, but the action was anticlimactic, since by then the CIO had gone its own way and did not even send representatives to the convention.[1]

Between the AFL conventions of 1935 and 1936, CIO-minded unionists in region after region challenged craft unionism in the regional bodies of the AFL. In early May 1936, at the yearly convention of the BFL, regional delegates from the Amalgamated Clothing Workers (ACW) and the International Ladies' Garment Workers Union (ILGWU) offered a resolution of support for the CIO, which failed, but only by 60 out of 375 votes. In addition, a CIO-oriented candidate, J. Fred Rausch of the Building Trades Council and the People's Unemployment League (PUL), challenged the AFL stalwart Joseph McCurdy for the presidency of the BFL and lost by only eighty-eight votes. Despite these indications of a developing insurgency within organized labor in the region, the BFL majority stood fast beside the national AFL leadership. The only significant break with the tradition at the BFL convention of 1936 was the election of the first female delegate ever to the executive board.[2]

At its annual convention later that month, the Maryland–District of Columbia Federation of Labor (MDCFL), the state-level affiliate of the AFL, also faced an industrial-unionist upsurge. Besides the Baltimore-based industrial unionists, opposition forces at that convention included the UMW from Western Maryland; the CIO-oriented textile workers from the massive Celanese Corporation acetate plant in Cumberland, Maryland (who attended as observers without voting rights); and a number of militant unionists from Washington, D.C. Taking no chances, the MDCFL leadership, headed (like the BFL) by Joseph McCurdy, killed a resolution supporting industrial unionism in committee before the resolution made it to the convention floor. However, C. V. MacDonald of the Washington laundry workers' union managed to propose to the convention a resolution to ban Jim Crow in affiliated unions and to hire Black organizers. Despite receiving vocal support from progressives, industrial unionists, and radicals, including J. Fred Rausch, James Blackwell of the PUL, and Albert Blumberg of the Baltimore teachers' union and the Communist Party, the resolution lost in a close vote of eighty-two to seventy-six. McCurdy again managed to retain his leadership position, but the MDCFL was being battered from inside and out as waves of industrial-union organizing began to engulf the region.[3]

Over the next year, the split both ideologically and practically between the AFL and the emerging CIO deepened. Sometimes almost comically obsessed by the CIO threat, AFL leaders, including McCurdy locally and the AFL's national president, William Green, laced their condemnations of the CIO with anticommunism, claims that CIO leaders took orders from Moscow, predictions of chaos if the CIO prevailed, and racism. The conventions of the BFL and the MDCFL in 1937 formally expelled the region's CIO unions from both organizations; the CIO unions did not bother to send representatives. African American delegates at the MDCFL convention in 1937 submitted another resolution to organize unskilled Black workers; it was defeated, this time resoundingly.[4]

However, by 1937 the CIO, building on its considerable gains during the first organizing wave, had established its own metropolitan- and state-level structures. In July 1937, seventy-seven delegates from twenty-seven CIO unions in the Baltimore region met at the National Maritime Union hall and founded the Baltimore Industrial Union Council (BIUC). Frank Bender, director of the CIO in Maryland—who had come originally from the UMW (which was strong in western Maryland)—was elected president. Other key figures at the conference included representatives of the most vigorous industrial-union efforts in the region. Patrick Whalen, president of the Baltimore branch of the National Maritime Union (NMU), was elected first vice-president; William Hobbes, president of the Steel Workers Organizing Committee (SWOC) at Sparrows Point, became second vice-president; and the ILGWU organizer Angela Bambace was chosen fifth vice-president. Ulisse De Dominicis of the ACW was another of the influential conference leaders. The last four of these regional CIO leaders represented the three main pillars of the early CIO in the Baltimore region—garment workers, seamen, and steelworkers—and, it should be noted, they represented labor organizations with demonstrated commitments to interracialism. Other leading participants came from the Mine, Mill, and Smelter Workers, the Newspaper Guild, and the American Radio Telegraphists; all three had leftist leaderships and took strong antiracist stands.[5]

On November 8–10, 1937, five months after the creation of the BIUC, 215 delegates from 98 CIO locals participated in the founding convention of the Maryland and District of Columbia Industrial Union Council (MDCIUC) at Moose Hall in Baltimore. As with the BIUC, a leader from the UMW, John T. Jones of western Maryland, was elected president of the state-level body. Twelve vice-presidents were chosen, including representatives from the leading CIO unions in Baltimore, Washington, D.C., and western Maryland. Sidney Katz of the United Federal Workers of D.C. was elected secretary of the council, a position he would hold for the next eight years. The MDCIUC convention took an antiracist stance, electing two African American delegates to vice-presidential posts. The delegates discussed and voted on twenty-nine resolutions on economic and political matters, a number of which focused on racial questions. A resolution against Jim Crow in industry and in the unions passed overwhelmingly, as did several others concerning Black workers, including a solidarity resolution with the largely African American Comfort Springs strikers in Baltimore; a resolution supporting the Scottsboro Boys; a resolution calling for civil rights for everyone in Washington, D.C.; and a resolution advocating the extension of Social Security coverage to domestic and agricultural workers. During a lunch break, the African American delegates Jesse Smith of the NMU and Arthur Murphy of the SWOC were refused service at the Moose Hall cafeteria. In response, eight White CIO delegates who were present walked out, and the facility was boycotted for the rest of the convention, indicating that antiracism was more than just a matter of resolutions.[6]

The regional organizations of the AFL and the CIO also diverged on their relationship to radicalism. The AFL bodies, particularly the BFL, had long been officially anticommunist, but there had always been socialists and leftists in their ranks, and the radicals had sometimes been influential. That ended with the split, as the great majority of the Socialists and Communists moved to the CIO, and the regional AFL shifted sharply to the right, especially at its leadership levels. By contrast, a significant number of Socialists, Communists, and radical industrial unionists of various stripes were involved in the leadership of the regional CIO councils and the CIO unions affiliated with them—far more, it appears, than on the national level of the CIO. Based on an internal CP report by Mike Howard, a party member and steelworkers organizer who was elected secretary of the BIUC, the historian Vernon Pederson claims that five of the fourteen initial leaders of the BIUC were Communists, and seven more were "close sympathizers." The presence of Communists and radicals in leading circles of the BIUC and the MDCIUC was undoubtedly well known within these organizations at the time, but in the era of the Popular Front, as both historians and veterans of the era have pointed out, there were implicit rules against most Communist labor activists' identifying themselves as such. Still, their presence in the leadership ranks of the Baltimore CIO must have been something of an open secret. Similarly, the industrial-unionist rhetoric of the regional CIO bodies and meetings, while often class-conscious and militant, tended, Popular Front–style, to stop well short of socialist and revolutionary formulations.[7]

By the time that the MDCIUC was formed, the economic recovery was faltering, along with the first organizing wave of the late Depression. Nonetheless, the CIO on the ground in the Baltimore region had chalked up substantial organizing gains, giving the BIUC and the MDCIUC a solid foundation.

The Garment Workers–CIO

From early 1936, before disputes around the CIO and industrial unionism had torn apart the AFL's city and state federations, the CIO was already making its presence felt in the industries and the workplaces of the Baltimore region. During the strike and organizing wave of 1936–37, three groups of workers—the garment workers, the seamen, and the steelworkers—took the lead in shaping the industrial class struggle and thereby giving the CIO in the region its initial form.

The city's garment workers and their unions, the ACW and the ILGWU, provided the fledgling CIO in the region with its most important industrial-union base and its most deeply rooted "indigenous" foundations. Together, they were the largest, oldest, and—since their revival starting in 1932—most successful industrial unions in the region. Like their national affiliates, these unions aligned themselves from the beginning with the CIO project and became mainstays of the new organizing wave in the city. In April 1936, the ILGWU, for example, brought John Brophy, national director of the CIO, to town for an open meeting to build support for a regional industrial union campaign. At the time of this meeting, the ILGWU was already five weeks into a strike at S. Cohen and Sons, which, although marred by multiple fights, injuries, and arrests, was eventually won.[8]

The ILGWU caused a much bigger ruckus some months later, when in

March 1937 seventy-five women stopped work, and twenty-five of them sat down at the Roberts Dress Company. At the time, sit-down strikes were proliferating across the country, and the press in Baltimore responded to the Roberts sit-down with prominent headlines such as "City's First Strike of This Type Starts in South Paca Street Factory" (actually, a number of sit-downs had already occurred on ships in Baltimore harbor). The sit-down at Roberts Dress Company caused a particular stir because it involved women workers. In reality, this sit-down, called by the ILGWU national office to stop the company from sending work from the organized shop in Baltimore to non-union shops in New York, was a fairly mild affair compared with some of the workplace occupations of the era. The police were polite and unobtrusive, and the Baltimore plant manager offered the strikers sandwiches, cake, and coffee (which they refused). After two weeks, the union announced a settlement, and the workers who had remained in the building emerged victorious. The sit-down tactic had been successfully used in Baltimore in a well-planned, well-executed, very visible, nationally coordinated strike led by a union affiliated with the CIO.[9]

The impact of the larger Baltimore ACW on emerging industrial unionism was, naturally, greater. The ACW had mounted a series of organizing drives that began with its 1932 strike and continued with the National Recovery Administration (NRA) code fights of the first New Deal period, then with the post-NRA struggles. Now the ACW launched further actions during the wave in 1936–37 both to defend ground previously won and to expand its power and reach (see figure 28). In late 1936, a half-dozen clothing firms tried to break the ACW by lowering wages from former NRA levels and disregarding agreements with the union. The ACW struck the companies, which responded with strikebreakers and periodic violence but ultimately backed down in the face of the union's determination. Then, in February 1937, the ACW, with a membership then variously estimated at 7,000–10,000 in the city, pressured the national men's clothing manufacturers to raise the wages of their workers in Baltimore by the same 12 percent negotiated for workers in northern cities, thereby challenging management's practice of giving garment workers in the "border town" of Baltimore smaller wage increases than their compatriots to the north. After a couple of weeks of resistance, the employers capitulated, evidently unwilling to risk confrontation with such a formidable foe in the midst of a growing strike wave.[10]

These victories demonstrated the viability of the regional CIO's most established union, and thereby of CIO industrial unionism, to many of the workers of Baltimore. Also, during the wave of 1936–37, the ACW Joint

28. Throughout the second half of the 1930s, the largely female and increasingly multiethnic workers of Baltimore's garment industry, such as these pickets during the Kaylon strike in 1940, were key participants in the waves of industrial organizing. *Courtesy of the Kheel Center for Labor-Management Documentation and Archives, Cornell University.*

Board again demonstrated its commitment to interracialism by expanding its organizing drives into the unorganized segments of the men's clothing industry with the largest concentrations of African American workers and by doing so in an ongoing alliance with the Baltimore Urban League and Negro Labor Committee. Moreover, the ACW directly supported the CIO's organizing efforts in the textile industry, offering aid and guidance in 1937 to the fledgling Textile Workers Organizing Committee (TWOC). The success of the ACW, of industrial unionism, and of the incipient CIO was symbolized with some fanfare in October 1937 when the union moved into a new, larger headquarters building. Sidney Hillman, president of the ACW, and a number of other national union dignitaries joined local union leaders for an opening celebration.[11]

The Seamen–CIO

Along with the garment workers, the seamen played a crucially important role in shaping the emerging CIO in Baltimore during the wave of 1936–37, establishing themselves as the second pillar of the new regional industrial-union federation. The ACW and the ILGWU brought an older, tested, Baltimore-based industrial-unionist experience, with a developing interracial commitment, to the regional CIO. In contrast, the seamen brought an aggressive militancy, a willingness to directly take on both bosses and the AFL at once, and a forceful antiracism; they came to represent a somewhat more radical variant of CIO industrial unionism. In one of the most dramatic actions of the organizing wave, the militant seamen displayed these qualities when, on October 31, 1936, they struck the port of Baltimore.[12]

The seamen's strike of 1936–37, sometimes called the 100-Day Strike, involved all of the major Atlantic and Gulf ports. It was called with three interlocking objectives. First, it was a solidarity strike in support of the walkout of 40,000 marine workers on the West Coast led by Harry Bridges and the Maritime Federation of the Pacific. Second, it was a strike against the leadership of the AFL-affiliated International Seamen's Union (ISU) that had, without consulting the union's membership, made agreements with the shipping companies and refused to nullify them in the face of repudiation by the rank-and-file. Third, it was a strike against the shipping companies for improved contracts, a union hiring hall, the eight-hour day, overtime, and restrictions on port work on weekends. Accompanying these three objectives was the old left-wing project of building a national maritime federation of all marine workers.[13]

The seamen's strike was very much a left-led action, the work of an insurgent network within locals of the ISU called the Seamen's Defense Committee (SDC). The SDC was the direct descendant of the CP's Marine Workers Industrial Union (MWIU), which had dissolved into the ISU in early 1935. As such, the SDC drew heavily on the tactics, strategies, and overall vision of the earlier union. Although officially part of the ISU and the AFL, and not affiliated with the CIO, the SDC was an outgrowth of the broad industrial-unionist upsurge of the time that created the CIO. As an outcome of the 100-Day Strike, the insurgent ISU seamen's movement, nationally and in Baltimore, would transform itself into the NMU and join the CIO. The 100-Day Strike, therefore, shaped what became, especially in Baltimore, one of the CIO's most combative unions.

As discussed in chapter 7, the Baltimore local of the MWIU had been perhaps the most active local in the country and was responsible for the remarkable Baltimore Soviet of 1934. Drawing on this legacy, the Baltimore SDC proved to be one of the most vigorous organizing and antiracist networks operating in the ISU. While Joseph Curran and the New York–based SDC exercised overall leadership of the 100-Day Strike on the Gulf and Atlantic coasts, the strikers in Baltimore were often out in front of their colleagues in other ports. The Baltimore SDC initially contemplated a sit-down strike to support the maritime struggle on the West Coast but decided instead on a mass walkout. The strike grew from 800 seamen on the first day to 2,400 in a couple weeks, when as many as 28,000 walked off the job along the Gulf and Eastern coasts. In addition, the strike idled 2,000 longshoremen in Baltimore. As the strike grew, seamen in Baltimore started a series of sit-down strikes aboard freighters in the port.[14]

The reaction from the steamship companies was predictable and harsh. Up and down the coasts, they condemned the strike and refused to negotiate. Violence flared when the companies brought in goons and mobsters to intimidate and physically attack the strikers, resulting in several deaths; at least eight died in Baltimore alone. The seamen fought back to defend themselves and to drive off strikebreakers. The reaction from the ISU and AFL leadership to the seamen's strike was predictable. In Baltimore, Joseph McCurdy, head of the BFL — readier than ever to redbait dissident workers since the arrival of the CIO — denounced the strike on its first day, claiming that the strikers were not legitimate members of the AFL but were dominated by "members of the Communist Party." James Kelly, a local White leader of the largely segregated, though biracial, ILA, which felt particularly threatened by the strikers' antiracism and their call for a federation of all marine workers, immediately jumped into the fray on McCurdy's side. The ISU leadership, along with the Eastern and Gulf Coast Sailors Association of the AFL, joined the Steamship Trade Association of Baltimore and six major shipping corporations in getting a temporary injunction against the strike.[15]

Unions in Maryland affiliated with the AFL had been publicly supporting the ISU leadership against its rank-and-file insurgency and the SDC for some time. The convention of the MDCFL in May 1936 (the convention that rejected a ban on trade-union Jim Crow and quashed the resolution supporting the CIO) passed a resolution that described the ISU rank-and-filers as former MWIU members and Communists and supported the regional leadership's attempts "to purge their membership of proven Red termites." The national AFL and its unions were no more sympathetic to the seamen than their Baltimore affiliates. The AFL rejected the strikers' appeals at its national convention in Tampa, affirmed the disputed ISU contracts with the shippers, and branded the walkout an "outlaw strike."[16]

In Baltimore, the rank-and-file seamen countered by soliciting support from the broader progressive community. By late 1936, with the Popular Front an established fact in the city, the socialist, social liberal, and progressive labor circles that had ignored the Baltimore Soviet nearly two years earlier now responded favorably to appeals for solidarity from the left-wing leadership of the seamen. The Socialist matriarch Elisabeth Gilman became a fervent supporter of the SDC, and under her leadership, a citizens' committee was formed to support the strike and provide the strikers with food and clothing. Prominent members of this committee included CIO and PUL leaders such as James Blackwell and Lloyd Leigh; a grouping of progressive religious leaders, including Rabbi Edward Israel and Reverend Asbury Smith; and academics such as Gertrude Bussey of Goucher College. To broaden the strike support network beyond the Baltimore region, a team headed by the SDC leader Patrick Whalen traveled the labor circuit in eastern Maryland raising funds and making contacts.[17]

In addition, the support efforts for the 100-Day Strike attracted the attention of a recent arrival in Baltimore, I. Duke Avnet, who had graduated not long before from law school in New York City and had just passed the Maryland bar. Avnet came from a family of Jewish immigrants from "the Pale" of Russia and Poland; his parents became financially secure by operating a hotel in the Catskills. In an interview five decades after his first appearance in the city, he remembered his family being apolitical, although he recalled his father taking the side of the "underdogs." Avnet's college education, however, had left him "liberally inclined." He characterized his motivation in moving to Baltimore as simply a desire to live in a smaller city than New York, and he arrived with a strong interest in social justice. After a short time in the city, he attended a meeting at Westminster church and was much impressed with "a labor representative who was making an appeal to the congregation that night. He was a young man, a seaman, named Frank Dunlavey. There was a big labor strike afoot at the time. It was a strike by the rebels in the AFL International Seamen's Union against the ship owners. They were also rebelling against the leadership of the International Seamen's Union." Dunlavey described the desperate conditions of the striking seamen and told the crowd, "They need everything": food, medical care, and, "because an injunction had just been obtained against their striking and picketing," legal services. As Avnet put it, "I being a young lawyer, not having much of a practice at that time, went up to him and volunteered. And he said, 'Well all right, we'll be glad to have you.'" The next day, Avnet visited the strike headquarters and met Pat Whalen, who handed Avnet the injunction and asked him to do something about it. Avnet researched the question; then, with the help of an older and more experienced lawyer in Baltimore, he went to court and had the injunction overturned.[18]

So began the career of the city's most important labor lawyer of the period, who during the ensuing years worked closely with much of the regional CIO leadership and represented scores of CIO locals and activists in Baltimore and Maryland in key legal disputes. In addition, Avnet became an important activist outside the labor movement, especially in challenging segregation in Maryland's legal system. One of the main forces behind the Baltimore chapter of the National Lawyers Guild (NLG), Avnet said he was inspired to work with the guild because, while African American and female lawyers were barred from the Baltimore Bar Association, the NLG chapter was fully integrated. In many ways, Avnet became the successor to Bernard Ades, who earlier was the region's most prominent progressive, socially active lawyer. Avnet never met Ades, who had left Baltimore before he arrived. But Avnet later recalled that, during his first years in Baltimore, he was warned by other lawyers that "if you get into these civil rights cases, the same thing will happen to you as happened to him"—that is, disbarment. There were "very few lawyers in those days that would represent a union, even an AFL union," Avnet said. "They were afraid." Some years later, according to Avnet, Ades called him up and said, "I want to encourage you in doing the work you are doing. That's what I would have liked to have done. He said he was not practicing law any more. And he said he had a rough time of it."[19]

By the last week of November, the seamen's strike was picking up steam. With the marine workers on the West Coast holding firm, and the walkout gaining ground in Eastern and Gulf Coast ports, the specter of a nationwide general maritime strike loomed. At this point, cracks in the AFL anti-strike coalition began to appear, and the balance of forces on the waterfront seemed to be shifting in the seamen's direction, especially in Baltimore. On the national level, the AFL officers' union—the Masters, Mates, and Pilots Association—officially joined the strike with its own demands. In Baltimore, the unaffiliated Marine Engineers Beneficial Association went out at the same time as the Masters, Mates, and Pilots' local, together adding about 700 strikers to the battle. More important, mainly African American longshoremen in the ILA were showing signs of restlessness. In mid-November, the *Afro* reported widespread sympathy for the striking seamen among the Black longshoremen of Local 858 (see figure 29). To prevent a massive defection, the local ILA explicitly ordered its members to cross picket lines and begin loading and unloading ships.[20]

As discussed in chapter 7, the Baltimore MWIU had actively courted the

The First Wave 229

29. Black longshoremen were the dominant force on the docks in Baltimore throughout the 1930s. *Courtesy of Legacy Web, Baltimore County Public Library.*

ILA longshoremen in the early 1930s in its campaign to build a federation of all marine workers by focusing its efforts on the African American longshoremen majority and by contrasting its own antiracism with the segregationism of the ILA and the AFL. The MWIU's success, however, had been limited. Now the militant seamen of Baltimore saw another opportunity to establish an all-waterfront, interracial alliance while advancing the current strike. In mid-December, the SDC brought Harry Bridges., the leader of the Maritime Federation of the Pacific (who was then on a tour of Eastern and Gulf ports), and a group of approximately fifty longshoremen from the West Coast to town to help persuade local longshoremen to join the strike. On the evening of December 17, approximately 5,000 longshoremen and seamen jammed the Fifth Regimental Armory in Baltimore. After messages of greeting from Mayor Howard Jackson and Governor Henry Nice were read (indicating the growing leverage of the striking seamen, even among conservative politicians) and introductory comments were made, Bridges made an impassioned address to those assembled, urging the local longshoremen to walk out and to help "end the East Coast strike quickly." During the next few days, as maritime workers from the East Coast and West Coast soap-boxed on the docks together, newspapers in Baltimore reported that rank-and-filers from the largest two ILA locals, Local 829 and Local 858, were beginning to join the strike, thereby increasing the number of strikers to 5,000. The port would be crippled, and, as the *Baltimore Sun* put it, "It was predicted freely by shippers and seamen alike that as Baltimore goes, so will go other East Coast ports."[21]

To stop the rebellion from spreading among their rank-and-file, the leaders of the ILA in Baltimore attempted what must have been a desperate ploy. They called their locals together to vote officially on the question of joining a strike that they had previously censured as illegal. Local 829, with an overwhelmingly White membership, voted 350 to 237 to strike. However, Local 858, whose membership was more than 90 percent African American, voted 804 to 11 *against* striking after strong appeals for a negative vote from its local leadership. As William N. Jones of the *Afro* put it, with some rhetorical flourish, "For the first time in labor history in America, the vote of a colored-dominated labor union threatened to play the major role in an international strike of the first importance."[22]

Despite the nearly unanimous vote, the Black longshoremen of Local 858, evidently fearing racist reprisals, were unwilling to return to work unless the White longshoremen of Local 829 did as well. Suspense continued for another two days, as both longshore locals prepared to meet before the morning shift on December 21 at their adjoining union halls on 1102 and 1104 Hull Street. The striking seamen announced that they would picket the union halls beginning at 6 AM. Nonetheless, on that morning, the White longshoremen of Local 829 reversed themselves and united with their Black compatriots in refusing to join the seamen's strike. The looming possibility of a complete shutdown of Baltimore's harbor passed, and the possibility of an industrial-unionist maritime alliance in Baltimore was averted.[23]

Why did the Black longshoremen of Local 858, despite earlier indications to the contrary, refuse to join the 100-Day Strike? It is possible that some of the militant tactics the seamen employed to win the support of the longshoremen backfired. A number of longshoremen told *Afro* reporters that they decided not to join the seamen's strike because strikers had prevented Joseph Ryan, the White national president of the ILA, from speaking in Baltimore and, in fact, had run him out of town. In addition, the *Baltimore Sun* reported that a mass picket line of seamen prevented a joint meeting of the two ILA locals at a church hall and thus "weaned many sympathizers from the seamen's cause." Whatever the effect of the seamen's tactics in this regard, though, it seems unlikely that they fully explain Local 858's decision.[24]

Earlier, when discussing the reluctance of the Black ILA longshoremen to ally with the MWIU or to join the Baltimore Soviet in 1934, I argued that, in the context of a Jim Crow city and labor movement, the longshoremen and their leaders simply had too much to lose by working with Communist-led seamen, no matter how antiracist those seamen were. This time, two years later, things were somewhat different. Now, the longshoremen of ILA Local 858 were confronted with a three-coast national strike that was the product of a new, broad-based industrial-unionist movement with real interracialist credentials, which was already beginning to eclipse the craft-unionist, segregationist AFL on a national basis. But the answer to the question is still the same. The longshoremen of Local 858, like other Black longshoremen on the Atlantic and Gulf coasts, had achieved a *modus vivendi* that placed them in a privileged position relative to other Black workers; they were the "aristocrat[s] of Southern black workers," according to a fellow stevedore. Despite the segregationism of the ILA, they had attained a kind of parity with White longshoremen that was rare among Black workers. Also, their *institutional* power within the established organized-labor movement was quite extraordinary, as their ability to force the White Local 829 to reverse its decision to join the seamen's strike indicates. They were Baltimore's most successful heirs to the long tradition of African American trade unionism that emerged in the post-Reconstruction era, and the power and privilege they possessed was both hard-won and, as long as Jim Crow existed, quite fragile. This power and privilege was not to be lightly risked, however ambivalent the Black workers involved might be about the ILA. This choice should remind us, as some recent scholarship has done, that under segregationism, the semiautonomous spaces opened by African Americans to exercise limited forms of self-determination were sometimes quite logically defended against forces that were disrupting segregationism itself.[25]

This interpretation of Local 858's decision not to join the 100-Day Strike seems to be supported by the fact that the local's president (who had the surprising name Jefferson Davis) subsequently went out of his way to emphasize that he and his followers were sympathetic to the striking seamen but that the longshoremen acted out of organizational necessity. However, there were lingering doubts about the ultimate loyalties of some African American longshoremen. William N. Jones reported in the *Afro* that the longshoremen of Local 858 were standing by the AFL for the moment but that they were apprehensive about the coming battle with the CIO and the prospect of a never-ending battle within the AFL over Jim Crow.[26]

Although the peak of the 100-Day Strike in Baltimore passed with the longshoremen's refusal to join, the walkout did not immediately collapse. Even as the longshoremen were returning to work, two locals of ships officers again went out, idling 225 non-striking ILA members in the process. In fact, although there was slippage, the rank-and-file seamen's strike lasted until January 26, 1937, and during its last month, it took up a whole new campaign against the new continuous discharge books. Authorized by the Copeland Maritime Act and implemented on December 26, 1936, continuous discharge books were to be a mandatory, permanent record of every seaman's employment. Militant seamen saw them as "fink books" that could lead to blacklisting. In his autobiography, Charles Rubin, former seaman and editor of the rank-and-file newspaper the *Pilot*, described a key incident in this campaign: "The most sensational event was led by Patty Whalen, and called the 'midnight march of the Baltimore Brigade,' through rain and slush all the way to Washington and the Capitol. Seamen came from every port on the Atlantic and the Gulf. . . . Pickets were thrown around the Department of Commerce. Committees were assigned to visit all the principal department heads, including the White House." Thousands demonstrated in Washington, not just against the fink books, but also against the legitimacy of the isu's contracts with the shipping companies, a question that was then before the National Labor Relations Board (NLRB). A march from Baltimore to Washington was, of course, an old MWIU tactic.[27]

In the end, with the ranks of strikers thinning and the strike in the West coming to a conclusion, the seamen called off the 100-Day Strike on January 25, 1937—after eighty-seven days. Although the potential of the strike was not fully realized, it was by no means a total defeat. First and foremost, as a solidarity strike it was a success. The West Coast maritime strikers won a big victory that helped to establish a greater sense of unity among marine workers on the three coasts. Moreover, strikers in Baltimore and the East claimed a scattering of gains in wages and working conditions, new ties to local officers' unions, and possible concessions on the provisions of the Copeland Act. More important, the seamen in Baltimore and other ports emerged from the strike greatly strengthened, with an experienced core of rank-and-filers and a tested leadership in almost every port. In May 1937, in the wake of the 100-Day Strike, the seamen's rank-and-file movement founded the National Maritime Union as a CIO affiliate, with New York's Joseph Curran, the national SDC leader, as its president. Simultaneously, the Baltimore movement established a local of the NMU led by Pat Whalen, the principal leader of the SDC and the 100-Day Strike in the region. Whalen was a remarkable individual. Just over five feet tall and weighing only 125 pounds, he was over fifty years old at the time of the 100-Day Strike. Born to a radical working-class family in the western United States, he had a long history of union activity on the railroads and in other industries across the country, and as an international seaman. An independent thinker and a revolutionary syndicalist in temperament, Whalen was a member of both the MWIU and the CP in the early 1930s and subsequently became one of the most important CIO leaders in the city.[28]

Throughout 1937, the waterfront remained the place where the most militant version of the young Baltimore CIO's industrial unionism was forged. The NMU kept the pressure up on the shipping companies with frequent job actions and sit-down strikes; in some cases, the mere threat of a sit-down was enough to win a settlement from the company. However, in September of that year, thirty-seven NMU crewmen staged a sit-down on Bethlehem Steel's *Oakmar* after it tied up at Sparrows Point. As support for the *Oakmar*'s crew spread throughout the port, the company tried but failed to starve the crew out. Under threat of a broad solidarity strike, authorities in Baltimore took pre-emptive action and evicted the sit-down strikers by means of armed force. Despite the CIO's official complaints to the city government and the NLRB, the evictions were upheld.[29] The NMU was also willing to offer assistance to struggles beyond the ranks of the seamen, such as its support for the organizing drive of the CIO's Industrial Union of Marine and Shipbuilding Workers of America (IUMSWA), which in 1937 began establishing locals at the Maryland Drydock Shipyard and at Bethlehem's Sparrows Point and Key Highway shipyards.[30]

As the prime site of industrial-unionist militancy, the harbor also became a critical arena of contention between the advancing CIO and the defensive but reviving AFL. To counter the seamen's continuing project of building a federation of all marine workers and of rallying AFL forces on the waterfront to the CIO cause, the AFL set up the American Marine Labor Council as an umbrella for all AFL maritime unions. The Baltimore Marine Labor Council achieved a victory of sorts in June when one hundred ILA longshoremen refused to load the *Steel Exporter* until its NMU crew was replaced with a crew from the ISU. A few days later, the ILA attempted the same tactic by striking a ship named *City of Newport News*, but this time the NMU refused to back down, and a fight broke out between CIO seamen and AFL longshoremen. Also, competition between the AFL and the CIO over tugboat workers precipitated tugboat strikes that twice tied up the port for extended periods; the second of these strikes, however, resulted in significant gains for the workers. Ultimately, although the ILA and some other AFL unions were showing new vigor, the AFL counterattack against the CIO on the waterfront failed to progress very far. Severely damaged by the 100-Day Strike and undermined by a subsequent decision by the NLRB disallowing its contracts with the shipping companies, the ISU all but collapsed during 1937. More-over, in at least one case, an industrial-unionist versus craft-unionist conflict with strong racial undertones erupted *between* AFL unions. In mid-summer 1937, the ILA organized unskilled workers, many of whom were Black, at the Summers Fertilizer Plant, while the AFL Chemical Workers of America had organized the plant's skilled workers. The two unions fell into a jurisdictional dispute, and after arbitration failed, the longshoremen struck in opposition to the chemical workers.[31]

Finally, it should be reiterated that the seamen's and the NMU's struggles in the harbor during the first wave of CIO organizing offered the fledgling Balti-more CIO a very important model of antiracist organizing. Despite the over-whelming refusal of the Black longshoremen of the ILA to join the 100-Day Strike and the continuing, intermittent conflict between the NMU and the ILA on the docks, there was no racist backlash against the Black longshore-men among the interracial, though mainly White, seamen in Baltimore. On the contrary, the NMU continued to cultivate relationships with rank-and-file longshoremen, Black and White. Furthermore, the leadership of the NMU worked hard to instill a thoroughgoing antiracism in its own rank-and-file. Avnet, who became close to Whalen during the 100-Day Strike, later wrote an admiring biographical sketch of the NMU leader, which included an ac-count of an incident that occurred in early 1937. According to Avnet, an inte-grated crew that had been dispatched to a ship met a hasty rejection:

> The Captain of the vessel phoned and complained that some of the crewmem-bers were not satisfactory. There were three Negro members who had been assigned to the deck and engine departments. Previously Negroes had been segregated on the ships to the steward's department only. Pat [Whalen] held his ground and refused to withdraw these three crewmembers. Shortly after-ward, the crew itself arrived at the union hall and [the white crew members] announced that they would not sail with Negroes.
>
> Whalen called a general membership meeting for that night to try the white crewmembers for undemocratic conduct. During this meeting several seamen of color spoke against the white crew's actions, and a number of whites spoke in favor of it. Whalen took the floor and harangued the membership on how racism created a reservoir of strikebreakers and how the enemy ISU had always stood for Jim Crow.
>
> He spoke of trade union democracy where all were equal regardless of race, color or creed, and shook his head and vowed sadly that the new union would be better dead aborning than to follow in old ways. . . . The men understood him and the membership voted that the crew either sail with Negro members

or that they should turn in their union books. Some books were thrown upon the table. But the ship sailed with a mixed crew and this policy has since largely prevailed in the port of Baltimore.[32]

George Meyers, a White CIO leader and CP member during the period, recalled another way in which the radical seamen quite dramatically enforced integration: "The National Maritime Union always worked integrated crews, and we'd go to the bar and order up a bottle. The bartenders would serve the white seamen and refuse the others because, they said, it was against the law. So Paddy's [Whalen] boys would pick the bottle up and throw it in the mirror . . . and that was the way that the waterfront was integrated. After that, anyone could be served, no problem."[33]

There was, however, some resistance to interracialism in the NMU itself, and there were lapses. In August 1937, a group of Black and Filipino seamen wrote a letter to Joseph Curran in New York complaining that some NMU officials in Baltimore had been assigning them to all-colored crews. The *Afro* obtained a copy of the letter and wrote about it with an editorial entitled "Nip It in the Bud," predicting dire consequences for African American workers if the CIO should renege on its promises of racial equality. In response, Charles Hanson, an NMU official, responded immediately to the *Afro*, pledging that the NMU would not tolerate a color bar and declaring that the union was initiating an education campaign around racism. However, Charles Rubin, a White NMU activist, remembered telling an African American seaman in Baltimore in the late 1930s that the union was fully committed to eliminating racism, although "we are having a hell of a tough time doing it." But the commitment was there. Pat Whalen wrote to the NMU membership in January 1938 that "true unionism" stood in opposition to racial discrimination: "It is a very fundamental problem and cannot be compromised, and those of you who compromise are cowards."[34]

The Steel Campaign–CIO

As the CIO gained momentum in 1936, it turned its attention to an organizing campaign in the steel industry, which top leaders saw as the potential vanguard for the new industrial union movement. The United Mine Workers (UMW), a prime national mover behind the CIO, for years had suffered as the non-union steel industry bought up coal mines and squeezed the miners' union. Soon after the CIO was formed as a committee within the AFL, John L. Lewis of the UMW asked the AFL executive committee to fund a campaign in steel, offering to contribute $500,000 from the UMW's treasury. Receiving little more than vacillation and derision in return, Lewis wooed the AFL's Amalgamated Association of Iron, Steel, and Tin Workers (AAISTW) into alliance with the CIO for the proposed steel campaign, and the UMW put up the money. Philip Murray, vice-president of the UMW, mapped out an elaborate national strategy to unionize steel and hired scores of the best available organizers to carry it out, including (in a break with earlier UMW practices) some sixty Communists. In June 1936, in an irrevocable split from the AFL leadership, the Steel Workers' Organizing Committee (SWOC), absorbing the AAISTW, and the CIO launched a steel organizing campaign. However, in late 1936 and early 1937, just as the steel campaign was getting started, a series of sit-down strikes in automobile plants in Flint, Michigan, catapulted the United Auto Workers (UAW) and the CIO drive among autoworkers, to the foreground. In Baltimore, the SWOC's designated leading role was also overshadowed, not by the autoworkers, but by the garment workers and, even more so, by the seamen with their 100-Day Strike and the creation of the NMU. Nonetheless, the protracted SWOC campaign in the region — which included years of relentless organizing, outreach into working-class neighborhoods, and countless initiatives in alliance with the the Black freedom movement — did much to shape the industrial union struggle in Baltimore. Along with the garment workers and the seamen, the steelworkers formed the third pillar on which the region's CIO was built.[35]

The national leadership of the SWOC was extremely interested in Baltimore's important iron and steel industry, and organizing prospects there must have looked good, for steelworkers in the region were already on the move. In one of the earliest mass actions of the organizing wave of 1936–37, 900 workers at Eastern Rolling Mill went out on strike during March 1936. This strike occurred as the rubber workers' strike in Akron, the strike that essentially set off the national organizing wave, was heading toward victory. Moreover, this strike, like the later 100-Day Strike, was led by industrial unionists who were not yet affiliated with the CIO — in this case, members of the AFL-affiliated AAISTW, whose national officers were still discussing a possible country-wide steel campaign with Lewis and the CIO. In response to a 10 percent wage cut, 400 workers at Eastern Rolling Mill mounted a picket line to keep strikebreakers out of the plant, and they successfully resisted a number of police attacks. The strikers succumbed, however, when the combined forces of the Baltimore County, Baltimore City, and Towson police forces dispersed their picket lines and made arrests. In June 1936, Eastern Rolling Mill's workers struck again, and this time, after two weeks, the company backed down, canceling a scheduled pay cut, granting a forty-hour week with overtime, and giving partial recognition to Eastern Lodge No. 16

of the AAISTW. The lodge thanked the BFL, the ILGWU, and the ACW for their support, and along with its national union joined the SWOC and the CIO steel drive. The Eastern Rolling Mill workers provided the SWOC with a base from which to begin unionizing other steel mills in the region, especially the gigantic Bethlehem Steel emplacement at Sparrows Point.[36]

In early August 1936, amid great fanfare, the SWOC opened its official Baltimore drive. Because the situation at the Sparrows Point mill was rigidly antiunion and highly repressive, the SWOC supplemented its factory-floor organizing with a systematic strategy of base building in the various racial and ethnic neighborhoods where Bethlehem steelworkers lived. Of the major union campaigns in Baltimore launched in the late 1930s, only the SWOC's included a real focus on the neighborhood level. Initially, the SWOC launched a house-to-house canvass in the eastern Baltimore communities of Highlandtown and Essex and in the Bethlehem company town at Sparrows Point, signing up 156 steelworkers. After the canvassing, the SWOC began a series of open-air meetings with a rally at Eden and Monument streets in East Baltimore. It also cultivated alliances with community organizations and institutions. Organizers held numerous meetings at locations such as East Baltimore's Finnish Hall, sponsored events in conjunction with a variety of ethnic associations, distributed leaflets at churches, and sought coverage in the ethnic and radical press. The *Maryland Labor Herald*, edited by Charles Bernstein of the Workmen's Circle, became for a time a major voice of the SWOC campaign. The SWOC also organized in Baltimore's African American neighborhoods, connected with Black community institutions, and cultivated a relationship with the *Afro-American*.[37]

The SWOC's strikingly public interracialist approach was essential if it hoped to organize the plant, since approximately a third of the steelworkers at Sparrows Point were African American. In segregated Baltimore, the Black steelworkers could be won to the union only if opposition to racism were a first principle of the organizing drive. In addition, given the antiracist activity in the region in the early 1930s, the organizers may have felt that there was space in the border city to persuade a significant section of the White steelworkers of the wisdom of interracialism. Moreover, the SWOC drew on the experiences of its main progenitor, the UMW, which, whatever its weaknesses on the question of race, traditionally had one of the largest African American memberships of any national union. The SWOC assigned the former Pennsylvania steelworker Arthur Murphy, an experienced Black industrial unionist with a radical outlook, to lead the campaign in Maryland, along with the White organizers Israel Zimmerman and State Senator Robert Kimball.[38]

The SWOC's interracialism in the Baltimore region also had local roots. The failed Communist attempt to organize the steel industry in the early '30s had probably established some foundation for interracial unionism at the Bethlehem plant. In early 1935, when four Baltimore lodges and three Pennsylvania lodges of the AAISTW founded that union's Tenth District, the delegates had passed a strong resolution "against the practice of the steel trust of jim-crowism and discrimination." The antidiscrimination position of the AAISTW was fully vindicated during the struggle at Eastern Rolling Mill of early 1936, during which large numbers of the Black and White workers (some of them Communists) in the plant united and successfully forced concessions from management. When the SWOC in Baltimore absorbed the regional lodges of the AAISTW, it also absorbed their interracialism.[39]

The SWOC in Baltimore worked especially closely with the local council of the National Negro Congress (NNC) on its drive to organize African American steelworkers. The NNC defined itself as a nationwide militant, working-class-oriented freedom organization that sought to embrace and extend the existing freedom organizations. Comprising a remarkably broad coalition of political tendencies, the NNC had a strong orientation toward the labor movement and a natural affinity to the CIO. The socialist A. Philip Randolph, leader of the Brotherhood of Sleeping Car Porters, was the NNC's founding president while members came from a wide swath of radicals and progressives, including Communists and Socialists. In mid-1935, activists in the region joined others across the country in sponsoring the NNC's founding congress, and sixteen of them, including familiar figures such as Bernard Ades, George Murphy Sr., Ashbie Hawkins, Edward Lewis, William N. Jones, and Charles Houston signed the congress call. A Baltimore delegation led by Reverend D. E. Rice of the Payne African Methodist Episcopal church attended the NNC's founding congress on February 14–16, 1936 (see figure 30). By June, the Baltimore Council of the NNC had become one of twenty-six in the nation that was "fully formed," according to a national report by the NNC; it had taken up a voter registration drive, and that had become involved in the campaign to organize steelworkers.[40]

At the beginning of the steel drive in Baltimore, the SWOC organizers Murphy (who had spent the previous months organizing the NNC in the South and West), Kimball, and Zimmerman enlisted Baltimore's NNC as an organizational ally, and then met with important Black community leaders, including Thurgood Marshall of the NAACP, Edward Lewis of the BUL, William N. Jones of the *Afro*, and Reverend D. E. Rice to discuss their plans to organize the 5,000 African American steelworkers at Sparrows Point. Subsequently, the SWOC, along with the NNC and other supporters, sponsored an "all-city"

30. Baltimore delegates (*right to left*) Edward Lewis of the BUL, Reverend Roy Peters, and Reverend David Rice, with a porter, leaving by train for the founding meeting of the National Negro Congress in February 1936. *Courtesy of the Afro-American Newspapers Archives and Research Center.*

conference at Pythias Hall and an open mass meeting at Faith Baptist church, supplemented by a series of street rallies in the Black community. Since the *Afro* reported on all of these events, African Americans in the city became familiar with the organizing drive and the CIO. The SWOC, however, did not confine its appeals for racial unity to meetings in the city's Black neighborhoods. Through mass leafleting and general press releases, the SWOC and the Labor Committee of the NNC accused Bethlehem Steel of "gross discrimination" against Black workers before regional audiences, a charge that the company's management hastily attempted to refute. At the first SWOC outdoor rally in overwhelmingly White East Baltimore—the kick-off event for the whole steel campaign—both Thurgood Marshall and the national secretary of the NNC, John P. Davis, spoke. Subsequently, the SWOC sponsored similar interracial rallies in various working-class neighborhoods of the region.

Furthermore, to avoid the appearance that it practiced any type of Jim Crow, the SWOC assigned Arthur Murphy and its White organizers to all work with both Black and White workers.[41]

The SWOC campaign probably reached out, more often than any other CIO effort in Baltimore of the late 1930s, to the African American community at large and to the mainstream of the rapidly growing freedom movement. Still, the resulting cooperation between the SWOC and the mainstream of the freedom movement was somewhat episodic, partly because the forces led by the NAACP were so absorbed in their own neighborhood-based campaigns. In truth, though, the SWOC's forays into local Black neighborhoods aimed mainly to bolster support for its own workplace activities, not to build an ongoing neighborhood-based alliance. Hence, the SWOC's main allies in the freedom movement were the NNC and the BUL, organizations that were strongly oriented toward the workplace, but not really at the center of the burgeoning African American struggle.

Nationally, 1937 was the year of a great breakthrough for the CIO in steel. On March 2, United States Steel Corporation, the largest in the country, capitulated to the SWOC without a strike. It was also the year of a great setback, when the SWOC's strike against Little Steel (as the Bethlehem, Republic, National, Youngstown, and Inland companies were collectively known) collapsed in a wave of violence and repression epitomized by the famous Memorial Day Massacre on May 30, 1937, when police shot and killed ten strikers. Baltimore was a Little Steel town, and although the workers at Sparrows Point did not join the strike in 1937, the tragic events elsewhere temporarily derailed the local organizing campaign. Mike Howard, a former SWOC organizer in Baltimore, told the author Mark Reutter that, after the collapse of that strike, "It was a low, low time."[42]

Still, the SWOC drive in Baltimore made gains in 1937, in part because of the committee's success in organizing across racial lines. In early March, with the Bethlehem Steel plant running at capacity due to the worldwide arms buildup, union pressure helped to raise the minimum wage at Sparrows Point to $5 a day. At this point, the SWOC claimed that 4,000 of the 15,500 workers at Sparrows Point had joined the union, a big increase over the 400 or so members the AAISTW had a year previously. In July, as more and more workers joined, hope grew that a collective-bargaining election might be held soon. The SWOC organizer Arthur Murphy claimed that more than 4,000 Black workers had signed union cards. Bethlehem stonewalled, however, claiming that its employees were able to bargain through its "employee representation plan." The SWOC replied by filing a petition with the

NLRB charging that the plan was a company union and as such was in violation of the Wagner Act. In the meantime, the management at Sparrows Point was using armed company police and hired Pinkerton agents to physically intimidate organizers and disrupt the drive.[43]

The SWOC was more successful at some smaller plants. As the result of the previous year's strikes, Eastern Rolling Mill's workers, in an NLRB election in early June 1937, chose the CIO as their collective-bargaining representative by a four-to-one margin and quickly ratified a contract. The SWOC won another victory at Standard Sanitary Manufacturing Company, a maker of plumbing fixtures, after the company locked its 600 workers out to pre-empt a strike. The workers, many of whom were African American, responded with mass picket lines augmented by workers from Eastern Rolling Mill and Bethlehem. The SWOC, with the assistance of a federal negotiator, negotiated a settlement that, while not granting formal union recognition, gave the workers raises and a week's vacation each year. According to the *Afro*, this strike "was the first to involve so large a number of colored workers."[44]

The CIO in Other Sectors

While the garment workers, the seamen, and the steelworkers led in shaping the Baltimore CIO during the first wave, the industrial union struggle ranged far and wide throughout the region. Unionization efforts in the various economic sectors and industries all developed their own characteristic dynamics—including racial dynamics. An example of this was the CIO drive in the automobile industry.

Baltimore's relatively new auto industry must have looked like an enticing target for CIO organizers in early 1937, especially as sit-down strikes in auto plants spread across the country. Two General Motors plants stood side by side on Broening Avenue in southeastern Baltimore: a Chevrolet plant and a Fisher body plant, each employing 2,500–3,000 workers. Days after the beginning of the sit-downs in Flint, UAW organizers—including the seasoned local labor activists James Blackwell and J. Fred Rausch, both linked to the PUL and the Socialist Party—began organizing the Baltimore General Motors plants. Things did not go well, however. The management of both plants used supervisors, company unions, and, as the hearings of the La Follette Civil Liberties Committee of the U.S. Senate subsequently confirmed, Pinkerton agents to manipulate and intimidate the workers. The workforces at the plants were in large majority White, new to automobile manufacturing, and, in many cases, new to industrial employment; it appears that few of these workers had any previous contact with oppositional working-class or antiracist traditions. Consequently, in January 1937, the UAW organizers were literally run out of the plants by the workers. Subsequently, on February 24, workers shut down production for ninety minutes to protest the appearance of six UAW workers on the assembly line. As late as March 5, UAW members were still unable to enter the plants. Then, amazingly, everything changed. The national contract between the UAW and General Motors, signed in March 1937, recognized the union as the exclusive bargaining agent for *all* General Motors workers throughout the United States, including those in the Baltimore plants. In the wake of this agreement, the UAW made what appeared to be astonishing advances at General Motors in Baltimore. On June 8, 1937, 800 workers sat down at Fisher Body because the management would not remove an anti-union worker from the production line. The whole plant then walked out for a week in an unauthorized strike to protest anti-union harassment and assembly-line speedup.[45]

On the face of it, militant industrial unionism had taken root in the region's auto industry. However, these roots were still shallow, and General Motors workers in Baltimore remained volatile and unpredictable. Elsewhere in Baltimore, Black workers often gave CIO unions a stable anchor among the rank-and-file (even if there was some initial reluctance on their part to sign up with the union), but this potential anchor was all but absent in the General Motors plants. Moreover, the struggle against racism among White General Motors workers, which elsewhere challenged the antidemocratic character of Jim Crow ideology and strengthened industrial-unionist values, made little apparent progress on Broening Avenue.[46]

Beyond auto, CIO unions, including the United Shoe Workers; the United Furniture Workers; the United Sugar Workers; the Mine, Mill, and Smelter Workers; and the United Brick and Clay Workers, made gains in medium-size industries that had long been targeted by the labor movement. The organizing process was seldom easy, however, and often required tenacious, protracted struggle with assistance from the regional CIO. In August 1937, for example, the shoe workers won an NLRB election at the Chesapeake Shoe Manufacturing Company by a margin of 154 to 31. The company, like others in the city, refused to bargain, so the union struck. After twelve weeks and much support for the strikers from the ACW and the CIO, the company capitulated and signed a contract that included full union recognition, the eight-hour day, and a wage raise. Then, despite the contract, the company's president issued a statement to the press denying that the company had been defeated; a year and a half later, the NLRB finally ordered the company to live up to its agreement.[47]

Some medium-size industries had large concentrations of Black workers,

31. Although the main focus of the regenerating freedom movement was elsewhere during the late 1930s, Black workers struck, and Black leaders supported them. The picket in the center of this photograph from 1936 has been identified as Carl Murphy, publisher of the *Afro-American*. *Courtesy of the Afro-American Newspapers Archives and Research Center.*

and the regional CIO's interracialism was both rewarded with and strengthened by victories there (see figure 31). Three-quarters of the 800 workers at the American Sugar Refining Company in Baltimore harbor, the largest cane sugar refinery in the United States, were African American. In January 1938, after months of organizing, the workers at this refinery chose the United Sugar Workers–CIO over an AFL union as their collective-bargaining representative in an NLRB election. They elected an African American president and a Black majority to the leadership of the new Local 276. The Comfort Springs Corporation factory provided another example of a largely Black workforce that organized into the CIO—in fact, it became a cause célèbre of the regional CIO. About 70 percent of the 300 workers at Comfort Springs were African American, many of them women, and as soon as the organizing drive came to light, the management resorted to tried-and-true methods of race baiting to divide the workers. However, the CIO, in alliance with the local council of the NNC, countered the company's attack successfully, and both Black and White workers joined the United Spring and Accessory Workers' Local 539. In October 1937, after sixty Black (but no White) workers were laid off, more than 200 Whites and Blacks walked out together, mounted picket lines, and held out for a month and a half.[48]

By the time of the settlement at Comfort Springs, the MDCIUC had formed, and the region was beginning to feel the effects of the Roosevelt Recession. After seven years of Depression, the U.S. economy had started to reach pre-Crash levels of economic activity when, in late 1937, recession struck. In a few months, many of the employment gains made in the region and the country since the trough of early 1933 were reversed; unemployment rose rapidly across the board; and Black workers suffered immediately and disproportionately from the decline. By February 1938, the *Afro* estimated that the Sparrows Point steel plant had furloughed about 2,000 Black workers; for the first time since 1933, the number of strikes in Baltimore declined; and the work time lost to strikes fell by 55 percent. The first CIO organizing wave in the region had broken.[49]

10

The CIO, the AFL, and
the Baltimore Workers' Movement
The Second Wave, 1938–1941

In November 1937, in Baltimore when we met to form this organization, the economic recession . . . had begun to make itself felt. This recession continued on through most of the year. . . . Despite this obstacle, we have gone forward.
—JOHN T. JONES, President, Maryland and District of Columbia Industrial Union Council

With its organizing campaign stalled by the 1937–38 recession, the CIO in Baltimore and Maryland amplified its work in the political arena. Beginning in early 1938, as a part of the CIO's national strategy, the newly formed Labor's Non-Partisan League of Maryland worked with regional CIO bodies to elect progressive candidates—notably, David Lewis against Maryland's reactionary senator, Millard E. Tydings—and to promote state and national legislative initiatives on behalf of the multiracial working class. The Maryland and District of Columbia Industrial Union Council (MDCIUC) and the league supported wages legislation, labor rights bills, tax and budget laws, unemployment and relief measures, housing projects, and a federal anti-lynching bill. This venture into the realm of electoral and legislative politics broadened the scope of the regional CIO beyond the workplace, and its support for anti-lynching legislation put it at common cause with the rapidly growing NAACP branch. However, the economic struggle in the workplace remained the regional CIO's overwhelming concern.

By the time of the MDCIUC's second convention in early December 1938, President John T. Jones was able to discern "some slight indications of recovery trends." Actually, the second wave of CIO organizing was already under way, and this wave would be bigger than the first. By January 1939, the Baltimore regional CIO was again moving forward, claiming 40,000 members and growing. The momentum of the second wave would build over the next two years, as the Second World War overseas and war preparedness at home stimulated the U.S. economy, including many of the important industries in Baltimore.[1]

Three Pillars of the CIO

The three industrial union struggles—of garment workers, seamen, and steelworkers—that had most shaped the CIO in the Baltimore metropolitan region during its first organizing wave continued to do so during the second wave, although the role of each changed. The historian Robert Zieger, in his useful study of the CIO, characterizes the 1938–41 period as one of "stasis and schism" nationally. However, the epic national conflicts on which Zieger focuses, such as the defection of David Dubinsky and the International Ladies' Garment Workers Union (ILGWU) from the CIO, and the clash between John L. Lewis of the United Mine Workers (UMW) and Sidney Hillman of the Amalgamated Clothing Workers (ACW), were not major determinants of the grassroots struggles of the Baltimore region. Whatever the national disputes, locally the garment workers, especially the ACW, were a major force in the second organizing wave.[2]

The ACW's traditional base in men's garments was largely organized by 1938, apart from the anti-union bastion of the Gieif Company. But in the wake of the recession, the clothing industry faced further decline. In response, the ACW accelerated its major push into the cotton garments sector, an area of cheap clothing production that had actually grown during the Depression. Both the ACW and the ILGWU had conducted forays into cotton garments earlier in the decade, but this time the ACW campaign resulted in a series of major successes. The Marlboro Shirt Company settled with the union in April 1939; Stadium Manufacturing settled in November 1940; BVD, the largest cotton garment manufacturer in the region, with 800 workers in three plants, settled in March 1941; and Hanover Shirt settled in August 1941. In addition, through its cotton garments drive, the ACW increased its involvement on Maryland's Eastern Shore, organizing at several plants there, including one BVD factory. The struggle to organize these companies was intense, and despite the codified support of the right to organize under the Wagner Act, cotton garments employers put up stiff resistance. The workers at BVD, for example, were out for a month. However, no ACW cotton garments drive of this period was as difficult as the highly publicized campaign at the Kaylon Company, where victory for the 200 or so unionists finally came in July 1940, after twenty weeks of job actions, picket lines, litigation, and support activity from other unions. But even with so much of the ACW's energy and resources devoted to the cotton garments drive, and despite the specter of continued decline in the men's garments industry, the ACW's previously organized shops also won important gains, winning a large pay hike for 9,000 union members in June 1941. The Baltimore ACW could have been nothing other than an inspiration to industrial unionists in the region.[3]

In addition, both the ACW and the smaller ILGWU were prime backers of antidiscrimination resolutions and initiatives in the regional CIO. Both promoted interracialism among the mostly White, immigrant workers in their traditional base and supported the African American minority among their memberships. For example, when six Black women were fired for ILGWU activity at a non-union dress shop in 1937, the union fought for nearly a year and a half until it won their jobs back. Although the ACW's successful foray into the cotton garments industry increased its African American base, the union found itself frequently confronting bosses who systematically used racism to divide the workers and White workers with little union experience who reacted negatively to the union's integrationist approach. Organizing at the Marlboro and Aetna shirt factories was particularly tough in this regard. At one point, the Black ACW organizer Newman Jeffrey complained that racism "made it quite impossible to work here with any degree of effectiveness." During the grueling Kaylon strike, White ACW pickets shouted racial epithets at Black truck drivers who approached their picket line, drawing an embarrassing rebuke from Judge Eugene O'Dunne during an injunction hearing. As the ACW pursued its cotton garment campaign across the Chesapeake Bay to the Eastern Shore, it encountered a far more dangerous mixture of segregationist and anti-union attitudes. In November 1939, two White female ACW organizers had to disguise themselves and escape from a "drunken mob" that was looking for them in Salisbury, and the workers there who had joined the ACW were forced to sign union withdrawal forms. Nonetheless, the organizers returned to Salisbury, and the ACW pressed its campaign, step by step, with increasing levels of White–Black unity among cotton garments workers on the Eastern Shore.[4]

Expanding its organizing into other new areas, the ACW's Joint Board initiated a drive among the mainly African American workforce of the industrial laundries, strengthening its existing ties to the Black freedom movement in the process. In early 1939, ACW workers received support from other CIO unions and from freedom movement activists when they struck City Laundry in a bid to improve wages and working conditions. A few months later, ACW organizing efforts at Fish Dry Cleaning resulted in a strike by one hundred Black and White workers. As the strike dragged on for weeks, activists from the Black freedom movement formed a Citizens' Committee to support the strikers, with Elvira Bond (a former leader of the Buy Where You Can Work campaign) as its chairperson, and with the regional CIO lending its support. When Universal Clothing laid off forty-two Black workers in late 1938 to avoid paying them higher wages mandated by the new federal Wage and Hour Law, the ACW and the Baltimore Urban League (BUL) responded by creating a remarkably broad support committee that included many key forces from the labor, freedom, and social liberal communities, including Lillie Jackson of the NAACP; Carl Murphy of the *Afro*; Gough McDaniels, now of the National Negro Congress (NNC); Sidney Hollander of the BUL; Broadus Mitchell; and Rabbi Edward Israel. Initially, the company rebuffed the committee's efforts but then backed down in the face of a boycott against its products called by a coalition of the ACW, the League for Industrial Democracy (LID), the BUL, the Druid Hill YWCA, the Interdenominational Ministers Alliance, and the NAACP (which, despite its customary focus on neighborhood-based activities, was willing at times to intervene in workplace based struggles led by integrationalist unions like the ACW). Finally, as the ACW supported the organizing activities of CIO unions in other industries, it also worked to support their interracialism. For example, it helped the overwhelmingly White Textile Workers Organizing Committee (TWOC) to organize a local of African American rag graders. All in all, despite lapses, contradictions, and increasing challenges, the ACW used its leading role in the Baltimore CIO during the second wave to broaden the CIO's interracialist work.[5]

Like the ACW, the NMU and the seamen's movement also remained at the center of CIO efforts during the second organizing wave in the Baltimore region (see figure 32). As the Roosevelt Recession waned, the NMU mounted a series of shipping strikes that led to new contracts. A high point came in April and May 1939, when the NMU struck five major tanker companies along the Atlantic coast, idling ninety-two tankers in Baltimore Harbor; Pat Whalen, with some hyperbole, called this the most effective strike in maritime history. The Baltimore CIO again set up a Citizens' Committee, as it had during the 100-Day Strike, to support the seamen, and, signaling newly emerging cooperation between some AFL and CIO forces, the AFL's Teamsters Union honored the picket lines. The NMU continued to play a critical role in supporting union struggles, prompting the *CIO News* to remark, "It's safe to say that there isn't a union in town the National Maritime Union hasn't at one time or another aided with money or with counsel or with men." Most notably, the NMU continued to provide crucial aid to IUMSWA locals as the shipbuilding industry began to expand at an accelerating pace. Although most longshoremen remained in the ILA, the growth of the IUMSWA and

32. By the end of the second wave of industrial organizing, the NMU controlled the employment of seamen in Baltimore Harbor through its hiring halls. *Courtesy of the Albin O. Kuhn Library and Gallery, University of Maryland, Baltimore County. Reused with permission of the Baltimore Sun Media Group. All rights reserved.*

other CIO locals in the harbor area finally allowed the NMU to launch its long-desired federation of maritime workers, albeit in a somewhat truncated form without the participation of the longshoremen. In late 1939, the Baltimore Maritime Council was established as part of a coastwise effort to build an Atlantic Maritime Federation.[6]

The NMU, even more than the ACW, provided leadership in the metropolitan and regional CIO bodies in promoting racial equality through resolutions, support work, educational activities, participation in coalitions, and legislative action. As a result of the NMU's leading position in the Baltimore CIO, Pat Whalen was elected president of the Baltimore Industrial Union Council (BIUC) for two terms during the second wave. Ever a larger-than-life figure, he came to embody the militancy and antiracism of the CIO throughout greater Baltimore as he intervened in union struggles, spoke to the press, involved himself in political issues, and even represented the CIO in neighborhood-based campaigns, such as the protests around public housing for African Americans in 1939.

The Steel Workers Organizing Committee (SWOC), the third pillar of the

33. African American steelworkers voting in the crucial union recognition election inside Bethlehem Steel's Sparrows Point plant, September 25, 1941. *Courtesy of Legacy Web, Baltimore County Public Library.*

regional CIO organizing campaign, saw the crucial Bethlehem Steel drive stall with the Roosevelt Recession, then advance only slowly as the second organizing wave took hold during late 1938 and early 1939. The drive took a step forward in August 1939 when the National Labor Relations Board (NLRB) disestablished the Bethlehem company union, although the management rapidly constituted another, slightly less obvious company union. The SWOC replied with a strategy used by organizers across the country: it "bored from within" by running candidates for offices within the company union while attacking it from without. As the war-preparedness economic expansion took off in late 1939 and 1940, organizing picked up, and in early 1941, the SWOC declared membership gains of 70 percent in one month, reaching a total of 16,000 members in August. Finally, in September, the steelworkers got their long-sought NLRB election and, by a vote of 10,813 to 4,198, gave SWOC a better than two-to-one victory (see figure 33). By late 1941, after a five-year battle, the 20,000 steelworkers at Bethlehem's Sparrows Point mill, the largest on the Eastern seaboard, won union recognition.[7]

Despite the protracted, sometimes discouraging course of the SWOC's Bethlehem Steel campaign, its ultimate success consolidated the CIO as a major social force in the Baltimore region. The victory at Sparrows Point was the capstone event of the pre–Second World War CIO organizing drives in the region and a major victory nationwide. The SWOC, throughout the second wave as during the first, offered a reasonably consistent model of interracial industrial unionism that focused on both the workplace and, somewhat unusually, the neighborhood. It probably would not have won without its antiracist neighborhood campaign. It set up special "divisional locals" in the Black communities of East Baltimore and West Baltimore, for example, sponsoring interracial social events for the rank-and-file. Indeed, on the eve of the NLRB collective bargaining election, SWOC held a major rally at Ebenezer African Methodist Episcopal church and brought John P. Davis, national secretary of the NNC, in to speak. As a result of these efforts, as many as 7,500 African American workers at Sparrows Point were SWOC members by late 1941, providing the deciding margin in the NLRB election. Throughout the period, the SWOC continued to receive public support from Black freedom movement forces, including the *Afro-American*, the BUL, the NNC, and some national figures affiliated with the NAACP, thereby providing an important example in this regard for other CIO efforts. The SWOC's collaboration with the rapidly growing Baltimore branch of the NAACP was minimal at best, however, for reasons that will be explored later.[8]

Beyond the Three Pillars

Beyond the big three constituencies of the Baltimore CIO during the late Depression, the industrial union struggle ebbed and flowed. It progressed in some industries that had been organized during the first organizing wave, made gains in places where the struggle had barely been initiated earlier, spread widely into sectors both large and small that previously had been almost untouched, and remained shut out by particular recalcitrant industries. Likewise, the practice of CIO antiracism and interracialism varied across all of these struggles, with some succeeding—as with the seamen, the garment workers, and the steelworkers—and some falling a good deal short of these levels. Nonetheless, given that this was Jim Crow Baltimore, where segregationist craft unionism had dominated the region, the CIO unions' overall gains around the question of race were significant. Moreover, given the large presence of African American workers in Baltimore, albeit mostly in the lower and more marginalized segments of the workforce, as the second organizing wave spread into the new sectors and niches of the region's capitalist economy, it more frequently engaged Black workers.

The UAW union in Baltimore maintained its hold on the important General Motors plants, with their overwhelmingly White workforces, throughout the second wave of organizing, but the General Motors locals remained conflicted and unstable. In early 1939, for example, after Homer Martin had been ousted as national president of the UAW in favor of R. J. Thomas, the local at Fisher Body in Baltimore voted to support Martin and to reject the "Communists"; workers there again ejected James Blackwell, along with a number of CIO leaders from the plant. Subsequently, when the local realized that its stand took it outside the UAW, it reversed itself completely and voted its support for Thomas.[9]

During the second wave, the TWOC succeeded in organizing the largely White Baltimore and Maryland textile industry. In 1938 and early 1939, the TWOC, with continuing support from the ACW, won collective-bargaining recognition in mill after mill in the Hampden-Woodberry section of Baltimore City, capping its success with an agreement with the union-resistant Mt. Vernon-Woodberry Company in April 1939. But the biggest victory in textiles came in September 1939 when the giant Celanese Mill in Cumberland, Maryland, capitulated to the Textile Workers Union (the TWOC, renamed as the TWU) after a massive walkout of most of the mill's 9,000 workers. The struggle produced one of the most important labor leaders in the region, George Meyers, who became the president of the Celanese local, one of the largest in the national CIO at the time, in 1940. Meyers, who grew up in a German and Irish mining family in western Maryland, left school in 1930, in his late teens, and began looking for work. However, as he remarked during a later interview, "There were no jobs in the mines or anywhere else." He finally got a job at the Celanese Mill and found, to his shock, that "conditions were really terrible." Drawing on his family's mine-working background, he and a small group of Celanese workers built a local union by 1935; when the TWOC emerged over a year later, they joined. In the face of company intransigence, the workers launched a series of sit-down strikes beginning "at the same time as the big sit-down strike in Flint" in 1937. During the second organizing wave, they followed these up with the mass strike of 1939, which led to victory. From its early phases, the organizing drive at Celanese had been influenced not only by the Baltimore ACW, but also by the Baltimore NMU, most notably in the person of Patrick Whalen, who met Meyers and other Celanese activists during the fundraising visit of an NMU delegation during the 100-Day Strike. Whalen became a mentor to Meyers, who rose through the ranks of the CIO to become president of the MDCIUC in 1941 and, like Whalen, joined the Communist Party (CP). Also like Whalen, Meyers became an effective antiracist leader, as he and the workers at the Cumberland mill successfully integrated Celanese and other all-White plants.[10]

Black workers were also on the move in mass production in the late 1930s. The United Sugar Workers, with their Black-majority workforce, had won collective-bargaining status at the large American Sugar Refining Company in Baltimore Harbor as the region's first organizing wave was waning. During the second wave, this union, with support from the NMU, waged a determined struggle that resulted in improved wages and working conditions for its members. The sugar workers' leaders also played increasingly important roles in metropolitan and regional CIO bodies; by late 1940, Local 276's African American president, Alvin Sampson, was a member of the MDCIUC leadership. Similar to sugar refineries, the fertilizer industry, also located in the harbor, had a largely African American workforce. Little CIO activity occurred in this industry during the first organizing wave, although two AFL unions were attempting to organize the Summers Fertilizer plant, leading to an intra–Baltimore Federation of Labor (BFL) jurisdictional conflict. At the beginning of the second wave, Standard Wholesale Phosphate and Acid Works, a large fertilizer plant at Curtis Bay, were organized in the AFL Chemical Workers' Local 100. Standard Phosphate workers clearly continued to be unhappy with their wages and working conditions, and very likely with their union, and they struck repeatedly. In August 1939, these workers walked out for the third time in eighteen months, and both the NMU and the ILA supported them. Contention between the AFL and the CIO at the plant resulted, and the workers abandoned the AFL for the CIO, ultimately winning company recognition as a United Mine Workers local in April 1940.[11]

The Baltimore CIO opened new economic sectors to organizing during the second wave. An important example of this was the plastics industry, which saw a sometimes violent, but ultimately successful, organizing campaign at the large plastics manufacturer Standard Cap and Molding. Another drive in a new organizing sector—this time among commercial workers—was the well-planned and publicized campaign focusing on the Read's drugstore chain. The regional CIO's scope, especially during the second wave, became very broad: CIO organizing drives were mounted among cafeteria, laundry, office, newspaper, aircraft, electrical, cannery, and federal workers; among waitresses, porters, insurance agents, donut makers, and crab pickers. The CIO even announced plans to launch its own construction workers union in July 1939 to compete with the BFL's building trades unions.[12]

A number of CIO initiatives outside the mass-production sector entailed significant interracial organizing during the second wave, included the Mine, Mill, and Smelter Workers' campaign to organize the construction labor force on the Montebello tunnel—a campaign that made headway despite repeated racial conflicts among workers. Also, the United Federal Workers

(UFW) emerged during these years as a combative and outspokenly anti-racist union that organized workers in all occupational categories—"white," "blue," and "pink" collar—in the federal institutions of Baltimore and Washington, D.C. In January 1939, for example, Baltimore Local 106 of the UFW announced a drive among federally employed attendants and porters, the majority of whom were African American. By the early 1940s, the local, ultimately one of the most active in the union, had developed a large, mostly Black membership under the leadership of Albert Benjamin, a former African American college athlete who was then in his early twenties.[13]

Moreover, the interracial commitment of many of the leading activists of the CIO in the Baltimore region was demonstrated by their organizing efforts among Black workers in a number of relatively small-scale, dispersed work situations; these efforts were often given front-page publicity in the regional CIO News. In late 1939, a reported 500 of the 700 African American pinsetters working in Baltimore's forty-odd bowling alleys joined the United Recreation Workers–CIO, delivered demands for better wages and work hours to their employers, then struck four selected alleys. William Dixon, a well-known figure in the Black freedom movement, served as treasurer of the pinsetters union, which launched a strike in 1940 that, despite militant picketing and support, failed. The African American redcaps at Baltimore's railroad stations were another example of the CIO's efforts to organize interracially in small workplaces during the period. In 1934, the redcaps had established an independent Black union and were soon courted by the International Brotherhood of Redcaps–AFL, with which they affiliated in 1938. Subsequently, however, the redcaps rejected the AFL union, with its segregated locals, and affiliated with the United Transport Workers–CIO.[14]

Also, in early 1939, the CIO called for a drive to organize Black waitresses in the taverns in the Black community. The CIO News wrote, "Miserable serfdom wages as low as $1.50 a WEEK are forcing some 600 Negro girls working in Baltimore taverns and restaurants to turn to prostitution for a living." Frank Bender, regional director of the CIO, called a meeting at the Druid Hill YMCA to explore the feasibility of the campaign. Simultaneously, the CIO announced its intention to mount a drive among domestic workers in Baltimore and nationally, but little came of this before the Second World War.[15] Finally, the CIO opened a whole new front in Baltimore's hinterlands by establishing the United Cannery, Agricultural, Packing, and Allied Workers of America–CIO among the mostly Black crab pickers on the Eastern Shore in 1938. As a result, 350 crab pickers in Crisfield walked out of eight canneries and won a contract (see figure 34). A photograph in the *Afro* showing the

34. Workers in the seafood industry in Crisfield and other places on the Eastern Shore of Maryland joined the second wave of industrial unionism in the late 1930s. *Courtesy of the Enoch Pratt Free Library, Baltimore.*

overturned and burned car of the CIO organizer Mike Howard of Baltimore testified that the campaign in the Eastern Shore was no picnic.[16]

At one point, the CIO's organizing drives among Black workers in the late 1930s threatened to create conflict with, and within, the freedom movement. In 1938, as an outgrowth of its campaign among newspaper employees in Baltimore, the Newspaper Guild–CIO began organizing the staff of the *Afro-American* newspapers. According to Juanita Jackson Mitchell's later testimony, one of Carl Murphy's nephews—probably George B. Murphy Jr.— was involved in the drive at the *Afro*. Murphy had previously worked on the Washington edition of the *Afro*, directed publicity for the national NAACP from 1938 to 1941, and became the national administrative secretary of the left-wing NNC. The CIO complained to the NLRB when management fired several union members, and the NLRB ordered the fired workers reinstated with back pay. The *Afro* stopped firing pro-union employees, but it continued to resist unionization until the mid-1940s. Interestingly, the *Afro*, which had always been a stalwart supporter of the CIO, continued to report favorably on union campaigns while pursuing its own internal union busting. Clarence Mitchell, in an interview many years later, argued that Carl Murphy and the *Afro* were consistent in their support for interracial and African American trade unionism, especially the efforts of the CIO, with the exception of this one drive. The *Afro*'s own defense was that, as a newspaper serving a poor community, it could not afford union wages.[17]

In sum, the CIO was involved in industrial union struggles far and wide during the second wave in Baltimore and Maryland and made great gains. However, in some major sectors of the economy, including electronics and aircraft manufacturing, its progress was minimal. Both industries had overwhelmingly White workforces, and both remained largely immune to CIO organizing initiatives before 1941. By the end of 1940, both were on the very top of the CIO's list of targets.

The Center of Gravity Shifts

Since shipbuilding had long been important to the Baltimore region, it was natural that the Industrial Union of Marine and Shipbuilding Workers of America (IUMSWA) would become important to the regional CIO — especially so since it was strongly supported by the NMU as part of the organizing campaign in the harbor area. By the time the IUMSWA joined the NMU in the Baltimore Maritime Council in late 1939, the shipbuilding workers had made significant organizing advances. As the war in Europe, North Africa, and Asia intensified, and as industries at home stepped up production, the tempo of organizing in shipbuilding quickened. In Baltimore, a milestone was passed when the IUMSWA negotiated its first major contract with the management of Maryland Drydock in late 1938, giving the 1,000 workers employed by the firm wage increases totaling $160,000. By the end of 1939, the IUMSWA's locals were making headway at the rapidly expanding Bethlehem shipyards at Key Highway and Sparrows Point, where war preparedness was shifting into high gear. The IUMSWA organizer James "Scotty" Atkins wrote with evident glee that the SWOC organizers at the Sparrows Point steel mill were "peeved" at the more rapid gains the IUMSWA was making at the point's shipyard. In September 1940, Local 33 at the Sparrows Point shipyard emerged as a major regional center of struggle as 900 welders struck, followed by 4,000 other shipyard workers. Five hundred workers paraded through Sparrows Point in support of the strike, and the *CIO News* claimed that the strike was 95 percent effective. Although the workers called off the strike without a settlement in early October, it was clear that the IUMSWA was gaining momentum. In June 1941, IUMSWA's Local 24 won the biggest NLRB election to date at Bethlehem's Key Highway yard, and Local 33 won an even bigger one in October at the Sparrows Point shipyard. More than a year later, with the United States fully engaged in the Second World War, the IUMSWA claimed 25,000 members under union contract; it had become a major force within the Baltimore CIO.[18]

In the shipbuilding industry, where Black workers in this period were employed in far smaller proportions than at Bethlehem Steel, IUMSWA organizers, like SWOC organizers, implemented an interracialist approach. In late summer 1938, the IUMSWA's Scotty Atkins got a Black worker reinstated in his job and signed up fifty Black laborers at Maryland Drydock Company; he claimed, "The fact that the union is going to the front for the colored laborer has its effect on the morale at the yard." Although relatively few in number overall, African Americans were most numerous and active in Local 31 at Maryland Drydock, which elected an African American officer. However, on some occasions, the IUMSWA had difficulties integrating Black workers into the life of the union. A White national organizer noted that none of the 220 Black members of Local 33 of Bethlehem's Sparrows Point shipyard reported for picket duty during a strike in September 1940. Moreover, racial tensions in the region's shipyards grew as production picked up and as rapidly growing numbers of Whites and Blacks, many of both racial-ethnicities from the rural South, poured into the shipyards. Under these circumstances, the IUMSWA's implementation of interracialism became increasingly uneven.[19]

The IUMSWA's victory at Bethlehem Steel's Key Highway shipyard in June 1941, followed by the SWOC's "capstone" victory at Bethlehem's Sparrows Point mill three months later, represented the dramatic finale to the CIO's second organizing wave in the Baltimore region. The size and power of the shipbuilding and steel unions at the end of the second wave inevitably resulted in a power shift within the CIO in the Baltimore region away from its two main foundational unions, the NMU and the ACW, toward the SWOC (soon to be the United Steel Workers of America) and the IUMSWA. With the upswing in war production concentrated in other economic sectors, the garment industry, which had been weakening for two decades, went into a relative decline, as did its leading union, the ACW. And while the waterfront as a whole dramatically increased in economic importance with preparedness, and maritime unionism was increasingly important to the Baltimore CIO, the center of gravity in this sector moved away from the NMU toward the IUMSWA. This shift was already evident in late 1939, when, in the election for the first chair of the new Baltimore Maritime Council, Scotty Atkins of the IUMSWA beat Pat Whalen of the NMU, who had just finished his second term as head of the BIUC. Still, this shift occurred slowly and unevenly; the NMU and the ACW, and leading industrial unionists from their ranks, continued to wield considerable influence well into the Second World War period.[20]

The AFL Resurgence

During the last part of the first wave and throughout the second wave, the BFL began to reactivate. Indeed, the Baltimore region was not unique in this regard, for across the country AFL unions regained their footing and attempted comebacks, some quite successfully. In Baltimore, some unions affiliated with the BFL regrouped, responded to the unrest in their constituencies, and began to reactivate. These resurgent unions used a variety of organizing approaches and treated the question of racial unity in a number of ways, with varying results.

Some BFL unions expanded with some success within classic craft and White-dominant structures. The heavily Jim Crow construction trades grew in importance as increased federal funding and war preparedness caused an upturn in construction. So did some smaller craft unions. In late 1937, for example, the all-White Local 40 of the American Federation of Musicians (AFM) mounted a tenacious three-month strike to guarantee that only union musicians would be permitted to play at private parties in the hotels. As the Christmas season approached, the hotel managements finally agreed to a compromise that gave the musicians most of what they wanted. In addition, a number of BFL-affiliated unions that were semi-industrial in character became active, such as the Amalgamated Association of Street, Electric Railway, and Motor Coach Employees, which in mid-1936 launched a promising drive at the Baltimore Transit Company. With 3,000 or so employees, including a small number of Blacks, Baltimore Transit monopolized the street railroad and bus system in Baltimore and appeared to be an excellent organizing target. However, the union ran up against a hardline management that repeatedly blocked organizing efforts and a company union that it failed to dislodge until well into the war years. Moreover, the union failed to break with some of the more conservative AFL traditions, and although it claimed to be interracialist, its practice proved otherwise, to its own detriment.[21]

The BFL attempted to break new ground by targeting Baltimore's municipal employees for an organizing campaign, but after some initial successes with the truck drivers in the Street Cleaning Department, the City Services Commission banned unions among municipal workers. The BFL backed off, sought to negotiate the ban with the city, and unilaterally offered a number of concessions such as a no-strike clause in future contracts. For eight months the city government stalled, once postponing a meeting in August between the mayor and the BFL until cooler weather arrived. Finally, in early March 1938, Mayor Jackson conferred with both the BFL and the CIO and affirmed the right of city workers to organize. By this time, though, much of the BFL's original momentum was lost.²²

Other BFL drives were more successful. In West Baltimore beginning in late 1936, the Distillery Workers Union–AFL initiated a determined drive to organize the Calvert Distilling Company. The company resisted, and the union persisted through the discharge of union workers, a strike, an intervention by the NLRB, and the disestablishment of the company union. Finally, in April 1938, as the second organizing wave was beginning, the Distillery Workers won a closed shop contract. However, the AFL union faced stiff competition from CIO organizers in the liquor industry. In September 1940 the CIO's Distillery Workers Organizing Committee (DWOC) won an election at Roma Wine Company, the first winery organized in Baltimore, and in October 1940, the CIO union organized Pure Rye Company, the second biggest distiller in the state. By 1941, DWOC — now renamed the United Distillery Workers–CIO — with its more aggressive industrial-unionist approach, was challenging the AFL union on its home ground at the Calvert distillery.²³

In contrast to the BFL's Distillery Union, the Baltimore Teamsters Union was not to be outflanked by the CIO. The Teamsters Union was one of the most important and militant unions remaining in the BFL, and, as we saw during the early New Deal period, it was imbued with something of an industrial-unionist and interracialist spirit. There were a significant number of Black drivers in Baltimore in the 1930s, especially on local routes, and many of the helpers in the trucking industry were African American. The Teamsters organized both groups. In 1935, the Teamsters Union was involved in a tumultuous taxicab strike that ended in an ambiguous settlement. In late 1936, this strike was renewed, followed by a truce, then renewed again in early 1937. Police repression, retaliation by strikers, and general disorder grew until Judge Eugene O'Dunne and Joseph McCurdy of the BFL negotiated a settlement, but unrest continued, culminating in the arrest of the Teamsters' organizer Harry Cohen. Serving a three-month prison term for inciting to riot, Cohen became a BFL cause célèbre and even won the support of activists in the emerging CIO unions.²⁴

In late 1938, as the second wave was growing, the Teamsters Union again went into action, this time by initiating a massive interracial trucking strike after contract talks with the owners failed. On September 1, 1938, 2,000 drivers and helpers, Black and White, walked away from some 500 trucks owned by thirty to forty intrastate and interstate trucking firms, thereby shutting down approximately 80 percent of the trucking industry in the metropolitan area and threatening to bring regional commerce to a standstill. In the midst of heavy police activity and periodic violence, including gunfire, the strike remained solid, and after six weeks, the Teamsters prevailed. Harry Cohen, who led the strike even though he was still on parole from his arrest during the taxicab strike, stayed out of public view; his fellow Teamster leaders repeatedly explained, with apparent enjoyment, that he had "gone fishing." In a strange turn of events, Cohen, the parolee, asked the State Parole Commissioner to act as conciliator in the strike negotiations, and a settlement acceptable to the union was thereby reached.[25]

Cohen, one of the most widely known AFL leaders in the region at the end of the truckers' strike, was a polar opposite to the BFL's Joseph McCurdy, not just because of his industrial unionist-like militancy and interracialist outlook, but because he lacked McCurdy's knee-jerk hostility to the CIO. I. Duke Avnet recalled years later that Cohen was often "a bridge between the AFL and the CIO." Indeed, especially during the second wave, the Teamsters "played both sides," as Avnet put it, often supporting the struggles of CIO unions and, in turn, receiving support from the CIO. As Cohen's star rose, he began to contest McCurdy's leadership of the AFL in the region. In 1942, shortly after the United States entered the Second World War, Cohen was elected president of the BFL after McCurdy declined to run for re-election. Edward Lewis of the BUL wrote at the time that an organized bloc of African Americans in the BFL helped elect Cohen because of his opposition to Jim Crow. According to Lewis, Cohen had promised that if he was elected, he would place Blacks on all of the major BFL committees, a promise he subsequently seems to have kept. Cohen's ascension to the top leadership post of the BFL would open more opportunities to Black workers and for interracialist organizing in the federation during the coming war.[26]

Like the Teamsters Union, the ILA played a role in the AFL's counteroffensive against the CIO, although after the collapse of the AFL's ISU, the ILA would periodically cooperate with the CIO in the harbor area. The ILA Local 858, the main carrier of the African American trade union tradition that developed under Jim Crow, weathered an internal crisis stemming from corruption charges in 1939–40 and developed an association with the burgeoning Baltimore branch of the NAACP. In late 1939, the local entered into joint litigation with the branch against miscegenation laws, and in June 1941, it became the first organization to take out a special life branch membership. The close relationship of the NAACP branch and Local 858 was unusual during the second half of the Depression, but it foreshadowed the branch's frequent collaboration with unions during the Second World War.[27]

Under the pressure of interracial organizing advances by the CIO, and with the example of successful participation of African American workers within the ranks of the AFL-affiliated Teamsters and the ILA, the BFL's approach to racial unity began to change. Toward the end of the decade, even President Joseph McCurdy of the BFL began to openly criticize racism among White AFL organizers. Furthermore, in alliance with some of its more racially progressive affiliates, the BFL began to participate in organizing campaigns in small industries and enterprises with large proportions of Black employees. In late April 1939, the Hotel Restaurant and Hotel Service Workers Local 695 and the Bartenders Union 532 launched an interracial organizing drive among restaurant, tavern, hotel, and fountain workers at a mass meeting at the Monumental Elks Lodge in northwestern Baltimore. The ILA, the BFL, and the state's AFL federation extended their support, and Jefferson Davis of Local 858 was the featured speaker. By early June, the two unions had signed up 350 Black and White members and had opened an employment bureau for the membership of the locals.[28]

In late 1939, the Teamsters, Local 858, and the BFL became involved in an interracial organizing initiative among commercial laundry workers, most of whom were Black women. In August of that year, thirty workers at White Swan Laundry in northwestern Baltimore, organized by the AFL-affiliated Laundry Workers International Union (LWIU), struck after several workers were dismissed. The AFL affiliates and the Baltimore NAACP backed the strikers, and when arrests occurred, the NAACP attorney W. A. C. Hughes stepped in to defend those jailed. Also in August 1939, forty workers backed by both LWIU and the Linen Supply and Dry Cleaning Drivers Union–AFL (evidently, a Teamster affiliate) struck the Troy Laundry Company. Feelings ran high during the strike: the White manager of the laundry publicly called the Black workers "dumb," and on several occasions, company property was damaged. A few months later, in April 1940, the mainly Black workers of the Overall Dry Cleaning Company, organized with the Teamsters Union and won a closed shop agreement; as an indication of the growing, if intermittent, cooperation between the AFL and CIO unions, the IUMSWA supported that struggle and called on its membership to patronize laundries organized by the Teamsters. In the wake of the settlement at Overall Dry Cleaning, three more laundry companies signed contracts with AFL unions. Although the ACW was also organizing commercial and industrial laundries largely staffed by African American workers at this time, no record has been discovered of any friction or jurisdictional conflicts between the ACW and AFL laundry organizers.[29]

The increasing openness of the BFL to interracial organizing was further evident when an independent interracial labor organization—possibly a company union in origin—chose to affiliate with the federation. Some 1,100

Black and White street cleaners, members of the Baltimore Street Cleaning Labor-Social Association, struck on January 18, 1941, after the city fired one of their leaders. Nearly two months later, the remaining 600 of the original strikers (250 of whom were African American) returned to work with a five cent an hour raise and back pay for the time on strike. Upon returning, the strikers declared their intention to join the AFL. Four locals of the IUMSWA and several top CIO officials supported the AFL-oriented streetcleaners.[30]

The changing approach to race among some of the BFL affiliates complicated racial dynamics within older, established craft-oriented locals. The Hod Carriers No. 194 is a case in point. While some hod carrier locals had been segregated, this local had apparently been integrated since its founding in 1934. According to the *Afro-American*, the union had made such progress in organizing Black workers and winning wage gains throughout the late 1930s that its membership in 1941 comprised 1,400 Blacks and 300 Whites, and all of the local's officers were Black, with the exception of the White president. Nonetheless, certain Jim Crow practices survived. In April 1941, the local held a ceremony at its new, larger headquarters to commemorate its seventh anniversary, and an international vice-president of the union (and former organizer in Baltimore) was the guest speaker. After the ceremony, to the surprise of an *Afro* reporter who had been invited to cover the event, the membership divided along racial lines and left for separate banquets. The White members ended up "making merry" in a downtown hotel, and the Black members celebrated at the Elks Home in the African American community. Neither the White president nor the Black officers would discuss the separate banquets with the *Afro* reporter, and the reporter was prevented from entering the Elks Home. The event outraged the *Afro*'s editors, who headlined their article, "AFL Union Gives Jim Crow Dinner" and "Colored Officials Try to Keep Biased Affair Secret." It is unclear how common racially separate union-sponsored social events were in the BFL's integrated locals, but the union adamantly claimed that its Black and White members had equal status and benefits.[31]

Finally, an organizing drive by an African American AFL local precipitated an unusual, multifaceted controversy. Late in 1937, the Musians Protective Association, the African American Local 543 of the AMF, moved to organize the City Colored Orchestra, a valued institution in Black Baltimore. The City Colored Orchestra was formed in the 1930s after years of complaint that the city only supported an all-White orchestra; an unnamed philanthropist donated $2,000 to the city to redress the grievance. Dr. Llewellyn Wilson, a music teacher at Douglass High School and music columnist for the *Afro*, became the orchestra's director; Dr. Francis Woods, the director of colored schools, was appointed chair; and Violet Hill Whyte (who would become Baltimore's first Black police officer) was named secretary. During its organizing drive, Local 543 demanded that the musicians of the Colored Orchestra be classified as professionals like the White city-employed musicians, not as amateurs, and that they be paid a formal wage at the union rate of $4 a performance and $8 for a concert, rather than an informal stipend of $2–$3 for "expenses." In response to the objection that such pay would raise the orchestral budget by nearly $1,000 over its $2,000 limit, Charles F. Gwynn, the president of Local 543, remarked that the city was paying $64,000 for its music program for Whites, so it could afford $3,000 for Blacks. In addition, the union demanded a closed shop contract for the Colored Orchestra like that in effect for the city's White musicians. The White city director of music, Frederick Huber, with the concurrence of Llewellyn Wilson, rejected the union's demands, and the contest was on.[32]

Local 543 called on the other locals of the AFM throughout the city to put Huber on its unfair list. However, Oscar Apple, president of the overwhelmingly White regional AFM that had recently won a strike in the hotels, demurred. Local 543 pressed the issue, implying that the racism of the White musicians' leadership was undermining the AFM's support for its Black co-unionists, and Apple somewhat ambiguously reversed himself. Then Local 543's members withdrew from the City Colored Orchestra until a contract was offered, decimating the body. Director Wilson vowed that the orchestra's shows would go on anyway, but they did not. With the situation deadlocked, Huber announced that there would be no concerts for Blacks during that season, triggering an outcry in the Black community that targeted the city government. Finally, in March 1938, after six months of contention, Mayor Howard Jackson agreed to provide the funds to cover the union's wage demands, and Local 543 temporarily withdrew its demand for a full closed shop agreement. The local announced that Wilson, the orchestra's director, also had to join the union or resign; however, when Wilson angrily refused to do either, Local 543 dropped the issue.

Edward Lewis and the Black Carpenters

While some affiliates of the BFL were integrating to varying degrees and in various ways, others, such as the BFL construction unions, simply refused to change. During the second organizing wave, a remarkable campaign launched a frontal attack on the racial division of labor in construction work by seeking to bring Black workers into racially proscribed occupations. Not surprisingly, given his activities earlier in the 1930s, it was Edward S. Lewis of the BUL who headed the campaign.

In April 1938, the U.S. Housing Authority announced plans to spend $15 million on public housing in Baltimore. Since by federal statute 4.6 percent of the jobs on the resulting construction projects were reserved for Black workers, Lewis moved immediately to organize Black construction craftsmen to take advantage of the mandated jobs. The problem was that the skilled jobs on these projects were to go to union workers, but the construction unions affiliated with the BTC by and large barred Black workers from membership. A significant number of skilled Black construction workers were present in Baltimore, but because of the Jim Crow unions, they could only find work as laborers. Lewis initially investigated whether the regional CIO, of which he was an active supporter, was in a position to organize integrated construction unions to rival the AFL unions. Despite the beginnings of a CIO construction workers' drive as early as 1936, the first local was not yet chartered in the region. Deciding that the CIO was not an alternative, Lewis drew on the experience of the National Urban League's Negro Workers' Councils in the mid-1930s, and he organized an independent group of Black construction workers.[33]

In June 1939, the resulting Building Trades Association (BTA) of Baltimore formed a committee including about seventy skilled Black construction workers, with Robert De S. Tutman as president and Edward Lewis as adviser, to integrate the White construction workers' locals. Although the BTA faced stiff resistance from Whites in the building trades, they succeeded in integrating the Bricklayers Union working on the Edgar Allan Poe housing project in 1939 and obtaining non-binding agreement from the exclusively White construction union affiliates to work toward racial integration on others. The BTA also requested that the local Housing Authority employ Black architects for federal projects, and shortly thereafter, Albert I. Cassell was hired. Faced initially with resentment from Whites on the construction sites, the Bricklayers Union in particular succeeded in breaking down racist resistance and opening the door to greater racial integration.[34]

In March 1940, Local 544 of the United Brotherhood of Carpenters–AFL, an all-African American local, was born, and several Black carpenters went to work on the Poe project. Although three Black union carpenters were subsequently fired and replaced with White union carpenters, causing a controversy, African Americans had successfully broken into the city's construction carpentry trade. By January 1941, 110 African American carpenters, members of Local 544, were at work on government projects. Another breakthrough then occurred on the Poe project when David Leigh, a member of the BTA who had attempted to get into the local Plasterers Union for ten years, was finally admitted to that union and given a job.[35] Despite setbacks, on the eve of the U.S. entry into the Second World War, African Americans had made substantial progress in entering the AFL building trades unions in Baltimore and in integrating important sectors of the construction industry. The National Urban League hailed this campaign, and its leader, Edward Lewis, and others in the national freedom movement took notice. As it turned out, the construction workers' campaign capped the decade-long Baltimore phase of Lewis's career, for he was promoted to the position of executive secretary of the New York City Urban League in 1942. Before he left the Baltimore region, Lewis summed up the progress of this campaign in *Opportunity*, the journal of the National Urban League, stating that the White construction unions were not the only obstacles that the BTA faced, for the Black community and its leadership were often indifferent to the drive to integrate trade unions. Lewis, probably more than any other social activist in the region, had worked from his base in the Baltimore freedom movement throughout the 1930s to bridge the gap between the freedom and labor movements. However, as indicated by his remarks in *Opportunity*, the distance between the movements at the end of the 1936–42 phase was still significant.[36]

Factionalism, Anticommunism, and the Popular Front

As military activity and the threat of all-out war spread in Asia, North Africa, and Europe toward the end of the decade, many radicals and progressives in the Baltimore workers' and freedom movements participated in activities that both favored peace and opposed fascism. The Baltimore League against War and Fascism embodied this dual focus and functioned as a prototypical Popular Front organization. The liberals and leftists in the league, while working to avoid another world war, actively supported armed resistance to fascist aggression in Ethiopia and Spain. However, the nonaggression pact signed by the Soviet Union and Nazi Germany on August 23, 1939, followed by the German invasion of Poland and the beginning of the Second World War, disrupted the Popular Front alliance in Baltimore, as it did throughout the United States. Many activists oriented toward the Soviet Union and the Communist Party of the USA all but dropped the public fight against international fascism, and they increasingly contested the Roosevelt administration's covert support to the allies and growing emphasis on war preparation. Other activists (including some who had left the CP) were shocked by the eruption of war in Europe and appalled by the party's about-face on fascism.

As tension arose between former Popular Front allies in the labor and social movements, outside forces mounted a major attack on the CP. Representative Martin Dies of Texas chaired the House Un-American Activities Committee and led a frontal assault on Communists and progressives, including New Dealers and union organizers, that reverberated across the United States.

In Baltimore, in a much publicized action, a group of Jewish First World War veterans invaded a CP meeting in December 1939 and heckled the national Communist leader Elizabeth Gurley Flynn over the partition of Finland by Germany and the Soviet Union. Then, in early 1940, the Dies Committee trained its sights on the Baltimore CP, ordering a raid on its offices and dragging leading Maryland Communists to Washington to testify on ostensibly subversive materials found in the raid. Albert Blumberg, secretary of the Maryland and District of Columbia branch of the party and an activist in the CIO from its inception, refused to answer most of the committee's questions and for months was threatened with jail. Later that year, the committee found supposed evidence of fraudulent signatures on Baltimore CP election petitions, and in a major media event, several Communists, including Blumberg's wife, Dorothy, were tried and convicted on charges stemming from the investigation. The heavy publicity around the allegedly fraudulent signatures, and the fact that they were purportedly those of African Americans, reinforced the growing hysteria around Communism and race. In June, the Works Progress Administration required all of its workers to take an oath swearing that they were neither Communists nor fascists; shortly after, Rabbi Edward Israel, the well-known social liberal, resigned from the Maryland branch of the Youth Council after public accusations that the organization was dominated by the Communists.[37]

Under these conditions, the Popular Front alliance of radical industrial unionists, antiracists, Socialists, and Communists that had been crucial to the transformation of the Baltimore workers' movement began to unravel, and factionalism grew. The fact that an international issue could so directly affect the workers' movement in the metropolitan area was, of course, testimony to the degree to which that movement had joined the national and international mainstream in the previous four years. But the matter was divisive: for the first time, the presence of Communists and radicals among the leadership and rank-and-file of the regional CIO became an important issue rather than an open secret. Participating in a national trend, the ACW submitted a resolution against communism and fascism at the convention of the MDCIUC in December 1940. The resolutions committee, however, replaced it with an "Americanism" resolution, which was adopted without discussion in order, as the CIO News put it, to "avoid disruptive name calling." In response,

Ulisse De Dominicis and other ACW delegates, followed by a number of delegates from the TWU, walked out of the convention. Over the previous year, De Dominicis, a socialist and key figure in the Baltimore Popular Front, had become progressively more hostile to the CP, contesting the leadership of his old colleague Pat Whalen, a non-public Communist, within regional bodies of the CIO, calling him on one occasion "a Communist tool." Whalen was having problems within the NMU leadership at this time, perhaps because of his well-known independence, or perhaps because he was becoming something of a lightning rod for the anticommunists. In early 1940, he took a leave to "work on his power boat," and in mid-1940, the NMU transferred Whalen to Tampa, Florida. The man who had contributed so much to the militant industrial unionism and antiracism of the Baltimore CIO left town with little fanfare. After the United States entered the Second World War, Whalen joined the Merchant Marine to fight fascism in the Pacific. He was killed on June 1, 1942, by a Japanese torpedo.[38]

In early 1941, an anticommunist crisis erupted in the IUMSWA, by then well on its way to becoming the largest union in Baltimore. Nationally, the Socialist-led IUMSWA was working closely with federal national defense efforts. In January, the union's General Executive Council (GEC) passed a resolution threatening expulsion to any member "furthering the cause of Communism, Nazism, or Fascism." In April, William Smith, the IUMSWA's regional director for Baltimore and a member of the GEC, charged Carl Bradley, the business agent for Local 31, and Norman Edward Dorland, the local's president, with "reflecting the attitude of the CP in criticizing national defense, the Office of Production Management, and the Shipbuilding Stabilization Committee." (It appears that Bradley's and Dorland's opposition to the Shipbuilding Stabilization Committee, of which the IUMSWA's president John Green was a member, may have been of more concern to the national leadership than their organizational memberships.) In the first action of its kind, the GEC tried and expelled Bradley and Dorland and suspended Local 31's autonomy. In mid-May, the secretary of the Navy, citing Bradley's and Dorland's expulsions from the IUMSWA, ordered Maryland Drydock to fire them. The company willingly complied.[39]

Carl Bradley had been involved in a wide variety of labor and Communist activities in the city since 1926. In 1931, he even ran for mayor on the CP ticket. His politics were a mystery to no one. Dorland had been in Baltimore only a year and a half. Both he and Bradley were veterans of the Abraham Lincoln Brigade in the Spanish Civil War and were celebrated as such in local Popular Front circles. At the time of their expulsion, both were rising not only in Local 31, but also in the regional structures of the CIO. Bradley was frequently mentioned in the *CIO News*; was a leader in the CIO-endorsed peace movement; and gave a rousing antiracist speech that brought the audience to its feet at the MDCIUC convention in December 1940. Dorland had been elected president of the BIUC just before he was expelled from the IUMSWA.[40]

The anticommunist expulsion of Bradley and Dorland sharply raised tensions in the Baltimore CIO. Bradley and Dorland refused to accept their expulsion, kept many of Local 31's records, and formed a "rump" organization. The NMU supported their efforts and allowed their organization to meet in the NMU hall. The GEC sent a trustee to take over Local 31 and demand Bradley's and Dorland's expulsion from the BIUC and the MDCIUC. He was ignored. Local 31 withdrew from the BIUC amid a hue and cry of threatening lawsuits and sharpening conflict. But despite months of agitation, Bradley and Dorland failed to win reinstatement. The Popular Front compromise of don't ask, don't tell for Communists in the CIO was falling apart, and those accused of being Communists found it very hard to mount an effective public defense. Sidney Katz, secretary of the MDCIUC and almost certainly a CP member, claimed that the Maryland–Washington, D.C., CIO had previously "condemned" Communism and that the current controversy was nothing more than a "smear."[41]

As the second organizing wave climaxed with its amazing gains, the Popular Front in the Baltimore region—as in the United States as a whole—was dissolving, the anti-labor right wing was launching a broad "anticommunist" offensive, and serious factionalism was rising in the CIO. Then in late 1941, the Japanese imperial government bombed Pearl Harbor, and everything changed.

11

The New Baltimore NAACP
and the Metropolitan Region, 1936–1941

My Mother [Lillie Jackson] used to say God doesn't want any mealy
mouth Christians—he can't stand those. You got to speak up and stand
up and speak out and let people know what you are standing for! She
was fearless, and sometimes she conveyed all of that to the people,
it was contagious, you know
—JUANITA JACKSON MITCHELL

If the big story for the Baltimore workers' movement from mid-1936 through
1941 was the rapid expansion and transformation of the union struggle under
the leadership of the CIO, the big story for the region's freedom movement
was the rapid expansion and transformation of the neighborhood-based
freedom struggle under the leadership of the "new" branch of the NAACP.

The "New" Baltimore NAACP

The new Baltimore branch of the NAACP was a mixture of continuities
and discontinuities with the past. Many of the issues and campaigns the
branch would take up during the years after its reorganization had been addressed earlier by the Baltimore freedom movement, and some had been on
the movement's traditional agenda for decades. The very fact that the new
branch quickly became the leading organization of the regional freedom
struggle seemed to represent a return to the 1910s and '20s, when the old
NAACP branch led the movement. However, despite some similarities with
the past, the post-1935 Baltimore branch of the NAACP and the regional freedom movement that it led represented a qualitative break with tradition.
The pre-Crash Baltimore NAACP, during times of high activity and low, was
always a small, relatively elite organization that attempted to serve the Black
community "from above," largely through litigation. By contrast, the new

NAACP branch, while not abandoning legal action as a strategy, sought more than ever before to organize the Black community as a whole to participate in its own liberation by means of mass mobilization, including direct action. The mass orientation of the new branch was, of course, largely the result of the experiences of the freedom movement during the early 1930s: the Euel Lee defense campaign, the Buy Where You Can Work movement, the response to the lynching of George Armwood, and other activities led especially by the City-Wide Young People's Forum and the Communist Party. Even Donald Gaines Murray's lawsuit against the University of Maryland Law School had a mass dimension. In addition, the Baltimore CIO's mobilizations in the workers' movement provided powerful examples of the gains possible through mass action. The outlook of the new branch president, Lillie Jackson, was emblematic of this orientation. As her daughter Juanita Jackson Mitchell later remembered, "She kept preaching about the masses: 'The NAACP has got to get away from just the classes, the teachers and doctors and lawyers; we've got to have the masses.'" The new Baltimore NAACP aimed to become a mass organization that led a mass movement, and by 1941 it had largely succeeded.[1]

However, if the post-1935 NAACP branch, with its mass orientation and mass-action approach, was heir to the movement of the early 1930s centered on the Forum, its tendency toward multifaceted involvement with the workers' movement was less pronounced. The Forum, through the labor speakers it hosted at its Friday night meetings, its coalition with the People's Unemployment League (PUL), and its work with the labor-oriented radicals of the Socialist and Communist parties, was building foundations for what might have become a substantial freedom–workers' movement alliance. During the 1936–41 period, while contacts between the two developing movements, often mediated by the Baltimore Urban League (BUL) and National Negro Congress (NNC), continued, and each movement significantly influenced the other, they tended more often to operate in parallel than in concert. The NAACP, increasingly the center of a growing freedom movement, focused its energy in the neighborhood and public spheres, and the labor movement led by the CIO focused just as strongly on the workplace. Hence, while the successes of the reorganized NAACP branch built on the pioneering practices of the Forum, in some ways the range of activities of the Baltimore NAACP was—at least until the onset of the Second World War—narrower than that of the Forum.

One indication of the Baltimore NAACP's success was the rapid growth and diversification of its membership. At mid-decade, there were probably about one hundred NAACP members in the city, most of them inactive; a year later, there were approximately 2,500 members, and the branch was one of the four top contributors of dues to the national organization. By the end of 1939, the branch's membership had climbed to nearly 3,500, second only to the Detroit branch in size; these two branches remained the largest in the country through the Second World War years. By 1941, the Baltimore branch's membership had grown to 4,263.[2]

By the middle of 1941, the NAACP in Baltimore looked very different from how it had looked half a decade earlier, in terms of both its size and class character. There are few direct data on the social class of Baltimore NAACP members during these years, but given the overwhelmingly working-class nature of Black Baltimore and the dramatic increase in membership, logic and anecdotal evidence indicate that vastly growing numbers of working-class African Americans joined and supported the local NAACP during these years. Earl Barnes, who became an activist in the shipyard union during the Second World War, remembered how his whole family and many other working-class people were drawn into the NAACP's activities in the late 1930s; he became a member at fifteen. In addition, Juanita Jackson Mitchell later recalled domestic workers with "run over shoes" coming into the office with their membership fee of $1. She also remembered recruiting members among the African American hod carriers and longshoremen, the latter because President Jefferson Davis of International Longshoremen's Association (ILA) Local 858 "taught the men to contribute to the NAACP." In fact, in June 1941 Local 858 took out a $500 organizational life membership in the NAACP, and a meeting was held at the Sharp Street Methodist church to mark the event. Executive Secretary Walter White of the national NAACP addressed the meeting and presented the leadership of Local 858 with a Life Membership Medal.[3]

There was, however, one way that the social base of the Baltimore branch of the NAACP remained unchanged during the 1936–41 period: its membership remained almost entirely Black, with no Whites in any leadership capacity. Of the $2,134 collected in dues in the membership drive of 1935, only $200 came from Whites, and this included several special $25 "sustainer" memberships. The Baltimore NAACP may have been integrationist in philosophy, but it certainly was not integrated in racial composition during the late 1930s — less so, it seems, than branches in the North. Perhaps the racial-ethnic character of the reorganized branch simply reflected the sharply segregated environment of Baltimore's "border city" neighborhoods. However, there was fervor to the branch's approach to racial advancement that at times had almost Black nationalist overtones, which might have seemed off-putting to Whites. Whatever the reason, very few White social liberals and radicals, such as those who sat on the various boards of the BUL, joined or participated in the local NAACP branch.[4]

An important feature of the work of the new Baltimore NAACP during the 1936–41 period—and this, too, was a change—was that it organized in two related but distinct geographical spaces. The first arena was the Baltimore metropolitan region proper, and the branch's success there is suggested by the membership figures noted earlier. The second arena was the region's hinterlands, for during these years the NAACP expanded throughout Maryland. By late 1937, the Baltimore branch was conducting its annual membership drive in several Maryland counties adjacent to the city and was receiving as much as one-sixth of its membership from those areas. The goal, however, was not to extend the Baltimore branch over the state like an umbrella but, rather, to help other locales develop their own branches. As Juanita Jackson Mitchell recalled, Lillie Jackson traveled all over Maryland in the late 1930s, "talking freedom's message." In alliance with the national office of the NAACP and the Maryland Colored Teachers Association, Jackson and her branch built a statewide movement that revived or initiated many county NAACP branches. As a much younger Juanita Jackson reported to Walter White in November 1937, "Mrs. L.M. Jackson, president of the Baltimore branch, has set as her goal for the N.A.A.C.P. in Maryland the organization of a Maryland State Conference of N.A.A.C.P. Branches." The state conference formed less than four years later.[5]

The branch's work "at home" in the metropolitan region and the extension of its work across the state were distinct, although deeply interrelated and interdependent processes. The best-known NAACP activities in Maryland in the late 1930s and early 1940s were without a doubt its state campaign, which had a major impact across the country. However, the campaigns outside the city's borders were possible only because the reorganized NAACP branch was already successfully building a broad, foundational movement in the African American neighborhoods of Baltimore. It therefore makes sense to begin by investigating the branch's activities in the city.

The Struggle in the Baltimore Metropolitan Region

One of the most striking things about the history of the Baltimore branch in the late 1930s and early 1940s is just how much activity it generated within the metropolitan region. In alliance with other community forces or the national office of the NAACP or on its own, the branch was involved in campaigns against discrimination in education, lynching, restrictive residential covenants, and segregation in high-profile public employment; in addition, it engaged in more spontaneous actions against discrimination by taxicab companies, department stores, and golf courses. While pursuing these protest activities, the branch honed its organizational structure, engaged in broad public education, and sponsored a series of activities that raised funds from and created a sense of identity within its mass base. Simultaneously, a number of the branch's leading members created a network of neighborhood protective associations, which, although not officially NAACP organs, provided the branch with a grassroots infrastructure. The new NAACP branch became not just a mass organization but a deeply rooted, very activist one.

Community interest in the fight against discrimination in education was particularly high because of the watershed success of the Murray case in 1935. Therefore, the branch, in cooperation with the national NAACP, worked to defend and extend the gains of that case. At the end of 1936, a second African American student gained entry to the University of Maryland Law School, followed by a third in late 1939. Still, segregationist forces attempted to roll back these gains, prompting an immediate response from the NAACP. In March 1937, H. C. "Curly" Byrd, president of the University of Maryland; Attorney-General Herbert O'Conor; and State Senator Ridgely Melvin proposed a bill to raise the state's subsidy to Morgan College and to create a new scholarship fund for Black students to study out of state so segregation could be retained at the university. The NAACP's national office and the Baltimore branch condemned the bill, threatened legal action, and began to mobilize community opinion against it. The bill died.[6]

The reorganized branch also challenged racial discrimination in Baltimore's system of elementary and secondary education. In early 1937, the NAACP renewed the freedom movement's long-standing demand for the immediate appointment of an African American to the all-White Baltimore school board. In 1937 and 1938, the Forum, working now as a semiautonomous organ of the branch, sponsored Friday night mass meetings on this issue and invited Mary Church Terrell, the first Black woman to sit on a city board of education (in Washington, D.C.), to speak. By the early 1940s, a broad coalition of churches and social organizations publicly supported this demand; even the Baltimore Industrial Union Council of the CIO and some prominent White figures joined in. Victory, however, was delayed until March 1944, during the war years, when the newly elected Republican mayor, Theodore McKeldin, appointed the veteran freedom movement attorney and NAACP activist George McMechen to the school board.[7]

The Baltimore branch also challenged discrimination in other facets of the education system. It repeatedly protested the living conditions at the Cheltenham Reform School for African American boys and called on the state to take it over from its private owners. Under pressure from the NAACP, a grand jury recommended a complete change of personnel on the reform school's board in mid-1938, a call echoed later that year by Governor Harry Nice. During the same period, the branch called for better schooling for Black children with disabilities and for a "decent" African American orphanage. And in 1941, the NAACP supported George Brown's suit against the Baltimore school board over the lack of suitable playing fields at schools for Black students; the board and the courts brushed that suit aside.[8]

Lynching was another central concern of the Baltimore NAACP from 1936 to 1941. Building on the momentum of the Baltimore freedom movement's anti-lynching protests of 1933–35, the branch, the *Afro-American*, the Forum, the emerging NAACP Youth Councils in the city, and allies at Morgan College mounted sizable meetings and actions during the National Youth Demonstrations against Lynching in 1937 and 1938. In January 1938, Lillie Jackson reported on the branch's campaign to pass anti-lynching legislation: "We have been busy calling up preachers, attending preachers' meetings, various Fraternal groups, Social clubs and individuals, asking them to write and send telegrams to our Senators in the State of Maryland urging them to vote for the anti-lynching bill as it is." After Congress rejected the bill, the branch and its allies sponsored a large demonstration in the middle of a snowstorm against Maryland's Senator George Radcliffe, who had opposed the measure.[9]

While the national NAACP campaign provided the main framework for the anti-lynching activities of the Baltimore branch, the branch also supported the local anti-lynching and defense campaign work of other groups in Baltimore, some of which was led by radicals. In 1936, the Scottsboro Defense Committee, led by the Communist Party, formed a Baltimore chapter. The branch provided the committee with meeting space, and several leading NAACP figures joined its steering committee, including Gough McDaniels, who became its chair. Both Lillie Jackson and Thurgood Marshall spoke at its mass meetings. In ensuing years, as the Baltimore council of the NNC carried on the work around the Scottsboro Boys, NAACP forces—especially the NAACP youth movement and the Forum—and the *Afro* supported its activities.[10]

The Baltimore NAACP and its allies remained particularly vigilant against the possibility of another lynching in the region. While the protests after the murder of George Armwood in 1933 had turned large sections of public and official opinion in Maryland against racialized lynching, the arbitrary murder of Black people remained a constant threat, especially on the Eastern Shore. In Snow Hill in 1938, the White chief of police reportedly

35. While continuing her involvement in the struggle in Baltimore, Juanita Jackson's main responsibility from 1936 through 1938 was to organize the national NAACP's youth movement. In January 1937, she (*left*) and another NAACP staff member visited the Scottsboro Boys in prison and then launched a national support campaign for them among African American youth. *Courtesy of the Library of Congress.*

shot a seventeen-year-old Black boy dead, point blank, without provocation, then shot into a crowd demonstrating against the killing. The Baltimore branch protested; the *Afro* gave the shootings prominent coverage; and the NAACP's national office investigated. In 1940, a crowd of 1,000 Whites broke into the Worcester County jail, seized a thirty-one-year-old woman and her fourteen-year-old daughter, and threatened to lynch them if they did not help to find the woman's husband, who was accused of rape and murder. The branch raised a clamor in Baltimore and Annapolis, and the governor sent in twenty-five State Troopers, who successfully rescued the captives.[11]

The old Baltimore NAACP had achieved its first victories over Jim Crow in the 1910s, not long after it was founded, by overturning city ordinances that mandated segregated housing. In the late 1930s, housing discrimination was still an important issue, for racially restrictive covenants—stipulations placed in the deeds of houses owned by Whites that prohibited sale to African Americans—were common, and the White tradition of using violence to uphold residential segregation still flourished. The problem of restrictive covenants was particularly severe in Baltimore because, unlike in many other cities, African American neighborhoods were "ringed" by White neighborhoods and could not expand without running into Jim Crow barriers. In fact, ringing Black neighborhoods by means of restrictive covenants was a conscious and ongoing policy of White neighborhood associations in the region.

In 1940, Orris S. Byrd of the Mount Royal Improvement Association claimed that of 3,000 White-owned properties in his neighborhood, which bordered on African American northwestern Baltimore, 2,800 were restricted by covenants. And John P. Raffety of the Tolson Springs Improvement Association stated that his area was entirely "protected" by covenants, effectively sealing off a Black neighborhood to its west.[12]

In late 1936, an African American couple, Reverend and Mrs. E. D. Meade, bought a house on an all-White block, despite a restrictive covenant written into its deed. They became the object of violent attacks from White neighbors and were forced to abandon the home. The NAACP branch's legal committee decided to make the case a legal test of restrictive covenants. When the attorney W. A. C. Hughes, with the backing of Thurgood Marshall from the NAACP's national office, filed suit in lower court and lost, the branch appealed to a higher court. Funds for the appeal came from local Baptist ministers and a fundraising campaign that included a mass meeting at which Thurgood Marshall spoke. Then, as Juanita Jackson Mitchell recalled, "The NAACP took that case to the highest court in Maryland, and we lost it there." The Court of Appeals held that the Fourteenth Amendment only covered the public sphere and that restrictive covenants were a private matter. The case ended there, because in 1937 an appeal to the U.S. Supreme Court was beyond the means of the Baltimore NAACP. In 1948, Thurgood Marshall and the NAACP took a restrictive covenant case from Missouri to the U.S. Supreme Court, and, as Juanita Jackson Mitchell put it, "Every argument raised in [the Meade] case was raised in *Shelley v. Kraemer*, which ten years later was won in the Supreme Court."[13]

Despite the legal obstacles, Blacks continued to attempt to move into "White" areas during the last years of the Depression, and Whites continued to respond with violence. While the Meade case was still in litigation in May 1937, the Slingluff Russell family moved to an all-White block, and a mob of Whites broke the windows of their house and splattered its walls with paint. In April 1939, a mob numbering as many as 1,000 White people attacked the home of Reverend and Mrs. Charles Randall, the first Black residents on the 1800 block of Baker Street, destroying their furniture. Police were called in; nine members of the mob were arrested; and two were injured. The branch sued, but the suit was unsuccessful, and the Randalls were served with an injunction that prevented them from staying in their home.[14]

As important as its activities in the educational, anti-lynching, and housing arenas were, the movement led by the NAACP achieved its most famous victory in the city during the late 1930s in a campaign against the color bar in public jobs. The immediate purpose of the campaign was not to destroy racial barriers throughout the public employment sector—that would come during the Second World War—but to place African Americans in relatively high-profile positions that provided services for, or held authority over, the Black community. In 1937, the NAACP and the Forum were eager to try again to breach Jim Crow employment at Baltimore's Enoch Pratt Free Library, a campaign they had lost three years earlier. They lost again in 1937 when, despite vigorous agitation and support, the library refused to hire Jean Blackwell, a woman whose excellent qualifications included a degree from Columbia University and experience as a librarian at the New York Public Library. The staff at the Pratt Library remained segregated until 1944. At about the same time they lost the Enoch Pratt case, the branch and its allies scored a victory for a job candidate at the city morgue. In Juanita Jackson Mitchell's words, "Bernard Martin had taken the exam for city morgue keeper and had passed it, but they wouldn't appoint him because it wasn't a Black man's job, it was a White man's job." So the branch "went to court and got him installed as a city morgue keeper."[15]

The really big victory came, however, with the appointment of the first African Americans to the city's police force. The demand for Black police officers had long been one of the freedom movement's cornerstone issues; the police, after all, literally had the power of life and death over Black residents. The Forum was particularly active in this campaign, bringing Black police and firefighters from Philadelphia, Atlantic City, and Washington, D.C., to its Friday night meetings to persuade people in Baltimore that their demands for African Americans in such positions were attainable. Then, as Juanita Jackson Mitchell later remembered, "We began to picket and do everything to demand colored policemen." Finally, in the fall of 1936, following an initial round of agitation by freedom forces, Governor Harry Nice announced in a speech at a Forum meeting that, after the retirement of Baltimore's serving police commissioner, he would appoint a commissioner who would be willing to hire Black officers. In May 1937, a grand jury recommended that the city hire African Americans to handle crime among Blacks, and public discussion of the issue grew, with stories on the subject appearing in both the *Afro* and the mainstream White press. The NAACP and the Forum mounted a letter-writing campaign, followed by a petition drive that collected 5,000 signatures in favor of the hiring of African American police. In response, Governor Nice appointed William P. Lawlor police commissioner, and in December 1937, Lawlor appointed Violet Hill Whyte to the Baltimore police force. A partially and symbolically important Jim Crow barrier fell.[16]

It is interesting to review Violet Hill Whyte's background as an indication of the kind of qualifications Jim Crow Baltimore required of its first African

American police officer. At forty, she was a high school and college graduate, had worked as a teacher in the public school system, and was the mother of four children. She was active in the School of Christian Education, a member of the advisory board of the Civic League, the president of the Intercity Child Study Association, the executive secretary of the Parent–Teacher Federation, and a member of the Negro State Republican League. As the daughter of Reverend Daniel G. Hill, former pastor of the Bethel AME church, and the wife of a school principal, she was from a distinguished Black family. One of her siblings was vice-president of Howard University, and three others were college instructors. In summary, Baltimore's first police officer came from a solidly upper-middle-class background; she was well educated, well connected in community circles, and part of the social stratum that included much of the freedom movement's leadership. Officer Whyte was assigned to northwestern Baltimore to work with "delinquent" Black girls. As the *Baltimore Evening Sun* noted, "A police-box key and a badge [were] the only marks of authority" that Whyte carried. Baltimore was not yet ready for an officer with a uniform and a gun, even if she came from the upper levels of the Black community.[17]

The movement did not rest with Violet Whyte's appointment but immediately called for more African American officers and demanded that they be uniformed. The previous September, Marse Calloway and the Maryland Colored Republican Voters' League, with support from the NAACP, had opened a free school to train Black candidates for the police force. In late February 1938, 183 men and women graduated, having completed the police school's three-month course. Although four of the male graduates joined the force in July 1938, it would be more than four years before another African American (a woman) was finally hired, and Blacks on the force were still denied uniforms. Finally, in 1943, in the middle of the Second World War, another new police commissioner, Hamilton Atkinson, gave uniformed assignments to the Black men on the force for the first time.[18]

In addition to its protest activities against lynching and discrimination in education, housing, and public employment, the Baltimore NAACP attempted to respond to incidents of racial oppression whenever and wherever they occurred. One of the first things that Lillie Jackson did as the branch president was to establish an NAACP office in one of her buildings that was easily accessible to the public. Through notices in the *Afro* and other means, the NAACP invited people to come by with their problems, promising that the branch would address them. In addition, as Juanita Jackson Mitchell recalled, the branch often attempted to get young men from the community out of prison: Lillie Jackson "would go to the judges, to the governor, to the parole board. . . . She would get them out on parole and encourage them. . . . The NAACP would help get them jobs." In another example, W. A. C. Hughes and the NAACP, working with ILA Local 858, defended a Black longshoreman and a White woman accused of violating miscegenation laws by marrying. In a partial victory, the couple received a ten-year suspended sentence, but the antimiscegenation laws remained on the books. The branch also monitored situations that seemed potentially threatening to community members. In a report to the national NAACP office in February 1937, Lillie Jackson wrote that the branch was watching the case of a thirty-one-year-old White man who was charged with raping a fourteen-year-old Black girl: "There have been a number of cases of White men attacking Colored girls and light sentences imposed. We feel that Negro womanhood should be protected and will do all we can to put a stop to this most brutal crime." Finally, in early 1938, Lillie Jackson experienced a racial slight that others had complained about for years: she was refused service by White cab drivers at the Pennsylvania Railroad station. The local NAACP sharply protested the incident to the Pennsylvania Railroad Company, and in response, the company promised to punish any drivers who practiced discrimination. When another racist incident involving a White taxicab driver occurred, Lillie Jackson and Thurgood Marshal pressed their complaints higher, but with ambiguous results.[19]

Jim Crow Department Stores

Black Baltimoreans during the late 1930s complained, as they had done for years, about racial discrimination in downtown department stores, and the reorganized branch took up the problem. While the department store struggle was intermittent, and not a major, ongoing focus of branch activity, it represented perhaps the most important attempt at interracial protest activity in the public sphere in Baltimore during this period, when truly interracial campaigns were rare in the NAACP-led freedom movement. The campaign also indicates something about Black–Jewish relationships in the region and how they affected the new freedom movement.

The issue itself was simple: the downtown department stores were hostile to Blacks shopping in their facilities. Walter Sondheim, a manager during the 1930s at the prestigious Hothschild Kohn store, later testified to the ways the downtown stores discriminated against African Americans. Some stores, he said, "had a policy of actually discouraging black customers. . . . Then there was a practice of not discouraging these customers, except in departments where you sold things that were tried on, like dresses, hats, and underwear—things of this sort. Then there got to be this incredibly insulting policy of saying that blacks could buy things in stores, but weren't allowed to return them." Of course, few African Americans could afford to shop often in the downtown stores during the Depression, so this form of discrimination was something of a middle-class issue. Nevertheless, many Blacks—especially Black women—were deeply offended by it. Lillie Jackson herself was infuriated when she was refused service while shopping for wedding apparel for her daughter Virginia at a downtown department store in 1933. Three years later, after the successful reorganization of the NAACP branch, anger about the department stores' practices flared again.[20]

In February 1936, the question of discrimination at department stores came up during an open discussion at a Friday night mass meeting of the Forum, and Lillie Jackson and other NAACP activists expressed themselves forcefully on the issue. Then in May 1938, Lillie Jackson described in a letter to the *Afro* how she had been refused service at Hothschild Kohn, and the Baltimore NAACP branch publicly launched a campaign against the downtown stores. Direct action soon followed as African Americans who were refused the right to shop confronted top managers and complained. The NAACP leader J. E. T. Camper later recalled accompanying Lillie Jackson and a male activist to shop at Hutzler's, another leading department store. After being rebuffed, Jackson directly challenged the owner, Albert Hutzler, who then offered to let her in to shop after closing time. She indignantly refused. On another occasion, Georgia McMechan, a NAACP activist, went into Hothschild Kohn to test discrimination and was prevented from trying on shoes. Juanita Jackson Mitchell later remembered that Lillie Jackson and Charles Houston discussed the possibility of taking a test case on the issue to court. Houston came to Baltimore to observe Jackson being refused service, but the department stores apparently got wind of the plot, and Jackson got prompt, courteous service for the first time in memory—and ended up buying items she did not really want. "Charlie never did come up with a suit he could file," Juanita Jackson Mitchell added.[21]

White activists entered this struggle because of the rationale some department store managers offered for their segregationist policies. The managers claimed that they personally wanted to end Jim Crow practices in their stores, but if they did, their White customers would flock to the competition. With the support of the NAACP and the Baltimore Urban League, a committee of progressive White women that included Peggy Ewing Waxter, the wife of the liberal Judge Thomas J. S. Waxter, met with Albert Hutzler, a leading figure among the owners, to discuss racial discrimination in his store. As Juanita Jackson Mitchell remembered it, Hutzler told the committee that he would consider ending discrimination if the committee brought him 1,000 signatures from White women in the wealthy northern suburbs of Green Spring and Delaney Valley pledging to shop at Hutzler's if it desegregated. The committee of White women took up the task with great energy; they were, in Juanita Jackson Mitchell's words, on "a real crusade." The women obtained the requisite signatures, but when they presented them to Hutzler, he raised concern about the reaction of less affluent White customers. The committee then obtained the signatures of more middle-class Whites, only to have Hutzler balk again and suggest that the women convince his competitors to end segregation in their stores. Juanita Jackson Mitchell recalled tears running down the faces of Peggy Waxter and the others because Hutzler had "just played with them like a cat with a mouse, they were so bitterly deceived." The campaign, and the involvement of White female activists in it, was revived during the Second World War, although little was won until the postwar years.[22]

For the freedom movement, the department store issue was especially complicated for two related reasons. First, some of the owners and managers of the stores were themselves otherwise fairly liberal, even on racial issues. Hutzler was on the Board of Governors of Morgan College and was appointed in the early 1940s to the Governor's Interracial Commission. At least two others served on the executive board of the BUL, including Walter Sondheim, a middle manager (who later claimed that he worked behind the scenes to overturn the stores' racist policies), who was friendly with Walter White, the NAACP's national executive secretary. Nonetheless, neither the liberalism nor the connections of some department store managers deterred the activists. Clarence Mitchell, in an interview in 1977, remembered that an unnamed White civil rights supporter who had ties to the department stores tried to get Walter White to stop Lillie Jackson from pursuing the issue for fear of its divisiveness. "But," Clarence Mitchell added, "that didn't help, because she just took on both Walter White and this man."[23]

The second complication of the department store issue was that many of the downtown stores had Jewish owners and managers. This fact adversely affected Black–Jewish relations in Baltimore, just as the predominantly Jewish ownership of shops on the 1700 block of Pennsylvania Avenue had created tension during the Buy Where You Can Work campaign of 1934. Just a couple of months after the reorganization of the Baltimore NAACP, a controversy erupted at a Forum Friday night meeting devoted to the question, "Germany's Treatment of the Jews: Is It Justified?" The meeting featured a mock debate between Baltimore's social-liberal activist Rabbi Edward Israel and a sociology professor from Johns Hopkins University. Rabbi Israel condemned Nazi persecution of Jews, and the professor, for purposes of the meeting, explained Nazi self-justifications.[24]

In a commentary on the Forum meeting in *The Crisis*, Rabbi Israel wrote that he was appalled by the seemingly sincere applause the Nazi position received from some portions of the overwhelmingly Black audience: "There seemed to be a yearning . . . to pour certain perceptible sympathies into that applause." During the discussion period, Israel's "anguish increased" as discrimination against Blacks by Jewish-owned department stores was raised. In his article, Israel minimized racism by the department stores, writing that it was true "in one or two instances," while he emphasized his own staunch opposition to all such racist practices. He was further horrified about what happened after the chairperson of the meeting, Juanita Jackson, responded to his suggestion and moved a resolution to oppose the participation of the U.S. team in the Berlin Olympics in 1936 because of Germany's persecution of Jews. Several well-known community figures got up and spoke in opposition because this was the first Olympics in which African Americans could compete. Under the guidance of the Forum's leadership, nonetheless, the resolution passed. Overall, Israel feared that what he witnessed at the meeting was not an isolated incident but that, "as a by-product of Hitlerism . . . there seems to be a great increase in anti-Semitism among Negroes."[25]

The "Letters from Readers" section in subsequent issues of *The Crisis* printed a variety of responses, most of them critical in one way or another of Israel's conclusions. One from an African American woman, who signed her name "Mig," deplored prejudice everywhere but questioned the existence of serious problems between Blacks and Jews: "The problems I think are more economic than racial." The other was from a Jewish progressive who pretty much accepted Israel's point of view, though with less anxiety, and counseled that "sympathetic unity" was necessary between Blacks and Jews, but this could occur only if "the Negro as well as the Jew extends the hand of friendship." Two letters from Baltimore were highly critical of Israel. One was from Lillie Jackson, and in it she claimed that there were "four things that have aroused the ire of all Negroes": discrimination in Jewish-owned department stores; high rent and housing prices in the Black community due to Jewish real-estate interests; Jewish home owners' working their Black domestic help hard for low wages; and Jewish politicians who solicited the Black vote, thereby displacing Black politicians, and who then did nothing for the Black community. Generally, Jackson compared Jews unfavorably to Gentiles (a term she used to identify White Christians) in their treatment of Blacks. The second was written by Reverend John T. Colbert, pastor of the Grace Presbyterian church, a member of the executive board of the NAACP branch, and a grandson of the abolitionist Henry Highland Garnet. Colbert made points similar to those in Jackson's letter but gave his argument a strongly anti-communist twist by remarking that "the small number of Negroes who have become Communists have become so because of Jewish agitation."[26]

The final letter of the debate came from Edward Lewis of the BUL. His letter was unique in the exchange because he alone took a consistent class point of view. He criticized some of the Black respondents for failing to see that Black landlords and merchants, not only Jews, exploited Black people; that some Jewish real estate brokers exploited White Gentile *and* Jewish renters; and that in the workers' movement Blacks sometimes undermined their own interests because of their ethnic hostility to Jews. Lewis wrote about his work during the previous six weeks attempting to persuade Black clothing workers to join the International Ladies' Garment Workers Union—work that was made difficult, he claimed, because Blacks often distrusted the union's Jewish leadership. Lewis, however, had few criticisms of Jewish department store owners, repeating their dubious claim they would gladly remove Jim Crow restrictions if other stores did.[27]

What can be made of this debate? First, although the number of participants was small, the debate pointed to ongoing friction between African Americans, including some of those involved in the freedom movement, and Jewish Americans in Baltimore in the late 1930s. Some reminiscences have even suggested that Blacks' alienation from Jews was greater in Baltimore than elsewhere because it was believed that Jewish liberals there were less involved in the freedom struggle than in other cities. More important was the fact that in Baltimore relatively large Jewish and Black communities were juxtaposed in a southern-like Jim Crow environment, in which some upper- and middle-class elements of the Jewish community participated in the segregationism of their milieu. In the sphere of retail commerce, in particular, Jews and Blacks often faced each other across the front lines of Jim Crow.[28]

Second, there was a definite tendency in Israel's article and in some of the letters to underplay the degree of exploitation and oppression suffered by African Americans in Baltimore in relationship to some Jewish commercial interests. Most of the points in Lillie Jackson's letter were based in lived experience and were substantially factual, even if they were given a particular ideological twist. Moreover, there was a structural asymmetry to the positions of Blacks and Jews in the city that cannot be ignored. While some portions of the Jewish community were involved in the oppression and exploitation of Blacks, almost no Blacks were involved in such practices toward Jews.

Third, there were strains of a narrow ethnic nationalism in the Black community, evident in Colbert's letter and to a lesser degree in Lillie Jackson's, that at times reproduced elements of anti-Semitism. In Jackson's letter, there was a strong tendency toward ethnic stereotyping of Jews by implicitly attributing the discriminatory actions of Jewish landlords and department store owners to their religion/ethnicity, while the question of class was ignored. Moreover, Lillie Jackson raised the specter of Jewish conspiracy with her improbable arguments that the Jewish-owned department stores downtown refused to serve Blacks to force them to shop at Jewish-owned stores in the Black community, or that Jews were generally responsible for *initiating* Jim Crow in the department stores in Baltimore. The anti-Semitic overtones in Colbert's letter were stronger. He constantly used the phrase "the Jews" without qualifiers, as in "the Jews take the lead in this pernicious practice," and he clearly had a hard time viewing Jewish people as anything but a racialized monolith. Moreover, he chose to reintroduce the reactionary myth that blamed Jews for Communism into the discussion.

This is not to argue that the leading elements of the local NAACP were essentially anti-Jewish. Walter Sondheim, who had some difficult interactions with Lillie Jackson over the years, emphatically stated, "There was no indication ever of an anti-Semitic feeling on Mrs. Jackson's part." Nevertheless, anti-Semitic myths and stereotypes existed in the movement. In later interviews, Juanita Jackson Mitchell admitted the existence of anti-Jewish sentiment in the freedom struggle of the period but always pointed to concrete experiences of racial discrimination as its source. Few in the Black community or in the older adult segment of the freedom movement had had much experience with the labor movement or with the poor, often militant working-class majority of the Baltimore Jewish community. In fact, few seem to have realized that there were two sections to the Baltimore Jewish community: the more affluent, settled, and assimilated German Jews and the largely working-class Eastern European Jews who had arrived in the United States more recently. Moreover, active Jewish social liberals did not share the racism of the Jewish department store owners and managers. Even if some had narrow understandings of the effects of Jim Crow on African Americans, a number of them proved to be committed to antiracist struggle. Rabbi Israel himself, in the years after the *Crisis* controversy, continued to work closely with the NAACP and the freedom movement. Many of the White women who petitioned to desegregate the department stores and who participated in the interracial shopping teams were Jewish. And then there was the industrialist Sidney Hollander, a long-time leader of the BUL and an important figure in national Jewish circles, who had worked for decades in support of the Black freedom movement. Perhaps, though, Hollander is a good symbol of the per-

sistent character for Black–Jewish tension in segments of the freedom movement, for his relationship with Lillie Jackson was often uneasy and sometimes contentious, especially around the department store issue. In 1947, the
strains between Hollander and Jackson reached the point at which Hollander wrote to Walter White in the national NAACP office citing "Mrs. Jackson's
anti-Jewish bias" and asking White to help "to get rid of her" as the NAACP
branch president. The national office rejected Hollander's plea.[29]

Consolidating the Branch

By the middle of 1941, the Baltimore branch of the NAACP had consolidated
its leading role in the region's new, mass-based freedom movement and had
placed itself at the center of the political culture of African American Baltimore. The branch developed an organizational system to engage its most
active supporters in a variety of offices, boards, and committees, all with their
own designated functions. As of 1937, it had a thirty-one-member Executive Committee and seven standing committees—Legal Redress and Legislation, Education, Membership, Entertainment, Publicity, Junior Division,
and Interracial—as well as grassroots neighborhood organizations for specific campaigns, such as membership drives and voter registration. Drawing on the tradition of the Forum Friday night meetings, the branch sought
to educate its membership on important issues of the day at mass meetings
every third Sunday at 3 PM at the Sharp Street Methodist Episcopal church.
These gatherings often featured well-known speakers, many from outside
the city. According to Juanita Jackson Mitchell, Lillie Jackson would "tell the
ministers to stay off the third Sunday of the month, because that's Freedom
Sunday." The Sunday educational meetings continued for decades, and in
the 1950s they featured speakers such as Jackie Robinson, Rosa Parks, Fred
Shuttlesworth, and Medgar Evers.[30]

Moreover, as a mass organization leading a mass movement, the Baltimore NAACP sought to keep its base active socially and culturally, beyond the
periodic petitions, letter-writing drives, rallies, mass meetings, and demonstrations that it sponsored. It involved large numbers of its constituents in
its annual membership drives, Christmas seal sales, baby contests, and similar special events. Most of these were important for fundraising, for unlike
the BUL, which was funded by the Community Chest and wealthy White
backers, the NAACP branch had to raise its own money largely from the African American community. But these events were also mass community ritu-
als that always took place amid much publicity and celebration, where the
people participating in them affirmed their identity as part of the NAACP-led

36. Juanita Jackson and Clarence Mitchell were married with great fanfare before hundreds of well-wishers on September 7, 1938. They then left for Minnesota, where Clarence Mitchell became the director of the St. Paul Urban League, and returned to Baltimore in 1941. *Courtesy of the Afro-American Newspapers Archives and Research Center.*

movement. For similar purposes, the branch officially supported the *Afro-American*'s annual Clean Block campaigns, which (starting in 1935 and continuing into the 1970s) involved thousands of children and adults for several months in organized self-help neighborhood improvement; the best-looking and most improved blocks received community recognition and prizes.[31]

The Infrastructure: Neighborhood Protective Associations

Underlying the formal structure of the Baltimore NAACP was a remarkable infrastructure: a network of neighborhood protection associations that developed in the city's African American communities during the late 1930s. This network provides striking evidence that the Baltimore freedom movement was becoming increasingly grassroots in character, even as its national ties strengthened. Starting in 1936 under Lillie Jackson's leadership, but not as an official project of the NAACP, the protective associations were organized to rid Black neighborhoods of unwanted commercial ventures, especially taverns and liquor outlets. There were precursors to these associations in Baltimore, the most recent being the Forum's public opposition in 1934 to liquor sellers in the community because they threatened "the morality of today's youth," but in the late 1930s and early '40s, the campaign assumed citywide and even national importance.[32]

The battle against taverns in Black neighborhoods was Lillie Jackson's particular passion, derived partly from her Methodist Episcopal morality. As the NAACP activist and fellow anti-tavern campaigner Verda Welcome later remarked, Lillie Jackson "was a teetotaler, she and her children." It also resulted, as Clarence Mitchell explained, from Jackson's desire to defend the neighborhood not just from taverns, but also from the destructive effects of various types of commercial and industrial enterprises, including barbershops, funeral parlors, horse stables, and factories that were to be inappropriately located in Black residential areas. Nevertheless, for Lillie Jackson, liquor outlets were the greatest threat because, according to her daughter Juanita, bars and taverns were a particular danger to family and children: "My mother was later to preach this at NAACP meetings—protect your family. She crusaded against an aspect of racial discrimination, the bringing in of alcoholic beverage outlets, taverns, in the same area as churches and schools."[33]

William L. Adams, who made a fortune from the proceeds of the taverns he owned, surprised an oral history interviewer in 1977 when he explained why he supported Jackson's opposition to taverns in the community. Adams argued that the problem was with White-run taverns, not those owned by Blacks, such as himself: "Let's face it, if a white man wanted to open a place of business, he would come and put it right in the neighborhood. . . . They didn't care about the community, except to take the money out of it. . . . They didn't even have black bartenders." Adams, who was over six feet tall and known as "Little Willie," began opening taverns in the Black community in 1935 ("Nice places," he claimed, "with black bartenders") and became a banker for the illegal numbers racket. He was also, however, an important financial supporter of the local NAACP.[34]

Initially, Lillie Jackson opposed commercial intrusions in the community as an individual. In 1936, she helped to form the Northwest Residential Protective Association. Juanita Jackson Mitchell recalled the origin of the association and the grassroots organizing philosophy that underlay it:

> My mother said you start with what you have. You start with your family, then you go to your church, and your neighbors, organize the neighborhood. Dr. George B. Murphy was a great educator and was the brother of Carl Murphy. In the grocery store diagonally across from where he lived, they wanted to put in a tavern. My mother told him to organize. The Northwest Residential Protective Association — the first — was organized. And its first battle was to keep that tavern out. They did everything on that, they picketed — they won! That gave a push to organize neighborhood protective associations all over the ghetto.

Like the NAACP itself, the neighborhood associations combined mass mobilization with litigation, but it was often an uphill fight, as Mitchell pointed out:

> Now the liquor boards were under the state. [Lillie Jackson] went with many groups to Annapolis to protest. We found that where there wasn't much money being paid, we won. But the bottom line was that where a lot of money was being put out to get a tavern in whatever neighborhood, they usually got the license.
>
> We won a number of them in court, but it was an arduous, hard struggle. Finally, they adopted a policy that a tavern couldn't be within a hundred and fifty feet of a school. You know, a hundred and fifty feet is not very far.

While the associations were autonomous neighborhood-based organizations, many leading people from the NAACP were involved. For example, Florence Snowden, Lillie Jackson's sister, was the president of the association organized in 1938 to prevent the opening of a tavern on Druid Hill Avenue. As Juanita Jackson Mitchell recalled, "These neighborhood associations, backed by the NAACP, would go to court, and we would provide the lawyers, and the like." In return, the associations strengthened the NAACP branch as a mass organization, and "they also became wonderful assets in our voter registration campaigns."[35]

Clarence Mitchell later stated that some activists in the freedom movement were less than happy with the anti-tavern campaigning. Controversy
ensued when a neighborhood association, backed by the NAACP leadership, moved to block a liquor license sought by the Walter Green Post of the
American Legion. Lillie Jackson (who owned property on the same block)
and the neighborhood association prevailed at the hearings with the license
commission, and the Legionnaires responded angrily, one declaring, "We
bought fifteen dollars of her 'Anti-Lynch buttons,' we have backed them in
all their campaigns. . . . We have been cheek to jowl with the NAACP, but this
is too much." The post's leader, Linwood Koger, a past president of the Baltimore NAACP and a prominent figure during the Armwood lynching protests,
complained about the Baltimore branch's involvement in the controversy directly to Roy Wilkins in the NAACP's national office. In a letter to Wilkins,
Juanita Jackson countered Koger's complaint by emphasizing that it was the
neighborhood association, not the Baltimore NAACP, that had defeated the
post's bid for a liquor license. Surprisingly and with doubtful accuracy, she
also dismissed Koger and the Legion post as a group that had "never participated wholeheartedly" in the freedom movement.[36]

Whatever the controversy they sometimes stirred, the associations were
clearly seen by most in the local and the national NAACP as an asset. In
1943, *The Crisis* profiled Lillie Jackson and enumerated the three major accomplishments of her leadership to that date: the 5,000 member Baltimore
branch, the Maryland State Conference of Branches, and the network of
neighborhood associations. There was, though, concern among national
NAACP staff that the anti-tavern sentiment in the freedom movement limited
the appeal of the branch. The NAACP field organizer Ella Baker (then early
in her career as one of the twentieth century's most effective freedom movement leaders), after conducting the membership drive in Baltimore in 1941,
argued that the branch was "challenged by the need for a more dramatic and
mass encompassing technique" for base building. Her example was recruitment in beer gardens, nightclubs, and other such locales: "We went in, addressed the crowds and secured memberships and campaign workers [w]ith
the results that are well summed up in a comment overheard in a club, 'You
certainly have some nerve coming in here, talking, but I'm going to join the
doggone organization.'" Nevertheless, whatever the shortcomings of their
approach, the neighborhood associations assisted the branch in deepening
its roots in Baltimore's Black neighborhoods. They provided a crucial foundation for the transformation of the late Depression freedom movement in
the metropolitan region into a fully fledged popular struggle.[37]

12

The New Baltimore NAACP, the State, and the Country, 1936–1941

God opened my mouth, and no man can shut it.
—LILLIE M. JACKSON

As it built the freedom movement within the Baltimore metropolitan region, the leadership of the reorganized Baltimore NAACP branch worked successfully to spread the struggle and the organization throughout the state of Maryland. By 1941, the branch and the movement it led in Baltimore, and Maryland, had consolidated into a significant social force, an important regional expression of the long civil rights movement that had been developing in various places around the country since the early 1930s. And on the eve of the U.S. entry into the Second World War, the orientation of the Baltimore-based movement was shifting, as its Maryland-wide ascendancy combined with a growing involvement with working-class issues, and with segments of the region's CIO-led workers' movement.

The Statewide Movement

The first major involvement of the Baltimore NAACP beyond municipal borders began even before the branch was fully reorganized. In 1935, Baltimore County had eleven high schools for White children and none for Black children. Black children who wanted to continue their education beyond the segregated elementary schools (which covered first through seventh grade) had to travel to a high school in the city of Baltimore, and they had to pass a special examination to become eligible to do so. While White children also took an exam before going on to high school, the two exams were different in content and were administered differently; the White students could repeat the exam if they failed. Whites also received tutoring to help them with their second attempt, while the Black students had only one chance to pass each year and little or no tutorial support. As a result, fewer than half of the Black elementary school graduates passed. The families of those students who managed to enroll in high school in Baltimore had to pay a significant share of the costs, because the payments from the county failed to fully cover them. The Black community of Baltimore County had objected for years to these discriminatory arrangements and had repeatedly requested that a high school for African Americans be built locally. Their requests were ignored.[1]

In August 1935, while the Baltimore branch was in the process of reorganizing, NAACP activists in the city, who were itching for a follow-up to the Donald Gaines Murray case, became interested in the high school situation in Baltimore County. Thurgood Marshall, then counsel to the emerging branch, found that a number of county residents were eager to challenge the status quo, and in collaboration with Charles Houston he decided to develop a test case. After rejecting several possible plaintiffs, Marshall filed suit on March 14, 1936, in the name of Margaret Williams against the Baltimore County Board of Education in the Circuit Court in Towson. Margaret Williams had graduated from elementary school but had twice failed the required high school examination, the second time by only a few points, and she was therefore turned down for funding. Before going to court, Marshall and a number of local residents again attempted and failed to convince the Baltimore County Board of Education to build a high school for African American students, and they tried and failed to enroll Williams in a county high school through standard administrative means.[2]

Although it was initiated rather spontaneously, the Margaret Williams case fit naturally into the NAACP's emerging campaign to fight racial inequities in education. In fact, the case was particularly welcome to some in Black Baltimore, for it demonstrated that the NAACP was willing to challenge discrimination not only at the university level, as it had with the Murray case and others, but also at the secondary level. Submitting a petition for a writ of mandamus, the NAACP argued that Williams had to be admitted to the Whites-only Catonsville High School because the county lacked separate but equal facilities for Blacks, in violation of the due process guarantees of the U.S. Constitution. Like the Murray case, the Williams case was handled in a manner consistent with Charles Houston's overall approach, combining litigation with mass education and mass mobilization. The Baltimore NAACP branch, relying heavily on the pages of the *Afro-American* for publicity, called meetings for support and fundraising, sought out organizational allies in the community, and circulated petitions. The initial round of the mobilization in the county coincided with the first membership drive for the reorganized Baltimore NAACP; county supporters of the high school protest joined the city branch, and city members made financial commitments in support of the Williams case.[3]

Unfortunately, the Williams case did not duplicate the success of the Murray case in the lower court. After pretrial maneuvering, the case was finally heard before Judge Frank I. Duncan in September 1936. While Marshall argued vigorously that the high school eligibility examination for Black students was blatantly discriminatory, it made no difference. In late October, the judge ruled that the question of enrolling Williams in Catonsville High School could be considered only after she passed the eligibility examination, which he found to be "fair and reasonable and . . . fairly conducted." Houston and Marshall immediately appealed the decision. The national office and the Baltimore branch were optimistic, since the Maryland Court of Appeals had previously supported the NAACP's position in the Murray case. However, in May 1937, the court agreed with the lower court's decision denying Williams a writ of mandamus. Although there was talk among activists of a further appeal or of a new test case with a plaintiff who had passed the eligibility examination, the local NAACP was by then absorbed by other struggles; the cost of the Williams case had proved much higher than expected; and attempts to get increased funding from the national NAACP were causing tension. Moreover, Thurgood Marshall, who had taken a position in the national office in New York assisting Charles Houston in developing a coordinated national assault on segregation, was less available locally. The Baltimore County high school issue was, for the time being, dropped.[4]

The historian Bruce Thompson has proposed that this case represented a defeat for the Baltimore NAACP, and from a legal point of view, he is right. However, from an organizing point of view, the case represented an advance. The new branch had acted publicly to defend African Americans outside Baltimore and to extend the struggle throughout Maryland; the local and national NAACP had gained valuable experience from this experiment in their Maryland "legal laboratory"; and the Black community in Baltimore County had founded its own NAACP branch during the process. And even before the Williams case had drawn to a close, the branch was again involved beyond the city limits in a campaign to equalize teachers' salaries across racial lines throughout Maryland.[5]

The Campaign to Equalize Teachers' Salaries

The struggle to equalize teachers' salaries is today, as it was nearly eight decades ago, the best-known NAACP campaign in Maryland during the late Depression years, since it provided an exceptional series of victories over Jim

Crow that reverberated across the U.S. South. Most accounts tend to treat the campaign as an important episode in the legal history of the national NAACP, all but ignoring the grassroots mobilization of Black teachers and community members that was at the center of the struggle. Led by an alliance of the Baltimore branch of the NAACP, the Maryland State Colored Teachers Association, and the NAACP's national office, the campaign was successful not only in the victories that it won in equalizing salaries, but also in expanding the freedom struggle and its mass organizations throughout the state.[6]

The struggle to equalize teachers' salaries addressed a grievance long held by Black communities throughout the state, but no longer in the city of Baltimore where teachers' salaries had been essentially equalized in 1925. In the late 1930s, the minimum salary for Black teachers in the counties of Maryland was, by state law, about half that of White teachers. Since state law only set minimum salaries for each racial-ethnic group, and White school boards often paid White teachers above the minimum salary scale, Black teachers were frequently left at an even greater income disadvantage than the law mandated. State and county officials often attributed the salary differentials to the superior training of White teachers, but in fact African American teachers across the state had almost identical qualifications to those of their White counterparts. Attempts at salary equalization in the counties, especially Baltimore County, began immediately in the wake of the equalization of salaries in the city of Baltimore and continued intermittently into the early 1930s under the prodding of Carl Murphy and the *Afro-American*. Little, however, was accomplished. During this period, the Maryland State Colored Teachers Association lobbied the state legislature to change the salary law, also to no avail. Enolia McMillan (then Enolia Pettigen), who became president of the teachers' association while serving as principal of Pomonkey High School in Charles County, Maryland, later remembered that the organization worked "very hard on this matter of unequal pay and unequal school terms. We had bills before the Legislature every year, but they, for some reason, never got passed. . . . I remember one year they couldn't even find the bill, and the session closed without any action. So we decided that there was only one thing left for us to do, and that was to take our case to court."[7]

Shortly after arriving in Baltimore, Pettigen became involved in reestablishing the NAACP branch, serving as the head of the Women's Division during the membership drive of 1935. In the process, she met Thurgood Marshall, Charles Houston, and Carl Murphy. Immediately after the membership drive, the reorganized branch announced that it was launching a new statewide campaign to equalize teachers' salaries. As Enolia Pettigen

McMillan later remembered, "A joint committee of our Teachers Association and the Baltimore branch of the NAACP, of which I happened to serve as chairperson," was formed. Known officially as the Joint Committee on the Teachers' Salary Case, the group was responsible for finding plaintiffs for the court cases to be filed, and for building broad public support for the issue. The committee set up a special teachers' association trust fund "to get money together for the court case"; contributions to the fund came not only from the allied organizations, but also, increasingly, from community groups, local teachers, and individual members of the community. In addition to Pettigen as chair, the leadership of the committee included Lillie Jackson, Carl Murphy, and George Murphy, all of whom worked closely with the NAACP attorneys Charles Houston, Thurgood Marshall, and W. A. C. Hughes.[8]

On December 31, 1936, in Montgomery County, after a petition to the school board requesting the equalization of salaries had been unceremoniously rejected, the NAACP lawyers filed a petition for a writ of mandamus on behalf of William B. Gibbs Jr., principal of Rockwell Colored Elementary School. The filing was followed by a spate of publicity in the *Afro* and other media, as well as an organizing drive in the Black community and among the teachers, resulting in a letter-writing campaign and the creation of a new county NAACP branch. To the surprise of the county's Board of Education, the court showed a positive attitude toward the petition. After brief negotiations, the board capitulated and settled out of court. The salaries of African American teachers in Montgomery County were to be raised to the levels of White teachers over a period of two school years. The salary equalization campaign had its first victory.[9]

The campaign moved on to Calvert County, where, in November 1937, the newly formed NAACP branch filed an equalization suit. Under pressure, the county's Board of Education followed the example of Montgomery County, entered out-of-court negotiations with the teachers' representatives, and agreed to equalize salaries over a two-year period. These two surprising victories attracted much attention in county and state government circles. As a result, Republican Governor Harry Nice decided to call for the repeal of the "unconstitutional" state salary statutes that were the legal foundation for the Jim Crow teacher salaries. Despite Nice's efforts, the legislature dragged its feet on the question, while the movement kept rolling into county after county—educating, organizing, and litigating. Five more county Boards of Education surrendered without significant resistance; one more county board made a partial salary adjustment; another resisted for a while, then capitulated. Some county boards refused to budge, and a few retaliated against activists, firing teachers and principals. However, by the end of 1938, nine of

Baltimore's twenty-three counties were equalizing salaries, and the movement had not yet really gone to court.[10]

Seeking to circumvent the expensive and drawn-out process of county-by-county litigation, the NAACP lawyers decided to change their legal strategy by filing a suit for one plaintiff in a higher court in the hope of establishing a statewide precedent. They sued the Maryland State Board of Education on behalf of the elementary school principal Walter Mills of Anne Arundel County in federal court instead of state court and asked for an injunction instead of a writ of mandamus. When the suit against the state board was thrown out, the lawyers immediately re-filed, again in federal court, to enjoin the Anne Arundel Board of Education from salary discrimination. With White anger raging over a proposed Black housing project in the county, the Anne Arundel board decided to fight, and the case went to court with the board pulling out all stops to win. The board even attempted bribery: Mills testified in court that he had been offered a 10 percent pay increase if he would drop the suit. The litigation dragged on for months, with demoralizing effects on the rank-and-file, until in late November 1939 Judge W. Calvin Chesnut of the U.S. District Court decided for the plaintiffs, agreeing that the unequal salaries were a violation of the Fourteenth Amendment. As Roy Wilkins ecstatically editorialized in *The Crisis*: "The latest victory of NAACP attorneys in the courts is one of the most significant ones in recent years. . . . This decision is the first one ever to be handed down by a Federal court upon the unusual practice in vogue in the South of paying Negro teachers much less than Whites doing essentially the same work." Complaining that the equalization of salaries would bankrupt its budget, the Anne Arundel board considered appealing the decision, but facing stiff resistance from Black teachers, it came up with the necessary money by the start of the next school year. The resistance to salary equalization in Maryland was broken. Prince Georges County, followed by Maryland's southernmost county, St. Mary's, agreed to equalization. Finally, in early 1941, the legislature capitulated and equalized teachers' salaries throughout Maryland.[11]

The campaign to equalize teachers' salaries in Maryland had at its inception attracted attention in the U.S. freedom movement, and this attention grew as the campaign proceeded from victory to victory. At the national NAACP convention in 1936, Enolia Pettigen and Thurgood Marshall had presented the plans for a joint assault on unequal teachers' salaries in Maryland by the NAACP and the Maryland Teachers Association, and delegates from around the country had shown great interest. Two years later, at the 1938 national convention in Columbus, Ohio, the NAACP awarded Enolia Pettigen McMillan its Merit Medal for her work on teachers' salary equalization. But some in the national movement did more than just congratulate the Maryland activists for their work; they began to follow their example. In late 1937, after a presentation by Thurgood Marshall on the victorious campaign in Montgomery County, the Virginia State Teachers Association voted unanimously to take similar action and pledged to raise $5,000 to do so. And in March 1941, as Maryland's campaign achieved final victory, *The Crisis* reported successes in equalizing teachers' salaries in Virginia, Missouri, and Kentucky; the next month, it announced that New Orleans was initiating a test equalization case under Thurgood Marshall's direction.[12]

The campaign in Maryland was an important factor in the resurgence of the freedom movement in the "border" and southern states of the late 1930s and early 1940s. Moreover, the success of the equalization campaign in Charles Houston's "Maryland legal laboratory" again vindicated his strategic vision of combining litigation based on the Fourteenth Amendment with mass mobilization to overturn Jim Crow in the educational sphere. In the following decade and a half, the national NAACP devoted major resources to pursuing this vision (although the mass-mobilization component of Houston's original strategy declined in importance as the years passed), leading ultimately to the U.S. Supreme Court's decision in *Brown v. Board of Education* in 1954.

In Maryland, the victory resulted in real economic gains for the state's African American teachers and for the Black population as a whole. As the NAACP happily pointed out, the salary increases by 1941 represented more than $5 million in additional income flowing annually into the African American communities of the state. The freedom movement itself came out ahead financially, too. The grassroots and institutional fundraising for the equalization struggle was so successful that, according to Thompson, the amount raised by the joint committee more than paid the bills, and the campaign may actually have been "a money maker for the NAACP"—a most unusual occurrence and an indication of the depth of the mass participation. Just as important, the mobilization around salary equalization resulted in organizing gains for the freedom movement as community activists and teachers in county after county revived old NAACP branches, founded new ones, and revitalized the Maryland State Colored Teachers Association. These organizational gains culminated in the inaugural meeting of the Maryland State Conference of NAACP Branches at the Sharp Street Methodist Episcopal church on May 24–25, 1941, shortly after the state's legislature abolished the teachers' salary code. Two hundred and three delegates from sixteen Maryland counties attended, along with representatives of various labor unions as "special guests at this meeting." Those present heard leaders from both the

37. Delegates to the first Maryland State Conference of NAACP Branches, 1941. The arrows indicate (*left to right*) Enolia Pettigen McMillan, George B. Murphy, and Lillie Jackson, leaders of the salary equalization campaign and the new state conference. *Courtesy of the Library of Congress.*

local and the national freedom movement, including the NAACP's executive secretary, Walter White, speak; ratified a statewide program; and elected a statewide leadership, with Enolia Pettigen McMillan as president and Lillie Jackson as first vice-president (see figure 37).[13]

The campaign to equalize teachers' salaries was important for another reason. The Baltimore branch of the NAACP rebuilt the freedom movement in the metropolitan region during the late Depression by organizing almost exclusively in the neighborhood and public spheres. Unlike the City-Wide Young People's Forum in the early 1930s, the Baltimore Urban League (BUL), or the National Negro Congress (NNC), the branch showed little sustained interest in workplace struggles or the workers' movement in the city. In the statewide equalization campaign, the branch was intimately involved in a struggle at the intersection of the neighborhood and the workplace—one that entailed mobilizing the community and the employees involved for better wages and working conditions and for improved community life. Furthermore, although the Maryland State Colored Teachers Association, with which the branch allied, was not a labor union of workers in the strong sense of the term, it was an employees' organization of proletarianized and marginalized professionals. The equalization campaign demonstrated that the Baltimore branch was willing to intervene in the workplace sphere and to ally with employees' organizations in campaigns that, in its view, corresponded to the interests of the Black community. Moreover, during the last phases of the statewide equalization campaign, the Baltimore branch was beginning to increase its involvement in workplace issues, and in alliances with the workers' movement in the city. This involvement would deepen significantly as U.S. intervention in the Second World War approached.

Public Housing, the March on Washington Movement, and Glenn L. Martin

If the salary equalization campaign in the state foreshadowed the growing involvement of the NAACP-led freedom movement in workplace issues during the Second World War, three campaigns in the city at the end of the preintervention period drew the freedom much closer to the workers' movement: the drive for public housing, the March on Washington Movement (MOWM), and the desegregation of the Glenn L. Martin Aircraft Company.

Housing conditions, which were already bad for African Americans in Baltimore, deteriorated during the Depression as residential construction and maintenance languished and immigration continued. In the mid-1930s, federal Public Works Administration funds became available for urban housing, raising the possibility that the residential crisis in Black Baltimore might be eased. However, the region's real estate interests were cool to such funding, especially for housing for African Americans, and city and state officials failed to pursue this possibility. The *Afro-American* criticized these failures angrily. In 1937, Congress created the U.S. Housing Authority to channel federal public housing funds to local communities, and in response, the Baltimore Citizens' Housing Committee (BCHA) was formed to demand that the city government apply for the funds. The BCHA was an alliance of thirty-two Black and White groups, including, significantly, representatives of both the freedom movement led by the NAACP and the workers' movement led by the CIO. It called for housing for both Blacks and Whites and for a metropolitan housing authority that included Black representation. In response, Mayor Howard Jackson and the city government reversed their earlier opposition to public housing and created the Baltimore Housing Authority (BHA); after more pressure, they appointed the freedom movement veteran George B. Murphy as one of the BHA's five directors.[14]

Initially, the prospect of public housing for the region looked good: nine projects were proposed, six of them for Blacks. To realize these proposals, freedom activists, especially from the NAACP wing of the movement, mobilized, attended or organized community meetings, and formed neighborhood-based committees. In one of its largest forays into neighborhood-based campaigning before the Second World War, the CIO sent representatives to community committees, participated in meetings, and raised its own demands, such as housing for Black workers at Bethlehem Steel and other large plants. On one occasion in 1939, Patrick Whalen, head of the Baltimore Industrial Union Council (BIUC), silenced a hostile White crowd at a public meeting with a passionate defense of public housing for all. The nature of the coalition emerging in the new housing movement is evident in the committee formed in northwestern Baltimore, which included representatives from the NAACP, the NNC, the BUL, the CIO, and some social liberal groupings. Both Lillie Jackson of the NAACP and Albert Blumberg of the Communist Party were among its leaders.[15]

In late 1940, with war preparedness now in full swing, the public housing movement achieved its first big victory with the opening of the 278 unit Edgar Allan Poe Homes for African Americans, the city's first public housing project. The Poe project, like much public housing born of "slum clearance," was a mixed blessing for the Black community. Of the 3,000 tenants displaced by the construction of the project, only forty-seven became residents there, while more than half of the rest ended up paying higher rents than they had before. However, with the Poe project, public housing in Baltimore became a reality, and the right of African Americans to it was established. As defense-boom immigration surged, the pressure for more public housing for both Whites and Blacks intensified, and the question of race and public housing was raised again and again. Whites' opposition to public housing for Blacks, catalyzed by racist neighborhood associations, real estate interests, and some public officials, spread throughout the Baltimore region to areas that included East Baltimore, Towson, Glen Burnie, Herring Run, Turner Station, Dundalk, Moore's Run, and Cherry Hill. The pro-housing movement attempted to meet the opposition head on, mobilizing its forces, pressuring politicians, and publicizing the housing issue in the *Afro*, the *CIO News*, and (as far as possible) in the *Baltimore Sun* newspapers. The entry of the United States into the Second World War greatly exacerbated the controversy around public housing, and the efforts of the NAACP, the CIO, and their allies in the public housing movement of the prewar years became a much more concerted and collaborative alliance during the war.[16]

Toward the end of the preparedness period, the NAACP-led movement in Baltimore also shifted its focus toward more working-class and workplace issues when it joined the national March on Washington Movement (MOWM). In January 1941 A. Philip Randolph of the Brotherhood of Sleeping

Car Porters proposed a march of 10,000 African Americans on Washington, D.C., to demand that federal government end racial discrimination in defense-related industries and in the armed forces. Initially attracting little more than skepticism, the idea spread slowly, then grew with increasing momentum. A mass call for a July 1 march on D.C. was issued in April in the name of a national coalition led by Randolph that included the Brotherhood, the NAACP, and the National Urban League. In actuality, neither the NAACP nor the Urban League seriously mobilized nationally to build the march, but the MOWM campaign caught the imagination of Black people across the country, and it took off on its own. With the Black press actively publicizing the march, activists in local Black communities came together and threw themselves into MOWM activities. In Baltimore, Edward Lewis, long a leading advocate of the freedom movement's involvement in working-class issues, publicly supported Randolph's proposal for the march as early as mid-January 1941. During the ensuing months, with the MOWM receiving coverage in the *Afro*, an energetic alliance of movement activists, community organizations, churches, and fraternal groups coalesced in the region. Significantly, many of them were affiliated with the sector of the Baltimore movement led by the NAACP—forces that had not been deeply involved in such work-related issues in the past. As Juanita Jackson Mitchell later remarked, "People were ready to march" for jobs. Unlike the national NAACP and the Urban League, the local NAACP, the BUL, and their allies immersed themselves in preparations for the march.[17]

The NNC, though, which was deeply committed to workplace activism in Baltimore and elsewhere, played no direct role in the MOWM, despite substantial agreement with the goals of the proposed march. The previous year, Randolph had resigned as national president of the NNC during sharp organizational and ideological disputes. In the wake of his resignation, he became increasingly hostile to the NNC and to the Communists, whom he accused of taking over the organization. Partially as a result of this hostility, he and the MOWM leadership defined the march as an all-Black, not an integrated, affair. Neither the NNC nor its ally, the CIO, would participate due to exaggerated fears of "narrow" Black Nationalism. Nevertheless, the NNC's Jobs Conference in Baltimore in April, supported by the CIO, sharply criticized FDR for his failure to issue an executive order banning discrimination in war industries, in effect giving tacit support to the MOWM's goals.[18]

The MOWM grew rapidly in Baltimore and across the United States during May and June, and Randolph began predicting that 100,000 Black demonstrators would show up in Washington. The Roosevelt administration, clearly alarmed at the MOWM mobilization, asked the movement's leaders to call off the march. Randolph refused, and the movement kept building. Finally, on June 25, FDR relented and promised that, if the march were canceled, he would issue an executive order banning racial discrimination in government employment and in the war industries—but not in the armed forces. The MOWM leadership agreed. Roosevelt issued Executive Order 8802 and established the Fair Employment Practices Commission (FEPC) to implement his order. Despite some confusion over the last-minute cancellation of the march, and some unhappiness that the armed forces remained segregated, activists in Baltimore and across the country celebrated Executive Order 8802 as a big victory for the freedom movement, which, as the movement's wartime experience would demonstrate, it was. Moreover, for the first time the new Baltimore NAACP branch and its allies had poured their energy into fighting the color bar in working-class employment, and the victory they helped to secure had, in effect, amounted to a profound commitment to continuing this struggle.[19]

The campaign to integrate the workforce at the Glenn L. Martin Aircraft Company overlapped and drew strength from the MOWM campaign; it represented another important moment in the reorientation of the Baltimore social movements toward joint activities in the workplace. The initiative for the campaign came largely from the workers' movement—the CIO, specifically—but forces from the freedom movement rapidly became involved.

Glenn L. Martin Aircraft was critically important to the emerging war economy in the Baltimore metropolitan region. An icon of Baltimore's industrialization during the 1920s and the 1930s, Martin became one of the region's fastest growing enterprises in the late 1930s and early 1940s. In January 1938, the company employed 2,370 workers; by June 1941, after receiving $400 million in military contracts, it employed 18,000, with the expectation that its workforce would number 45,000 before the end of that year. However, as of mid-1941, Martin had no legitimate union and no known African American employees. As C. E. Crowley, a top official at the company, adamantly declared in May of that year, "The company will not employ colored."[20]

At the conference of the Maryland and District of Columbia Industrial Union Council (MDCIUC) in December 1940, the CIO designated Martin the top organizing priority for the new year, demanding that the company immediately begin to hire Black workers. While the organizing campaign proceeded on the shop floor, the CIO mobilized its allies to pressure the company on its segregationist policies. In late December 1940, a delegation from the NNC, including CIO unionists and a representative of the AFL Glassblowers

Association, visited Martin to press the company to change its racist hiring policy. They were rebuffed. In late January and early February 1941, several CIO unions joined with the Maryland Youth Congress, the BUL, some church-related groups, the AFL Maryland Teachers Union, and the NNC to send thousands of postcards denouncing the company's refusal to hire Blacks. "Maryland citizens of both races" signed the cards. The postcard blitz was followed by another delegation to Martin and another rebuff. In early May, a third delegation of NNC, CIO, and Black community leaders visited the company; it was led by two national officers of the NNC and accompanied by nine African Americans who wanted to apply for employment. The company reiterated its exclusionary policy but gave the nine prospective workers application forms. The UAW, the CIO union organizing at Martin, began exposing the company's housing for its inadequacies and its Jim Crow character.[21]

On May 3, in the middle of the Martin campaign, the NNC held its Jobs Conference in Baltimore. The conference was co-sponsored by the Civil Liberties Department of the Colored Elks and endorsed by the BIUC plus a number of individual CIO unions. More than 600 delegates reportedly attended, including 200 from trade unions; the delegates claimed to represent 250,000 people. The conference focused on the Glenn L. Martin Company and demanded that 7,000 of the 20,000 jobs to be created at Martin go to African Americans. By then, the MOWM was picking up steam and, along with the Glenn Martin campaign and other similar struggles around the country, was making racial job discrimination in the defense industry an increasingly visible public issue. The federal government could not ignore the clamor. Around this time, William Knudsen, director of the Office of Production Management, wrote to Martin urging it to hire Black workers in Baltimore rather than fostering the "unnecessary migration of labor by recruiting White workers out of town." Subsequently, Sidney Hillman, then the co-director of the Office of Production Management, also wrote to the company asking that it not discriminate in hiring. Neither letter had any discernible effect.[22]

Subsequently, the NNC, CIO, and BUL became involved with the Select Committee of the House of Representatives Investigating National Defense Migration, chaired by Representative John H. Tolan of California. The Tolan Committee, as it was known, scheduled hearings in Baltimore for July 1–2, 1941, on the impact of the defense emergency on the people and economy of the region. Edward Lewis collaborated with Palmer Weber, a White labor progressive from Virginia who served on the Tolan Committee's staff, to ensure that the hearings highlighted discrimination in regional industries. Weber also remembered, in a later oral history interview, working with the leadership of the Baltimore NAACP branch (in the process beginning a decades-long friendship with Lillie Jackson) even though this organization played little public role in the hearings. Under way just days after FDR capitulated to the MOWM and issued Executive Order 8802, the proceedings began with a long list of witnesses testifying from many points of view. Lewis's meticulously researched testimony thoroughly exposed the role of racial discrimination in Baltimore's preparedness boom. Frank Bender of the Maryland CIO argued forcefully that inadequate and overpriced housing, anti-union employers, and racial discrimination in industry were disrupting defense production. But perhaps the most interesting testimony before the committee was that of Glenn L. Martin himself. He admitted that his plant had "practically no Negroes," stated that Jim Crow there was necessary "because Baltimore has segregation," and claimed that White workers would strike if he tried to introduce Black workers into his factories. At the same time, however, he professed that he did not "have a thing in the world against the Negro" and claimed that there were no restrictions on employment at his company "other than the man's ability to do a job." Martin seemed to be temporizing, even vacillating.[23]

In the days following Martin's testimony to the Tolan Committee, his company began to change its hiring policies, and in late July, the NNC reported that its conversations with Martin officials were at last making progress. Then, in October, the NNC, the CIO, and the freedom movement celebrated victory as the first Black skilled workers started work at the Martin aviation factory. A year later, in September 1942, Edward Lewis reported that "upwards of 300 men and women of color" had been employed in skilled positions at the Glenn L. Martin Company during its first year of desegregated hiring, and more were in training (see figure 38). The combined effect of the Martin campaign, the MOWM, and Executive Order 8802 had done the job. Overturning Martin's racial hiring ban was an important advance on two levels. Nationally, it represented an early breach of Jim Crow hiring practices in the utterly recalcitrant aircraft industry. Regionally, it represented an important breach of Jim Crow hiring in the Baltimore defense industry as a whole, as Martin became one of only a handful of production facilities in Baltimore that hired any Blacks for skilled or semiskilled work. Furthermore, the victory at Glenn L. Martin represented an initial step in allied action on the part of the freedom movement and the CIO to open all defense industries and all categories of jobs to Black workers.[24]

38. Black workers at the newly integrated Glenn L. Martin Company aircraft plant, 1942. *Courtesy of the Enoch Pratt Free Library, Baltimore.*

The National and the Local

By 1941, the Baltimore branch of the NAACP had fully consolidated and developed a seasoned, effective leadership. It was now the undisputed center of the regional freedom movement, the leading force in a statewide network of NAACP branches, a contributor to the reinvigorating national freedom movement, and a close collaborator with the NAACP's national office. The importance of the Baltimore movement for the national organization is suggested by the fact that, between 1935 and 1938, two of the seven full-time national staff members—Juanita Jackson and Thurgood Marshall—were from the Baltimore movement, and a third, Charles Houston, had for years been intimately involved with it.

However, the relationship between the national and the local NAACP bodies was not always smooth. The Baltimore branch had a history and autonomy of its own that sometimes conflicted with the national leadership. Tension sometimes arose when the leadership of the Baltimore branch felt that demands from the national office were undermining its efforts to develop the movement in Baltimore. "I cannot understand," Lillie Jackson wrote to Walter White in May 1937, "how the National Office expects the President of a Local Branch to keep alive the interest of its Community by always raising money to help others, and not to help ourselves." In mid-1937 the branch asked permission to keep all of the proceeds of a rally and mass meeting rather than send a portion of the funds to the national office, as normally required. The money was needed locally to cover the costs of the Meade restrictive covenant case and of delegates' expenses to the national NAACP convention. The national office very reluctantly agreed, and Walter White bristled at the independence of the Baltimore branch, questioning its decision to take on the Meade case. "Should not these branches," he asked, "unite on a single case in which the issue is clearly raised instead of [spending] money on separate cases all over the country?" A difference of perspective underlies the contention here: the Baltimore branch took up cases like Meade's to better the conditions in its community and to build the movement locally; White saw such cases as part of a national litigation-based strategy to develop a string of legal precedents.[25]

In addition, the national office sometimes felt that the Baltimore branch failed to fulfill its responsibilities. In April 1937, Thurgood Marshall, then writing as the assistant special counsel of the NAACP, complained that Baltimore had failed to mobilize support for his efforts to get an open hearing on a pending bill in the Maryland legislature. Sometime later, Field Secretary Ella Baker criticized the effectiveness of the branch's leadership during the membership drive of 1941, stating that "in Baltimore a functioning publicity committee and speakers bureau were not obtainable for the short duration of two-weeks of campaigning, although the branch membership was nearly three thousand." As the historian Barbara Ransby has shown in her fine biography of Ella Baker, the long-term relationship between Baker and Lillie Jackson was marked by a good deal of friction and conflict, with the leaders of the national NAACP often siding with Baker over what they saw as Jackson's localism and arrogance.[26]

The leadership of the Baltimore branch was, in fact, quite protective of its autonomy. Lillie Jackson, for example, vehemently protested what she felt was Thurgood Marshall's failure to inform the branch about his activities in Annapolis around the Melvin scholarship bill (and Marshall vehemently denied any wrongdoing). In late 1938, W. A. C. Hughes wrote to Walter White "at the request of the Executive Committee of the Baltimore Branch" claiming that "there has not been enough cooperation between the National and the Local Legal Department." He then suggested that, if the situation did not improve, the branch would "not promise financial or other aid" to the national NAACP. After a stern response from White, the branch, in a letter from Enolia McMillan, retracted Hughes's threat but not his criticisms.[27]

Strains between the local branch and the national office were often revealed in tension between Lillie Jackson and Walter White. Differences between the two were often compounded by divergences in their lifestyles. After delivering a speech at the Forum in the early 1930s, the urbane White walked into Lillie Jackson's house and pulled out a cigarette. According to Juanita Jackson Mitchell, Lillie Jackson immediately told him, "Oh, Mr. White, you can't smoke in *my* home. This is a Christian home!" White put the cigarette away. Over time, White saw Jackson as contentious and overly willful, while she reportedly found him aloof and manipulative; the relationship continued to be strained even after Lillie Jackson joined the national board of the NAACP in 1947. White is said to have opposed her membership. Ultimately, the real causes of the friction between Jackson and White, and between Baltimore and national NAACP leaders, was not personal but the struggle to define the proper relationship between a national organization and a local branch with a mass membership that had its own, distinct dynamic and needs. Juanita Jackson Mitchell remembered that, to encourage recruitment and to lure rank-and-file activists to leadership, the Baltimore branch devised a policy that gave any recruiter who signed up one hundred or more members during a membership drive a seat on the branch's board. While visiting Baltimore, Roy Wilkins became concerned that the branch was exceeding the constitutional limit on board size. Lillie Jackson pointedly reminded Wilkins that the branch sent in its national dues and told him, "You run your little red wagon and I'll run mine."[28]

Women, the Regional NAACP, and Lillie Jackson

One of the most striking features of the Baltimore and Maryland freedom movements between 1936 and 1941 was the prominence of women in leadership. This can be seen clearly in the salary equalization campaign, where two of the four leaders, including the chair of the joint committee, were women. In addition, the leadership of the NAACP's new statewide organization, the Maryland State Conference of NAACP Branches, was overwhelmingly female, with four out of the six top offices, including the presidency, occupied by women. In the Baltimore branch of the NAACP, the situation was similar. Throughout the period, the local NAACP president was, of course, a woman, as were most of the active officers. In 1937, for example, six of nine committee chairs were female, as were four of seven vice-presidents. The executive committee, by contrast, was largely male, but membership there was often honorific, symbolic of status in the African American community. Not only were women predominant in the real leadership; they were prominent in the active rank-and-file. The majority of teachers involved at the grassroots of the statewide equalization struggle were women, and anecdotal evidence indicates that many of the most active rank-and-filers in the Baltimore branch were female. Perhaps the large number of women in the ranks of the NAACP was not surprising. As Juanita Jackson Mitchell, Evelyn Burrell, and Verda Welcome—all Baltimore-based Black female activists during this period—pointed out in oral history interviews, women were a majority in many of the institutions in the local Black community, especially the churches, which provided infrastructure for the new NAACP-led movement.[29]

Of course, the broad participation of African American women in many of the community's institutions, or in the movement led by the NAACP in the late 1930s and early '40s, was not unique to Baltimore or Maryland. Other studies have commented on women's roles in such movements elsewhere in these years, and a perusal of The Crisis for the period indicates that women were present in significant numbers on the leading bodies of NAACP branches across the country. What is more striking, though, is how women in Maryland occupied top positions. In this, the new NAACP movement carried on the tradition of the Forum, where women—especially Juanita Jackson and, indeed, Lillie Jackson in her role as adult adviser—were the top leaders. This is not to argue that the Maryland freedom movement was dominated by women, for men played many important roles. Nor is it to suggest that, in the freedom movement, male chauvinism played no role. The point is simply that no other social movement of the era in Baltimore or Maryland approached the freedom movement in terms of its prominent female leadership or its apparent gender egalitarianism—and those facts are in themselves worth noting.

By 1941, Lillie Jackson was well on her way to becoming the paramount, almost mythic, leader of the increasingly powerful Baltimore freedom movement (see figure 39). In Lillie Jackson, the Baltimore freedom movement found an exceptionally capable and charismatic leader and a person of great religious belief who had a deep commitment to her people, a secure sense of herself as a strong woman, and enormous energy. From 1935 almost until her death in 1975, she threw herself into the movement, seeing it as both a politi-

39. Lillie Jackson in the late 1930s. *Courtesy of the Afro-American Newspapers Archives and Research Center.*

cal and a religious imperative, a "holy crusade," with the NAACP as "freedom's army." Participation in the struggle was a transcendent duty, a way of life, taught through the slogans she coined, such as, "Every day a voter registration day, every day a membership day in the NAACP." However, for all of her ideological fervor, she was a pragmatic leader who believed in working outside and inside the system at the same time. Her leadership was based on tremendous moral authority, with remarkable abilities to mobilize others, as Evelyn Burrell related in an oral history interview:

> Miss Lillie was so dedicated! She was such an inspiration! You couldn't say no to Miss Lillie, do you hear me? I remember after I had gotten married and was living here, Miss Lillie would call me up at 3 o'clock in the morning, and she would say, "Evelyn." I'd say "Yes, Miss Lillie." "I want you to do such and such a thing. Be here at such and such a time tomorrow. Is that understood?" I'd say, "But Miss Lillie, I—" "I don't care. Whatever it is, it can wait, Evelyn, it can wait."

Lillie Jackson could be intimidating, but she was also loved; she was widely known as "Ma Jackson" and "Miss Lillie." As the years passed, no one else in the movement approached her stature, and only her ally and friend from childhood, Carl Murphy of the *Afro-American*, came close. Parren Mitchell later remembered that Jackson and Murphy developed a brother–sister relationship, and Juanita Jackson Mitchell later recalled that her mother was the only one who could call Murphy, who was barely over five feet tall, "Little Man," though she would often add, "but he's mighty." In many ways, Lillie Jackson personified the Baltimore NAACP during the three and a half decades she led it.[30]

However, Lillie Jackson's dynamic, personal, larger-than-life style of leadership sometimes caused tension not only with the national office but also within the regional movement. Enolia McMillan was one of the most accomplished leaders of the freedom movement in the state and worked closely with Jackson for many years. (McMillan succeeded Jackson as president of the Baltimore NAACP in 1969 and held the post until she was elected national NAACP president in 1984, serving in that capacity for six years.) However, sometime in the mid-1940s, McMillan found herself in opposition to Jackson. In an interview in 1976, McMillan offered her retrospective view of Jackson's leadership, a view that, while critical of Jackson, attempts balance. She is worth quoting at length:

> Mrs. Jackson was a very dynamic leader and, as such, she usually formulated the plans herself and told you what they were. The discussion usually centered around her. It was more or less a one-way street whereby she would indicate what we would be working on next and how we proposed to do it and what she wanted us to do. . . .
>
> We concurred with her in the goals, and since she was accepting the leadership, we supported her. We'd agree with the goal 100%, and, if there was a difference of opinion regarding method, she was given the benefit of the doubt. . . .
>
> I think the courage that she displayed and the faith that she had in the American way of life was the secret of her success. Courage and faith—and hers was an active courage.

The interviewer asked whether the leadership or the executive board of the Baltimore branch was "ever at serious odds with Mrs. Jackson over any policy or goal." McMillan then replied, "No. I think what happened was that those of us who tended to be at odds stopped going to board meetings. . . . A lot of folks decided the same thing, because you were a bad fellow if you disagreed. And I felt that the benefits that the NAACP had to offer were more important than any particular issue. So I worked in the membership campaigns right straight through, but I stopped going to board meetings."[31]

While Lillie Jackson's leadership drew on pre-1930 traditions in the Baltimore freedom movement, the legacy of the Forum period, and the evolving national movement, it was, in its tremendous strengths and in its weaknesses, hers alone. Jackson was unquestionably one of the great freedom movement leaders of the pre-1960 era. However, in viewing Baltimore of the 1930s as a whole, it is hard not to feel that, under her leadership, with its middle-class (she always emphasized the importance of property owning) and religiously tinged radicalism and nationalistic populism, something of the raggedly democratic, secularly political, and socialist-tinged impulses of the Forum and the earlier youth movement was lost. Nonetheless, the resurrection and ascension of the Baltimore branch of the NAACP, and the creation of the Maryland State Conference of NAACP Branches, are impossible to imagine without Lillie Jackson's guiding hand. And she was loved. As the writer and social activist Langston Hughes put it in 1962, "She was born in Baltimore, educated in Baltimore, taught school in Baltimore, and has lived most of her seventy-odd years in Baltimore. She lives, works, eats, and sleeps the NAACP. It is her heart and soul. They call her 'Ma' Jackson, but her real name is Lillie—Dr. Lillie M. Jackson. . . . Thousands of Baltimoreans know her as 'that NAACP lady.'"[32]

The Fate of the Forum

Juanita Jackson Mitchell remarked in an oral history interview, "The ferment of the City-Wide Young People's Forum created the climate for the revival of the NAACP." She was right. But in 1941, with the NAACP branch fully re-established and flourishing, the Forum disappeared. For a time after the reorganization of the Baltimore NAACP in 1935, the Forum continued as a key center of freedom activity, albeit one closely aligned with the NAACP branch. The Forum, for example, claimed primary responsibility for gathering the 5,000 signatures on the petition in 1937 demanding Black police, was vital to the anti-lynching efforts, and continued to organize important Friday night meetings. Moreover, it continued its activities within the peace movement, something with which the NAACP branch was little involved. However, by 1938 the importance of the Forum to the Baltimore freedom movement was diminishing. It continued to function, "but," to quote Juanita Jackson Mitchell again, "politely so." The center of gravity had shifted toward the NAACP, in which some former Forum activists had immersed themselves; others had left town for other pursuits; others still, under the leadership of

Howard Cornish, Juanita Jackson's successor as president, maintained the Forum the best they could. In early 1938, the *Afro-American* editorialized, "We would like to see the City-Wide Young People's Forum incorporate as a permanent agency, resume its civic program, keep its platform open to all schools of thought, and begin a permanent endowment fund to insure its life and activities."[33]

This was not to be. The Forum continued for three more years but at declining levels of activity. During its heyday in the early 1930s, the Forum held mass educational meetings literally *every* Friday from October to April—some twenty-nine or thirty meetings a year. During the 1938–39 season, there were only fifteen Friday evening meetings, and during the 1939–40 season and the final 1940–41 season, there were just thirteen each. Once the speakers for the Friday night meetings had come from far and wide and included some of the leading Black and White thinkers of the day, but in later years, they came increasingly from Baltimore and were seldom of national stature. The Forum's own sketch of its history, contained in the program booklet for the last Friday meeting of the 1941 season (and apparently the last such meeting ever), enumerated no new activities or accomplishments after 1937. Nonetheless, the booklet made a remarkable claim: "It is estimated that during the ten years of its activity the Forum has had an estimated total attendance of 330,000 persons."[34]

Evelyn Burrell, who was the Forum's youngest member when she joined in 1933, later recalled a key factor in the Forum's demise: "By 1941, in comparison with 1933, the young people of the Forum could no longer be called young people. We had acquired certain positions in life. . . . By '41, those of us in the City-Wide Young People's Forum were practically doing the same things as the NAACP. So we merged. We were the NAACP youth division then." It is not surprising that the NAACP youth movement ultimately absorbed the Forum, since the Forum was its prototype; it is, though, a bit surprising that this did not occur until 1941, for the Youth Councils were launched in 1936. Clearly, the leadership of the NAACP branch decided to keep the Forum operating with an identity separate from the emerging Youth Councils, which did take root in Baltimore during these years. (The Youth Council at Morgan College in particular seems to have been durable.) Baltimore, however, did not become a leading center for the NAACP's youth movement in the United States in these years. It seems that during the late 1930s, despite the crucial role that it had played in the early 1930s, the African American youth rebellion in Baltimore ebbed, and its importance to the regional freedom movement declined.[35]

This is not to say that Black young people in the region no longer had the capacity to rebel. In an oral history interview, Evelyn Burrell told the story of a student protest at Morgan College in 1941, during her senior year. A number of students were "horsing around" in the college's Rabble Room, a center for students' social activities. In the jostling, a female student was pushed and landed on a male student's lap just as the dean walked in. The dean immediately expelled the two students and refused to listen to the explanations from other students about what had happened. So the students decided to go out on strike. As Burrell put it, "We were very well organized. That's one thing I might say the City-Wide Young People's Forum taught us." Days passed, and the strike held. With graduation approaching and the seniors becoming increasingly nervous about the future, the strikers appealed to Dwight Holmes, the president of Morgan College, who agreed to take the situation under advisement. Several days later, Holmes announced that the two students who had been expelled would be reinstated and that there would be no repercussions against the strikers. "We carried out an extensive ten-day strike that was really effective, very effective," Burrell remarked. "Incidentally," she added, the male student "went on to become an outstanding policeman [who] headed up the Boy's Clubs." And the female student "went on to become one of Baltimore city's best supervisors."[36]

There are high tides and low tides of youth rebellion. The Morgan student rebellion of 1941 occurred at low tide in Baltimore and had little effect on the region's freedom movement. Still, it is a fitting coda to the story of the pioneering City-Wide Young People's Forum.

Epilogue

We must either unite the Negro people as full-fledged American citizens with
the rest of us in the war against tyranny and fascism, or we will alienate the
Negro people from us, thereby serving the Axis enemies of democracy.
—GEORGE MEYERS, President, Maryland and District of
Columbia Industrial Union Council

In the dozen years after the Great Crash, the Black freedom struggle and
the workers' struggle in the Baltimore metropolitan region, located on the
border of North and South, constructed two substantially new popular social movements, led by two powerful mass organizations. In the freedom
struggle, the reorganized Baltimore branch of the NAACP, over the previous half-decade, had emerged as the leading force in the regional and statewide freedom movements and was an important contributor to the growing
national freedom movement. It, in alliance with other smaller groupings in
the movement, had challenged Jim Crow in many arenas and venues and
had won some important victories. In the workers' struggle, the CIO, after
a period of rapid growth and development, had consolidated itself as the
leading mass organization—or, more accurately, a federation of mass organizations—in the regional movement, and also had won important victories.
Segments of the AFL had also been caught up in the waves of activity, and
while it remained a rival to the CIO, the AFL in a real sense had fallen under
the CIO's hegemony. Moreover, the struggle against racism in the workplace
and in the unions had significantly advanced, creating something of a freedom movement within the ranks of the workers' movement.

However, despite their simultaneous growth within the same metropolitan region, their shared and intertwined roots in struggles before 1936, and
their involvement with each other, the movements led by the CIO and the
NAACP did not consummate a functioning, ongoing alliance during the late
1930s. Nonetheless, by evolving in the same social space and by expressing
their ideologies and demands in the same cultural atmosphere, they influenced each other quite profoundly. In addition, because of the activities of
the Baltimore Council of the National Negro Congress and the Baltimore
branch of the Urban League, two freedom organizations deeply involved

with the workers' and workplace struggles, and because of radical groupings that operated across the movements, the two were constantly linked.
Moreover as the movements grew, there was increasing convergence between
them due to the changing class and racial/ethnic compositions of both. Then,
during the war-preparedness period, as U.S. entry into the Second World
War approached, the NAACP and its allies, and sections of the CIO began to
work together around issues of public housing and the racial-ethnic division
of labor in the defense industry. The opening of the Edgar Allan Poe housing
project, the desegregation of hiring at the Glenn L. Martin Company, and the
national victory of the March on Washington Movement (MOWM), to which
many in the Baltimore movements contributed were indicators of the potential for new, more sustained collaborations between the two movements.
By the time the United States declared war on Japan, the two movements
had accomplished much, and the possibility that the Baltimore freedom and
workers' movements might realize great levels of unity seemed strong.

So what happened to these movements during the years of U.S. involvement in the Second World War and after? While the answer to that question
takes us beyond the boundaries of this book, a few tentative projections are
in order.[1]

First, despite the myth that social struggle was generally subsumed to wartime unity, both of the movements in Baltimore continued to make substantial gains in terms of influence and impact. While generally honoring the no
strike pledge (the promise to avoid striking and disrupting the war effort),
the CIO continued to organize new industries and shops and to recruit large
numbers of war workers. Moreover, many of its leading activists continued
to struggle against racism in the workplace, although those efforts sometimes produced controversy within the unions and real battles on the shop
floor. The Baltimore branch of the NAACP and its allies pressed the struggle
against Jim Crow under the "Double-V" campaign (victory at home over
racism; victory abroad over fascism) and succeeded on many fronts. Indeed,
one of the most famous mobilizations of the Baltimore NAACP, the march
of several thousand people on Annapolis against police brutality, occurred
in April 1942. One measure of the NAACP branch's achievements during the
war was the amazing growth of its membership from just over 4,000 in 1941
to just under 20,000 in 1945. Only the Detroit branch was larger.

Second, the possibility of an enhanced alliance between the regional
workers' and freedom movements, glimpsed on the eve of Pearl Harbor, was
substantially realized during the war years, although the character of this alliance requires more research and analysis. The main arenas of collaboration,
as in 1939–41, were public housing and defense employment, with the latter

becoming the most important. The wartime workers' and freedom movement worked together in a number of important coalitions, including the Total War Employment Committee to integrate employment in public utilities and transportation, the campaign to resist resegregation at Western Electric (which, after a U.S. Army occupation of the plant, was lost) and activities to oppose hate strikes and actions by White workers who were objecting to the upgrading of Black workers.

Third, in the struggle to destroy the racialized division of labor in wartime employment, the freedom and workers' movements found an unusual and effective ally in the Fair Employment Practices Committee (FEPC). In mid-1941, in response to the MOWM, President Franklin D. Roosevelt had issued Executive Order 8802, prohibiting discrimination in defense employment and establishing the FEPC to ensure that the order was implemented. The FEPC, however, never had the power needed to carry out its mandate and frequently received as much opposition from other government agencies as it did from employers. As a result, the personnel of Region IV of the FEPC, which oversaw war-related employment in the Baltimore region, turned to the freedom and workers' movements for help in carrying out its work and in the process the two movements enhanced their alliance (see figure 40).

As the Second World War ended and reconversion began, there is much evidence that the Baltimore workers' and freedom movements were at the peak of their strength and influence and appeared, individually and together, to be poised for greater advances in ensuing years. However, this was not to be. During the postwar period, the region's workers' movement, like the workers' movement nationally, was subjected to a series of anticommunist assaults that precipitated what some have called a "civil war" in the ranks of organized labor. The witch hunting of Reds that had begun to destabilize the Baltimore movement on the eve of the war, only to recede during wartime unity, returned with a vengeance after the war, much strengthened by the overall Cold War atmosphere and augmented by local Jim Crow culture. The unions were not destroyed, but they were weakened by dissention and splits, and they retreated from the broader social struggle to the narrow economic struggle in the workplace. Simultaneously, the antiracist struggle within the unions ebbed, and the alliance with the freedom movement deteriorated.

The freedom movement was also affected by the Cold War at home, but it did not withdraw substantially from broad social struggle. During the dog days of the Red scare, available evidence indicates that the movement in the region led by the NAACP continued to challenge Jim Crow, perhaps at a slowed pace, in the neighborhood and public sphere although seldom in the workplace, since the workers' movement was no longer much oriented

40. This photo of African American workers on the liberty ship *Frederick Douglass*, named in honor of the great Black abolitionist, in the Bethlehem-Fairfield shipyard in 1943 suggests some of the gains made by Africa Americans in Baltimore during the Second World War. Photograph by Roger Smith. *Courtesy of the Farm Security Administration, Office of War Information Photograph Collection, Library of Congress.*

toward alliance. Then in 1951, the regional freedom movement began to win a remarkable series of victories: theaters, parks, recreation facilities, dime-store lunch counters, department stores, and the Maryland National Guard began to desegregate; African Americans were hired for the first time by the public library, the fire department, and some government departments and as skilled workers in public utilities and transportation; nursing and other schools at the University of Maryland began admitting Black students; and, two years before the Supreme Court's landmark decision in *Brown v. Board of Education*, the top White vocational high school in the city admitted thirteen African American students. Then in 1954 came *Brown v. Board* mandating the desegregation of schools nationally. In most Jim Crow locales, it took years and much struggle to implement the *Brown* decision, but because of pressure by the already-mobilized freedom movement, schools in Baltimore desegregated almost immediately—Baltimore was, according to Juanita Jackson Mitchell, "the first city south of Mason-Dixon that complied." All indications are that the long modern freedom movement in the border city of Baltimore, which was inaugurated in 1931, entered its Civil Rights Movement phase several years before the bus boycott in Montgomery, Alabama, in 1955 and 1966. Tragically, though, despite the promise of 1941 and of 1945, the region's workers' movement was no longer in a position to join the freedom movement as a firm ally.[2]

An influential interpretation, advanced by some historians who are closely related to the long civil rights movement historiographical trend, holds that in a number of regions, a "labor-based civil rights movement" arose within the workers' movement during the years of the Second World War, presenting a "moment of opportunity" for the emergence of a working-class-based, antiracist social movement that might have substantially transformed U.S. society. This moment, it is argued, passed with the defeat of "civil rights unionism" during the anticommunist reaction of the postwar years, ensuring, in the words of two leading historians, that "when the civil rights struggle of the 1960s emerged it would have a different social character and an alternative political agenda, which eventually proved inadequate to the immense social problems that lay before it." This interpretative framework may work for some locales, but it seems only partially satisfactory for the history of the social movements of the Baltimore metropolitan region. "Civil rights unionism" did emerge during the preparedness period in Baltimore and, evidence suggests, expanded during the war, but it was the product of alliances between the workplace-based labor movement and the neighborhood-based freedom movement—both of which had been developing together and interacting with one another from the early Depression period—not an outgrowth of the radical activities in the labor movement alone. And while it appears true that "civil rights unionism" was largely defeated in postwar Baltimore, along with the labor left, as the workers' movement was contained and set back, the neighborhood-based freedom movement in Baltimore, which was also a major determinant of the region's failed "civil rights unionism," was not defeated. In fact, it moved forward, but without its earlier alliances with the workers' movement.

Finally, when the modern civil rights phase of the freedom movement arose in the region, it did so not on the basis of some more recent "alternative agenda" that was less adequate than that of wartime "civil rights unionism," but on the basis of the long-evolving, deeply rooted agenda of the Baltimore freedom movement. This agenda ensured the movement's survival as a center for broad mass struggle throughout the Cold War years; again, the region's workers' movement, although surviving, did not endure as such a center. Indeed, the new freedom movement that had emerged in the Baltimore Metropolitan Region in the early 1930s, in dialectical interaction with the reviving regional workers' movement, maintained and evolved over decades, even after the workers' movement retreated and stagnated, to lay foundations for the upsurges of the 1950s, '60s, and beyond. And while more study is required into these questions, we must applaud the remarkable endurance of the long Black freedom movement in Baltimore, Maryland, and across the United States, for this movement, without a doubt, has proved utterly crucial to the reshaping of the modern world. But, as I wrote, these questions need much more investigation.[3]

Notes

Introduction

Epigraph: Juanita Jackson Mitchell, "Welcome to Baltimore" speech delivered at the Annual Meeting of the Oral History Association, Baltimore, October 13, 1988.

1. The question of whether or not to capitalize terms of color associated with racial groups, particularly with African Americans and European Americans, has been a subject of much controversy, and there is still little agreement among otherwise like-minded scholars. In this study, the term "Black," with the initial letter capitalized, is used to refer to African Americans because it refers to a people, an ethnicity or nationality, a social-cultural group, not a biologically determined "race." "White" when it is used as an ethnic descriptor to refer to European Americans is also capitalized. Both of these capitalizations are now recommended by the American Psychological Association and are accepted by the *Chicago Manual of Style*.

2. Hall, "The Long Civil Rights Movement and the Political Uses of the Past," is perhaps the founding statement of the "long civil rights movement" scholarly trend. This trend is growing and institutionalizing at a remarkable rate, as indicated by the Long Civil Rights Movement Conference held on April 2–4, 2009, at the University of North Carolina, Chapel Hill, and the related scholarly website at https://lcrm.lib.unc.edu/blog (accessed July 26, 2010).

3. Castells, *Urban Question*, 23. See also Harvey, *Social Justice and the City*; Katznelson, *Marxism and the City*, esp. chap. 3.

Chapter 1: Traditions of Opposition

Epigraph: Johnson, "Negroes at Work in Baltimore, Maryland," 12.

1. U.S. Bureau of the Census, *Fifteenth Census of the United States: Population* (1930), vol. 3, pt. 1, 1061; Casey et al., *Second Industrial Survey of Baltimore*, 7–24; Bruchley, "The Development of Baltimore Business, 1880–1914," pt. 1, 18–21, 32–40, pt. 2, 144–55.

2. U.S. Bureau of the Census, *Fifteenth Census of the United States: Population* (1930), vol. 4, 661–65, 674–76; Callcott, *Maryland and America*, 16–19; Brown, "Maryland between the Wars," 757.

3. The southern character of Baltimore City is explored in Ryon, "Baltimore Workers and Industrial Decision-Making, 1890–1917," 564–66.

4. Callcott, *Maryland and America*, 10–16; Moore, *Murder on Maryland's Eastern Shore*, 10–12.

5. Casey et al., *Second Industrial Survey of Baltimore*, map no. 3; Olson, *Baltimore*, 302–8.

6. Olson, *Baltimore*, 212–17, 254–56, 303; Beirne, "Hampden-Woodberry"; Beirne, "The Impact of Black Labor on European Immigration into Baltimore's Oldtown, 1790–1910"; Beirne, "Late Nineteenth Century Industrial Communities in Baltimore"; Beirne, "Residential Growth and Stability in the Baltimore Industrial Community of Canton during the Late Nineteenth Century"; Durr, "People of the Peninsula"; Ryon, "Baltimore Workers and Industrial Decision-Making, 1890–1917," 569–70; Fee et al., *The Baltimore Book*, chaps. 3, 7.

7. Sigmund Diamond interview, by Andor Skotnes; Fein, *The Making of an American Jewish Community, 1773-1920*, 178–79; Torrieri, "Residential Dispersal and the Survival of the Italian Community in Metropolitan Baltimore, 1920–1980," 56–68; Orser, "The Making of a Baltimore Rowhouse Community"; Fee et al., *The Baltimore Book*, chaps. 6, 9–10.

8. Callcott, *Maryland and America*, 19–20; Olson, *Baltimore*, 303–4.

9. Reid, *The Negro Community of Baltimore*, 15–17, 19–21, 39; West, "Urban Life and Spatial Distribution of Blacks in Baltimore, Maryland, 1940–70," 17–29, 36–39; Olson, *Baltimore*, 275–79, 324–28, 338–39; Groves and Muller, "The Evolution of Black Residential Areas in Nineteenth-Century Cities"; Ryon, "Old West Baltimore," 54–69; Fee et al., *The Baltimore Book*, chap. 4.

10. Casey et al., *Second Industrial Survey of Baltimore*, 23–27; Reutter, *Sparrows Point*, chap. 3; Olson, *Baltimore*, 212–15.

11. Casey et al., *Second Industrial Survey of Baltimore*, 18–21, 25, 89–90, "Supplement," 119–21; Brown, "Maryland between the Wars," 697–700.

12. Reutter, *Sparrows Point*, 103–8; Casey, et al., *Second Industrial Survey of Baltimore*, 18–21, 89–90; Olson, *Baltimore*, 239–44, 292–95, 304–5; Brown, "Maryland between the Wars," 697–700; Fee et al., *The Baltimore Book*, xiii.

13. Casey et al., *Second Industrial Survey of Baltimore*, "Supplement," 17; Arnold, "The Last of the Good Old Days"; Brown, "Maryland between the Wars," 724–25. For an overall account, see Crooks, *Politics and Progress*.

14. Casey et al., *Second Industrial Survey of Baltimore*, 18–20, 89–90; Goldberg, "Party Competition and Black Politics in Baltimore and Philadelphia," 47–51; Arnold, "The Last of the Good Old Days," 445; Brown, "Maryland between the Wars," 674–76, 684–85, 697–701; Olson, *Baltimore*, 322–23; Argersinger, *Toward a New Deal in Baltimore*, 12–15.

15. Skotnes, "Structural Determination of the Proletariat and the Petty Bourgeoisie"; Ehrenreich and Ehrenreich, "The Professional–Managerial Class."

16. U.S. Bureau of the Census, *Fifteenth Census of the United States: Population* (1930), vol. 4, 661–65, 674–76.

17. Ibid.

18. Ibid.

19. Ryon, "Baltimore Workers and Industrial Decision-Making, 1890–1917," 568; *Monthly Labor Review*, vol. 36, January 1933, 72; U.S. Bureau of the Census, *Fifteenth Census of the United States: Population* (1930), vol. 2, 67–73; Casey et al., *Second Industrial Survey of Baltimore*, "Supplement," 35.

20. Argersinger, *Toward a New Deal in Baltimore*, 10–11, 147; Johnson, "Negroes at Work in Baltimore, Maryland," 19; Reid, *The Negro Community of Baltimore*, 59; Brown, "Maryland between the Wars," 690; Farrar, *The Baltimore* Afro-American, *1892–1950*, 70–71.

21. Interview with Sara Barron, by Barbara Wertheimer, New York State School of Industrial and Labor Relations Library, Cornell University, New York, 14–16; Argersinger, *Making the Amalgamated*, chaps. 1–6, 73–82; Ryon, "Human Creatures' Lives," 356–58; Fee et al., *The Baltimore Book*, 95, 101.

22. Jo Ann Argersinger, "Comment," Southern Labor Studies Conference, Austin, October 29, 1985; Argersinger, *Making the Amalgamated*, chap. 6.

23. Sigmund Diamond interview; Interview with Sara Barron, 14–18; Asher, "Dorothy Jacobs Bellanca," 62–65; Argersinger, *Toward a New Deal in Baltimore*, 153–54; Argersinger, *Making the Amalgamated*, chap. 5.

24. Thomas, "A Nineteenth Century Black Operated Shipyard, 1866–1884," 2; Reid, *Negro Membership in American Labor Unions*, 23, 94, 106, 121–23, 126–27, 139–41, 166; Reid, *The Negro Community of Baltimore*, 46, 59–64; Johnson, "Negroes at Work in Baltimore, Maryland," 19; Graham, *Baltimore*, chap. 5; Spero and Harris, *The Black Worker*, 183, 192.

25. Johnson, "Negroes at Work in Baltimore, Maryland," 16; Reid, *Negro Membership in American Labor Unions*, 49–50; "Longshore Labor Conditions in the United States—Part I," *Monthly Labor Review*, vol. 31, October 1930, 18–20; Reid, *The Negro Community of Baltimore*, 59–61; Spero and Harris, *The Black Worker*, 193–94.

26. Fee et al., *The Baltimore Book*, 49, 95; Argersinger, *Making the Amalgamated*, 137–39; Reid, *The Negro Community of Baltimore*, 65–69; Argersinger, *Toward a New Deal in Baltimore*, 2–3.

27. Andor Skotnes, "On the Theory of Racism: Critique of the Primary Working Paper," unpublished paper presented at the Southern California Conference on Racism and National Oppression, Los Angeles, October 9–11, 1981. Since I wrote the paper, my formulations on race and ethnicity have been especially influenced by Ringer, *"We the People" and Others*, esp. "Book One." For a classic example of the "whiteness" approach, see Roediger, *The Wages of Whiteness*.

28. Olson, *Baltimore*, 279; Fein, *The Making of an American Jewish Community, 1773–1920*, 149–50.

29. Sigmund Diamond interview.

30. Ibid.; Argersinger, *Toward a New Deal in Baltimore*, 6; Olson, *Baltimore*, 279–81; Fein, *The Making of an American Jewish Community, 1773–1920*, 158–65.

31. *Landsmanshaftn* were Jewish aid societies formed by immigrants from the same regions in their countries of origin.

32. Sigmund Diamond interview; Olson, *Baltimore*, 279–81; Fein, *The Making of an American Jewish Community, 1773–1920*, 158–65; Kartman, "Jewish Occupational Roots in Baltimore at the Turn of the Century."

33. Sigmund Diamond interview; interview with Sara Barron; Kartman, "Jewish Occupational Roots in Baltimore at the Turn of the Century"; Fein, *The Making of an American Jewish Community, 1773–1920*, 165–71; Olson, *Baltimore*, 281–85; Asher, "Dorothy Jacobs Bellanca," 62–65; Argersinger, *Making the Amalgamated*, 69–73, 78–79, 133–34; Fee et al., *The Baltimore Book*, 101.

34. U.S. Bureau of the Census, *Fifteenth Census of the United States: Population* (1930), vol. 3, pt. 1, 1059.

35. Juanita Jackson Mitchell interview, by Andor Skotnes; Juanita Jackson Mitchell and Virginia Jackson Kiah, no. OH 8094, McKeldin-Jackson Oral History Collection, MHS, 48; "Thurgood Marshall," documentary movie produced by Carl Rowan, 1988; Reid, *The Negro Community of Baltimore*, chaps. 4–7, 10.

36. Juanita Jackson Mitchell interview; Greene, "Black Republicans on the Baltimore City Council, 1890–1931," 203. Reid, *The Negro Community of Baltimore*, chapters 3, 5.

37. Reid, *The Negro Community of Baltimore*, 47–50, chaps. 8–9; *Baltimore Evening Sun*, June 7, 1936.

38. Reid, *The Negro Community of Baltimore*, chaps. 8–9; Juanita Jackson Mitchell interview; Nathan, "Chasing the Shadows."

39. Reid, *The Negro Community of Baltimore*, chap. 9; *Baltimore Evening Sun*, June 7, 1936.

40. Reid, *The Negro Community of Baltimore*, 186–204; *Baltimore Sun*, February 1, 2, 4, 5, 6, and 7, 1932; Reid, *Negro Membership in American Labor Unions*, 106, 139–41.

41. Thomas, "Public Education and Black Protest in Baltimore, 1865–1900"; Reid, *The Negro Community of Baltimore*, 97–105; Farrar, "See What the *Afro* Says," 192–204; Juanita Jackson Mitchell interview; Ryon, "Old West Baltimore," 57.

42. Reid, *The Negro Community of Baltimore*, 160–82.

43. Ibid., 182–186; Evelyn Burrell interview, by Andor Skotnes; Edward S. Lewis interview, by Andor Skotnes.

44. Reid, *The Negro Community of Baltimore*, 168–71; Juanita Jackson Mitchell interview; Evelyn Burrell interview.

45. Neverdon-Morton, "Black Housing Patterns in Baltimore City, 1885–1953," 28–31; Reid, *The Negro Community of Baltimore*, 194; Juanita Jackson Mitchell interview.

46. Reid, *The Negro Community of Baltimore*, 199; Hunter, "Don't Buy Where You Can't Work," 53, 111, 124n.

47. "Reminiscences of Broadus Mitchell," Oral History Collection, Columbia University, 115–18; Edward S. Lewis interview; Pearson, "The National Urban League Comes to Baltimore," 523–31; Reid, *The Negro Community of Baltimore*,

128–29, 187–88; Power, "Apartheid Baltimore Style," 295–97, 317–18; Farrar, *The Baltimore* Afro-American, *1892-1950*, 103–5.

48. McGuinn, "The Courts and the Occupational Status of Negroes in Maryland," 256–57; Thomas, "Public Education and Black Protest in Baltimore, 1865–1900," 385–88; Ryon, "Old West Baltimore," 59; Greene, "Black Republicans on the Baltimore City Council, 1890–1931," 206–7, 213–20; Power, "Apartheid Baltimore Style," 317–19; Neverdon-Morton, "Black Housing Patterns in Baltimore City, 1885–1953," 26–28; Musgrove, "Early History," 4–16; Farrar, *The Baltimore* Afro-American, *1892-1950*, 60–64, 101–3. See the biographical profiles "George W. F. McMechen (1871–1961)," "W. Ashbie Hawkins (1861–1941)," "Warner T. McGuinn (1859–1937)," in the Archives of Maryland Biographical Series, available online at www.mdarchives.state.md.us/msa/refserv/html/bioinfo.html (accessed September 4, 2008).

49. Farrar, *The Baltimore* Afro-American, *1892-1950*, 7–15; Farrar, "See What the *Afro* Says," 77–105. A random survey of the *Afro-American* in the 1920s and 1930s will demonstrate the variety of its articles and its racial-ethnic consciousness.

50. This agenda appeared regularly in the *Afro*: see, e.g., *Afro-American*, January 10, 1931.

51. Farrar, "See What the *Afro* Says," 10, 20, 22, 30–31, 41, 46, 50–51.

52. Juanita Jackson Mitchell interview; Farrar, *The Baltimore* Afro-American, *1892-1950*, 8–9.

53. Farrar, *The Baltimore* Afro-American, *1892-1950*, 139–47.

54. Frazier, *The Black Bourgeoisie*.

55. Farrar, *The Baltimore* Afro-American, *1892-1950*, 178–79; *Afro-American*, July 6 and 13, 1929.

56. Farrar, *The Baltimore* Afro-American, *1892-1950*, 179; *Afro-American*, July 27, 1929.

Chapter 2: Communist Party in Baltimore

Epigraph: Carl Murphy, *Afro-American*, May 9, 1931.

1. *Afro-American*, May 9, 1931.

2. U.S. Bureau of the Census, *Fifteenth Census: Unemployment* (1930), vol. 1, 28–39; Argersinger, *Toward a New Deal in Baltimore*, 7–8.

3. *Baltimore Sun*, January 15, February 27, August 15, November 11, 1930; *Afro-American*, January 10, 1931, September 3, 1932.

4. *Baltimore Sun*, January 9, February 13, 20, May 15, 17, June 22, 26, July 9–10, 23, 31, August 17, October 6, 8, November 11, 20, 1930; Argersinger, *Toward a New Deal in Baltimore*, 11; Spero and Harris, *The Black Worker*, 194; Reid, *The Negro Community of Baltimore*, 60.

5. Some social historians discuss the Baltimore CP intermittently in their studies: Argersinger, *Toward a New Deal in Baltimore*, 117–18, 124, 137, 146, 152, 163, 166,

197; Nelson, *Workers on the Waterfront*, 96–100; Fee et al., *The Baltimore Book*, 167–68, 193–97; Reutter, *Sparrows Point*, 214–16, 311–16, 352–58; Callcott, *Maryland and America*, 109–11; Durr, *Behind the Backlash*, 29, 32–33, 39–40, 48. Moore, *Murder on Maryland's Eastern Shore*, focuses more consistently on the Baltimore Communist Party, as do Pedersen, *The Communist Party in Maryland, 1919–57*, and Skotnes, "The Communist Party, Anti-Racism, and the Freedom Movement in Baltimore."

6. *Baltimore Sun*, November 11, 1933, March 30, 1940, January 15, 1947; *Baltimore Evening Sun*, March 28, 1947, February 19, 1951; Callcott, *Maryland and America*, 109–10; Pedersen, "Red, White, and Blue," 71–73, 163, 196–97.

7. *Party Organizer*, March 1934, 28–29, April 1934, 19–22, May–June 1934, 30–34; interview with Dr. and Mrs. Albert E. Blumberg, by George Callcott; Pedersen, "Red, White, and Blue," 124.

8. Brown et al., *New Studies in the Politics and Culture of U.S. Communism*, 242–46.

9. Executive Committee of the Comintern, "Resolution on the Negro Question," October 28, 1928, in Degras, *The Communist International, 1919–1943*, 552–54; "Extracts from a Resolution of the ECCI Political Secretariat of the Negro Question in the United States," October 26, 1930, in ibid., 124–35; Campbell, "'Black Bolsheviks' and Recognition of African America's Right to Self-Determination by the Communist Party USA"; Haywood, *Black Bolshevik*, chap. 8.

10. *Baltimore Evening Sun*, March 6, April 8, 1930; *Baltimore Sun*, March 7–8, 1930; Rosenzweig, "Organizing the Unemployed," 41–43.

11. Richmond, *A Long View from the Left*, 114–23; *Baltimore Sun*, January 15, February 11, April 1–2, December 5–6, 9, 1931, November 24, 1932; *Baltimore Evening Sun*, April 1, 1931.

12. Bailey, *The Kid from Hoboken*, 226; *Baltimore Sun*, January 21, January 24, February 26, November 11, 1931, February 2, 1932; *Afro-American*, April 21, 1934.

13. *Baltimore Evening Sun*, April 8, 1930, April 1, 1931.

14. *Baltimore Sun*, January 15, February 25, September 11, 1931, February 2, 1932; "Reminiscences of Clarence Mitchell," Oral History Collection, Columbia University, 21–22.

15. Katznelson, *Marxism and the City*, 275–76.

16. Leab, "United We Eat," 313–15.

17. On the TUUL, see Honig, *The Trade Union Unity League*; Barrett, *William Z. Foster and the Tragedy of American Radicalism*, 168–71; Johanningsmeier, *Forging American Communism*, 256–58. On the BFL in this period, see Argersinger, *Toward a New Deal in Baltimore*, 147, 151–53.

18. Richmond, *A Long View from the Left*, 101–7; Kutnik, "The Revolutionary T.U. Movement in the U.S.A. in the Conditions of the 'New Deal' of Trustified Capital," 702; Reutter, *Sparrows Point*, 214–16; Honig, *The Trade Union Unity League*, 22.

19. U.S. Bureau of the Census, *Fifteenth Census of the United States: Population* (1930), 4:674–76; Marine Workers Industrial Union, *Centralized Shipping Bu-*

reau, 13; Bailey, *The Kid from Hoboken*, 223–31; interview with Bill Bailey, by Bruce Nelson; Rubin, *The Log of Rubin the Sailor*, 111–12, 139–42. Both Jo Ann E. Argersinger and Bruce Nelson have written on the Baltimore seamen's movement of 1934: Argersinger, "Assisting the 'Loafers,'"; Argersinger, *Toward a New Deal in Baltimore*, 122–24; Nelson, *Workers on the Waterfront*, 96–100. I am indebted to both of them personally for many insights and much guidance in conversation. I am grateful to Nelson for giving me access to his oral history interview with Bill Bailey and to Bill Bailey for informative discussion and providing me with an advance copy of his book.

20. *Marine Workers Voice*, October 1929; Nelson, *Workers on the Waterfront*, 79, 93. Nelson is skeptical about the claim by the *Marine Workers Voice* of 123 visits by ships in one month. Wobblies were members of the anarcho-syndicalist Industrial Workers of the World, a revolutionary union founded in 1905, whose membership peaked in the mid-1920s.

21. Nelson, *Workers on the Waterfront*, 75–96. Many articles on Third Period trade union policy, strategy, and tactics appeared in the *Communist*, in the *Communist International*, and in a plethora of pamphlets in the early 1930s.

22. *Marine Workers Voice*, May 1934; *Baltimore Sun*, June 27, July 29, September 25, October 23, 1932; Richmond, *A Long View from the Left*, 110–11.

23. *Marine Workers Voice*, September 1933; *Baltimore Sun*, August 20, 1933.

24. Naison, *Communists in Harlem during the Depression*, 34. The best overall treatment of the Scottsboro case remains Carter, *Scottsboro*.

25. *Afro-American*, October 28, 1933; *Baltimore Evening Sun*, October 14, November 4, 1931; *Baltimore Sun*, November 5, 1931; *New York Times*, November 5, 1931; Moore, *Murder on Maryland's Eastern Shore*, chaps. 4–7.

26. *Baltimore Evening Sun*, November 5, 26, 1931; *Baltimore Sun*, October 14–15, November 11, 29, December 1, 1931. During the early 1930s, women still did not appear on jury panels in Maryland.

27. *Baltimore Evening Sun*, December 4, 1931; *Baltimore Sun*, December 5–6, 9–10, 1931; *Afro-American*, December 12, 1931; Ifill, *On the Court-House Lawn*, 46.

28. *Baltimore Evening Sun*, December 4, 1931; *Baltimore Sun*, December 5, 6, 9–10, 1931; *Afro-American*, December 12, 1931, January 30, 1932; "Reminiscences of Broadus Mitchell," 150–55; Moore, *Murder on Maryland's Eastern Shore*, 8, 76–80.

29. *Afro-American*, January 23, 30, 1932, February 23, 1935; *Baltimore Sun*, December 27, 31, 1935.

30. *Afro-American*, November 29, 1932; *Baltimore Evening Sun*, September 26, 29, 1932.

31. *Afro-American*, January 30, 1932.

32. *The Crisis*, April 1932, 117–19, May 1932, 154–56, 170–71, June 1932, 190.

33. *Afro-American*, January 23, 1932; Walter White to William N. Jones, November 13, 1931, Records of the NAACP, Library of Congress, group I, series G, container 85.

34. Interview with Juanita Jackson Mitchell, by the author; City-Wide Young

People's Forum (hereafter CWYPF), "The Second Annual Inter Collegiate Oratorical, Vocal and Instrumental Contest," 1933, 34, Juanita Jackson Mitchell personal collection; *Afro-American*, October 22, 29, 1932; Farrar, *The Baltimore* Afro-
American, *1892–1950*, 151; *Baltimore Evening Sun*, May 5, 1932, March 16, 1933;
Opportunity, July 1933, 212.
   35. *Baltimore Sun*, May 9, 1933; *Baltimore Evening Sun*, May 8, 1933.
   36. *Baltimore Sun*, May 9, 1933; *Baltimore Evening Sun*, May 8, 1933.
   37. *Baltimore Evening Sun*, October 9, 1933; *Baltimore Sun*, October 10, 1933.
   38. Bailey, *The Kid from Hoboken*, 225–26; Juanita Jackson Mitchell interview.
   39. Haywood, *Black Bolshevik*, 347–58; Sitkoff, *A New Deal for Blacks*, 156–60;
Pedersen, *The Communist Party in Maryland, 1919–57*, 81.
   40. Haywood, *Black Bolshevik*, 347–58.
   41. *Afro-American*, January 13, 28, 1933; *Baltimore Sun*, January 9, 1933.
   42. *Afro-American*, January 13, 1933; *Baltimore Sun*, January 9, 1933.
   43. *Afro-American*, January 28, 1933 (the *Baltimore World* article is quoted in this
issue).
   44. Ibid.
   45. *Baltimore Sun*, January 22–23, 26, 28–29, 1933.
   46. *Baltimore Evening Sun*, January 26, 1933; *Baltimore Sun*, May 27, 1934.

Chapter 3: City-Wide Young People's Forum

Epigraphs: City-Wide Young People's Forum, program for the Annual Inter Collegiate Oratorical, Vocal and Instrumental Contest (CWYPF contest program), held
in 1935, 18; Reid, *The Negro Community of Baltimore*, 191.

   1. Interview with Juanita Jackson Mitchell, by the author; Reid, *The Negro Community of Baltimore*, 65.
   2. Juanita Jackson Mitchell interview.
   3. CWYPF contest program (1934), 1; Juanita Jackson Mitchell and Virginia Jackson Kiah, no. OH 8094, McKeldin-Jackson Oral History Collection, MHS.
   4. CWYPF contest program (1939), 21; Juanita Jackson Mitchell interview. The
only focused, scholarly treatment the Forum has received, apart from my earlier
work, is Genna Rae McNeil, "Youth Initiative in the African American Struggle for
Racial Justice and Constitutional Rights: The City-Wide Young People's Forum of
Baltimore, 1931–1941," in Franklin and McNeil, *African Americans and the Living
Constitution*, 56–80.
   5. Juanita Jackson Mitchell interview; interview with Evelyn Burrell, by the author; CWYPF 1987 reunion (videotape); Mitchell and Kiah, no. OH 8094; CWYPF
contest program (1934).
   6. The account of the early lives of the Jackson sisters is drawn from the following, overlapping sources: Juanita Jackson Mitchell interview; interview with
Juanita Jackson Mitchell and Virginia Jackson Kiah, by the author; Mitchell and

Kiah, no. OH 8094; Skotnes, "Narratives of Juanita Jackson Mitchell," 44–66; "Juanita Mitchell (1913–): Lawyer, Community Activist, Civil Rights Leader," in Smith, *Notable Black American Women*, 757–58; Hathaway, "Lillie May Jackson, 1889–1975."

7. After Lillie Jackson's death, an NAACP membership card in her name dating from the 1920s was found among her possessions; there is also evidence that she was briefly vice-president of the dormant Baltimore branch in 1929. Juanita Jackson Mitchell interview; Musgrove, "An Early History of the Baltimore Branch of the NAACP: 1912–1936," 15.

8. Juanita Jackson Mitchell interview.

9. On Black fraternities and sororities, see Giddings, *In Search of Sisterhood*, 15–22, 126–30; Randolph Edmonds, "Fraternities at the Crossroads," *The Crisis*, vol. 46, October 1939, 301–2.

10. Juanita Jackson Mitchell interview; Clarence Mitchell, no. OH 8209, 8, no. OH 8154, 6, McKeldin-Jackson Oral History Collection, MHS; "Reminiscences of Clarence Mitchell," Oral History Collection, Columbia University, 1–3; Watson, *Lion in the Lobby*, 61–76.

11. Juanita Jackson Mitchell interview; CWYPF contest program (1934); "Reminiscences of Thurgood Marshall," Oral History Collection, Columbia University; Williams, *Thurgood Marshall, American Revolutionary*, 22–60.

12. Juanita Jackson Mitchell interview; CWYPF contest program (1934), back cover.

13. Juanita Jackson Mitchell interview; "William A. C. Hughes, Jr. (1905–1966), MSA SC 3520–13492," Archives of Maryland (Biographical Series), available online at http://www.msa.md.gov/msa/speccol/sc3500/sc3520/013400/013492/html/msa 13492.html (accessed August 8, 2008); *New York Times*, July 19, 2001; *Afro-American*, November 4, 1933; CWYPF contest program (1934), 3, 34; Donald Gaines Murray, no. OH 8139 (tape), McKeldin-Jackson Oral History Collection, MHS.

14. Evelyn Burrell interview; Evelyn T. Burrell, no. OH 8138, "Biography" sheet, McKeldin-Jackson Oral History Collection, MHS.

15. Juanita Jackson Mitchell interview; Williams, *Thurgood Marshall, American Revolutionary*; Watson, *Lion in the Lobby*; "Juanita Mitchell (1913–)."

16. Juanita Jackson Mitchell interview; *New York Times*, July 19, 2001; Clarence M. Mitchell to Will Maslow, February 10, 1944, Papers of Clarence Mitchell and the NAACP Washington Bureau, 1942–78, available online at http://www .clarencemitchellpapers.com/SampleDocumentsI.htm (accessed August 8, 2008).

17. CWYPF contest program (1934), 1–3; Juanita Jackson Mitchell interview.

18. CWYPF contest program (1934), 1–3; Juanita Jackson Mitchell interview; Mitchell and Kiah interview, no. OH 8094; *Afro-American* (Washington, D.C., ed.), October 22, 1932; McNeil, "Youth Initiative in the African American Struggle for Racial Justice and Constitutional Rights," 63–64.

19. CWYPF contest programs (1934), 2–3, (1935), 2–3; Juanita Jackson Mitchell interview.

20. CWYPF contest programs (1934), 2–3, (1935), 2–3; Juanita Jackson Mitchell interview.

21. CWYPF contest programs (1934), 2–3, (1935), 2–3; Juanita Jackson Mitchell interview.

22. CWYPF contest programs (1934), 2–3, (1935), 2–3; Juanita Jackson Mitchell interview.

23. CWYPF, 1987 reunion (videotape).

24. CWYPF contest programs (1934), 1–5, (1935), 1–5; Juanita Jackson Mitchell and Virginia Jackson Kiah, no. OH 8097, 1–2, McKeldin-Jackson Oral History Collection, MHS; *Afro-American*, April 1, 1933.

25. CWYPF contest programs (1934), 1–5, (1935), 1–5, 12; Juanita Jackson Mitchell interview.

26. CWYPF contest program (1934), 1; Juanita Jackson Mitchell interview.

27. Evelyn Burrell interview; CWYPF contest programs (1934), 1–5, (1935), 1–5, 12, (1939), 2–3, 5–8, (1940), 2–3, 5–8, (1941), 1; Juanita Jackson Mitchell interview.

28. CWYPF contest programs (1934), back cover, (1935), back cover, (1939), first page, back cover, (1940), first page, back cover, (1941), last page; Juanita Jackson Mitchell interview; CWYPF, *Minutes of the Executive Board of the City-Wide Young People's Forum* (hereafter, *Minutes*), 1936–38.

29. CWYPF contest programs (1934), back cover, (1935), back cover; Evelyn T. Burrell, no. OH 8138, 6.

30. Juanita Jackson Mitchell interview; CWYPF contest programs (1934), back cover, (1935), back cover, (1939), back cover, (1940), back cover, (1941), last page; CWYPF, *Minutes*, passim.

31. Juanita Jackson Mitchell interview; CWYPF, *Minutes*, September 26, 1933.

32. McNeil, "Youth Initiative in the African American Struggle for Racial Justice and Constitutional Rights," 70–72; Juanita Jackson Mitchell interview; CWYPF contest programs (1933–41).

33. CWYPF contest programs (1934), 1 (1936), 3–5; Juanita Jackson Mitchell interview.

34. Juanita Jackson Mitchell interview.

35. CWYPF contest program (1934), 4; Juanita Jackson Mitchell interview; Evelyn Burrell interview.

36. *Afro-American*, April 1, 1933. Copies of the untitled statement and petitions were given to me by Juanita Jackson Mitchell and are in my possession.

37. Untitled petition statement; Juanita Jackson Mitchell interview.

38. CWYPF contest program (1934), 3; *Baltimore Sun*, April 19, 26, 1933; *Baltimore Evening Sun*, April 18, 1933; CWYPF, *Minutes*, September 12, October 10, November 14, 1933.

39. CWYPF contest program (1934), 3; Reid, *The Negro Community of Baltimore*, 194; Juanita Jackson Mitchell interview; CWYPF, *Minutes*, September 12, October 10, November 14, 1933. Anna Ward is profiled in Argersinger, *Toward a New Deal in Baltimore*, 31, 38–39, and Durr, "The Conscience of the City."

40. Reid, *The Negro Community of Baltimore*, 148; Juanita Jackson Mitchell interview.

41. Juanita Jackson Mitchell interview.

42. Clarence Mitchell, no. OH 8154; Juanita Jackson Mitchell interview.

43. Wolters, *Negroes and the Great Depression*, 219–29; McNeil, *Groundwork*, 87–88; Juanita Jackson Mitchell interview.

44. Sitkoff, *A New Deal for Blacks*, 250–51; Zangrando, *The NAACP Crusade against Lynching, 1909–1950*, 109; McNeil, *Groundwork*, 88; Juanita Jackson Mitchell interview; W. E. B. Du Bois to Juanita E. Jackson, February 20, 1934 (copy in the author's possession).

Chapter 4: People's Unemployment League

Epigraph: "Initiation Procedure and Pledge of Loyalty," People's Unemployment League, Vertical Files, Enoch Pratt Free Library.

1. Argersinger, "The Right to Strike," 299; *Monthly Labor Review*, January 1933.

2. *Baltimore Sun*, September 13, 1932; Argersinger, *Toward a New Deal in Baltimore*, 144–46; Argersinger, *Making the Amalgamated*, 36–39, 140–42; Fraser, *Labor Will Rule*, 101–7, 207. I am grateful to Jo Ann Argersinger for introducing me to the Baltimore labor movement of the 1930s, including the ACW, in conversations that began a long time ago.

3. *Baltimore Sun*, September 13, 1932; Argersinger, *Making the Amalgamated*, 140–44; Fraser, *Labor Will Rule*, 207, 240, 242.

4. The following account of the AWC strike in 1932 and its aftermath is drawn from the *Baltimore Sun*, September 13, November 13, 1932, February 28, 1933; *Baltimore Evening Sun*, October 27, 1932; interview with Sara Barron, New York State School of Industrial and Labor Relations Library, Cornell University, New York City, 49–50, 57–58; Argersinger, *Making the Amalgamated*, 143–48; Argersinger, "The Right to Strike," 301–4; Argersinger, *Toward a New Deal in Baltimore*, 144–46; Argersinger, "The City That Tries to Suit Everybody," 96–101; Fraser, *Labor Will Rule*, 255–57.

5. Reid, *The Negro Community of Baltimore*, 63; *Afro-American*, July 15, August 12, 1933.

6. Bernstein, *The Lean Years*, 341–43, 421–22; Bernstein, *The Turbulent Years*, chaps. 4, 6.

7. Brown, "Maryland between the Wars," 697; Argersinger, *Toward a New Deal in Baltimore*, 12–13.

8. Interview with Frank Trager, by Roy Rosenzweig, and Naomi Riches to Roy Rosenzweig, April 7, 1973. I am grateful to Roy Rosenzweig for sharing these two documents with me. Clarence Whitmore to Harriet P. Turner of Pratt Library, June 21, 1934, Vertical Files, Enoch Pratt Free Library; Rosenzweig, "Socialism in Our Time," 489–96.

9. Frank Trager interview; Rosenzweig, "Socialism in Our Time," 489–96.

10. *Baltimore Sun*, January 13, 1933; Frank Trager to Norman Thomas, March 7, 1934, Norman Thomas Papers, NYPL; Whitmore to Turner; "Weekly Bulletin of the People's Unemployment League," December 11, 1933, Vertical Files, Enoch Pratt Free Library; "Conference: People's Unemployment League, Baltimore, Maryland, and Aubrey Williams," August 24, 1934, Federal Emergency Relief Administration records, NARA; *Baltimore Sun*, January 22, 1933, March 27, 1934; *Monthly Labor Review*, May 1933, 1025; *Maryland Leader*, February 17, 1934. I am grateful to Rosenzweig and Argersinger for discussions of the PUL.

11. Riches to Rosenzweig; "Constitution of the People's' Unemployment League of Maryland, Incorporated," 1937, Vertical Files, Enoch Pratt Free Library; Trager to Thomas; Whitmore to Turner; Frank Trager interview; *Baltimore Sun*, March 6, 1933; *Monthly Labor Review*, May 1933, 1025–26; "Conference."

12. Frank Trager interview; Trager to Thomas; *Monthly Labor Review*, May 1933, 1025–26.

13. *Baltimore Sun*, February 19, March 14, March 29, April 2–3, July 30, 1933; "Conference."

14. *Maryland Leader*, February 17, February 24, April 14, 21, 28, May 5, June 7, 16, 23, 30, July 7, 14, August 11, 25, September 1, 8, October 1, 20, November 24, December 11, 15, 22, 1934, January 12, 1935; Bennet Mead to Jacob Baker, July 25, 1933, Federal Emergency Relief Administration records, NARA.

15. Frank Trager interview; *Monthly Labor Review*, May 1933, 1025–26.

16. Report to the Executive Committee, PUL, from L. L. Leith, December 9, 1933, Vertical Files, Enoch Pratt Free Library; *Maryland Leader*, April 21, 1934; "Weekly Bulletin of the People's Unemployment League," December 11, 1933; *Baltimore Sun*, July 14, 1933.

17. Whitmore to Turner; *Baltimore Sun*, May 2–3, July 15, September 1, 1933; "Weekly Bulletin of the People's Unemployment League," December 11, 1933; *Baltimore Sun*, April 13, June 22, October 22, 1933.

18. Frank Trager interview.

19. "Constitution of the PUL"; Frank Trager interview; Trager to Thomas; Reid, *The Negro Community of Baltimore*, 210; *Afro-American*, June 1, 1935.

20. *Maryland Leader*, January 12, 1935.

21. Frank Trager interview; Riches to Rosenzweig; Broadus Mitchell, "Gilman, Elisabeth," in James et al., *Notable American Women, 1607-1950*, 42–43; Hall, "Broadus Mitchell (1892–1988)"; "Frank Trager Obituary," *New York Times*, August 31, 1984; "Joel Seidman Obituary," *Chicago Tribune*, October 18, 1977; Argersinger, *Toward a New Deal in Baltimore*, 127–40; Rosenzweig, "Socialism in Our Time."

22. *Baltimore Evening Sun*, November 29, 1934; Rosenzweig, "Socialism in Our Time," 488–89; Trager to Thomas; "Platform of the Socialist Party of Maryland," 1930, Vertical Files, Enoch Pratt Free Library; *Maryland Leader*, February 17, 1934.

23. Frank Trager interview.

24. *Baltimore Sun*, January 1, 1933; Riches to Rosenzweig; Frank Trager to Norman Thomas, March 7, 1934, Norman Thomas Papers, NYPL; *Baltimore Sun*, January 13, 1933; Frank Trager interview.

25. Sara Barron interview, 21, 39.

26. Frank Trager interview; *Baltimore Sun*, January 13, 1933, February 4, March 2–3, 1934; Sara Barron interview, 10; Whitmore to Turner; Sigmund Diamond interview, by the author; *Maryland Leader*, July 21, 1934.

27. *Baltimore Sun*, January 13, 1933; Markowitz, *The Rise and Fall of the People's Century*, esp. 3–9.

28. Mitchell, "Gilman, Elisabeth."

29. Ibid.; *Baltimore Evening Sun*, November 12, 1934.

30. Mitchell, "Gilman, Elisabeth"; "Reminiscences of Broadus Mitchell," Oral History Collection, Columbia University, 85–89; Kim, "The Integration of Socialism and Feminism."

31. Report to the Executive Committee, PUL, December 9, 1933; "Weekly Bulletin of the People's Unemployment League"; Riches to Rosenzweig; Frank Trager interview.

32. Hall, "Broadus Mitchell (1892–1988)," 31.

33. Ibid., 31–32; "Reminiscences of Broadus Mitchell"; Pearson, "The National Urban League Comes to Baltimore."

34. "Reminiscences of Broadus Mitchell"; Pearson, "The National Urban League Comes to Baltimore."

35. Pearson, "The National Urban League Comes to Baltimore"; Farrar, *The Baltimore Afro-American, 1892–1950*, 103–5; Fee et al., *The Baltimore Book*, 76; "Reminiscences of Broadus Mitchell"; Hall, "Broadus Mitchell (1892–1988)," 43; interview with Evelyn Burrell, by the author; interview with Juanita Jackson Mitchell, by the author; Forum contest program (1935).

36. Interview with Edward S. Lewis, by the author; Frank Trager interview; *Afro-American*, February 4, 1933.

37. Frank Trager interview.

38. Comment at the Southern Labor History Conference, Austin, October 26–29, 1995.

39. For the classic statement of the Popular Front, see Dimitroff, *The United Front*, 182–99.

40. Riches to Rosenzweig; Frank Trager interview; quote in Argersinger, *Toward a New Deal in Baltimore*, 139.

41. Frank Trager interview; Whitmore to Turner.

42. Riches to Rosenzweig; Trager to Thomas; Whitmore to Turner; Frank Trager interview; *Baltimore Sun*, May 2–3, July 15, September 1, 1933; Cohen, "A Socialist Training School," 6.

43. Trager to Thomas; Norman Thomas to Frank Trager, March 15, 1934; Elisabeth Gilman to Norman Thomas, March 26, 1934; Frank Trager to Norman Thomas, April 19, 1934, all in Norman Thomas Papers, NYPL.

44. Riches to Rosenzweig; Trager to Thomas; *Baltimore Sun*, March 1, 1936; Frank Trager interview; Pedersen, *The Communist Party in Maryland, 1919–1957*, 44–45. According to Pedersen, Ceattei/Chatty had been expelled from the Maryland Communist Party in 1929.

Chapter 5: The Lynching of George Armwood

Epigraph: Donald Smith, *Afro-American*, October 28, 1933.

1. *Afro-American*, July 29, September 9, 21, October 28, 1933; Zangrando, *The NAACP Crusade against Lynching, 1909–1950*, 5–6. Various ages are given for Armwood; the age used here comes from his mother's testimony. On the lynching of Armwood, see Ifill, *On the Courthouse Lawn*; Moore, *Murder on Maryland's Eastern Shore*.

2. *Afro-American*, October 28, 1933. In its issue dated November 1940, *The Crisis* published another poem on its cover about the Armwood lynching by Esther Pope entitled "Flag Salute"; it is reproduced in Garfinkel, *When Negroes March*, 35–36.

3. Zangrando, *The NAACP Crusade against Lynching, 1909–1950*, 72–106.

4. *Baltimore Evening Sun*, October 18–19, 1933; *Afro-American*, October 21, 1933. Mary Denston was seventy-one, according to the *Afro*, and eighty-two, according to the *Baltimore Evening Sun*. "Reminiscences of Clarence Mitchell," Oral History Collection, Columbia University, 5; Clarence Mitchell, no. OH 8209, McKeldin-Jackson Oral History Collection, MHS, 9–12. Ifill argues that claims that lynching victims had mental disabilities were surprisingly frequent and should be regarded with some skepticism: Ifill, *On the Courthouse Lawn*, 34.

5. *Afro-American*, October 21, 28, 1933; interview with Juanita Jackson Mitchell, by the author; "Reminiscences of Clarence Mitchell"; Clarence Mitchell, no. OH 8209, 9–12. Spencer is partially quoted in Ifill, *On the Courthouse Lawn*, 38.

6. *Baltimore Evening Sun*, October 19, 1933; *Afro-American*, October 21, 1933; *New York Times*, October 19, 1933; Ifill, *On the Courthouse Lawn*, 42.

7. *Baltimore Evening Sun*, October 19–20, 1933; *Afro-American*, October 21, 1933; *New York Times*, October 19, 1933.

8. *Baltimore Evening Sun*, October 19–20, 1933; *Afro-American*, October 28, 1933.

9. *Baltimore Evening Sun*, October 19–20, 1933; *Afro-American*, October 21, 1933; Clarence Mitchell, no. OH 8209, 9–14.

10. *Baltimore Evening Sun*, October 20, 1933; *Afro-American*, November 25, 1933; *New York Times*, October 19, 1933.

11. See Wells-Barnett, *Southern Horrors and Other Writings*. Recent studies of lynching include Brundage, *Under Sentence of Death*; Brundage, *Lynching in the New South*; Ifill, *On the Courthouse Lawn*. The quote is from *Afro-American*, November 4, 1933.

12. *Afro-American*, October 21, 28, 1933; "Reminiscences of Clarence Mitchell"; Clarence Mitchell, no. OH 8209, 9–12; Parren Mitchell, no. OH 8170, McKeldin-Jackson Oral History Collection, MHS, 1–2; Juanita Jackson Mitchell interview.

13. *Afro-American*, October 21, 28, 1933; *Baltimore Sun*, October 25, 1933; *Baltimore Evening Sun*, October 19, 1933; Juanita Jackson Mitchell interview.

14. *Afro-American*, October 21, 28, 1933.

15. *Baltimore Evening Sun*, October 24, 1933; *Baltimore Sun*, October 25, 1933.

16. *Baltimore Evening Sun*, October 25–26, 1933; *Afro-American*, October 28, 1933; Ifill, *On the Courthouse Lawn*, 38.

17. *Afro-American*, October 21, 28, November 11, 1933; *Baltimore Sun*, October 26, 1933; Forum contest program (1934), 4; Moore, *Murder on Maryland's Eastern Shore*, 182.

18. *Afro-American*, October 21, 29, 1933; *Baltimore Evening Sun*, October 19, 25, 1933; Roy Wilkins to Governor Albert Ritchie, October 27, 1933, Records of the NAACP, container 85, group I, series G, Library of Congress.

19. *Afro-American*, October 28, 1933.

20. Ibid.

21. Ibid.; Forum contest program (1934), 4.

22. *Afro-American*, October 21, 28, November 4, 11, 18–19, 1933; *Baltimore Evening Sun*, October 24, 26, 1933; *Baltimore Sun*, November 19–20, 1933; Musgrove, "An Early History of the Baltimore Branch of the NAACP," 15–16.

23. *Afro-American*, October 28, 1933.

24. Ibid., November 4, 1933; Forum, *Minutes*, October 31, 1933.

25. *Afro-American*, November 4, 11, 1933.

26. Ibid., November 18, 25, 1933; *Baltimore Sun*, November 19–20, 1933.

27. *Afro-American*, November 18, 25, 1933; *Baltimore Sun*, November 19–20, 1933; Forum, *Minutes*, October 24, 1933.

28. *Afro-American*, November 18, 25, 1933; *Baltimore Sun*, October 19, 1933.

29. *Afro-American*, November 4, 1933.

30. Ibid.

31. Ibid., October 28, 1933.

32. Ibid., November 11, 1933.

33. Ibid., November 18, 1933.

34. "Reminiscences of Clarence Mitchell," 22–23; *Afro-American*, November 25, December 9, 1933.

35. *Afro-American*, November 4, 1933.

36. Ibid.; *Baltimore Evening Sun*, October 30, 1933; *Baltimore Sun*, March 3, 1934; Juanita Jackson Mitchell interview.

37. *Afro-American*, November 25, December 9, 1933; Ifill, *On the Courthouse Lawn*, 68–69, 89–91, 101–3.

38. *Afro-American*, December 2, 1933; "Reminiscences of Clarence Mitchell," 6–7; Clarence Mitchell, no. OH 8209, 13–14.

39. *Afro-American*, December 9, 1933; "Reminiscences of Clarence Mitchell," 6–7; Clarence Mitchell, no. OH 8209, 13–14.

40. *Afro-American*, December 16, 23, 1933; Ifill, *On the Courthouse Lawn*, 70–73, 185n.

41. Charles Trigg to Walter White, January 10, 1934, Charles Trigg to Walter White, January 12, 1934, Walter White to Charles Trigg, January 26, 1934, Juanita Jackson to Walter White, February 7, 1934, Walter White to Juanita Jackson, February 8, 1934, Walter White to Charles Trigg, February 8, 1934, Branch Files, Records of the NAACP, container 84, group I, series G, Library of Congress; *New York Times*, January 8, 1934; *Baltimore Sun*, February 4, 1934; *Maryland Leader*, May 12, 1934.

Chapter 6: Buy Where You Can Work

Epigraph: Interview with Juanita Jackson Mitchell, by the author.

1. *Afro-American*, June 17, 1933.

2. McKay, *Harlem*, 73–85; interview with Evelyn Burrell, by the author; *Afro-American*, June 3, 17, 24, August 5, September 23, 30, October 7, December 23, 1933, April 14, 1934; interview with Juanita Jackson Mitchell, by the author. This chapter is based on Skotnes, "Buy Where You Can Work."

3. *Afro-American*, September 30, 1933; Evelyn Burrell interview; Reid, *The Negro Community of Baltimore*, 172–73.

4. *Afro-American*, June 3, 17, September 30, October 7, 1933.

5. Juanita Jackson Mitchell interview; *Afro-American*, June 3, 1933.

6. *Afro-American*, June 17, October 7, 1933; *Daily Record*, April 10, 1935; Toni Costonie, "Prophet Kiowa Costonie," available online at http://www.african americanworld.com/reparations-1.htm (accessed October 15, 2004).

7. *Afro-American*, June 17, 24, October 7, 1933; Costonie, "Prophet Kiowa Costonie."

8. *Afro-American*, September 23, 30, October 7, 1933; Evelyn Burrell interview; Juanita Jackson Mitchell interview.

9. *Afro-American*, September 30, October 7, December 23, 1933; McGuinn, "The Courts and the Occupational Status of Negroes in Maryland," 259.

10. Juanita Jackson Mitchell interview; *Afro-American*, January 10, August 12, September 30, October 7, 14, 1933; Meier and Rudwick, "The Origins of Nonviolent Direct Action in Afro-American Protest," 315–16; Hunter, "Don't Buy Where You Can't Work," 77–102; Jones, "A History and Appraisal of the Economic Consequences of Negro Trade Boycotts," 17–33.

11. *Afro-American*, September 23, 30, October 7, 14, 1933.

12. Ibid., October 14, November 18, 1933.

13. CWYPF, 1987 reunion (videotape); Juanita Jackson Mitchell interview; CWYPF, *Minutes*, November 15, 1933.

14. Juanita Jackson Mitchell interview; Evelyn Burrell interview; CWYPF, *Minutes*, November 14, 1933; *Daily Record*, April 10, 1935. MacNeal is quoted in Hunter, "Don't Buy Where You Can't Work," 114; McGuinn, "The Courts and Equality of Educational Opportunity," 259.

15. Evelyn Burrell interview.

16. CWYPF, *Minutes*, November 28, 1933; CWYPF contest program (1934), 3;

Juanita Jackson Mitchell interview; *Afro-American*, November 25, December 2, 15, 1933.

17. CWYPF, *Minutes*, December 12, 1933, 5; *Afro-American*, December 16, 23, 26, 1933; Evelyn Burrell interview; Juanita Jackson Mitchell interview; *Daily Record*, May 26, 1934.

18. *Afro-American*, December 16, 23, 1933, May 5, 1934; *Daily Record*, April 10, 1935; Hunter, "Don't Buy Where You Can't Work," 118.

19. *Afro-American*, December 16, 23, 1933; CWYPF, *Minutes*, December 19, 1933.

20. Evelyn Burrell interview; *Afro-American*, December 16, 1933; McGuinn, "The Courts and Equality of Educational Opportunity," 263.

21. *Afro-American*, December 16, 1933.

22. Ibid., November 18, 25, December 16, 1933.

23. Ibid., December 16, 1933.

24. Clarence Mitchell, no. OH 8154, McKeldin-Jackson Oral History Collection, MHS; CWYPF, *Minutes*, December 19, 1933; *Afro-American*, December 23, 1933, January 6, 1934.

25. CWYPF, *Minutes*, January 16, February 6, 1934; CWYPF contest program (1934), 3–4; *Afro-American*, January 6, 13, March 17, 1934; Juanita Jackson Mitchell interview.

26. *Afro-American*, November 4, December 23, 30, 1933; McGuinn, "The Courts and Equality of Educational Opportunity," 260.

27. *Afro-American*, March 17, 1934.

28. Ibid., May 26, 1934; McGuinn, "The Courts and Equality of Educational Opportunity," 260, 264n; Hunter, "Don't Buy Where You Can't Work," 120.

29. "Baltimore, Md., Chain Store Picketing," in Baltimore, Maryland, 1933, file, Records of the NAACP, container 85, group I, series G, Library of Congress; *Afro-American*, May 17, June 2, 9, 16, 1934; CWYPF contest program (1935), 12.

30. *Afro-American*, June 30, July 7, 1934.

31. Ibid., January 13, July 7, 1934; Juanita Jackson Mitchell interview; Evelyn Burrell interview.

32. *Afro-American*, January 13, June 30, July 7, 1934.

33. Ibid., June 30, 1934; *Daily Record*, April 10, 1935; *Baltimore Sun*, April 11, 1935; CWYPF, *Minutes*, May 22, 1934; Juanita Jackson Mitchell interview.

34. Juanita Jackson Mitchell interview; *Afro-American*, April 9, 1938.

35. Meier and Rudwick, "The Origins of Nonviolent Direct Action in Afro-American Protest," 315–16.

36. Myrdal, *An American Dilemma*, 803; Frazier, *Negro Youth at the Crossroads*, 288; Bunche, "The Program, Ideologies, Tactics, and Achievements of Negro Betterment and Interracial Organizations," 391–92; Reid, "The Negro in the American Economic Order," 1, 165; Harris, *The Negro as Capitalist*, 181–84; Meier and Rudwick, "The Origins of Nonviolent Direct Action in Afro-American Protest," 323; Hunter, "Don't Buy Where You Can't Work," 31–40.

37. *Afro-American*, December 16, 1933.

38. Ibid., June 2, 16, August 25, 1934 (emphasis added); McGuinn, "The Courts and Equality of Educational Opportunity"; *Baltimore Evening Sun*, August 22, 1934; *Maryland Leader*, August 25, September 1, 8, October 1, 1934; Clarence Mitchell, no. OH 8154.

39. Lillie Jackson to Walter White, June 30, 1934, "Baltimore, Md. Chain Store Picketing," in Baltimore, Maryland, 1933, file, Records of the NAACP, container 85, group I, series G, Library of Congress; *Afro-American*, June 16, August 25, 1934; *Baltimore Evening Sun*, August 22, 1934; CWYPF, *Minutes*, April 24, May 8, 1934; *Baltimore Sun*, November 1, 1942.

40. *Afro-American*, June 22, 1935; *The Crisis*, January 1937, 8; Farrar, *The Baltimore* Afro-American, *1892–1950*, 146; Costonie, "Prophet Kiowa Costonie"; Kiowa Costonie Jr. to the author, December 29, 2002, e-mail correspondence. Prophet Costonie's son Kiowa Costonie Jr. recalled that in Chicago, his father had sold healing water and prayer cloths as part of a mail order business. Also, the elder Costonie included his son in his performances as a child prodigy with a photographic memory. Kiowa Costonie Jr. even appeared in this capacity on television and was covered in *Jet* magazine. However, according to him, his memory really was not exceptional; he and his father used a system of "simple word association."

41. *Afro-American*, December 16, 1933, June 30, 1934; Juanita Jackson Mitchell interview.

42. *Afro-American*, March 17, 1934; Henry Louis Gates Jr., "Black Demagogues and Pseudo-Scholars," *New York Times*, July 20, 1992.

43. Juanita Jackson Mitchell interview; CWYPF contest program (1934), back cover; Reid, *The Negro Community of Baltimore*, 199; *Afro-American*, December 16, 23, 1933.

44. Walter White to Reverend Charles Y. Trigg, December 5, 1933, Walter White to Juanita E. Jackson, December 5, 1933, Juanita E. Jackson to Walter White, December 7, 1933, Walter White to Juanita E. Jackson, December 13, 1933, George W. Mitchell to the NAACP, December 17, 1933, all in Baltimore, Maryland, 1933, file, Records of the NAACP, container 85, group I, series G, Library of Congress.

Chapter 7: The Baltimore Soviet

Epigraph: Interview with Bill Bailey, by Bruce Nelson, January 24, 1979.

1. Bernstein, *The Turbulent Years*, 30, 35, chaps. 3–4, 6.

2. Argersinger, *Toward a New Deal in Baltimore*, 150, 157, 163.

3. *Afro-American*, June 17, August 12, 26, 1933; *Baltimore Sun*, August 22, 26, 1933; *Baltimore Evening Sun*, August 21, 1933; Brown, "Maryland between the Wars," 749.

4. *Afro-American*, August 5, 12, 26, 1933; *Baltimore Evening Sun*, August 21, 1933; *Baltimore Sun*, August 22, 26, 1933; Trotter, "From Raw Deal to New Deal?"

5. *Maryland Leader*, June 1, 1935; *Baltimore Sun*, May 29–30, 1935; Brown, "Maryland between the Wars," 697, 750.

6. *Marine Workers Voice*, December 1933, January, May 1934; *Baltimore Sun*, October 21, November 24, 1933; interview with Bill Bailey, by Bruce Nelson; Nelson, *Workers on the Waterfront*, 96–100; Argersinger, "Assisting the 'Loafers'"; Argersinger, *Toward a New Deal in Baltimore*, 122–24.

7. Elizabeth Wickenden to William Plunkert, April 2, 1934, State File (Maryland), Federal Emergency Relief Administration records, no. 420, NARA; Argersinger, "Assisting the 'Loafers,'" 237–38; Bill Bailey interview.

8. Wickenden to Plunkert; Argersinger, "Assisting the 'Loafers,'" 237–38.

9. *Marine Workers Voice*, January 1934; Wickenden to Plunkert; Argersinger, "Assisting the 'Loafers,'" 237–39.

10. Wickenden to Plunkert.

11. *Marine Workers Voice*, March, April, July 1934; Marine Workers Industrial Union, *Centralized Shipping Bureau*, 16–17; *Maryland Leader*, January 20, 1934; *Baltimore Sun*, February 11, 1934; Bailey, *The Kid from Hoboken*, 225; Marine Workers Industrial Union, *Centralized Shipping Bureau*, 12, 18, 30–32.

12. Reid, *The Negro Community of Baltimore*, 62. Reid mistook the seamen's relief program for the MWIU itself.

13. Joseph La Combe to William Plunkert, April 22, 1934, State File (Maryland), Federal Emergency Relief Administration records, no. 420, NARA.

14. *Marine Workers Voice*, November, December 1933, January 1934; *Baltimore Sun*, October 21, November 23, 24, 1933; Arnesen, "Bi-racial Waterfront Unionism in the Age of Segregation."

15. *Marine Workers Voice*, January 1934.

16. Ibid.; *Afro-American*, July 14, August 18, 1934.

17. *Baltimore Sun*, March 21, May 15, 29, 1934; Bailey, *The Kid from Hoboken*, 227–28; Marine Workers Industrial Union, *Centralized Shipping Bureau*, 9, 24.

18. *Maryland Leader*, October 6, 1934; *Marine Workers Voice*, May, September–October, November 1934; *Baltimore Evening Sun*, May 28, October 8, 1934; Elizabeth Wickenden to Janet Long, July 13, 1934, notes to meeting with Janet Long, November 11, 1934, MWIU to William J. Plunkert, October 10, 1934, WUC to William J. Plunkert, October 30, 1934, State File (Maryland), Federal Emergency Relief Administration records, no. 420, NARA; Argersinger, "Assisting the 'Loafers,'" 232–34.

19. Nelson, *Workers on the Waterfront*, 101; Bill Bailey interview; Rubin, *The Log of Rubin the Sailor*, 183–88, 191–97.

20. *Maryland Leader*, February 16, March 2, 1935; *Baltimore Sun*, February 10–11, 23, June 25, 1935.

21. *Baltimore Sun*, May 11, 23, July 10, August 5, September 13, 1933, February 24, 1934, March 22–23, May 29, 1935; *Afro-American*, July 15, 1933; *Maryland Leader*, March 3, December 1, 8, 1934, January 12, 26, March 2, July 20, 27, 1935; Argersinger, *Making the Amalgamated*, 152–54.

22. *Maryland Leader*, March 17, 24, April 14, 28, May 26, 1934, March 23, 30, April 6, June 15, July 20, 27, October 19, 1935.

23. *Afro-American*, August 12, 1933; Argersinger, *Making the Amalgamated*, 165–66.

24. *Baltimore Sun*, April 26, 1935; *Maryland Leader*, May 4, August 3, 1935, April 11, May 2, 1936.

25. *Maryland Leader*, March 3, 17, 24, 31, May 12, 19, 26, June 7, 16, 23, 30, August 31, September 15, 22, October 27, November 3, 11, 1934, February 2, 26, March 2, 9, April 13, May 18–19, June 8, September 7, 14, October 5, 27, 1935, January 18, February 8, March 7, 14, May 11, 30, June 27, 1936; *Baltimore Sun*, January 8, August 12, September 16, 1933, April 17, 27, May 13, June 8, July 7, 1934, March 5–6, June 15, 1936; Argersinger, *Toward a New Deal in Baltimore*, 150.

26. *Maryland Leader*, June 7, 16, 23, July 28, September 29, December 8, 1934, March 2, 1935; *Baltimore Sun*, April 17, June 8, 14, July 7, September 22, 1934, February 24, 25, 1935; Argersinger, *Toward a New Deal in Baltimore*, 151, 163–65.

27. *Maryland Leader*, March 24, April 21, 28, June 16, November 3, 1934; *Afro-American*, January 25, May 5, 1935; interview with Edward S. Lewis, by the author.

28. *Maryland Leader*, March 2, 24, April 28, July 7, November 10, 24, 1934, April 6, June 1, 8, August 10, October 26, December 21, 1935; Argersinger, *Toward a New Deal in Baltimore*, 152.

29. *Maryland Leader*, January 12, February 3, 17, April 28, 1934, June 7, 16, 23, July 13, November 16, December 1, 28, 1935, January 25, 1936.

30. Ibid., November 11, 1934, January 5, 26, February 2, March 7, 14, June 22, July 20, 27, 1936.

31. Ibid., February 17, 1934, May 18, 1935.

32. Reports of the PUL's activities appeared in almost every edition of the *Maryland Leader* during these years: see, e.g., ibid., February 17, 24, April 21, 28, May 5, June 7, 16, November 16, 1934, January 19, February 2, July 27, August 24, October 26, November 9, 16, 30, December 7, 21, 1935.

33. Ibid., January 5, 12, 1935, March 21, 1936.

34. Interview with Frank Trager, by Roy Rosenzweig; *Maryland Leader*, August 18, November 24, December 1, 1934, January 19, 1935; Rosenzweig, "Socialism in Our Time," 502.

35. *Maryland Leader*, January 19, February 9, June 22, November 30, 1935; *Baltimore Sun*, February 2, 1935; Frank Trager interview.

36. *Maryland Leader*, July 7, August 24, October 26, 1935.

37. Ibid., November 2, 9, 16, December 7, 14, 21, 1935.

38. Ibid., January 18, 25, 1935; Argersinger, *Toward a New Deal in Baltimore*, 136.

39. *Maryland Leader*, October 26, December 14, 21, 1935.

40. Rosenzweig, "Socialism in Our Time," 501. See also Oppenheimer, "The Organizations of the Unemployed, 1930–1940," 36; Piven and Cloward, *Poor People's Movements*, chap. 2; Argersinger, *Toward a New Deal in Baltimore*, 138–40; *Baltimore Sun*, August 23, 1937, January 10, 1938.

41. *Afro-American*, September 16, October 15, 1933, July 7, 19, 1934, January 12,

July 20, October 12, 26, November 1, December 7, 14, 1935; Farrar, *The Baltimore Afro-American, 1892–1950*, 92–94.

42. *Afro-American*, August 12, 1933, October 12, 1934, January 12, 1935, January 1, 1938; *Baltimore Sun*, May 17, 1934; *Maryland Leader*, March 7, 21, 1936; Edward S. Lewis interview; Parris and Brooks, *Blacks in the City*, 248–60.

43. *Afro-American*, October 12, October 26, November 16, December 7, 14, 1935; Parris and Brooks, *Blacks in the City*, 257–58; Zieger, *The CIO, 1935–1955*, 22–24.

Chapter 8: Seeking Directions

Epigraph: Interview with Juanita Jackson Mitchell, by the author.

1. Interview with Juanita Jackson Mitchell, by the author; CWYPF contest programs (1934), 3, (1935), 4; CWYPF, *Minutes*, April 10, 1934; *Baltimore Sun*, February 27, March 13, 1934; Reid, *The Negro Community of Baltimore*, 44–45.

2. Juanita Jackson Mitchell interview; CWYPF, *Minutes*, January 16, 1934, March 23, 1935; CWYPF contest program (1935). For the national dimensions of the NAACP campaign at this time, see Zangrando, *The NAACP Crusade against Lynching, 1909–1950*, 113–21.

3. Juanita Jackson Mitchell interview; CWYPF contest program (1935), 4; *Baltimore Sun*, February 20, 22, 1934.

4. Reid, *The Negro Community of Baltimore*, 210–11.

5. CWYPF contest program (1935), 12; *Baltimore Sun*, May 13, 17, November 9, 1934; *Maryland Leader*, May 19, 1934; Juanita Jackson Mitchell interview; CWYPF song card, n.d. (in my possession).

6. *Afro-American*, January 25, 1936; CWYPF, *Minutes*, September 23, November 12, 27, 1935; *Afro-American*, April 25, 1936; *Maryland Leader*, March 10, May 19, 1934, April 6, November 9, 1935, February 8, 1936; Wittner, *Rebels against War*, 5–15.

7. *Maryland Leader*, April 18, 1936; CWYPF, *Minutes*, March 14, April 15, 1936; *Afro-American*, April 25, 1936; interview with Albert Blumberg, by the author; Pedersen, *The Communist Party in Maryland, 1919–1957*, 88.

8. Juanita Jackson Mitchell interview; Wittner, *Rebels against War*, 8; Broadus Mitchell, "Gilman, Elisabeth," in James et al., *Notable American Women, 1607–1950*, 42–43.

9. Juanita Jackson Mitchell interview; *Baltimore Sun*, July 21, 29, September 17, 1934; *Afro-American*, August 4, 1934; *Maryland Leader*, September 22, 1934.

10. "What Socialists Stand For: Platform of the Socialist Party of Maryland," May 1934, Vertical Files, Enoch Pratt Free Library 4; *Baltimore Sun*, September 11, 1934; *Maryland Leader*, July 21, 1934.

11. Watson, *Lion in the Lobby*, 97–100; *Maryland Leader*, September 22, 1934.

12. Juanita Jackson Mitchell interview; interview with Evelyn Burrell, by the author; *Afro-American*, November 3, 1934. *Baltimore Sun*, November 7, 1934; *Baltimore Evening Sun*, November 7, 1934; *Maryland Leader*, November 10, November 17,

1934; CWYPF contest program (1935), 5; "Reminiscences of Broadus Mitchell," Oral History Collection, Columbia University, 5. The *Baltimore Evening Sun*, November 29, 1934, gave the counts for previous Socialist Party gubernatorial candidates: A. L. Blessing in 1920, 2,799; W. H. Champlin in 1923, 1,456; T. G. Dill in 1926, 2,495; Elisabeth Gilman in 1930, 4,178.

13. *Maryland Leader*, November 24, 1935; CWYPF contest program (1935), 2, 21; *Baltimore Sun*, February 1, 1935; *Afro-American*, February 2, 1935.

14. Joel Seidman left for the Brookwood Labor College; Frank Trager left to work with the LID in New York; and Juanita Jackson left for the national NAACP office in New York; she then married Clarence Mitchell, and they both traveled to Minneapolis to work with the local Urban League. Juanita Jackson Mitchell interview; Cohen, "A Socialist Training School," 6. Robert D. McFadden, "Frank N. Trager, 78, an Expert on Asia, Dies," *New York Times*, August 31, 1984.

15. *Afro-American*, October 28, November 11, 1933; *Baltimore Sun*, January 24, March 20, 1934; *Baltimore Evening Sun*, October 10, 1933. Quoted in McNeil, *Groundwork*, 96.

16. *Baltimore Sun*, March 20, May 18, 1933, April 19, 27, June 26, July 27, December 2, 6–8, 1934.

17. *Afro-American*, March 10, 1934; *Baltimore Sun*, March 2, 10, June 7, 14, July 16, December 16, 29, 1934; McNeil, *Groundwork*, 98–101, 119–20.

18. *Baltimore Sun*, February 22, 1934; *Afro-American*, March 3, October 27, 1934; Juanita Jackson Mitchell interview.

19. *Afro-American*, October 27, 1934, November 3, 1934.

20. Ibid., January 25, 1936; Charles Houston, "An Approach to Better Race Relations," speech to the National YWCA Convention, Philadelphia, May 5, 1934 (in my possession).

21. Juanita Jackson Mitchell interview; McNeil, *Groundwork*, 113–18, 131–39; Tushnet, *The NAACP's Legal Strategy against Segregated Education, 1925–1950*, 53–58; Seawright, "Desegregation at Maryland"; Kuebler, "The Desegregation of the University of Maryland."

22. McNeil, *Groundwork*, pts. 1–2; Douglas O. Linder, "Before *Brown*: Charles H. Houston and the *Gaines* Case," available online at http://www.law.umkc.edu/faculty/projects/ftrials/trialheroes/charleshoustonessayF.html (accessed July 25, 2007), 1–12.

23. Ibid.

24. Juanita Jackson Mitchell interview; McNeil, *Groundwork*, 137–39; Seawright, "Desegregation at Maryland," 60–65.

25. Juanita Jackson Mitchell interview; Clarence Mitchell Jr., no. OH 8154, McKeldin-Jackson Oral History Collection, MHS, 42.

26. Juanita Jackson Mitchell interview; Juan Williams, "Marshall's Law," *Washington Post Magazine*, January 7, 1990, 17; Williams, *Thurgood Marshall, American Revolutionary*, 52–53; Seawright, "Desegregation at Maryland," 61–62. Marshall's bitterness toward the University of Maryland remained with him throughout his

life. When the University of Maryland Law School named its new library after him in 1980, Marshall, by then a Supreme Court Justice, refused to attend the dedication ceremony, saying that the university had wanted nothing to do with him when he was young, and he wanted nothing to do with it now. In fact, Clarence Mitchell had to persuade a reluctant Marshall to allow the law school to use his name at all: Williams, *Thurgood Marshall, American Revolutionary*, 371–72.

27. Seawright, "Desegregation at Maryland," 65–66; Farrar, *The Baltimore* Afro-American, *1892–1950*, 47–48.

28. Juanita Jackson Mitchell interview; Williams, "Marshall's Law," 17; Seawright, "Desegregation at Maryland," 66–67; Kuebler, "The Desegregation of the University of Maryland," 41–45.

29. Juanita Jackson Mitchell interview; Seawright, "Desegregation at Maryland," 67–68; Kuebler, "The Desegregation of the University of Maryland," 45–47.

30. Ibid.

31. *Afro-American*, June 22, 1935; Juanita Jackson Mitchell interview.

32. Juanita Jackson Mitchell interview; Walter White to Carl Murphy, November 22, 1934, Murphy to White, November 23, 1934, White to Murphy, November 27, 1934, Baltimore, Maryland, 1934, file, Records of the NAACP, group I, series G, container 35, Library of Congress; *The Crisis*, September 1935, 272, October 1935, 312; "Report of the Department of Branches," October 9, 1936, pt. 1: "1909–1950 Meetings of the Board of Directors," Papers of the NAACP (microfilm), reel 6, Library of Congress; Wolters, *Negroes and the Great Depression*, 327; Meier and Rudwick, *Black Detroit and the Rise of the UAW*, 80–99.

33. *Afro-American*, June 7, 1930; Robert W. Bagnall to Carl Murphy, June 12, 1931, Bagnall to Murphy, June 14, 1931, Baltimore, Maryland, January–June 1931, file, Bagnall to A. C. Clark, September 30, 1931, Bagnall to Walter White, September 30, 1931, Baltimore, Maryland, July–October 1931, file, Murphy to White, November 12, 1931, White to Murphy, November 19, 1931, November–December 1931 folder, all in Records of the NAACP, group I, series G, container 85, Library of Congress; Farrar, *The Baltimore* Afro-American, *1892–1950*, 180.

34. Carl Murphy to Walter White, October 12, 1932, Robert Bagnall to Carl Murphy, October 14, 1932, and other correspondence in Baltimore, Maryland, 1932, file, Walter White to Charles Trigg, December 5, 1933, Walter White to Juanita Jackson, December 5, 1933, Juanita Jackson to Walter White, December 7, 1933, Walter White to Juanita Jackson, December 13, 1933, George W. Mitchell to the NAACP, December 17, 1933, and other correspondence in Baltimore, Maryland, 1933, file, all in Records of the NAACP, group I, series G, container 85, Library of Congress; *Afro-American*, September 17, 1932, November 11, 1933; Farrar, *The Baltimore* Afro-American, *1892–1950*, 180–81.

35. See the large correspondence on this topic in Baltimore, Maryland, 1935, file, Records of the NAACP, group I, series G, container 85, Library of Congress; Juanita Jackson Mitchell interview; Clarence Mitchell, no. OH 8154, 78; Juanita Jackson

Mitchell, no. OH 8095, McKeldin-Jackson Oral History Collection, MHS, 4; *The Crisis*, October 1935, 312; Farrar, *The Baltimore* Afro-American, *1892–1950*, 181–83.

36. Musgrove, "An Early History of the Baltimore Branch of the NAACP," 15; Hughes, *Fight for Freedom*, 176; Juanita Jackson Mitchell interview.

37. *The Crisis*, October 1935, 312, December 1935, 374; *Baltimore Sun*, October 10–11, 1935; Juanita Jackson Mitchell interview.

38. *The Crisis*, December 1935, 374–75.

39. Ibid., July 1936, 200–201, 208, August 1936, 246–49, September 1936, 277, 281–83; *Baltimore Evening Sun*, June 30, July 5, 1936; program for the Twenty-Seventh Annual Conference of the NAACP, Baltimore, June 29–July 5, 1936 (photocopy in my possession); Clarence Mitchell Jr., no. 8154, 76–82; Juanita Jackson Mitchell interview.

Chapter 9: The First Wave

Epigraph: Avnet, "Pat Whalen," 249.

1. Zieger, *The CIO, 1935–1955*, 22–41.

2. *Baltimore Sun*, May 7, 1936; Argersinger, *Toward a New Deal in Baltimore*, 161.

3. *Maryland Leader*, May 30, 1936; *Afro-American*, May 23, 1936; *Baltimore Sun*, May 17–21, 1936.

4. *Afro-American*, May 22, 1937; *Baltimore Sun*, May 18–20, 1937; *Baltimore Evening Sun*, May 17, 1937.

5. *Baltimore Sun*, July 29, October 15, 1937; Pedersen, *The Communist Party in Maryland, 1919–1957*, 101.

6. MDCIUC, "Summary of the Proceedings of the First Convention," November 8–10, 1937, Vertical Files, Enoch Pratt Free Library; *Afro-American*, November 13, 1937.

7. Pedersen, *The Communist Party in Maryland, 1919–1957*, 101–2.

8. *Maryland Leader*, March 21, April 4, 11, 18, June 20, 1936.

9. *Baltimore Sun*, February 24, March 12, 19, 27, 1937.

10. Ibid., February 15–16, February 28, June 11, October 21–22, 1937; *Baltimore Evening Sun*, October 21, 1937; Argersinger, *Making the Amalgamated*, 143–57, 164–65; Argersinger, *Toward a New Deal in Baltimore*, 144–47, 168–70.

11. Ibid.

12. *Baltimore Sun*, November 1, 1936.

13. Ibid., November 1, 5, 18, 1936; interview with I. Duke Avnet, by the author; Nelson, *Workers on the Waterfront*, 213–18; Fee et al., *The Baltimore Book*, 169–72; Argersinger, *Toward a New Deal in Baltimore*, 166–68.

14. *Baltimore Sun*, October 31, November 1, 5, 20, 24, 1936; Rubin, *The Log of Rubin the Sailor*, 238.

15. *Baltimore Sun*, October 31, November 1, 5, 20, 24, 1936; I. Duke Avnet interview; Fee et al., *The Baltimore Book*, 170; Nelson, *Workers on the Waterfront*, 215.

16. Maryland-D.C. Federation of Labor, *32nd Annual Convention Book*, Enoch Pratt Free Library Vertical Files, 65–66.

17. *Baltimore Sun*, November 10, 21, 1936; I. Duke Avnet interview; Avnet, "Pat Whalen," 250.

18. I. Duke Avnet interview.

19. Ibid.

20. *Baltimore Sun*, November 24, 1936; *Baltimore Evening Sun*, November 24, 1936; *Afro-American*, November 14, 1936.

21. *Baltimore Sun*, December 18, 21, 1936; *Baltimore Evening Sun*, December 19, 1936.

22. *Afro-American*, December 26, 1936.

23. *Baltimore Sun*, December 20–22, 1936; *Afro-American*, December 26, 1936.

24. *Afro-American*, December 26, 1936; *Baltimore Sun*, December 20, 1936.

25. *Afro-American*, December 26, 1936, June 26, 1937; Fee et al., *The Baltimore Book*, 171–72; Arnesen, *Waterfront Workers of New Orleans*; Arnesen, "Bi-racial Waterfront Unionism."

26. *Afro-American*, June 26, 1937.

27. *Baltimore Sun*, December 22, 30, 1936, January 26, March 5, 1937; Rubin, *The Log of Rubin the Sailor*, 249–50.

28. *Baltimore Sun*, January 26, 1936, March 5, 1937; Fee et al., *The Baltimore Book*, 172; Nelson, *Workers on the Waterfront*, 218, 228–30; Avnet, "Pat Whalen," 249; Rubin, *The Log of Rubin the Sailor*, 160–61.

29. *Baltimore Sun*, September 3–4, 6, 29, 1937, December 2, 1939, August 1, 1940; *Baltimore Evening Sun*, September 24, 1937; NLRB, releases, July 31, 1940, February 21, 1941, Vertical Files, Enoch Pratt Free Library.

30. *Baltimore Sun*, March 22, April 23, May 24, 26, June 13, 1937.

31. *Afro-American*, October 10, 1937; *Baltimore Sun*, June 13, 16, 22–23, 27, October 30, December 10, 1937; *Baltimore Evening Sun*, November 12, 1937.

32. Avnet, "Pat Whalen," 251–52.

33. Quoted in Fee et al., *The Baltimore Book*, 192.

34. *Afro-American*, November 14, 21, 1937; Rubin, *The Log of Rubin the Sailor*, 235.

35. Bernstein, *The Turbulent Years*, 435–41, 519–51; Reutter, *Sparrows Point*, 247–51; Zieger, *The CIO, 1935–1955*, 34–39, 46–54.

36. *Maryland Leader*, March 14, June 27, July 11, August 1, 1936; *Baltimore Sun*, March 5–6, 15, June 21, 1936; Zieger, *The CIO, 1935–1955*, 33–34.

37. *Afro-American*, August 15, 1936; Reutter, *Sparrows Point*, 252–53.

38. Bernstein, *The Turbulent Years*, 453–54.

39. *Afro-American*, January 25, May 5, 1935, August 15, 29, October 3, 22, 1936; Reutter, *Sparrows Point*, 252.

40. *Afro-American*, February 22, October 22, 1936; FBI report dated January 9, 1941, file no. 100-154, and FBI report dated February 1, 1941, file no. 100-154, both in FBI Files on the National Negro Conference (microfilm), reel 1; Naison, *Com-*

munists in Harlem during the Depression, 177–84; Wolters, *Negroes and the Great Depression,* 359–61.

41. *Afro-American,* August 15, 19, 22, October 3, 1936.

42. Reutter, *Sparrows Point,* 257–65; Zieger, *The CIO, 1935–1955,* 54–65.

43. *Afro-American,* March 6, 1937; *Baltimore Sun,* February 22, March 18, June 21, July 24, 1937; Reutter, *Sparrows Point,* 253.

44. *Afro-American,* June 1, 1937; *Baltimore Evening Sun,* June 5, 10, 12, 21, 24, 1937; *Baltimore Sun,* June 5, 8, 10, 17, 20–22, 24, 1937.

45. *Baltimore Sun,* February 19, 22, 24, March 6, 1937; Reutter, *Sparrows Point,* 259–60.

46. *Baltimore Sun,* June 11, 14–16, 1937, February 6–7, 1939.

47. Ibid., November 4–5, 1937, November 14, 1939.

48. NLRB, release, January 15, 1938, Vertical Files, Enoch Pratt Free Library; *CIO News,* February 19, 1938, December 23, 1940; *Afro-American,* September 18, October 30, 1937, November 26, 1938; *Baltimore Sun,* December 10, 1937.

49. *Afro-American,* February 5, 1938; Argersinger, *Toward a New Deal in Baltimore,* 171.

Chapter 10: The Second Wave

Epigraph: "Report of John T. Jones to the Second Annual Convention of the Maryland and District of Columbia Industrial Union Council," December 7, 1938, in the Vertical Files, Enoch Pratt Free Library.

1. "Report of John T. Jones to the Second Annual Convention of the Maryland and District of Columbia Industrial Union Council"; *Baltimore Sun,* July 29, October 15, 1937.

2. Zieger, *The CIO, 1935–1955,* 90–110.

3. *CIO News,* April 21, October 23, 1939, March 18, 25, April 1, 15, 29, May 20, June 17, 24, July 22, November 18, 1940, January 13, February 24, March 17, 21, August 11, 18, 1941; *Baltimore Sun,* April 19, June 2, 1940; *Baltimore Evening Sun,* June 1, 1940; *Daily Record,* June 16, 1940. Argersinger, *Making the Amalgamated,* 165–67.

4. *CIO News,* November 20, 27, 1939; quoted in Argersinger, *Making the Amalgamated,* 165–66; *Daily Record,* June 16, 1940.

5. *CIO News,* May 29, 1939; *Afro-American,* November 19, 26, 1938, August 19, 1939; Argersinger, *Toward a New Deal in Baltimore,* 153–55.

6. *CIO News,* February 20, March 13, April 21, May 8, 29, June 5, October 2, 9, 23, December 18, 1939; *Baltimore Sun,* April 20, 22–23, 25, May 17–18, 1939; *Baltimore Evening Sun,* February 20, 1939.

7. *CIO News,* March 13, 20, May 8, August 21, 1939, December 16, 1940, March 10, 31, September 22, 29, 1941; *Baltimore Sun,* September 26, 1941; *Afro-American,* September 27, 1941; Reutter, *Sparrows Point,* 280–99.

8. Interview with I. Duke Avnet, by the author; *Afro-American,* June 5, Au-

gust 19, October 30, November 11, 1939, February 22, May 17, August 9, October 6, 13, 20, 1941; Reutter, *Sparrows Point*, 292–94, 298.

9. *Baltimore Sun*, February 6–7, 1939.

10. Fee et al., *The Baltimore Book*, 192–93; interview with George E. Meyers, by George Callcott. I thank Professor Callcott for sharing the interview notes with me.

11. NLRB, press release, January 15, 1938, Vertical Files, Enoch Pratt Free Library; *CIO News*, February 19, 1938, August 28, September 11, 18, 25, 1939, June 24, July 29, December 23, 1940; *Afro-American*, November 26, 1938.

12. *CIO News*, January 9, 23, February 6, 20, 27, April 13, June 12, July 31, August 7, 14, September 11, October 2, 23, December 11, 1939, January 15, 1940, May 6, 13, 20, June 17, July 15, 29, August 5, December 23, 1940, April 14, May 5, 1941; NLRB, press releases, June 9, 1938, May 15, July 18, August 22, 1939, January 31, 1940, Vertical Files, Enoch Pratt Free Library.

13. *CIO News*, January 16, March 6, June 12, September 25, December 18, 1939, June 17, 1940; *Afro-American*, August 6, 1938.

14. *CIO News*, November 20, 1939, January 1, 8, 22, 1940; *Afro-American*, January 12, October 29, 1938, November 25, December 16, 1939, January 27, July 20, August 3, 1940.

15. *CIO News*, January 9, 1939.

16. *Afro-American*, April 30, October 29, 1938, January 27, July 20, 1940; *CIO News*, January 9, January 23, 1939.

17. *CIO News*, January 30, February 27, March 27, April 17, 1939; Interview with Juanita Jackson Mitchell, by Andor Skotnes; Clarence Mitchell Jr., no. OH 8154, McKeldin-Jackson Oral History Collection, MHS, 27–39; Farrar, *The Baltimore Afro-American, 1892–1950*, 20; Ryon, "An Ambiguous Legacy," 23. On George B. Murphy Jr., see Naison, *Communists in Harlem during the Depression*, 303–4.

18. *CIO News*, February 20, May 29, June 5, December 18, 1939, January 1, 15, May 20, September 30, October 7, 1940, June 16, July 7, October 27, 1941; *Baltimore Sun*, June 18, September 20, 26–27, October 5, 8, 1940, June 13, July 3, 1941; *Baltimore Evening Sun*, February 20, 1939; *Afro-American*, October 5, 1940, October 4, 1941; James "Scotty" Atkins report (hereafter, Atkins report), June–December 1939, Local 28 folder, Records of the IUMSWA, University of Maryland, College Park.

19. Atkins report; *CIO News*, December 18, 1939, January 6, 1941; *Afro-American*, October 5, 1940.

20. *CIO News*, October 9, 23, 1939.

21. *Baltimore Sun*, August 12–13, 20, 31, October 8, November 14, 20, December 13, 1937, April 13, 18, 25–26, May 3, October 18, 1939; *Baltimore Evening Sun*, August 13, September 6, 17, October 22, December 3, 1937; *Baltimore News-Post*, December 15, 1937; report from Daniel Donovan to George Johnson, Fair Employment Practices Commission, June 10, 1943, Baltimore Transit Company, Baltimore, Maryland; 4-BR-92; William F. Hill, file, in Selected Documents of the Committee on Fair Employment Practices, 1941–46 (microfilm), NARA.

22. *Baltimore Sun*, July 17–18, August 22, October 25, 1937, January 22, February 10, March 4–5, 1938; Argersinger, *Toward a New Deal in Baltimore*, 160–61.

23. *CIO News*, September 23, October 14, 1940; NLRB, press release, June 25, 1941, Vertical Files, Enoch Pratt Free Library.

24. *Baltimore Evening Sun*, August 13, 31, 1937.

25. Ibid., August 13, 31, 1937, September 1, 16, October 5, 1938; *Baltimore Sun*, September 1, 13, 16–17, October 15, 1938.

26. *CIO News*, July 6, 1942; *Afro-American*, January 2, 1943; Duke I. Avnet interview.

27. *Afro-American*, May 20, November 18, 1939, September 21, 1940; Region IV Weekly Report, 10 March 1945, Selected Documents of the Committee on Fair Employment Practices, 1941–46 (microfilm), NARA.

28. *Afro-American*, May 6, 13, June 19, 1939.

29. Ibid., August 12, 26, September 2, 1939; *CIO News*, April 29, May 6, 1940.

30. *Afro-American*, March 8, 1941, *CIO News*, March 3, 1941.

31. *Afro-American*, July 29, 1939, November 9, 16, 1940, April 19, 1941.

32. The following account of the City Colored Orchestra drive draws on *Afro-American*, January 1, 15, 22, 29, February 12, 26, March 5, 19, 26, 1938.

33. Interview with Edward S. Lewis, by the author; Lewis, "We Tackled the Unions and Won," 138–40.

34. *Afro-American*, April 16, 23, May 14, 28, June 4, 25, August 3, October 22, November 19, April 1, 15, 19, May 6, July 29, 1939.

35. Ibid., March 30, April 6, 27, October 22, 1940, February 1, April 5, 1941; Sidney Hollander to Walter White, January 21, 1941, Papers of the NAACP (microfilm), part 18, series B, reel 2.

36. *Afro-American*, May 17, September 6, November 15, December 11, 1941; Lewis, "We Tackled the Unions and Won," 138–40; Edward S. Lewis interview.

37. *Baltimore Sun*, December 9, 1939, March 29–30, April 2, 11, 19, July 6, June 14, 23, July 17, August 9, 1940; *Baltimore Evening Sun*, March 29, April 11, June 5, 14, 19, 1940; Pedersen, *The Communist Party in Maryland, 1919–57*, 108–12.

38. *CIO News*, January 15, March 13, December 23, 1940; Argersinger, *Toward a New Deal in Baltimore*, 172–73; Avnet, "Pat Whalen," 254.

39. *Baltimore Sun*, April 22, May 14, 1941; January–April 1941 folder, May 1941 folder, June–August 1941 folder, September–December 1941 folder, Records of the IUMSWA, University of Maryland, College Park, box 72, series 2; Pedersen, *The Communist Party in Maryland, 1919–57*, 112–13.

40. *CIO News*, August 12, November 11, 25, December 23, 1940, April 14, 1941.

41. January–April 1941 folder, May 1941 folder, June–August 1941 folder, Records of the IUMSWA, University of Maryland, College Park; *Baltimore Sun*, December 16, 1940.

Chapter 11: The Metropolitan Region

Epigraph: Interview with Juanita Jackson Mitchell, by the author.

1. "Interview with Juanita Jackson Mitchell," by Andor Skotnes.

2. *The Crisis*, April 1936, 116, November 1940, 359–60; Walter White to Lillie Jackson, September 14, 1937, Papers of the NAACP (microfilm), pt. 12, series A, reel 17; "Report of Department of Branches for the December Meeting of the Board of Directors," June 1941, ibid., pt. 1, reel 6.

3. Interview with Earl Barnes, by the author; interview with Juanita Jackson Mitchell, by the author; "Report of Department of Branches for the December Meeting of the Board of Directors."

4. *The Crisis*, December 1935, 374.

5. Ibid., November 1937, 344–45, August 1941, 265; Juanita Jackson Mitchell interview; Juanita Jackson to Walter White, 24 November 1937, Papers of the NAACP (microfilm), pt. 12, series A, reel 17.

6. Lillie Jackson to Charles Houston, March 24, 1937, Papers of the NAACP (microfilm), pt. 12, series A, reel 17; Juanita Jackson Mitchell interview; *Baltimore Evening Sun*, March 9, 24, 1937; *The Crisis*, November 1936, 83, 87, November 1939, 341; *Afro-American*, August 13, 1938.

7. CWYPF, *Minutes*, January 5, 26, December 7, 1937; "Report on Branch Activities," February 4, 1937, Papers of the NAACP (microfilm), pt. 12, series A, reel 17; *The Crisis*, March 1937, 88; *Baltimore Sun*, March 3, May 5, 1942; *CIO News*, May 18, 1941, May 25, 1942; Farrar, *The Baltimore* Afro-American, *1892-1950*, 37.

8. "Report on Branch Activities"; Lillie Jackson to Thurgood Marshall, November 5, 1937, Papers of the NAACP (microfilm), pt. 12, series A, reel 17; *Afro-American*, January 1, September 24, 1938, February 25, 1939; *The Crisis*, September 1938, 304; *Baltimore Sun*, March 14, 1935, November 8, 20, 1941.

9. Correspondence from 1937–38, esp. Catherine Watt to Juanita Jackson, n.d. [January or February 1937], and Lillie Jackson to Walter White, Papers of the NAACP (microfilm), pt. 12, series A, reel 17; *Baltimore Sun*, January 10, October 10, 1938; *The Crisis*, February 1937, 52, 56, March 1937, 89, March 1938, 87. For background, see Zangrando, *The NAACP Crusade against Lynching, 1909-1950*, chaps. 6–7.

10. See Baltimore branch correspondence, 1936–39, esp. Lillie Jackson to Morris Shapiro, March 31, 1936, Morris Shapiro to Helen Alpert, April 8, 1936, Helen Alpert to Anna Damon and Morris Shapiro (three undated letters, clearly from 1936), Jesse Smith, acting secretary, Baltimore Scottsboro Committee, to Scottsboro Defense Committee, October 1, 1937, Rose Shapiro to Elisabeth Gilman, March 7, 1939, all in Papers of the NAACP (microfilm), pt. 6, reel 19; *Afro-American*, April 2, 1938.

11. See documents and correspondence in Snow Hill 1938, file, including Ralph Parsons to Walter White, September 23, 1938, Walter White to Lillie Jackson, telegram, September 30, Ralph Parsons to Walter White, September 23, 1938, Walter White to Lillie Jackson, October 5, 1938, Thurgood Marshall, October 5, 1938, all

in Papers of the NAACP (microfilm), pt. 8, series B, reel 14, and in Snow Hill, 1940, file, including Walter White to Governor Herbert O'Conor, telegram, February 14, 1940, Walter White to Senator Robert Wagner, February 15, 1940, Thurgood Marshall to Sara L. Taylor, March 11, 1940, in ibid., pt. 7, series A, reel 30; *Baltimore Sun*, September 19, 1938; *The Crisis*, March 1940, 81; *Afro-American*, January 7, 1939, December 30, 1939.

12. Citizens Planning and Housing Association of Baltimore, "Memorandum on Negro Housing in Metropolitan Baltimore," August 1944, Vertical Files, Enoch Pratt Free Library; *Baltimore Evening Sun*, February 12, 1940.

13. Appellants brief in Meade case, 1937, 1939, Papers of the NAACP (microfilm), reel 1; Meade case, ibid., pt. 5, reel 2; Lillie Jackson to Walter White, May 10, May 21, 1937, and Walter White to Lillie Jackson, May 22, 1937, ibid., pt. 12, series A, reel 17; Juanita Jackson Mitchell interview; Juanita Jackson Mitchell, no. OH 8183, McKeldin-Jackson Oral History Collection, MHS, 50–55; *The Crisis*, March 1937, 88; *Baltimore Sun*, October 14, 1937, January 12, 1938; *Afro-American*, January 15, 1938; Thompson, "The Civil Rights Vanguard," 258–61.

14. *Baltimore Sun*, May 13, October 15, 1937, April 15–16, May 26, November 17, 1939; *Afro-American*, January 13, 1938, December 30, 1939.

15. CWYPF, *Minutes*, March 2, 13, 27, 30, April 13, 1937; *Afro-American*, December 30, 1939; Thompson, "The Civil Rights Vanguard," 248; Juanita Jackson Mitchell interview.

16. Juanita Jackson Mitchell interview; Farrar, *The Baltimore Afro-American, 1892–1950*, 111–12; Thompson "The Civil Rights Vanguard," 248–50; CWYPF, *Minutes*, April 1, 1936, February 15, 1938; CWYPF contest program (1939), 7; *Afro-American*, January 1, 1938; *Baltimore Sun*, May 8–9, 1936, November 25, December 4, 6, 10, 1937; *Baltimore Evening Sun*, September 10, October 12, December 4, 6, 10, 1937; *Baltimore News Post*, December 6, 1937.

17. *Baltimore Evening Sun*, December 4, 1937; *Baltimore Sun*, December 4, 1937, *Baltimore News Post*, December 3, 1937.

18. *Baltimore Sun*, January 29, March 1, July 9–10, 28, 1938; *Baltimore Evening Sun*, October 26, 1937, February 17, April 23, July 23, 28, 1938, January 10, 1939; Juanita Jackson Mitchell, no. OH 8095, McKeldin-Jackson Oral History Collection, MHS, 33; *The Crisis*, March 1943, 91.

19. Juanita Jackson Mitchell, no. OH 8096, McKeldin-Jackson Oral History Collection, MHS, 43 (edited). *Afro-American*, January 1, 1938, November 18, December 30, 1939, January 2, 1943; *Baltimore Sun*, November 14, 1939; Juanita Jackson Mitchell interview; Lillie Jackson to Governor Harry Nice, March 15, 1937, Papers of the NAACP (microfilm), pt. 12, series A, reel 17; *The Crisis*, March 1937, 88, September 1938, 304; Thurgood Marshall to Lillie Jackson, January 4, 1938, Lillie Jackson to Thurgood Marshall, January 17, 1939, Papers of the NAACP (microfilm), pt. 12, series A, reel 17; Juanita Jackson Mitchell interview.

20. Juanita Jackson Mitchell interview; Clarence Mitchell, no. OH 8209,

McKeldin-Jackson Oral History Collection, MHS, 67–72; Hathaway, "Lillie May Jackson," 188; Walter Sondheim Jr., no. OH 8172, McKeldin-Jackson Oral History Collection, MHS, 1–6.

21. *The Crisis*, February 1936, 39, March 1936, 80, April 1936, 118; *Afro-American*, May 14, 1938; J. E. T. Camper, no. OH 8134, McKeldin-Jackson Oral History Collection, MHS, 14; Juanita Jackson Mitchell interview.

22. Juanita Jackson Mitchell interview; Sidney Hollander to Walter White, December 16, 1940, Hollander to Jacob Billikopf, September 2, 1942, Mrs. Joseph N. (Ella G.) Ulman, "A Project of Understanding," Papers of the NAACP (microfilm), pt. 18, series B, reel 22; Farrar, *The Baltimore* Afro-American, *1892–1950*, 183–84.

23. J. E. T. Camper, no. OH 8134, 16–17; Walter Sondheim Jr., no. OH 8172, 4; Juanita Jackson Mitchell interview; Clarence Mitchell, no. OH 8209, 33–34.

24. *The Crisis*, February 1936, 39, March 1936, 80, April 1936, 118, June 1936, 189.

25. Ibid., February 1936, 39, 50.

26. Ibid., March 1936, 80–81, April 1936, 122–23.

27. Ibid., June 1936, 189.

28. Juanita Jackson Mitchell interview; *The Crisis*, June 1938, 177.

29. Sidney Hollander to Walter White, August 22, 1947, Roy Wilkins to Walter White, August 28, 1947, Papers of the NAACP (microfilm), pt. 18, series B, reel 22.

30. Juanita Jackson Mitchell, no. OH 8095, 28–29; Juanita Jackson Mitchell interview.

31. The membership drives and Christmas seal campaigns were reported yearly in the *Afro-American* and *The Crisis*. For 1936–37, see, e.g., *The Crisis*, February 1936, 56, October 1936, 343, April 1937, 116, December 1937, 372–73. The yearly Clean Block campaigns were publicized in the *Afro*: see Farrar, *The Baltimore* Afro-American, *1892–1950*, 325, 327–30.

32. Juanita Jackson Mitchell interview; Lillie Jackson Report, February 4, 1937, Papers of the NAACP (microfilm), pt. 12, series A, reel 17; *The Crisis*, January 1943, 18; Thompson, "The Civil Rights Vanguard," 251–53.

33. Verda Welcome, no. OH 8145, McKeldin-Jackson Oral History Collection, MHS, 9; Clarence Mitchell, no. OH 8209, 29–30; Juanita Jackson Mitchell interview.

34. William L. Adams, no. OH 8210, McKeldin-Jackson Oral History Collection, MHS, 49–50; Karena Chatmon, "William L. (Little Willie) Adams: Everyone's Advocate," *Metropolitan*, 7–10, and Mark Bowden, "Making a Million Bucks in Baltimore," *Baltimore Magazine*, January 1979, 58–59, both in Vertical Files, Enoch Pratt Free Library.

35. Clarence Mitchell, no. OH 8209, 29–30; Juanita Jackson Mitchell interview; *Afro-American*, January 13, 1938.

36. Clarence Mitchell, no. OH 8209, 29–30; Juanita Jackson to Roy Wilkins, September 23, 1937 (with unidentified news clipping), Papers of the NAACP (microfilm), pt. 12, series A, reel 17; *Afro-American*, December 30, 1939.

37. *The Crisis*, January 1943, 18; Thompson, "The Civil Rights Vanguard," 253; "Report of Department of Branches for the December Meeting of the Board of Directors"; *Afro-American*, September 27, 1941.

Chapter 12: The State and the Country

Epigraph: Lillie M. Jackson, quoted in interview with Juanita Jackson Mitchell, by the author.

1. *Baltimore Sun*, March 29, April 15, 1936; *The Crisis*, March 1937, 88, June 1937, 184; Wennersten, "The Black School Teacher in Maryland, 1930s," 371–72; McGuinn, "The Courts and Equality of Educational Opportunity," 156–59; Thompson, "The Civil Rights Vanguard," 261–98.

2. *Baltimore Sun*, October 10–11, November 25, 1935, January 17, March 15, 29, September 16, 1936.

3. Ibid., October 10–11, 1935. On the Lloyd Gaines case, see Tushnet, *The NAACP's Legal Strategy against Segregated Education, 1925-1950*, 70–75; Williams, *Thurgood Marshall, American Revolutionary*, 97–99; McNeil, *Groundwork*, 143–45.

4. *Baltimore Sun*, September 15, 1936; *Baltimore Evening Sun*, October 22, 1936, April 22, 1937; "Report on Branch Activities," February 4, 1937, Papers of the NAACP (microfilm), pt. 12, series A, reel 17; *The Crisis*, July 1937, 214; Thompson, "The Civil Rights Vanguard," 292–98.

5. Thompson, "The Civil Rights Vanguard," 287–98.

6. Examples of the national-legal interpretation include Tushnet, *The NAACP Legal Strategy against Segregated Education, 1925-1950*, 58–69; Williams, *Thurgood Marshall, American Revolutionary*, 89–92. Genna Rae McNeil, however, discusses Houston's mass orientation: McNeil, *Groundwork*, 153. Bruce Thompson also addresses the mass aspect of the cases: Thompson, "The Civil Right Vanguard," 303–57.

7. Enolia McMillan, no. 8110, McKeldin-Jackson Oral History collection, MHS, 12; "Editorial Comment," 539–42; Farrar, *The Baltimore* Afro-American, *1892-1950*, 32–34.

8. Enolia McMillan, no. 8110, 3–4; Thompson, "The Civil War Vanguard," 312–313, 315.

9. Report of the Secretary, March 8, 1937, June 9, 1937, August 25, 1937, Report of the Department of Branches, October 11, 1937, Papers of the NAACP (microfilm), pt. 1, reel 6; Juanita Jackson to Enolia McMillan, September 10, 1937, Juanita Jackson to Walter White, November 24, 1937, ibid., pt. 12, series A, reel 17; *The Crisis*, January 1937, 22, February 1937, 53, October 1937, 312; Thompson, "The Civil Rights Vanguard," 310–18.

10. December 29–30, 1937, January 10, December 6, 1938; *Afro-American*, January 1, 1938; *The Crisis*, January 1938, 14; Report of Department of Branches, December 28, 1937, December 12, 1938, Papers of the NAACP (microfilm), pt. 1, reel 6; Thompson, "The Civil Rights Vanguard," 325–33.

11. *Baltimore Sun*, December 6, 1938, January 15, February 11–12, April 22, October 29, November 15–16, 23, 25, December 22, 1939, January 3, August 26, 1940, April 29, 1941; *Afro-American*, December 30, 1939; *The Crisis*, December 1939, 369, 372, January 1940, 10–11, March 1940, 85–86, March 1941, 83; Thompson, "The Civil Rights Vanguard," 339–45.

12. *The Crisis*, August 1936, 248, August 1938, 270, March 1941, 83, April 1941, 137.

13. Enolia McMillan, no. 8110, 15–18; Wennersten, "The Black School Teacher in Maryland, 1930s," 372; *The Crisis*, August 1941, 265, September 1941, 292; Thompson, "The Civil Rights Vanguard," 347–57.

14. "Testimony of Edward Lewis," *National Defense Migration Hearings before the Select Committee Investigating National Defense Migration*, Select Committee Investigating National Defense Migration, U.S. House of Representatives (hereafter, *Tolan Committee Hearings*), 6074; "Quoth the Raven, 'Nevermore,'" 18; Farrar, *The Baltimore Afro-American, 1892–1950*, 105–6; Argersinger, *Toward a New Deal in Baltimore*, 97–99.

15. *CIO News*, June 5, 1939; Argersinger, *Toward a New Deal in Baltimore*, 105; *Afro-American*, July 16, 23, September 10, 1938.

16. "Quoth the Raven, 'Nevermore,'" 17–21; *Baltimore Sun*, September 7, 1940, March 9, 1940, October 5, 1942, April 25–26, May 4, June 3, 19, 22, July 20–21, September 14, 19, October 5, 14–15, 22–23, 26, November 20, 1943, February 19, 1945; *Baltimore Evening Sun*, February 12, 1940; Argersinger, *Toward a New Deal in Baltimore*, 109–11.

17. *Afro-American*, January 21, 1941; interview with Juanita Jackson Mitchell, by the author; Farrar, *The Baltimore Afro-American, 1892–1950*, 95; Garfinkel, *When Negroes March*, 38–62; Naison, *Communists in Harlem during the Depression*, 310–12; Schultz, "The FEPC and the Legacy of the Labor-Based Civil Rights Movement of the 1940s," 74–75.

18. Ibid.

19. Juanita Jackson Mitchell interview; Garfinkel, *When Negroes March*, 56–77.

20. *Afro-American*, May 10, 1941; *Baltimore Evening Sun*, August 12, 1941, March 26, 1942.

21. *CIO News*, December 23, 1940, January 6, February 2, March 3, 1941; *Afro-American*, February 1, May 10, 1941.

22. *CIO News*, April 21, May 5, 1942.

23. "Reminiscences of Palmer Weber, Oral History Collection, Columbia University; *Afro-American*, July 12, 1941; "Testimony of Edward S. Lewis," *Tolan Committee Hearings*, 6067–95; "Testimony of Frank Bender," *Tolan Committee Hearings*, 6061–67; "Testimony of Joseph McCurdy," *Tolan Committee Hearings*, 6040–42; "Testimony of Glenn Martin," *Tolan Committee Hearings*, 6018–32.

24. *Afro-American*, September 27, October 4, November 8, 1941; *CIO News*, July 28, October 13, 1941; *Baltimore Evening Sun*, April 13, 1942; Lewis, "War Problems of Baltimore's Negro Community," 12.

25. Lillie Jackson to Walter White, May 27, 1937, Thurgood Marshall to Walter

White, June 12, 1937, Walter White to Lillie Jackson, June 18, 1937, Walter White to Thurgood Marshall, June 18, 1937, Papers of the NAACP (microfilm), pt. 12, series A, reel 17.

26. Thurgood Marshall to Walter White, April 23, 1937, ibid., pt. 12, series A, reel 17; "Report of the Department of Branches," December 1941, ibid., pt. 1, reel 6; Ransby, *Ella Baker and the Black Freedom Movement*, 122–24.

27. Thurgood Marshall to Walter White, April 23, 1937, W. A. C. Hughes Jr. to Walter White, November 4, 1938, Walter White to W. A. C. Hughes, November 10, 1938, Enolia P. McMillan to Walter White, November 27, 1938, Papers of the NAACP (microfilm), pt. 12, series A, reel 17.

28. Juanita Jackson Mitchell, no. OH 8095, McKeldin-Jackson Oral History Collection, MHS, page 6; Juanita Jackson Mitchell interview.

29. *The Crisis*, July 1941, 229, August 1941, 265; Baltimore NAACP letterhead for the years 1936 and 1941, Baltimore NAACP files, Papers of the NAACP (microfilm), pt. 12, series A, reel 17.

30. Juanita Jackson Mitchell interview; interview with Evelyn Burrell, by the author; Parren J. Mitchell, no. OH 8170, McKeldin-Jackson Oral History Collection, MHS, 3.

31. Enolia McMillan, no. OH 8110, 29–32; Mike Bowler, "Enolia McMillan's Life and NAACP History Go Together," *Baltimore Sun*, June 30, 1986; "Enolia Pettigen McMillan," Archives of Maryland (Biographical Series), MSA SC 3520–13576, available online at http://www.mdarchives.state.md.us (accessed 25 August 2008); "Enolia Pettigen McMillan," Maryland Women's Hall of Fame, available online at http://www.mdarchives.state.md.us (accessed 25 August 2008).

32. Hughes, *Fight for Freedom*, 176.

33. Juanita Jackson Mitchell interview; CWYPF contest program (1939), 4–9, (1940), 4–8, (1941), 1–3; *Afro-American*, January 13, 1938.

34. CWYPF contest program (1941), 1–3.

35. Evelyn Burrell interview; CWYPF, *Minutes*, January 7, 1936–October 25, 1938.

36. "Evelyn Burrell interview."

Epilogue

George Meyers, *CIO News*, July 20, 1942.

1. The following sketch of the workers' and freedom movements in the Baltimore region during the war and postwar periods is based on work in progress by the author.

2. Interview with Juanita Jackson Mitchell, by the author.

3. Korstad and Lichtenstein, "Opportunities Found and Lost," 799–800, 811. The concept of "civil rights unionism" is further developed in Korstad, *Civil Rights Unionism*.

Bibliography

Archives, Collections, and Documents

Afro-American Newspapers Archives and Research Center, Baltimore
Manuscript, periodical, and photograph collections

Albin O. Kuhn Library and Gallery, University of Maryland, Baltimore County
Baltimore Sun photograph collection

Center for Oral History, Butler Library, Columbia University, New York
Oral History (OH) Collection

Enoch Pratt Free Library, Baltimore
Maryland and African American departments
Vertical Files
Newspaper and digital collections

Federal Bureau of Investigation Files on the National Negro Conference
Scholarly Resources, Inc., microfilm no. 06061, 2 reels

Juanita Jackson Mitchell personal collection, Baltimore
Papers, letters, photographs, clippings, and publications (subsequently
donated to the Library of Congress)

Kheel Center for Labor-Management Documentation and Archives,
Cornell University, Ithaca
Photograph collection

Legacy Web, Baltimore County Public Library
Online photograph archive at
http://external.bcpl.lib.md.us/hcdo/lw_home.html

Library of Congress, Washington, D.C.
Records of the NAACP
NAACP and Farm Security Administration photograph collections
Papers of the NAACP (microfilm)

Lillie May Carroll Jackson Museum, Baltimore
Archive of papers, letters, photographs, clippings, and publications

Maryland Historical Society, Baltimore (MHS)
African American collection

McKeldin-Jackson Oral History Collection
Photograph collections

Maryland State Archives, Annapolis
Historical and biographical series—African Americans
Photograph collections

Rare Book and Manuscript Department, Milton S. Eisenhower Library,
Johns Hopkins University, Baltimore
Photograph collection

National Archives and Records Administration, Washington, D.C. (NARA)
Federal Emergency Relief Administration records, Record Group 69
Photograph collections
Record of Selected Documents of the U.S. Committee on Fair Employment
Practices, 1941–1946 (microfilm)

New York Public Library (NYPL)
Norman Thomas Papers
Periodicals and microfilm

New York State School of Industrial and Labor Relations Library,
New York City Division of Cornell University
Garment workers collection

Schomburg Center for Research in Black Culture, NYPL, New York
Carnegie-Myrdal Collection
Edward S. Lewis Collection
Periodicals and microfilm

Select Committee Investigating National Defense Migration,
U.S. House of Representatives, Washington, D.C.
National Defense Migration Hearings before the Select Committee Investigating
National Defense Migration. U.S. House of Representatives, 77th Con.,
1st[–2d] sess., pursuant to H. Res. 113, a resolution to inquire further
into the interstate migration of citizens, emphasizing the present and
potential consequences of the migration caused by the national defense
program, pt. 15, Baltimore hearings, July 1–2, 1941. Washington, D.C.: U.S.
Government Printing Office, 1941–42.

U.S. Bureau of the Census, Washington, D.C.
Fifteenth Census of the United States: Population (1930)
Fifteenth Census of the United States: Unemployment (1930)

University of Maryland Archive, College Park
Records of the Industrial Union of Marine and Shipyard Workers of
America (IUMSWA)

Newspapers and Periodicals

Afro-American, Baltimore and Washington, D.C., 1929–45
Baltimore Evening Sun, 1929–45
Baltimore Sun, 1929–45
CIO News, Maryland–Washington, D.C., ed., Maryland–District of Columbia
    Industrial Union Council, 1938–45
Councillor, Baltimore Council of Social Agencies, 1936–42
The Crisis: A Record of The Darker Races, NAACP, 1929–45
Daily Record, Baltimore
Marine Workers Voice, Marine Workers Industrial Union, 1929–34
Maryland Leader, State Committee, Socialist Party of Maryland, 1934–36
Monthly Labor Review, U.S. Bureau of Labor Statistics, 1929–45
Opportunity, National Urban League, 1929–45

Oral Histories and Personal Testimonies

By the Author (in my possession)
    I. Duke Avnet, September 29, 1989, Baltimore
    Earl Barnes, October 3, 1987, Baltimore
    Albert Blumberg, June 13, 1990, New York
    Evelyn Burrell, October 4, 1987, Baltimore
    Kiowa Costonie Jr. (correspondence), December 29, 2002
    Sigmund Diamond, April 19, 27, May 3, 1988, New York
    Edward S. Lewis, April 5, 1985, New York
    Juanita Jackson Mitchell, February 20, March 19, August 5, 12, 1987, June 11,
        1991, Baltimore
    Juanita Jackson Mitchell and Virginia Jackson Kiah, June 14, 1991, Baltimore
    Milton Seif, October 13, 1987, Baltimore

By Other Historians (copies in my possession)
    Interview with Bill Bailey, by Bruce Nelson, January 24, 1979
    Interview with Dr. and Mrs. Albert E. Blumberg, by George Callcott
        (interview notes), July 26, 1977
    Interview with George E. Meyers, by George Callcott (interview notes),
        December 27, 1977
    Interview with Frank Trager, by Roy Rosenzweig, May 17, 1973, New York
    Naomi Riches correspondence with Roy Rosenzweig, April 7, 1973

McKeldin-Jackson Oral History (OH) Collection, MHS
    William L. Adams, no. OH 8210
    Evelyn T. Burrell, no. OH 8138
    J. E. T. Camper, no. OH 8134
    Enolia McMillan, no. OH 8110

Clarence Mitchell, no. OH 8209
Clarence Mitchell, no. OH 8154
Juanita Jackson Mitchell, no. OH 8095
Juanita Jackson Mitchell, no. OH 8096
Juanita Jackson Mitchell and Virginia Jackson Kiah, no. OH 8094
Juanita Jackson Mitchell and Virginia Jackson Kiah, no. OH 8097
Parren Mitchell, no. OH 8170
Donald Gaines Murray, no. OH 8139
Walter Sondheim, Jr., no. OH 8172
Verda Welcome, no. OH 8145

New York State School of Industrial and Labor Relations Library, New York City Division of Cornell University
Interview with Sara Barron, by Barbara Wertheimer, June 4, 1975

Oral History Collection, Columbia University, New York
"Reminiscences of Thurgood Marshall," by Ed Edwin, 1977
"Reminiscences of Broadus Mitchell," by Daniel Joseph Singal, 1972
"Reminiscences of Clarence Mitchell," by Ed Edwin, 1981
"Reminiscences of Palmer Weber," by Andor Skotnes, 1985

Other Personal Testimony (in my possession)
City-Wide Young People's Forum, 1987 reunion (videotape), December 27, 1985, Baltimore
Juanita Jackson Mitchell, "Welcome to Baltimore," keynote speech delivered at the Annual Meeting of the Oral History Association, October 13, 1988, Baltimore (videotape)

Secondary Sources

Althusser, Louis. *For Marx*. New York: Pantheon, 1969.
Argersinger, Jo Ann E. "Assisting the 'Loafers': Transient Relief in Baltimore, 1933–37." *Labor History* 23 (1982), 226–45.
———. "The City That Tries to Suit Everybody: Baltimore's Clothing Industry." *The Baltimore Book: New Views of Local History*, ed. Elizabeth Fee, Linda Shopes, and Linda Zeidman, 81–102. Philadelphia: Temple University Press, 1991.
———. *Making the Amalgamated: Gender, Ethnicity, and Class in the Baltimore Clothing Industry, 1899–1939*. Baltimore: Johns Hopkins University Press, 1999.
———. "'The Right to Strike': Labor Organization and the New Deal in Baltimore." *Maryland Historical Magazine* 78 (1983), 299–318.
———. *Toward a New Deal in Baltimore: People and Government in the Great Depression*. Chapel Hill: University of North Carolina Press, 1988.

————. "Toward a Roosevelt Coalition: The Democratic Party and the New Deal in Baltimore." *Maryland Historical Magazine* 82 (1987), 288–301.

Arnesen, Eric. "Bi-racial Waterfront Unionism in the Age of Segregation." *Waterfront Workers: New Perspectives on Race and Class*, ed. Calvin Winslow, 19–61. Urbana: University of Illinois Press, 1998.

————. *Waterfront Workers of New Orleans: Race, Class, and Politics, 1863-1923.* New York: Oxford University Press, 1991.

Arnold, Joseph L. "The Last of the Good Old Days: Politics in Baltimore, 1920–1950." *Maryland Historical Magazine* 71 (Fall 1976), 443–48.

Asher, Nina. "Dorothy Jacobs Bellanca: Feminist Trade Unionist, 1894–1946." PhD diss., State University of New York, Binghamton, 1982.

Avnet, I. Duke. "Pat Whalen." *Phylon* 12 (1951), 249–54.

Bailey, Bill. *The Kid from Hoboken: An Autobiography.* San Francisco: Circus Lithographic Prepress, 1993.

Baltimore Gas and Electric Company. *Second Industrial Survey of Baltimore: A Quarter Century of Progress in the City of Industrial Advantages, 1914-1939.* Baltimore: Consolidated Gas Electric Light and Power Company of Baltimore, 1939.

Barrett, James R. *William Z. Foster and the Tragedy of American Radicalism.* Urbana: University of Illinois Press, 2002.

Beirne, D. Randall, "Hampden-Woodberry: The Mill Village in the Urban Setting." *Maryland Historical Magazine* 77 (March 1982), 6–26.

————. "The Impact of Black Labor on European Immigration into Baltimore's Oldtown, 1790–1910." *Maryland Historical Magazine* 83 (Winter 1988), 331–45.

————. "Late Nineteenth Century Industrial Communities in Baltimore." *Maryland Historian* 11 (Spring 1980), 39–49.

————. "Residential Growth and Stability in the Baltimore Industrial Community of Canton during the Late Nineteenth Century." *Maryland Historical Magazine* 74 (March 1979), 39–51.

Bernstein, Irving. *The Lean Years: A History of the American Worker.* Chicago: Haymarket Books, 2010.

————. *The Turbulent Years: A History of the American Worker, 1933-1941.* New York: Houghton Mifflin, 1970.

Braverman, Harry. *Labor and Monopoly Capital: The Degradation of Work in the Twentieth Century.* New York: Monthly Review Press, 1974.

Brown, Dorothy. "Maryland between the Wars." *Maryland: A History, 1632-1974*, ed. Richard Walsh and William Lloyd Fox, 405–21. Baltimore: Maryland Historical Society, 1974.

Brown, Michael, Randy Martin, Frank Rosengarten, and George Snedecker. *New Studies in the Politics and Culture of U.S. Communism.* New York: Monthly Review Press, 1993.

Bruchley, Eleanor. "The Development of Baltimore Business, 1880–1914." *Maryland Historical Magazine* 64 (Spring–Summer 1969), 18–42.

Brundage, W. Fitzhugh, *Lynching in the New South: Georgia and Virginia, 1880–1930.* Urbana: University of Illinois Press, 1993.

Brundage, W. Fitzhugh, ed. *Under Sentence of Death: Lynching in the South.* Chapel Hill: University of North Carolina Press, 1997.

Bunche, Ralph. "The Program, Ideologies, Tactics, and Achievements of Negro Betterment and Interracial Organizations." Unpublished ms., Carnegie-Myrdal Collection, Schomburg Center for the Study of Black Culture, New York Public Library, 1940.

Callcott, George H. *Maryland and America: 1940 to 1980.* Baltimore: Johns Hopkins University Press, 1985.

Campbell, Susan. "'Black Bolsheviks' and Recognition of African America's Right to Self-Determination by the Communist Party USA." *Science and Society* 58 (Winter 1994–95), 440–70.

Carter, Dan T. *Scottsboro: A Tragedy of the American South.* Baton Rouge: Louisiana State University Press, 1969.

Castells, Manuel. *Urban Question: A Marxist Approach.* Cambridge: MIT Press, 1977.

Claudin, Fernando. *The Communist Movement from Comintern to Cominform.* New York: Monthly Review Press, 1975.

Cohen, Lewis M. "A Socialist Training School." *Student Outlook* 4 (October 1935), 6–8.

Crooks, James B. *Politics and Progress: The Rise of Urban Progressivism in Baltimore.* Baton Rouge: Louisiana State University Press, 1968.

Degras, Jane T., ed. *The Communist International, 1919–1943,* vol. 2. London: Oxford University Press, 1956–65.

Dimitroff, Georgi. *The United Front: The Struggle against Fascism and War.* New York: International Publishers, 1938.

Durr, Kenneth D. *Behind the Backlash: White Working-Class Politics in Baltimore, 1940–1980.* Chapel Hill: University of North Carolina Press, 2003.

Durr, W. Theodore. "The Conscience of the City: A History of the Citizens' Planning and Housing Association and Efforts to Improve Housing for the Poor in Baltimore, Maryland, 1937–1954." PhD diss., Johns Hopkins University, Baltimore, 1972.

———. "People of the Peninsula." *Maryland Historical Magazine* 77 (March 1982), 27–53.

"Editorial Comment: Discrimination in Negro Teachers' Salaries in Maryland." *Journal of Negro Education* 5 (October 1936), 539–42.

Ehrenreich, Barbara, and John Ehrenreich. "The Professional–Managerial Class." *Between Capital and Labor,* ed. Pat Walker, 5–48. Boston: South End, 1979.

Engels, Friedrich. *The Condition of the Working Class in England.* Stanford: Stanford University Press, 1958.

Farrar, Hayward. *The Baltimore* Afro-American, *1892–1950.* Westport, Conn.: Greenwood, 1998.

————. "See What the *Afro* Says: The Baltimore *Afro-American*, 1892–1950." PhD diss., University of Chicago, 1983.

Fee, Elizabeth, Linda Shopes, and Linda Zeidman, eds. *The Baltimore Book: New Views of Local History*. Philadelphia: Temple University Press, 1991.

Fein, Isaac M. *The Making of an American Jewish Community: The History of Baltimore Jewry, 1773–1920*. Philadelphia: Jewish Publication Society of America, 1971.

Franklin, John Hope, and Genna Rae McNeil, eds. *African Americans and the Living Constitution*. Washington, D.C.: Smithsonian Institution Press, 1995.

Fraser, Steven. *Labor Will Rule: Sidney Hillman and the Rise of American Labor*. New York: Free Press, 1991.

Frazier, E. Franklin. *Black Bourgeoisie*. New York: Free Press, 1957.

————. *Negro Youth at the Crossroads: Their Personality Development in the Middle States*. New York: Schocken, 1967.

Frisch, Michael H. *A Shared Authority: Essays on the Craft and Meaning of Oral and Public History*. New York: State University of New York Press, 1990.

Garfinkel, Herbert. *When Negroes March: The March on Washington Movement in the Organizational Politics for FEPC*. Glencoe, Ill.: Free Press, 1959.

Giddings, Paula. *In Search of Sisterhood: Delta Sigma Theta and the Challenge of the Black Sorority Movement*. New York: William Morrow, 1988.

Goldberg, Robert. "Party Competition and Black Politics in Baltimore and Philadelphia." PhD diss., Brandeis University, Massachusetts, 1984.

Graham, Leroy. *Baltimore: The Nineteenth Century Black Capital*. Washington, D.C.: University Press of America, 1982.

Gramsci, Antonio. *Selections from the Prison Notebooks*. London: Lawrence and Wishart, 1971.

Greene, Suzanne E. "Black Republicans on the City Council, 1890–1931." *Maryland Historical Magazine* 74 (September 1979), 202–22.

Grele, Ronald J. *Envelopes of Sound*. Chicago: Precedent, 1975.

Groves, Paul A., and Edward K. Muller. "The Evolution of Black Residential Areas in Nineteenth-Century Cities." *Journal of Historical Geography* 1 (April 1975), 169–91.

Hall, Jacqueline Dowd. "Broadus Mitchell (1892–1988)." *Radical History Review* 45 (1989), 31–38.

Hall, Jacquelyn Dowd. "The Long Civil Rights Movement and the Political Uses of the Past." *Journal of American History* 91 (March 2005), 1233–63.

Harris, Abram L. *The Negro as Capitalist: A Study of Banking and Business among American Negroes* (1936), repr. ed. College Park, Md.: McGrath, 1968.

Harvey, David. *Social Justice and the City*. Baltimore: Johns Hopkins University Press, 1973.

Hathaway, Phyllis. "Lillie May Jackson." *Notable Maryland Women*, ed. Winifred G. Helmes, 187–91. Maryland: Tidewater, 1977.

Haywood, Harry. *Black Bolshevik: Autobiography of an Afro-American Communist*. Chicago: Liberator, 1978.

Hobsbawm, Eric J. *Labouring Men: Studies in the History of Labour*. New York: Basic, 1964.

Honig, Nathaniel. *The Trade Union Unity League: Its Structure, Policy, Program, and Growth*. New York: Labor Unity, 1934.

Hughes, Langston. *Fight for Freedom: The Story of the NAACP*. New York: Norton, 1962.

Hunter, Gary Jerome. "'Don't Buy Where You Can't Work': Black Urban Boycott Movements during the Depression, 1929–1941." PhD diss., University of Michigan, Ann Arbor, 1977.

Ifill, Sherrilyn A. *On the Courthouse Lawn: Confronting the Legacy of Lynching in the Twenty-First Century*. Boston: Beacon, 2007.

James, Edward T., Janet Wilson James, and Paul Boyer, eds. *Notable American Women, 1607–1950: A Biographical Dictionary*. Cambridge: Harvard University Press, 1971.

Johanningsmeier, Edward P. *Forging American Communism: The Life of William Z. Foster*. Princeton: Princeton University Press, 1994.

Johnson, Charles S. "Negroes at Work in Baltimore, Maryland." *Opportunity* 1 (June 1923), 12–19.

Jones, William. "A History and Appraisal of the Economic Consequences of Negro Trade Boycotts." Master's thesis, Atlanta University, 1940.

Kartman, Laurine Levy. "Jewish Occupational Roots in Baltimore at the Turn of the Century," *Maryland Historical Magazine* 74 (March 1979), 52–61.

Katznelson, Ira. *Marxism and the City*. New York: Oxford University Press, 1992.

Kelley, Robin D. G. *Hammer and Hoe: Alabama Communists during the Great Depression*. Chapel Hill: University of North Carolina Press, 1990.

Kim, Janice C. H. "The Integration of Socialism and Feminism: Elisabeth Gilman, 1900–1940." Master's thesis, Johns Hopkins University, Baltimore, 1996.

Korstad, Robert Rodgers. *Civil Rights Unionism: Tobacco Workers and the Struggle for Democracy in the Mid-Twentieth Century South*. Chapel Hill: University of North Carolina Press, 2003.

Korstad, Robert, and Nelson Lichtenstein. "Opportunities Found and Lost: Labor, Radicals, and the Early Civil Rights Movement." *Journal of American History* 75 (December 1988), 786–811.

Kuebler, Edward J. "The Desegregation of the University of Maryland." *Maryland Historical Magazine* 71 (Spring 1976), 37–49.

Kutnik, Lee. "The Revolutionary T.U. Movement in the U.S.A. in the Conditions of the 'New Deal' of Trustified Capital." *Communist International*, September 20, 1934, 702–10.

Leab, Daniel J. "'United We Eat': The Creation and Organization of the Unemployed Councils in 1930." *Labor History* 8 (Fall 1967): 300–315.

Lewis, Edward S. "War Problems of Baltimore's Negro Community." *Councillor* 7 (September 1942), 12–13.

———. "We Tackled the Unions and Won." *Opportunity* 18 (1940), 138–40.

Lichtenstein, Nelson. *Labor's War at Home: The CIO in World War II.* New York: Cambridge University Press, 1982.

Marine Workers Industrial Union. *Centralized Shipping Bureau.* New York: n.p, 1934.

Markowitz, Norman. *The Rise and Fall of the People's Century: Henry A. Wallace and American Liberalism, 1941–1948.* New York: Free Press, 1973.

Marx, Karl. *The Eighteenth Brumaire of Louis Bonaparte.* New York: International, 1994.

McGuinn, Henry J. "The Courts and Equality of Educational Opportunity." *Journal of Negro Education* 8 (April 1939), 150–63.

———. "The Courts and the Occupational Status of Negroes in Maryland." *Social Forces* 18 (December 1939), 256–68.

McKay, Claude. *Harlem: Negro Metropolis.* New York: E. P. Dutton, 1940.

McNeil, Genna Rae. *Groundwork: Charles Hamilton Houston and the Struggle for Civil Rights.* Philadelphia: University of Pennsylvania Press, 1983.

Meade, Teresa A. *"Civilizing" Rio: Reform and Resistance in a Brazilian City, 1889–1930.* State College: Pennsylvania State University Press, 1997.

Meier, August, and Elliot Rudwick. *Black Detroit and the Rise of the UAW.* New York, Oxford University Press, 1979.

———. "The Origins of Nonviolent Direct Action in Afro-American Protest: A Note on Historical Discontinuities." *Along the Color Line: Explorations in the Black Experience*, August Meier, Elliot Rudwick, and David Levering Lewis, 307–404. Urbana: University of Illinois Press, 2002.

Moore, Joseph E. *Murder on Maryland's Eastern Shore: Race, Politics, and the Case of Orphan Jones.* Charleston, S.C.: History Press, 2006.

Musgrove, George Derek. "An Early History of the Baltimore Branch of the NAACP: 1912–1936," Unpublished ms. in author's possession, May 1997.

Myrdal, Gunnar. *An American Dilemma: The Negro Problem and Modern Democracy.* New York: Harper and Row, 1962.

Naison, Mark. *Communists in Harlem during the Depression.* Urbana: University of Illinois Press, 1983.

Nathan, Daniel A. "Chasing the Shadows: The Baltimore Black Sox and the Perils of History." *Baseball in America and America in Baseball*, ed. Donald G. Kyle and Robert B. Fairbanks, 52–87. College Station: Texas A&M University Press, 2008.

Nelson, Bruce. *Workers on the Waterfront: Seamen, Longshoremen, and Unionism in the 1930s.* Urbana: University of Illinois Press, 1988.

Neverdon-Morton, Cynthia. "Black Housing Patterns in Baltimore City, 1885–1953." *Maryland Historian* 16 (Spring–Summer 1985), 23–39.

Olson, Sherry H. *Baltimore: The Building of an American City*. Baltimore: Johns Hopkins University Press, 1980.

Oppenheimer, Irene. "The Organizations of the Unemployed, 1930–1940." Master's thesis, Columbia University, New York, 1940.

Orser, W. Edward. "The Making of a Baltimore Rowhouse Community: The Edmonson Avenue Area, 1915–1945." *Maryland Historical Magazine* 80 (Fall 1985), 203–27.

Parris, Guichard, and Lester Brooks. *Blacks in the City: A History of the National Urban League*. Boston: Little, Brown, 1971.

Pearson, Ralph L. "The National Urban League Comes to Baltimore." *Maryland Historical Magazine* 72, no. 4 (1977), 523–33.

Pedersen, Vernon L. *The Communist Party in Maryland, 1919–57*. Urbana: University of Illinois Press, 2001.

———. "Red, White, and Blue: The Communist Party of Maryland, 1919–1949." PhD diss., Georgetown University, Washington, D.C., 1993.

Piven, Francis Fox, and Richard Cloward. *Poor People's Movements: How They Succeed and They Fail*. New York: Pantheon, 1977.

Poulantzas, Nicos. *Political Power and Social Classes*. London: New Left, 1973.

Power, Garrett. "Apartheid Baltimore Style: The Residential Segregation Ordinances of 1910–1913." *Maryland Law Review* 42 (1983), 289–328.

"Quoth the Raven, 'Nevermore.'" *Councillor* 6 (March–April 1941), 17–21.

Ransby, Barbara. *Ella Baker and the Black Freedom Movement: A Radical Democratic Vision*. Chapel Hill: University of North Carolina Press, 2003.

Reid, Ira De A. "The Negro in the American Economic Order." Unpublished ms., Carnegie-Myrdal Collection, Schomburg Center for the Study of Black Culture, New York Public Library, 1940.

———. *The Negro Community of Baltimore: A Social Survey*. New York: National Urban League, 1934.

———. *Negro Membership in American Labor Unions*. New York: Alexander, 1930.

Reutter, Mark. *Sparrows Point: Making Steel and the Rise and Ruin of American Industrial Might*. Urbana: University of Illinois Press, 2004.

Richmond, Al. *A Long View from the Left: Memoirs of an American Revolutionary*. Boston: Houghton Mifflin, 1973.

Ringer, Benjamin. *"We the People" and Others: Duality and America's Treatment of Its Racial Minorities*. New York: Tavistock, 1983.

Roediger, David A. *The Wages of Whiteness: Race and the Making of the American Working Class*. New York: Verso, 1999.

Rosenzweig, Roy. "Organizing the Unemployed: The Early Years of the Great Depression, 1929–1933," *Radical America* 10 (July–August 1976), 36–60.

———. "'Socialism in Our Time': The Socialist Party and the Unemployed, 1929–1936." *Labor History* 20 (Fall 1979), 485–509.

Rubin, Charles. *The Log of Rubin the Sailor*. New York: International, 1973.

Ryon, Roderick N. "An Ambiguous Legacy: Baltimore Blacks and the CIO, 1936–1941." *Journal of Negro History* 65 (1980), 18–33.

———. "Baltimore Workers and Industrial Decision-Making, 1890–1917." *Journal of Southern History* 51 (November 1985), 565–80.

———. "'Human Creatures' Lives': Baltimore Women and Work in Factories, 1880–1917." *Maryland Historical Magazine* 83 (Winter 1988), 346–64.

———. "Old West Baltimore." *Maryland Historical Magazine* 77 (Spring 1982), 55–69.

Schultz, Kevin M., "The FEPC and the Legacy of the Labor-Based Civil Rights Movement of the 1940s." *Labor History* 49 (February 2008), 71–92.

Seawright, Sally. "Desegregation at Maryland: The NAACP and the Murray Case in the 1930s." *Maryland Historian* 1 (Spring 1970), 59–73.

Sitkoff, Harvard. *A New Deal for Blacks: The Emergence of Civil Rights as a National Issue, the Depression Decade.* New York: Oxford University Press, 2009.

Skotnes, Andor. "The Black Freedom Movement and the Workers' Movement in Baltimore, 1930–1939." PhD diss., Rutgers University, New Brunswick, 1991.

———. "'Buy Where You Can Work': Boycotting for Jobs in African American Baltimore, 1933–1934." *Journal of Social History* 27 (Summer 1994), 735–61.

———. "The Communist Party, Anti-Racism, and the Freedom Movement in Baltimore, 1930–1935." *Science and Society* 60 (Summer 1996), 164–94.

———. "Narratives of Juanita Jackson Mitchell: The Making of a 1930s Freedom Movement Leader." *Maryland Historian* (Winter 2002), 44–66.

———. "Structural Determination of the Proletariat and the Petty Bourgeoisie: A Critique of Nicos Poulantzas." *Insurgent Sociologist* 9 (Summer 1979), 34–54.

Smith, Jessie Carney, ed. *Notable Black American Women.* Detroit: Gale Research, 1992.

Spero, Sterling D., and Abram L. Harris. *The Black Worker: The Negro and the Labor Movement.* New York: Columbia University Press, 1931.

Thomas, Bettye C. "A Nineteenth Century Black Operated Shipyard, 1866–1884: Reflections upon Its Inception and Ownership." *Journal of Negro History* 59 (January 1974), 1–12.

———. "Public Education and Black Protest in Baltimore, 1865–1900." *Maryland Historical Magazine* 71 (Fall 1976), 381–91.

Thompson, Bruce A. "The Civil Rights Vanguard: The NAACP and the Black Community in Baltimore." PhD diss., University of Maryland, College Park, 1996.

Thompson, E. P. *The Making of the English Working Class.* New York: Pantheon, 1963.

Torrieri, Nancy. "Residential Dispersal and the Survival of the Italian Community in Metropolitan Baltimore, 1920–1980." PhD diss., University of Maryland, College Park, 1982.

Trotter, Joe William, Jr. "From Raw Deal to New Deal?" *To Make Our World*

Anew: A History of African Americans from 1800, ed. Robin D. G. Kelley and Earl Lewis, 131–66. New York: Oxford University Press, 2000.

Tushnet, Mark. *The NAACP's Legal Strategy against Segregated Education, 1925– 1950*. Chapel Hill: University of North Carolina Press, 1987.

Walkowitz, Daniel J. *Worker City, Company Town: Iron and Cotton Worker Protest in Troy and Cohoes, New York, 1855–84*. Urbana: University of Illinois Press, 1978.

———. *Working with Class: Social Workers and the Politics of Middle-Class Identity*. Chapel Hill: University of North Carolina Press, 1999.

Watson, Denton L. *Lion in the Lobby: Clarence Mitchell Jr.'s Struggle for the Passage of Civil Rights Laws*. New York: William Morrow, 1990.

Wells-Barnett, Ida B., and Jacqueline Jones Royster. *Southern Horrors and Other Writings: The Anti-lynching Campaign of Ida B. Wells, 1892–1900*. Boston: Bedford, 1997.

Wennersten, John R. "The Black School Teacher in Maryland, 1930s." *Negro History Bulletin* 38 (April–May 1975), 370–73.

West, Herbert Lee. "Urban Life and Spatial Distribution of Blacks in Baltimore, Maryland, 1940–70." PhD diss., University of Minnesota, Minneapolis, 1973.

Williams, Juan. *Thurgood Marshall, American Revolutionary*. New York: Times, 1998.

Wittner, Lawrence S. *Rebels against War: The American Peace Movement, 1933– 1983*. Philadelphia: Temple University Press, 1984.

Wolters, Raymond. *Negroes and the Great Depression: The Problem of Economic Recovery*. Westport, Conn.: Greenwood, 1970.

Zangrando, Robert L. *The NAACP Crusade against Lynching, 1909–1950*. Philadelphia: Temple University Press, 1980.

Zeidman, Linda F. "A New World from the Ashes of the Old: History and Vision of Baltimore Steelworkers." Audio-visual presentation. Baltimore: Essex Community College, 1980.

Zieger, Robert. *The CIO, 1935–1955*. Chapel Hill: University of North Carolina Press, 1995.

Index

National Maritime Union (NMU), 173,
220–21, 225, 232–36, 248–50, 252–53,
256–57, 267–68
National Negro Congress (NNC), 238–40,
248, 251, 255, 270, 297, 299–302, 313–14
National Recovery Administration
(NRA), 96, 100, 105, 145, 164–65, 173–
74, 177, 184–85, 223
National Urban League, 11, 69, 96, 102,
108, 110, 169–70, 185–86, 286, 300. *See
also* Baltimore Urban League (BUL)
Negro Labor Committee (NLC), 96, 112,
174, 186, 189, 224
neighborhood protective associations,
273, 287–89
New Deal, 6, 80, 85, 97, 99–100, 102–3,
114–15, 163, 265–66, 300–301; Baltimore Emergency Relief Commis-
sion (BERC), 51, 88, 159, 179, 182; Civil
Works Administration (CWA), 100,
103, 115, 179; Federal Emergency Relief
Administration (FERA), 167–68, 171,
180; National Labor Relations Board
(NLRB), 232–64; National Recovery
Administration (NRA), 96–97, 164–65,
173, 177, 184–85, 223; Works Progress
Administration (WPA), 180–83
New Negro Alliance (NNA), 133, 156
Newspaper Guild, 178, 221, 255
Nice, Governor Harry W., 131, 138, 209,
229, 274, 277, 294
Norris–LaGuardia Act, 153, 156

O'Conor, Herbert, 194, 203, 273
O'Dunne, Judge Eugene, 127, 136, 203–4,
247, 259
Opportunity (NUL), 265
Opportunity Makers Club, 146, 151–52,
155
Ovington, Mary White (NAACP), 79–80
Owens, C. C., 135
Owens, Judge Albert S. J., 153, 159

Pancoast, Elinor (PUL), 94, 103, 105
Parker, Bruce, 171
Parks, Rosa, 285
Patterson, William (CP), 80, 126, 129, 131

Peeks, Robert, 142
People's Unemployment League of
Maryland (PUL), 91–92, 159, 163, 165,
172, 185, 187, 219–20, 241, 270; anti-
lynching protests, 120, 125, 130, 138;
BFL, 177–79; origins of, 97–112; peace
movement, 189–93; and Unemployed
Councils, 112–15; WAA and WPA orga-
nizing, 179–84, 193
Peters, Reverend Roy (NNC), 239
Pettigan, Enola. *See* McMillan, Enolia
Pettigen
Pickens, William, 79
Plessy v. Ferguson, 200–201
Poles and Polish Americans, 28, 66–67,
93, 227; neighborhoods, 15–16
Popular Front, 172, 216–17, 265–66;
in Baltimore, 178, 198–99, 222, 227,
265–68

race and ethnicity, definitions, 3n.1,
26–30
Raffety, John P., 276
Randolph, A. Philip, 186, 238; and
MOWM, 299–301
Rausch, J. Fred, 178, 219–20, 241
Reid, Ira De A. (NUL), 79, 89; on the
Black community in Baltimore, 23,
31–32, 36, 96, 102, 169–70, 188–89
Republican Party, 138, 197; and race/eth-
nicity, 18–19, 32, 37, 120, 144, 191–92,
273, 278, 294
Rhetta, B. M. (BUL), 110
Rice, Reverend D. E. (NNC), 238–39
Riches, Naomi (PUL), 94, 103, 105, 108,
115, 178, 191
Richmond, Al (CP), 53–54, 56
Ritchie, Governor Albert C., 51, 59, 64,
100, 123, 125–27, 134–35, 137–38
Robins, State's Attorney John B., 121, 123,
125, 137
Robinson, Jackie, 285
Roosevelt, President Franklin Delano,
80, 96–97, 99–100, 102, 114, 170, 180–
81, 188, 265, 300–301, 315; Roosevelt
Recession, 244, 248, 250
Rubin, Charles, 172, 232

ANDOR SKOTNES

is a professor of history in the
Department of History and Society at
the Sage Colleges, Troy, New York. He
edited (with Rina Benmayor) *Migration
and Identity* (1994; 2d ed., 2005).

Library of Congress Cataloging-in-Publication Data

Skotnes, Andor.
A new deal for all? : race and class struggles in Depression-era
Baltimore / Andor Skotnes.
p. cm. — (Radical perspectives)
Includes bibliographical references and index.
ISBN 978-0-8223-5347-8 (cloth : alk. paper)
ISBN 978-0-8223-5359-1 (pbk. : alk. paper)
1. New Deal, 1933–1939 — Maryland — Baltimore. 2. African
Americans — Maryland — Baltimore — History — 20th century.
3. Labor — Maryland — Baltimore — History — 20th century.
4. Baltimore (Md.) — Race relations — History — 20th century.
I. Title. II. Series: Radical perspectives.
F189.B19N475 2012
305.8009752′6 — dc23   2012011609